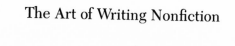

The Art of Writing Nonfiction

The ART of WRITING NONFICTION
NONFICTION
Second Edition

André Fontaine and
William A. Glavin, Jr.

SYRACUSE UNIVERSITY PRESS

The paper used in this publication meets the minimum requirements of American National Standard for Information Sciences—Permanence of Paper for Printed Library Materials, ANSI Z39.48-1984. ∞™

Library of Congress Cataloging-in-Publication Data

Fontaine, André, 1910–
  The art of writing nonfiction.

  Includes index.
  1. Journalism—Authorship. I. Glavin, William A.
II. Title.
PN4781.F65 1987   808'.06607   86-30212
ISBN 0-8156-2403-4 (alk. paper)

Manufactured in the United States of America

CONTENTS

Before he joined the faculty of the S.I. Newhouse School of Public Communications at Syracuse University, **André Fontaine** spent more than thirty years on newspapers and magazines in New York. He was City Editor of *Newsday*, Associate Editor of *Collier's*, Editor of *Bluebook*, and Senior Editor of *Redbook*. For more than a decade he was a free-lance writer, publishing over a hundred articles in major national magazines. He is now Professor Emeritus at Newhouse and is writing historical biographies.

William A. Glavin, Jr., is Associate Professor of magazine journalism at the S.I. Newhouse School of Public Communications at Syracuse University. He has worked as a newspaper reporter, a television news editor, and for four years as an associate editor at *Good Housekeeping* magazine, where he specialized in health-related topics.

PREFACE

*T*his book documents a major change in journalistic practice in the United States. It is a change that has been largely unnoticed outside the profession and not understood by thousands inside. It had its beginnings nearly half a century ago in the work of exceptionally talented writers and editors, then grew slowly as more and more practitioners saw, understood, and began to use the new techniques.

The change has been called many things—new journalism, literary journalism, advocacy journalism—and definitions of precisely what it is and how it differs from earlier forms have been elusive. With a boldness not warranted by our knowledge, we would like to offer one:

Interpretive journalism is a process, based on rigorous reportage, that employs the creativity and skills of the fiction writer and presents the judgment of the writer, after he or she has objectively evaluated the facts, of where the truth lies.

Interpretive stories can range in length from a 1,000-word newspaper story to a 3,500-word magazine article or even to a full-length book. In producing such stories, the journalist may use the fiction writer's techniques of plotting, suspense, dramatic conflict, and character development, but may not go beyond the facts unearthed during the research process. Though the story must present a conclusion, a point of view, that conclusion must be reached, as in the scientific method, only after all available evidence has been weighed and after as much bias and prejudice as is humanly possible has been ruled out. Thus the idea of journalistic objectivity is vital to the process. Though the methods of presentation may differ, the process is identical in all forms of interpretive journalism. Of the creativity involved, the late Truman Capote, in a *Playboy* interview, said, "Journalism is actually the last great unexplored literary frontier. . . . It's the only really serious and creative field of literary experimentation we have today."

This book explores and describes the process of interpretive journalism, and, to the best of our ability, tells how it is done. Starting with the inception and shaping of the idea for the story, the book takes the reader through the research process, the evaluation of the evidence, the organization and presentation of material, and a discussion of leads, endings, and the body of the story. Then it discusses different kinds of writing—dramatic, descriptive, explanatory, emotional, and profiles.

Originally published in 1974, *The Art of Writing Nonfiction* in this second edition adds a co-author, William A. Glavin, Jr., and new examples of outstanding journalism. The reader will find throughout the text frequent use of the first person singular "I"; these refer to the book's original author, André Fontaine. Pronouns were a further concern to us because we wanted the language in *The Art of Writing Nonfiction* to be free of sex bias. The book's first edition followed the long-accepted convention that says "he" or "him" may be used to refer to a person of unknown sex ("If you want to convince your reader, you have to give him the fact"). Today we are all more aware of the subtle ways language can fail to reflect the experiences and contributions of women, and we sought ways of reflecting that awareness in our writing.

We hope the book will be of practical value to journalism students, to practicing journalists who seek to expand the horizons of their craft, and to all aspiring writers who want to attempt this new and demanding art form.

We wish to thank those whose thought and advice were of inestimable help in creating this second edition of *The Art of Writing Nonfiction:* Diana J. Reinstein of Syracuse University's Bird Library, who offered valuable information about databases; Dean Edward C. Stephens of the S. I. Newhouse School of Public Communications, who freely offered assistance to both of us; Mary Kate Imbolli, whose help was invaluable, and who, among other things, spent hours teaching Glavin how to use a computer (which wasn't easy); and Isabel Pearce, who typed the manuscript and whose suggestions improved the work. We also wish to thank all of the writers whose work appears in the book. They are the practitioners of interpretive journalism, and the book could not have existed without their efforts. Finally, we wish to thank our students, past and present, who provided both the inspiration and the reason for the book.

ACKNOWLEDGMENTS

Grateful acknowledgment is made to the following for permission to use copyrighted material:

Ken Auletta, "Ralph Nader, Public Eye," *Esquire*, December 1983. Reprinted by permission of the author.

Joseph P. Blank, "A Boy's Trial by Fire," *Reader's Digest*, November 1963. Reprinted with permission.

Truman Capote, quoted in "The Story Behind a Nonfiction Novel,: by George Plimpton, *New York Times Book Review*, January 16, 1966. Copyright © 1966/67 by the New York Times Company. Reprinted by permission.

Randy Fitzgerald, "Time to Crack Down on Food Stamp Fraud," *Reader's Digest*, February 1983. Reprinted by permission.

Barbara Gelb, "Mike Nichols, The Special Risks and Rewards of the Director's Art," *New York Times Magazine*. Reprinted by permission of the author.

Dan Greenburg, "The Ninth Precinct Blues," *The New York Times Magazine*, January 21, 1979. Copyright © by Dan Greenburg. Reprinted by permission of the author.

Bob Greene, "Fifteen," in "American Beat," copyright © 1983 by John Deadline Enterprises, Inc. Reprinted by permission of the Sterling Lord Agency, Inc.

Rob Hoerburger, "Phil Collins Beats the Odds," *Rolling Stone*, May 23, 1985. Reprinted by permission of the author.

Bill Kovach, "Little Man Has His Day in Night Court," *The New York Times*, September 23, 1968. Reprinted by permission of the author.

Michael Lemonick, "Voyager's Triumph," *Time* Magazine. Copyright © 1986 by Time Inc. All rights reserved. Reprinted by permission of *Time*.

Andrew H. Malcolm, "Fateful Choice in Fatal Illness: How Long to Live," *The New York Times*, February 14, 1986. Copyright © 1986 by The New York Times Company. Reprinted by permission.

"100 Neediest Cases," 1967. Copyright © 1967 by The New York Times Company. Reprinted by permission.

Carl T. Rowan and David M. Mazie, "Hard Times in America's Heartland." *Reader's Digest,* November 1985. Reprinted with permission of the Readers Digest. Copyright © by the Reader's Digest Assn., Inc.

Bonnie Remsberg, "Beneath The Cloud," *Family Circle,* November 15, 1983. Reprinted by permission of the author.

Claire Safran, "The War on Toxic Waste," *Woman's Day,* October 4, 1983. Copyright © 1983 by Claire Safran. Reprinted by permission of the author.

Peter Wilkinson, "The Trim Man," *Manhattan Inc.,* April 1985. Reprinted by permission of the author.

The Art of Writing Nonfiction

1

A New Art Form

Almost since the days of Dr. Johnson's Grub Street, the literati have considered journalists as hacks. For the majority this is probably fair enough—even though Charles Dickens, Stephen Crane, Mark Twain, George Orwell, Ernest Hemingway, and dozens of other distinguished writers were also practicing journalists. But what most contemporary literary writers and critics have not fully realized is that during the last thirty years a new dimension in journalism has slowly emerged. Today some of the most vital and creative writing in the English language is being done by journalists. Perhaps this is insufficiently recognized because many critics, in and out of universities, don't understand the form.

For two centuries the novel has been one of our major art forms, but in recent years leading novelists like Truman Capote and Norman Mailer have turned to journalism, and other writers like John Hersey, Joan Didion, Nora Ephron, and Jimmy Breslin have worked in both forms. Meanwhile, nonfiction books have displaced novels as the most widely read and influential books on many publisher's lists.

During the sixties this new dimension in journalism became a kind of literary fad, identified by different names by its advocates and practitioners. Tom Wolfe, one of the most original of its practitioners, and Clay Felker, editor of *New York* magazine, called it "the new journalism." Harold Hayes, editor of *Esquire*, called it "literary journalism." Hobart Lewis, editor of *Reader's Digest*, called it simply "a new art form."

All except Lewis thought that this new form started in the early sixties, and all agreed that it was being practiced by a small group of New Yorkers that included Wolfe himself, Breslin, Gay Talese, and a few others. But while these men are unquestionably exceptional journalists, the list leaves out more names than it includes. Further, the history of the form was wrong.

Tom Wolfe has written that the new nonfiction was pioneered by *Esquire,* under editors Hayes and Felker in the early 1960s. He says the

1

characteristics of the new art form all developed about that time. But they actually had started to emerge at least ten and probably twenty years before. Wolfe calls one such characteristic "saturation reporting"; in it the reporter spends days or weeks with the subject of a story in order to observe first-hand the actions which reveal the person's character, the words which reveal motivation. But this kind of reportage was being done by several *Collier's* writers in the mid-forties, and I* can recall discussing with Harold Baron, of *Today's Woman,* the use of fiction plotting techniques for a nonfiction story as early as 1950.

Wolfe says all this came about in magazines, and most of it did, but the techniques also have been used in newspaper depth stories, in television documentaries, and in nonfiction books.

This type of writing is grounded almost equally in journalism and in what the English professors call creative writing—although all writing, of course, is creative. From journalism it takes the reporter's aggressive search for fact, a concern for accuracy, and a sensitive, trained observer's eye, as well as skepticism and adeptness at checking and cross-checking the things the reporter is told by his or her sources. From the "creative" or fiction writer the new journalism borrows imagination, skill at plotting and portraying character, the techniques of building a dramatic story and evoking the reader's emotions, and, most important, the imposition of the writer's judgment on the story.

The actual creative process was aptly described by the late Professor Cathy Covert of Syracuse University, herself a distinguished journalist. Creativity, she said, "is taking a bit of knowledge from one discipline, an insight from another, an experience you have lived, assimilating them in your mind, going through a process of complete chaos, and ultimately coming up with something quite new." And the chaos, she added, is absolutely essential.

This is an accurate description of what happens in the best journalism. Its practitioners—call them reporters, article writers, or nonfiction artists—go behind the facts to get the truth. They spend weeks—perhaps months—learning all they can about their subjects. They become experts by reading and interviewing experts. And they relate what they learn to the problems and worries and interests and yearnings of their readers. Then they write their stories in a way their readers can apprehend, in a way that becomes part of each reader's life experience.

Most people don't act simply on the basis of the things they perceive intellectually. They react to things they know, coupled with what they

---

*As noted in the Preface, the first person singular pronoun refers to André Fontaine.

sense intuitively, instinctually, as a result of an emotional conviction. The creative journalist looks for ways to involve these elements of a reader's personality, knowing that emotions are often more reliable than intellect.

For example, straight, factual accounts of traffic accidents are common in most newspapers:

Susan York, 7, daughter of Mr. and Mrs. Samuel York of 327 Livingston St., was struck and killed yesterday afternoon when she ran in the path of a car driven by Charles Williamson, 42, of 408 South George St.

We have all read such stories. Perhaps we have felt a pang of sadness before going on to look at other parts of the newspapers. But if we had actually seen the accident, we would have been affected far more deeply. We would have seen the little body lying the street, still and shockingly *wrong*, because a body doesn't belong in the middle of a street. Like all bodies, it looks flat, empty, doll-like. We would witness the horror of the mother, running out in the housedress and dirty sneakers she has been wearing to mop the kitchen floor, with none of her armor of makeup and with her hair in rollers. We would see her face stripped bare of the masks we all wear against the world as she kneels and picks up the child, see the way disbelief, then shock, then flooding grief wash over her face so nakedly it is oddly embarrassing, and we would want to turn away from this too-threatening emotion. And we would note the dulled expression on the face of the man whose car hit the child as he gropes to comprehend this thing he has done.

Anyone who has viewed such a scene never forgets it. Such a person is affected emotionally, and the creative journalist, in describing such a scene would attempt to make you, the reader, experience the emotions felt by a witness. The journalist does so by recreating the scene in print, making readers live the tragedy, making it a part of their view of life, and very probably causing them to think about their own driving habits.

So while the typical newspaper story conveys information that you perceive intellectually, creative journalism evokes your emotions, as the best fiction has been doing for centuries.

The difference between fiction and this type of journalism is that while fiction writers can create the characters and dramatic situations they need to get the underlying idea or theme of a story home to their readers, reporters may not. They are bound always by fact; they may make up nothing. This puts a tremendous burden on their ability to research a story and understand its depths, on their thoughtfulness in deciding what is important to report, and on their skill in organizing the story so that the essential truth they want to convey is not distorted.

To get an idea of how the two techniques differ, suppose a reporter and a fiction writer wanted to express this truth about modern living: in large, tightly structured organizations individuals are sometimes trapped between the practicalities of surviving in the organization and their own conception of what is ethical, or perhaps even lawful. The fiction writer would create a character, let's say a man in his middle thirties, married, with three children, a home in the suburbs, and all the familiar pressures to meet the ever-mounting expenses that maintain the family's position in the community, as well as his own status in the large corporation he works for. He also happens to be a man with an inordinate need for acceptance by other men because when he was six his father died, and he was brought up by a dominant and overprotective mother. After her husband died, the mother found some security in her fundamentalist religion, and as the years passed she became more and more rigid and simplistic in her ideas of right and wrong—a rigidity she passed on to her son.

When the reader discovers the man, he has just been given a promotion he has long worked for. But shortly he discovers that one part of his new job is to handle the arrangements his company continually makes with other firms in the same industry to rig the prices they charge for their products, both to government agencies and to the general public. The man knows such arrangements are a violation of antitrust laws, and his rigid conscience tells him he cannot allow himself to be a part of them. On the other hand, he knows that if he refuses to go along with the practice, his career in the corporation will be ended. He also knows enough about the lateral communication between corporations in the same industry to know he will not get a job with any of them.

There's his dilemma; what does he do? The fiction writer will work out the answer in terms of the man's character. Which of the conflicting traits will guide his decision—his need for acceptance or his rigid conscience? If the first, he will be diminished as a man; if the latter, he will be ruined economically.

A reporter, wanting to express the same dilemma, would search until he found a real situation that illuminated it. If he could find none, then he would conclude that his idea that such situations were common in today's life was false. Or if he did find one, he would dig and research and interview until he had all the factual material that would allow him to present the dilemma in terms of the man's internal struggle, just as the fiction writer does.

I ran across just such a situation while I was working on a different story. At an army base in Fort Lee, Virginia, there was a small airfield that could accommodate only light airplanes, and these only during daylight and in good weather. The commander of the base decided he wanted a larger field and asked the Department of Defense for money to build it. He was turned down, but he went ahead and built it anyway.

All base commanders have "operations and maintenance" funds of up to $25,000 a year, which they can spend without specific approval of Congress. At Fort Lee the commander decided to use these funds, but the improved airfield cost nearly $500,000. The difference was made up by falsifying invoices and purchase orders, so that airfield funds were officially listed as being spent for other purposes. After the field was built the whole scheme was uncovered by investigators from the General Accounting Office. It was reported to Congress, and special hearings were held on the affair. At these hearings the dilemma of some of the base officers was spelled out.

One colonel in the engineering office had to take care of the paperwork, developing fictitious projects to get the money and material needed for the airfield. He knew it was illegal and at one point he said to his superior officer, "I am not going to the pen for this." His superior responded ominously that he'd sign the papers.

The colonel told Congress, "I had to choose between violating the law or suffering as a result of the army's system." Those who know the "system" told me an uncooperative officer would likely be assigned to the worst posts, would get no more promotions, and would probably be discharged within a few years.

So here was the same dilemma. I never wrote the story, but if I should, I would tell it in terms of the colonel's personal struggle, I'd learn about his character and career, about the kind of thing that happens to officers who violate "the system." I'd report the things he actually did—how he struggled against the dilemma and finally reached the decision to go along, and what happened to him as a result. Nothing would be made up, but it would be necessary in the interviewing to get inside the officer himself and present the conflict from his point of view. Then the story would be organized to build up the drama of the dilemma, climax when he made his decision, and conclude with an account of what actually happened as a consequence of his choice.

To understand this kind of journalism, it is helpful to know how it came about, for it is a logical evolution in the development of the craft. In the nineteenth century journalistic writing was "personal," and much of it was magnificent. In *Pictures from Italy* in 1846. Charles Dickens reported the hanging of a highwayman in Rome with all the color and impact of his later novels. In 1865 George Alfred Townsend reported in the *New York World* on the capture of John Wilkes Booth with an artistry that put his readers on the spot and made them a part of the confusion and drama and tragedy. Writers such as these, many of whom later became outstanding novelists, used the dramatic techniques of fiction writers, evoking the emotions of their readers and certainly using their own judgment in evaluating the events they reported. The trouble was that many of them went too far and allowed their biases to override the facts. Often the ideal of objectivity never entered their calculations.

This kind of journalism was supplanted, about the turn of the century, by the "objective" reporting that dominated newspaper writing for the next fifty years. Objectivity resulted partly from changing economic conditions and partly from journalistic idealism. The first occurred largely through the growth of the Associated Press, because AP reports were distributed to newspapers representing all kinds of political opinion. Had the reports too obviously reflected any one point of view, they would have been unacceptable to many of the AP's potential customers. Objective reporting as a mark of professionalism spread largely through the leadership of *The New York Times* and a handful of other great newspapers that sought "objectivity" in pursuit of the ideal of impartiality.

This idea of "just the facts, Ma'am" added a great new ethic to reportage—fairness—and implanted it so firmly in the reporter's bag of disciplines that all journalism was elevated. But like all ideals, perfect objectivity was impossible to attain. In something as simple as an automobile accident, for example, what are the facts? Names, addresses, injuries, and what each car was doing. But if you didn't see the accident, how do you know what each was doing? You may ask the police. How do they know? They didn't see it either; they got the story from the drivers and from witnesses. So the reporter talks to witnesses and gets three conflicting stories. What are "the facts"?

Brock Brower, in *On Creative Writing* by Paul Engle, castigated this kind of journalism.

Journalism is routinely voiceless—but far worse, journalism is routinely mindless. Its vaunted objectivity . . . is only an escape from the need to reason. When finally faced with a controversial point which demands some interpretation, the journalist is famous for the "Lib-Lab"—i.e., on the one hand *this*, and on the other, *that*, but neither hand is his. The easy generalization . . . and the endless qualifier . . . are the two stylistic counterweights with which the journalist maintains his own commitment, and hence his own existence, at constant zero.

This type of writing became the norm, and newspapers followed it almost to destruction. Giving just the facts was fine in a simple society of uninformed people, content to be fooled and manipulated by their political and economic leaders.

But by the 1940s everything was suddenly more complicated. If a reporter were to give just the facts leading to the rise of Hitler, say, a newspaper had to find 500 pages to put them in, which it didn't have. And the endless, recitation of dry facts would not only lose readers in the first ten pages, but putting those facts in perspective would require an intimate knowledge of Germany that few readers had. Still, reporters tried to do this and newspapers stopped being pertinent and became mere news bulletin boards—a function television was soon to perform much better.

Meanwhile magazine writers had gone off on a new tack. Spurred by *Time* magazine and Henry Luce, who said frankly that objectivity was a myth and it was time to get the facts off the page and into the reader's mind and gut, magazine writers began to supply the expert knowledge and the perspective the reader needed. Nor did the best of them give up the ideal of objectivity; they simply moved it to another place in the writing process. They made judgments and expressed a point of view, but they concealed both behind the facts they selected to report. Thus they began to learn and use the skills of indirection (which we'll discuss later), and a new dimension was added to journalism.

Under the impact of this new pertinence the now familiar revolution in magazine content took place. Whereas before 1940 the mass magazines had contained about two-thirds fiction and one-third articles, they now reversed the ratio. And their circulations began to climb as readers increasingly found a medium that gave them information they needed in a way that made sense.

In the late forties a few of the top magazine writers began consciously adopting fiction techniques in writing their factual articles—which made everything more difficult, complicated, and effective. This process increased at a geometrical rate in the fifties, and the magazines ran into trouble. Spurred by their advertising departments and the competition of multimillion television audiences, magazine editors began wanting more and more fiction technique in their articles and less and less solid information. Or, put another way, in order to sell magazines, editors wanted more entertainment and less substance.

That was when readers were treated to endless recitals of the loves and difficulties of Liz Taylor and Richard Burton, to the Cinderella story of Grace Kelly and her celluloid romance with the man on top of the wedding cake, and similar vital information. Led by *McCall's,* in the 1960s many magazines also went in for packaging instead of substance, with page after page of huge, four-color pictures and little text. Magazines became more and more bland, further and further removed from the problems and triumphs and values of real people.

So, with some outstanding exceptions, magazines, too, failed their journalistic responsibility to tell people about their complicated world in a way that made sense. But a few years before, the best newspapers had caught the idea and started to do the job themselves. This was when the *Wall Street Journal,* for instance, began to carry the first "depth" stories on page one and showed the rest of the country's papers how it was done.

As the depth stories developed, they did precisely what the magazine articles had done. So did the best television documentaries, notably those produced by Edward R. Murrow and Fred Friendly for CBS. Indeed, television began to borrow magazine writers who understood the technique to do the job. Former magazine men like Arthur Morse, William Peters, Leslie Midgeley, and Gordon Manning moved to television. And several of them have said they made the documentaries the same way they had written magazine articles, except that they had available and learned to use the extra dimension of the camera and the sound track.

But of course television had its own built-in imperatives—so well documented by Friendly in his book *Due to Circumstances Beyond Our Control*—that soon caused the amount of this kind of superb journalism to decline. Then in the seventies more newspapers were getting the message, and the ten or twelve best papers in the country increasingly hired the writers, gave them the time and expenses they needed to do the job, and printed the interpretive stories that the times and their constitutional license demanded.

Today, large numbers of newspapers run sections with titles like "Style" or "Living," which contain some impressive interpretive pieces. While some of these sections also contain a great deal of pap, others contain fine stories, the result of good reporting done by reporters who are given the time and encouragement to do meaningful pieces. The increase has continued, but the need for this kind of journalism is so great that if all the mass media devoted twice the time and space that they currently do to it, the supply would still be too low.

One reason is the knowledge explosion. It has been said that the total of human knowledge since 1940 is equal to all human knowledge up to 1940.

Professor Bertram M. Gross, a noted social scientist, notes that in psychology, for instance, the amount of knowledge doubles every ten years. In this situation, the old cops-and-robbers type of reportage is as pertinent as a bicycle is to a fish. As knowledge expands it becomes more precise, more specialized, and more qualified. It gets further from the fund of knowledge of the average reader and thus needs to be related, interpreted, explained. This is the interpretive reporter's job. To do it properly he or she must master the broader implications of specialized knowledge and put them at the service of the average reader. The reporter must become a kind of communications bridge between the experts and the public.

Another dimension of the job facing journalism is the noninvolvement of people, what the social scientists call alienation. People are out of touch with their world and with other people, especially in the cities where some seven out of ten Americans live. Evidence erupts periodically all over the country. In a New Bedford, Massachusetts, bar a group of men raped a young woman on a pool table while the other patrons stood by, doing nothing. In Ohio, a woman driving to work one February morning skidded on a bridge and her car splashed into the river. The woman climbed out on the rear deck and, as the car slowly sank, screamed that she could not swim. Some thirty-five persons stood a mere fifteen feet away and watched her drown.

There are many causes of this alienation. A major one, we believe, is that increasingly over the past two or three generations, people have learned that they cannot control their own lives. With the growth of mass-production techniques, workers were no longer individual artisans who could make a chair, a suit, from start to finish, and who at the end had the satisfaction of holding a concrete expression of their work. They had become faceless parts of a great human machine. Once they sought to reassert their power as individuals by banding together into trade unions, and for a while they were effective. But the unions too grew into large, impersonal bureaucracies, at the same time the largest corporations began to operate on a multinational scale. Today unions are on the decline, and the economy is moved by forces too large and complex for most people to understand much less control.

Psychologists know that when people cannot control their own destiny, they often sink into apathy, sometimes too deeply ever to surface again. But they feel an internal, unexpressed rage, and perhaps when they see someone else being victimized, they express sadistic satisfaction by doing nothing. This process is reinforced, we believe, by the mass media. In movies, advertising, paperback and magazine fiction, and in the ceaseless drumfire of television commercials and "entertainment," people are presented from childhood with a picture of a never-never land in which all women are beautiful and happy, all men handsome, virile, and prosperous. They live in a suburban split-level with two gorgeous cars named after wild beasts and with smiling children who always learn, after minor peccadilloes, that the traditional values are best. Inevitably, after years of this, people find themselves trying to live in two worlds. They—not all and not all to the same degree—think the never-never land is the way life really is. But the realities of their own daily lives are uglier, less felicitous, pocked with loss, boredom, injustice, and problems that seem to have no solution. And when people measure this reality against the media's glamorous fictions, they feel both cheated and self-contemptuous, blaming themselves for not enjoying the kinds of lives the media portray. More apathy, more internal rage then may result.

This is one of the sicknesses of our times, and as the mass media have had a role in causing it, they have a responsibility to help cure it. It constitutes one of the challenges facing serious journalists today. To accept it and meet it successfully requires all the skills in communicating effectively that their profession has mobilized since Gutenberg.

Henry T. Yost, Sr., a biology professor at Amherst College, addressed an entering freshman class, which had been assigned to read *Don Quixote*, among other books, over the summer. His talk concluded:

> Someday we must see that freedom for the individual is not in acquiring better furniture, is not in being a success, is not in being pampered, is not even in being left alone. Our freedom lies in doing battle with giants wherever we may find them. We cannot be the New Men—a part of the establishment. We must be knights-errant and, like the Don, be willing to attempt the impossible—for that is the only true freedom. . . .
>
> For in reality, as in myth, man is always on a giant-hunt. If he does not find real ones, he will hunt mythical ones; and the role of the intellectual, be he scientist or humanist, is to replace the mythical giants with real ones, to direct the efforts of man to the searching out of those giants of our society that must be slain, and, in the process, to provide the encouragement to do battle with giants and to provide hope that the battle can be won.

No better statement of the job of the serious journalist has been made.

2

Where Do You Get Story Ideas?

*I*nterpretive writing requires changes throughout the reporting-writing process. The idea with which a story starts is a little different, the research is both broader and different in character from older reportage, the evaluation of the research is so changed it is almost a new process, and the writing itself is more highly crafted, difficult, creative.

The whole process starts, of course, with the story idea. Textbooks on magazine article writing say that ideas are everywhere, which is true but not very helpful. The problem is to know a good one when you see it. The solution starts not with the writer, but the reader.

The difference between amateur and professional writers is that amateurs write for themselves and professionals write for their readers. The reporter starting out on a newspaper quickly learns from her editor that readers are primarily interested in crime, sex, scandal, disaster, sports, society, and death, and the editors judgment of what makes up a good story is based on these values. If she goes to work for a magazine, she discovers that readers come in smaller groups and different sizes. At *Redbook,* for instance, I learned that our readers were primarily women between the ages of eighteen and thirty-five, married, with a home in the suburbs, two children, five and eight years old, and an interest in the P.T.A. If I had an idea for a story that involved teenagers, *Redbook* editors wouldn't listen to me; it was not for their readers.

If a writer today plans to sell an article to *Cosmopolitan,* she must know that *Cosmopolitan* readers are somewhat unlike the glamorous models who grace each issue's cover. The readers are primarily women between the ages of 18 and 34. They live in or near large cities, are employed, and earn about $14,000 a year. So *Cosmopolitan* is not the place for a story on how to choose the proper silver for a party at your Southampton beach cottage.

This kind of specialization, of course, was brought about not by editors, but by publishers who wanted to carve out a section of the reading audience and convince advertisers their magazine reached it more authoritatively than anyone else's. But whatever the cause, today's writers must think about their readers in more precise and subtle terms.

Thus the first, and simplest, step in writing is to know who your reader is. Is it a woman or a man? Aged fifteen, thirty-five, or fifty-five? College, high school, or grade school graduate? Skier, homeowner, scientist? Within these groupings you usually shoot for the idea that will affect the largest number the most intimately. (As Sumner Blossom, then editor of *American Magazine,* once said "I'd rather have a story on noses than on red hair: more people have noses than red hair.")

The key, as he indicated, is reader self-interest. People are primarily interested in themselves—their problems, the things they do every day, their hobbies, their relationships with others.

A good way to get the hang of this is to read and analyze some successful magazines. For example, anyone reading *Bicycling* magazine would know immediately that its editors want how-to pieces on nearly all aspects of bicycling, and pieces on fitness, bicycle trips, and tours. A reader of *Yankee* would realize that the magazine focuses on New England, and that the editors like articles on the region's history, places, and people. And a quick look at *Working Woman* tells us that the magazine wants material of interest to young, well-educated, busy career women.

A reader's self-interest may be as obvious as gender or as subtle as a psychological need. The writer must identify it and provide some satisfaction for it. When she does she will have a usable idea.

Such ideas provide a service to the reader—some simple, direct, practical, some complicated and subtle. For example, one day an observant writer may see a pet store with an unusual window display. It is the re-creation in miniature of a woodland pool, complete with rocks, overhanging branches of plants, a miniature waterfall, and a pool bright with darting tropical fish. The writer goes in, talks to the owner, and comes out with an article, perhaps for *Tropical Fish Hobbyist.*

This is fine. It has the elements of the craft: identifying the self-interest of a particular group of readers and finding new information that will serve their interest, getting it and presenting it in the proper medium and in a way that will be of value to them. It is creative in that the writer must conceive the idea, analyze the need for the information, and present it clearly and cogently. Great masses of useful information are supplied readers in this way via thousands of special-interest magazines ranging all the way from *Cats Magazine* to *Yachting.* Many features in newspapers (how to refinish your attic) and educational television programs ("This Old House") use the same basic techniques to supply similar needs.

But this kind of writing is also pretty elementary in the dynamic modern world of computers, heart transplants, and hunger that affects millions. Society is changing so fast today that none of us is living in the world we think we are, and the problems of people's relationships with each other and the systems they have created are so complex only the experts understand them, if anybody does. But people need the experts' knowledge, and it is the creative journalist's job to supply it. To do so effectively the journalist must develop skills that are considerably more sophisticated and subtle than those used by the writer dealing with the pet shop display.

This job starts in one of two ways. The writer either learns of some new information an expert has that can help solve a problem which large numbers of people face, or the writer first identifies the problem, then seeks out the information from experts to help solve it. Sometimes the two steps meld together so it's hard to tell which came first.

An example of the first is a piece I did some years ago for *Redbook*. It started with a small item in a New York newspaper, which reported a new technique some elementary school teachers were using in class. It was called sociometric testing and, like many sociological phenomena, the fancy name covered a simple process. They asked the kids in the class whom they liked best, like least, liked to work with, play with, and so on. And why.

I remembered an article I'd done two or three years before in which a sociologist at Ohio University had done a study which showed—vastly oversimplified—that the college students who had the most dates in college got the best marks. This seemed a contradiction, but when you learned why, it made sense: popular students felt accepted, secure, unthreatened; the resulting self-confidence released their energies for their studies. Question: if this was true for college students, wasn't it also true for grade school youngsters?

I went to see Dr. Helen Hall Jennings, a psychologist who had been mentioned in the newspaper story as an expert on sociometric testing, and she told me the answer was yes. But as I talked with her about the process, the subject began to broaden. When you looked at the answers of hundreds of children as to whom they liked best and least and why, you began to see emerging a whole system of values. This system was different from the one teachers and parents had for each other and, as I thought about it, I remembered that when I was a kid I felt and acted differently when I was with other kids than I did with adults. But now that I was an adult with kids of my own, I looked at them and their actions in terms of my adult value system. I never thought about theirs or that it might be different. I suspected most other parents did the same.

Now the idea began to take a different shape. Sociometric testing was a system by which educators could improve the learning ability of their pupils. But I wasn't writing for educators, I was writing for the general public. How could this insight be made valuable to general readers?

Obviously my target audience was parents and more specifically mothers, since typically they were more directly and consistently concerned with their children's development than fathers. Everybody knows that most parents want their kids to do well in school. But there was another element in the idea, too: if sociometric testing revealed the child's value system, it necessarily revealed, or could reveal, those qualities in youngsters which made others like them—made them, in other words, popular. I knew that Americans put a high value on popularity, so here was another reader self-interest that might be used.

Further research showed that there was a sound psychological reason for Americans' respect for popularity—that we all get a good deal of our feelings about ourselves from the way others react to us. If by their actions other people demonstrate that they find us valuable, respect and like us, we have a feeling of self-assurance, of confidence, a positive outlook on the world. If other people reject us, we tend to think they know what they're about and that we're not much good. So we become negative, sick with self-contempt, and we tend to withdraw.

Again the story idea changed shape and broadened. Now it would appeal not only to educators and parents, but would be of considerable help to them as they wrestled with the problems of raising emotionally healthy, competent youngsters. And it could be put to them in terms they were accustomed to dealing with, not in educators' gobbledygook. The title almost wrote itself: "What Makes Kids Popular?"

The market was also obvious—*Redbook*, because the article was a woman's piece, and because it dealt with younger children. The editors liked the idea and I went out and did the story. Here (with my comments interspersed) is the way it started and the way the original idea of sociometric testing was transformed into a story with a much broader reader self-interest:

What Makes Kids Popular?

Without meaning to, you can cripple or kill your child's chance of ever being popular. You won't do it intentionally, of course. If you do it, it's because, like almost all parents, you don't know what it is that makes one child respected and admired by his playmates and another baited and shunned.

If you'll remember back to your own school days, you'll doubtless recall that you felt and behaved entirely differently in front of parents and teachers than you did when you were alone with the other kids. You, like all children, lived in two worlds—the official one that adults saw and the "hidden" one you shared with your school and playmates. But now that you're a parent, the chances are you can't remember exactly what that hidden world was like.

Until recently, adults have never been able to enter a child's secret world. But within the past few years social scientists have developed a way to penetrate it. By means of a new kind of test they've explored that world and charted it. Their findings have surprised many who thought they were child experts.

If you want your child to be popular, you should try to understand this world, for it is often more powerful in determining what kind of person he'll be than you—or his teachers or any other adults—are.

The "you" lead was used in an attempt to get direct, immediate contact with the reader. The reader self-interest in raising popular kids is hit in the first paragraph, then expanded upon in a way designed to make the reader say, "Yes, that's the way it was." But after four paragraphs of abstract discussion I was afraid I was going to lose the reader, so I put in an anecdote that showed kids in action and also had some appeal for the reader. Of course it also indirectly made the point that kids knew how to operate effectively in their own world, which was often different from the world of the teacher or their parents.

Recently, for example, a boy in one school was fooling around and raising the roof instead of doing his work. The teacher was unable to do anything with him, even when she warned that if he didn't buckle down he might not be promoted. One day, in order to impress on him what it would be like to be left back, she said he would have to spend three or four days in the grade just below.

She told him this shortly before the noon hour. When lunch was over, she was presented with a petition signed by every member of the class except the "bad" boy. It said: "Joseph is our class member. It's our fault as much as his if he doesn't work. Please let him stay with us. We will see that he works."

Somewhat flabbergasted and a little proud, the teacher agreed. Joseph's work improved immediately and stayed at the higher level.

Now to explain the two reasons why it's important for kids to be popular, backed up by quotes from experts.

It is terribly important for a child to be popular in his own world—first, because his popularity will determine his attitude toward himself throughout his life, and second, because if he's popular he will learn more. Says Dr. Jean D. Grambs, professor of educational sociology at Stanford University, "The way one feels about oneself throughout life is affected by group atmospheres—the individual has a sense of personal security, poise, success, or the individual is suspicious, defensive, feels inferior, and dislikes others."

Thus if you can teach your child how to be popular in his hidden world you'll go a long way toward ensuring his success in his future marriage, his relations with others on his job, and his position among his friends and neighbors.

Furthermore, if a child is accepted, respected and admired by his mates, he learns more easily. Says Gordon Allport, distinguished Harvard psychologist, "The student's readiness to learn facts, it is now pretty well agreed, depends on the state of his attitudes. Information seldom sticks unless mixed with 'attitudinal glue.' And his attitudes are determined largely by what other kids think of him."

Now, after ten paragraphs, sociometric testing, which triggered the whole idea, is finally mentioned and explained. But the explanation is held to a minimum and includes no educator's jargon. To keep the reader going, there's a short, specific anecdote included. Immediately after the explanation of the device, we go back to the main reader self-interest: what makes kids popular.

A deceptively simple device has yielded these discoveries. It is called a sociometric test, and it measures children's popularity. The teacher asks each child whom he would most like to sit next to, or work on a committee with or play with.

Once she gets this information, she can draw up a chart showing which children are the most frequently chosen, and which are seldom or never chosen.

This is where the surprises start. In a New York City school, for example, there was a boy named Ronald who had an IQ of only seventy-five and whom the teacher thought "emotionally unstable, immature and below his grade level." But Ronald was chosen six times by other students, who apparently saw in him things that the teacher didn't. She put him with the six who had chosen him, and after two months she reported, "He reads nicely now and holds his own in class discussion." (Surprisingly often, the quiet, well-mannered and bright child is not wanted by his schoolmates.)

This teacher carried out the next step in sociometric testing—she rearranged the class so that the youngsters were with the ones they liked best. And, more important, she took steps to bring the unwanted children into the group.

To do this, a teacher must know what it is the other kids don't like about their less popular classmates, and this is where the testing gets tricky. Because finding out the real reasons—not the ones the kids tell you first—requires skill in what the psychologists call "depth interviewing." This may take hours, and usually the information is gotten indirectly, in reply to questions that seem inconsequential or downright silly.

It has taken years of such testing, plus the interviewing of thousands of children all over the country, for these scientists to compile any general list of the qualities that make children popular. Here are the highlights:

From here on the article lists the major attributes that make youngsters liked and respected by other kids. For emphasis the separate points are numbered and the first sentence set in boldface. In each case the point is stated, explained, then illustrated with an anecdote. There are four such points. Then there's one that lists the things that are in adult value systems, but not in the child's. Finally, the piece winds up with a "what can be done" section which suggests things parents can do to make their kids popular. This is a simple, practical structure; the artistry, if any, comes in thinking the basic idea through from a pedagogue's gimmick to something that would help parents, and in selecting and writing the anecdotes.

In the evolution of this idea, bits of information were taken from several sources and melded together to make something new. Here the process started with a new body of information from an expert; it could have started with the writer identifying a problem, a concern that is common to many readers, then seeking out the experts to find the answers, if any. But always the essential ingredient in shaping the idea is reader self-interest.

How does the writer identify self-interest? How does she learn about new information that the experts have? She arranges and maintains the broadest, most diverse intake of ideas, information, impressions, emotions that she can. She circulates and listens to people. She observes, not with the sightseer's bland gaze, but with the reporter's sharp eye that always asks why, and how does this fit. She reads enormously and as many different kinds of publications as possible. She watches television and movies, goes to plays and museums and concerts.

A writer learns to listen to everybody's shop talk as a possible source of ideas. She happens to go to a party at which are four aeronautical engineers who shortly huddle in one end of the room and talk shop. The writer probably knows nothing about aeronautical engineering, but she joins the group, listens, and gets involved, because if something concerns them, it may concern thousands of others in different jobs. It may not, too, but at least she's probably picked up some tidbits of information she didn't have before. Sometimes she tries to trigger the idea-formation process by asking a fuel oil dealer, say, what are the problems, headaches, gripes in his business. She may get a tip for an article for a home-and-garden magazine on ways to save money on oil heating or oil furnace repairs. It isn't earthshaking, but it's valuable to thousands of homeowners. Or the conversation may bring a tip-off on a racket-ridden union or city department that is victimizing homeowners and needs exposing.

A writer never knows where the next idea is coming from, so she makes the conglomeration of things she reads and experiences as rich as possible. Most writers I know read three or four newspapers a day, a couple of weekly newsmagazines, a dozen or so general magazines, plus scholarly or professional publications in the fields they are especially interested in. Medical writers read medical journals, political writers read the Congressional Record, and business writers read annual reports. Because universities are centers of research in many fields, many writers have had their names put on mailing lists of university news bureaus. All of these esoteric sources provide new bits of information which, when combined with the writer's own knowledge of people's self-interests, may trigger an idea for a new article, newspaper series, or a book.

For the creative journalist, the process of listening to people, of reading widely, of absorbing information, impressions, ideas, and emotions cannot be a passive pursuit. He or she also thinks about all these things trying to relate one to another, and juxtaposing bits of information to see if they add up to something new. It is in this process that good journalist spots trends and truths about the current scene that may have eluded others. The story idea mentioned in chapter 1, about the dilemma of a man caught in an organization trap, came while I was reading congressional testimony about the Fort Lee airfield scandal. As I thought about the situation later, it seemed likely that the colonel involved was only one of many caught in similar situations in other large organizations; checking around proved the hunch to be true.

Some years ago, the newspapers and magazines were full of stories about the horrible living conditions of migrant farm laborers. Question: Wasn't there some place in America where conditions weren't horrible, where the residents had accepted the migrants into their community's life? Some checking around revealed there was, and a report of what the town did and how it worked made an article.

Persistent thinking about what they are taking in provides writers with another great reservoir of ideas. Every writer I know agrees that some of the best story ideas can come while doing research for a quite different piece. Almost never when I have been out of town doing research on one story have I come back without an idea for one or two more. It usually happens while you're interviewing someone and the conversation wanders off the subject. Then a point she makes, an insight she shares, a story she tells opens a door to a whole new field of thought, and in the new vista you suddenly see the shape and color of a new story.

Finally, there are practical considerations in handling ideas that beginners often ignore. One of these is whether the story can actually be gotten. Many first-class ideas are too big, too diffuse to be practical. For example, medical fees had been rising faster than almost any other costs as this was written. A writer might think of doing a piece on exactly how much an appendectomy, an office visit, or a series of X-rays costs in fifty major cities across the country.

It's a good idea. It would be valuable both to document the rise in medical charges and to give millions a yardstick by which to measure their own doctor's fees. But how do you get the story? Is there time and money enough to visit each of the fifty cities and spend a week or two digging out the information? Keep in mind that it won't come easily. Most doctors won't tell you what they charge, and neither will the medical societies or medical schools. Insurance companies have schedules of fees for particular ailments, but everyone knows doctors frequently charge more than the scheduled price. Would you go door-to-door asking people? What people? How would you know that those you interviewed were a true cross-section of the city?

Labor unions might agree to poll their memberships, but less than twenty percent of American workers belong to unions, so how accurate would your sample be? Would an industry agree to such a poll? Probably not, but even if it did, wouldn't you have the same sample distortion? About the only way such an idea could be turned into a valid story would be for a magazine to hire a good polling organization to run a nationwide poll at great expense. Occasionally magazines do this, but usually the story idea originates with the editors rather than an individual writer.

A recent trend is for a publication to enlist a professional polling organization, usually in a university, to make broad, scientific studies of attitudes and happenings in its area of interest. The television networks and large newspapers like the *New York Times* and the *Washington Post* routinely use such polls to determine how Americans feel about particular issues or political candidates.

Another practical question that novice writers sometimes fail to consider is whether a story is publishable. Not whether it is well researched and written, but is the idea one that the mass media will use? The answer deals not with the audience or formula of a particular magazine or network, but with general attitudes that all media share.

The media try to be positive. A story about what's good is more acceptable than one about what's bad. Stories of a person's struggle to overcome obstacles usually must have a happy ending. Stories that explore a problem almost always must include a section at the end explaining what can be done to solve it. There are minor exceptions to this rule. Articles that expose a bad situation in the most dramatic possible terms are occasionally used for their shock value. But the market for this type of story is limited, and even then a "what can be done" section is usually included.

The reason is simple. The media are part of what we call the free enterprise system; most do not publish attacks on it. You can attack crime, labor unions, extreme leftists and rightists, politicians, and teachers, but seldom corporations or businessmen (except when some scoundrel embezzles $867,422.32 from some company, in which case you attack him, not the company). Book publishers are more likely to publish this kind of story—Ralph Nader's numerous books are examples.

Mass media editors want to keep their readers reading, their viewers watching. They know that factual, statistical presentations that appeal only to an audience's intellect are ignored in droves. So it's up to the writer to present his or her ideas and information in ways that appeal to reader's emotions and enable them to identify with the issue under discussion. One of the best ways of doing this is to personalize the situation. You write not about the problem but about a person experiencing the problem. For example, we all know that many of the people who say that the primary value of athletics is to teach teamwork and sportsmanship do not really believe that and are interested primarily in winning.

But to do an article on the subject, a reporter would have to find a way to personalize the issue. A few years ago, a student named Bob Lloyd did that. Lloyd, who came from Texas, heard about a high school football coach in the Texas town of Dripping Springs (really!) who was in danger of being fired because his team was losing. That was not unusual, but other facts were.

The coach had once been the town's hero, because he had coached the team to three division titles. He had also been praised because he had established a policy that every boy on the team would play in every game, no matter how important. Obviously his players loved him and when he was winning, the townspeople did too. But after the team was moved into a different division, containing considerably larger schools, the team started losing, and many of the townspeople turned on him. Lloyd's story beautifully captured all of these elements and showed that for some, at least, winning was the only thing. Lloyd sold the story to the *New York Times*.

With few exceptions, the mass media do not want essays in which writers expound their own ideas of the way things are or ought to be. They want reportage. Many times when I was first writing for magazines, editors tossed back a manuscript with, "This is just an essay, just you talking. Who the hell are you? The readers want to know what happened." It was hard on the ego, but it made the point.

All these media attitudes may offend your conception of journalistic truth and responsibility, as well as your ego. But a writer's obligation is to get published, and this is the way it is. If you want to write for a few select friends or people who are already convinced, that's fine. But if you want to reach millions with your message, you accept the strictures and figure a way to say what you want within their limits. In most cases it can be done. The flexibility and ingenuity required to shape your idea is also a part of the creative process.

3

How Do You Sell Ideas?

Once a writer has come up with an idea and decided on the magazine he or she thinks will use the article, the next job is to convince the magazine's editors to buy it. To do this, a magazine writer uses something called a query letter or outline (the two terms are interchangeable).

Like one or two other things in this business, the term "outline" is confusing. It has two meanings. One is the outline you produce for your own use when you are trying to figure out how to put the article together. It's informal, written for you, and takes whatever form you choose. But the outline an editor wants to see is different. It is a selling document, designed to sell the editor on your idea. It must convince the editor of four facts: (1) that the idea is valid; (2) that the story can be gotten; (3) that it will be right for his or her audience; and (4) that you can produce it—that is, that you know how to do the necessary research, and that the quality of your writing meets the magazine's standards.

Many textbooks on magazine writing say that the outline should be as short as possible, perhaps a single paragraph, certainly no more than a page. This may be all right for an editor with whom you have worked closely and who knows how you write and research. But if you want to do major articles for large magazines, or if you are unknown to the editor, a one-paragraph letter just won't do the job.

I have written outlines that were as long as six pages. That's long—two or three pages is better—but I always feel that the assignment is going to stand or fall on the basis of what's on the paper, and this is the only chance I'm going to have to convince the editor. And not just one editor; in the bigger markets, no single editor makes the decision on an idea. He or she passes it along to three or four others, and your outline must convince them too. An outline, then, is almost a telescoped article, and because it is, there are certain things you have to do before you can produce a good one.

First, you have to do enough preliminary research to make sure the idea is valid. You have to locate sources for material you will get and make sure they have the material, know what they're talking about, and are willing to talk to you. You have to figure out likely markets, which means, among other things, that you check *Reader's Guide to Periodical Literature* to see what else has been written on the subject and who has published it. It's not the smartest thing in the world to offer an article to *Good Housekeeping* on new discoveries in dieting if they published one two months ago. You must figure out the reader self-interests of the likely markets and the ways your article will appeal to them. You must gather two or three anecdotes that illustrate the theme or some of the points the article will make. Finally you must write the outline so that it will convince *by demonstration*.

It's no good to tell an editor, "There are a lot of good anecdotes." Get a couple and write them. That way you prove there are good ones and that you know how to handle them. It's no good to say, "This will be of great interest to your readers." You must isolate the particular self-interest and make it implicit to the outline so the editor will recognize it. It's no good to say, "There are many good authorities who will vouch for this idea." You must identify a couple and quote them in support of the idea. It does no good to say, "This is a great dramatic human narrative." You must indicate it by telling some of the story, or at least listing the elements of the drama, so the editor knows that you know what they are.

Obviously this kind of outline can't be written in fifteen minutes on a Friday afternoon. It takes work and thought. Further, while you're doing it, you know it may be wasted because the idea may never sell. That's the gamble you take, the investment you make in order to get a future reward. If you're not willing to do it, forget about the major markets and the lovely daydreams about showers of gold.

A good outline, then, should contain these elements:

1.   A title, if you can think of a clever one or one that expresses succinctly the theme of the piece.

2.   A clear, concise statement of the idea plus ways it appeals to reader self-interest.

3.   Evidence to support the idea, including a couple of anecdotes.

4.   Suggested sources for the material you will use.

5.   Suggestions for the "what can be done" section if it's a problem story.

6.   If you have to travel at the magazine's expense to get the material, some idea of where you'll go and about how much it will cost.

Here's an example of an outline that sold an idea to *Reader's Digest*. (The title isn't very catchy, but it does express the underlying idea; it was not used when the piece was published.)

Traffic Courts Are Unfair

Motorists all over the country are being whipsawed in traffic courts that are not courts at all, but collection agencies. They retain the power of courts to punish, yet ignore the safeguards for an individual's rights that the rest of our legal system has.

Thus, a startling statement for a lead and a succinct presentation of the basic idea. Next comes evidence to support the statement, written in a way that will also promote reader identification and appeal to his self-interest.

The pattern is familiar: you answer a summons for a minor violation. You wait for hours in a jammed, uncomfortable courtroom. The arresting officer is always right; your version is wrong. If you want to plead not guilty you're given another date for a hearing, you miss another day from work, and often the cop doesn't show up so you have another postponement, and another. Often you can't afford to miss more time from work so you give up and plead guilty.

Often when you say you want to plead not guilty the judge says, "Why not plead guilty. It will only cost you $5." What he doesn't say is that it is also a conviction on your record which, in states with a point system, may be the first step in the suspension of your license—and with it your only way to get to work, or get the kids to school, or shop for food. He also doesn't say the conviction may boost your insurance premiums: if you have three speeding violations in eighteen months, for example, your rate goes up 60 percent.

All this has been general; now come a couple of specific anecdotes, written very tightly.

If you plead guilty you may well be treated like a bank robber. Recently a young man answered a summons, but he hadn't brought enough money to pay his fine. Although he said his wife was outside in the car with additional cash, he was booked, fingerprinted, stripped, searched, and held in jail for eight hours before he could reach his wife and have her bring the additional money. A New York businessman was fined $15 at 11:50 A.M.; he'd forgotten his wallet. He telephoned his office and instructed an assistant to bring down the necessary amount; nevertheless he was handcuffed and thrown into the tank. The assistant arrived at 12:20 with the money, but he was not allowed to pay it until 4:00 P.M., and the businessman was not released until 4:45.

Now, another two points the article will make, both written to heighten reader identification.

Though the chief objective of these courts seems to be to collect money rather than to dispense justice, even the simplest modern traffic violation may not be an open-and-shut thing. For instance: you're driving at the speed limit in a 35-mile-an-hour zone. When you're seventy-five feet from the corner, the light turns red. You can stop in time, but there's a car tailgating you; if you stop quickly, it may hit you. You see there are no cars on the cross street, and you decide it's safer to run the light. You have had to make several fairly complicated decisions in a split second; certainly there's room for the argument that you were right—except in the collection-agency courts.

Further, there are many unrealistic speed limits in existence, as well as many bad traffic signals and confusing signs. A person can violate a law with the best will in the world, while trying hard to be lawful. Yet none of this is taken into consideration in thousands of traffic courts. Sometimes cops have a quota of tickets to give out and lay for victims until they fill it.

Now another anecdote to prove this last point.

Recently a woman stopped at an intersection unfamiliar to her and prepared to make a left turn. She had her blinker on and waited almost two minutes for traffic to clear before making the turn. She did not see a No Left Turn sign across the intersection, but she did see a parked police car with an officer watching her. He made no move to warn her the proposed turn was illegal but after she made it, he gave her a ticket.

Here comes the "what can be done section," plus identification of a major source for the story.

> But reform is possible. The American Bar Association has detailed a member, James Economos, to head up its Committee on Traffic Courts. Economos, whose headquarters is in Chicago, has traveled all over the country investigating abuses and has a store of facts about them. He has also helped communities fight to reform their traffic courts. One case I know of where he was successful was in Chenango County, New York. Here a citizens committee and the Chamber of Commerce banded together in a successful campaign of reform. But AAA officials assure me Economos has many other similar cases we could report on to tell people how to correct the abuses.

Finally, a suggestion of the travel—and expenses—necessary to get the story.

The way to do the story would be to go to Chicago and see Economos, and then if it proved necessary to visit some individual cities where abuses were taking place, do so.

After consulting with other editors, the man I worked with at the *Digest* told me to go ahead on the story. But he wanted me to get Economos to agree to sign the piece with an "as told to ———" by-line. I prefer not do that kind of story, because it restricts what you can write to what the other signer is willing to say publicly, and it means you have to do a good bit of negotiating on precisely how the final piece will be worded. But Economos proved to be willing to make many tough and truthful charges about this situation, and his name and position added authority to the piece, so that's the way we did it.

Of course, not all outlines have to be that long, and some are organized differently. Here's an outline done by one of Glavin's former students, Peter Wilkinson. The outline was sent to Christine Miles, the managing editor of *Manhattan, Inc.*, whom Wilkinson had met but had never worked with. The outline was the only basis Miles had of judging Wilkinson's ability.

Dear Chris:

Way back last year when you were still at *Forbes*, we talked about reporter/researcher jobs. I'm at Fairchild [a publisher] now and I want to propose an article that might fit in at *Manhattan, Inc.*

Al Wilburne was in the trimmings business. He sold buttons, bits of lace, piping, and ruffles to the big dress makers in New York's garment center. Through the years—Al opened his doors right after the Depression—his companies grew and prospered. But, in 1977, when in his 60s, Al saw an opportunity to increase his profits many times over. He started sending phony bills to his best customer, having them approved by a man inside, laundering the money, and using the loot to build a big house and buy furs and jewels for his wife.

In time, Al and others stole more then $4 million, pulling off the largest bogus billing scam in garment center history. Al had a partner in crime—his son Marc, who was a co-owner of several of the Wilburne companies. A shy, passive young man, Marc was a product of his father's influence and the two were nearly indistinguishable. Marc looked to Al for guidance in all aspects of business and his personal life.

Al had taken Marc into the family firm at 23—after one dismal year of dental school—and Marc performed well. But, before long, he too was consumed by the fraud. Ultimately, it would be Marc's unquenchable greed, his escalation of the scheme, that would attract the attention of federal agents. Together they were indicted, and together Al and Marc fled, first to Canada and then to Israel. And together they would come back to jail—Marc for five years, his dad for seven.

The Wilburnes had run a colorful series of crimes—hooking up with Israeli mafia figures, threatening grand jury witnesses, and framing other men. Both lived in million-dollar homes on Long Island and drove expensive cars. But later, when jail was only weeks away, the only job Marc could find was one driving an ice cream truck. And eventually, IRS agents, seeking restitution, would appraise everything the Wilburnes owned, right down to Marc's daughter's teddy bear.

Then, one night last month, Marc walked outside his "cell" at a minimum security prison in Connecticut (his father was asleep inside), tied together of couple of belts, and hanged himself from a tree. He was 35. The next day a federal judge in New York granted Al's pending request for a reduction in sentence. Al was free to go, the judge said, and Al buried Marc that afternoon.

As the court reporter for Fairchild News Service in New York, I've covered the Wilburnes since their return from Israel. I've written about their pleadings, sentencings, and Marc's death. As I see it, the article requires a detailed review of the extensive court file in the case, plus interviews with those who knew Al and his son—people in the garment center and, if possible, family members. I've gone to the prosecutor for help on this and can hope for a number of willing subjects.

Look forward to meeting with you to discuss the project further.

Note that the Wilkinson outline covers all of the basics. It tells Miles what the story is about, shows that it deals with *Manhattan, Inc.*'s area of interest (business in New York City), proves that Wilkinson knows how to conduct the necessary research, and gives an idea of the style in which he will write the story. (Mentioning the teddy bear indicated that Wilkinson had a reporter's eye for the telling detail.) No outline need do more than that. Miles says she grew interested in the story because of the outline. After reading it, she spoke with Wilkinson, gave him the assignment, and, a few months later, printed the article in *Manhattan, Inc.*

4

Research

*F*or the daily deadline reporter, research was much too fancy a word
for the process of getting a story. He called it legwork and it consisted of going where something was happening, looking acutely, listening
accurately, questioning participants to fill out the details, and checking
what he'd seen and heard with other participants or documentary sources
to make sure he hadn't been misled. In their book *The Reporter's Trade,*
Washington columnists Joseph and Stewart Alsop called this "the rule of
the feet" and added, "If you get out, and see what is going on for yourself,
and talk to a great many people who are responsibly involved in what is
going on, you can hardly help doing a good job of reporting."

True enough. The operative phrase is, "and talk to a great many
people who are responsibly involved." What people? Where?

A writer answering these questions calls upon his creativity in the
research part of the job. If he is going to use material from different
sources, different disciplines to create something new, this is the place
where he decides what sources and disciplines. If the disciplines are
diverse, varied, pertinent, and the sources valid, articulate, informed,
and imaginative, the resulting article will be also. If not, it won't.

That's easy to say, but how do you go about it? It helps, we think, if you
go back to thinking about your readers, realizing that you are their stand-
in, their eyes, ears, and nose, and mouth to ask the questions they would
ask. You think what their self-interest would be in the situation you're
reporting, what things would pique their emotions, why they would want
to read about it. It helps, too, to envision the forthcoming story as a
whole, to try to foresee all its different facts and make sure you explore
them all.

How do you get started? Let's say you have an idea for an article, and
you've checked *Reader's Guide to Periodical Literature* to see if any
magazine has done a similar one recently (none has). But you don't know

how to find out if the idea is valid—i.e., supported by fact—and you have no name or organization to start your research with.

Some of the most basic and helpful tools are located in the library. They are called databases, and they enable a writer to search through millions of documents to find material relevant to a particular subject.

There are three types of databases: bibliographic, full-text, and numeric. The first type gives you a bibliography of material that relates to your subject. The second (and much more expensive) type gives you the texts of any articles you are interested in. And the third offers numbers, rather than articles—for example, a numeric database might offer specific material from the last census.

Hundreds of databases are available, and even after you consult the directories that list them, you may need the help of an expert to decide which you should search. Ask the librarian. Most librarians we have dealt with have been eager to help.

Let's assume that you are doing a story on the problems of farmers who have lost their farms and moved to the city. If you want to know about the history of the farmer in America, you might search a database called *America: History and Life* or another called *Arts and Humanities Search*. Both will search the historical literature and offer you a list of citations to articles on the subject. You can then look up the articles in the appropriate journals.

If you wish to learn about the stress which the former farmers are experiencing, you might conduct a search of the *Psychological Abstract* database. If you wish to discover what the president of the United States has said and done about the farmers, you might search *Washington Presstext*, which contains all official information from the White House and the State Department, including presidential speeches, press conferences, vetoes, and executive orders. (It even includes State Department toasts, but they would probably be of little use in this context.)

The cost of such searches varies greatly, from $2 to hundreds of dollars, but most bibliographic searches cost between $5 and $50.

Among the cheapest of the databases are those produced by the US government. The *Government Printing Office's Monthly Catalog* lists citations to government-agency reports as well as to reports of Congressional hearings. The *NTIS* database offers more than a million citations to reports on government-sponsored research. *ERIC* makes available citations to educational research. and *Medline* contains citations to articles printed in thousands of medical journals worldwide. Remember as you conduct your research to think about the people your article is aimed at. Whose self-interest will be involved in it? Whose self-interest will be advanced? Whose injured? Once you've answered these questions you will have a direction, and most likely a source, to approach. For instance, once you have obtained the citations and read the articles, you might want to call some of the authors to get further information on the subject and to seek additional sources. One of the advantages of our overorganized world is that in America there is a society, a council, a club, for almost everything. You can find them listed in the *Encyclopedia of Associations,* which should be available in your library. You're almost certain to find one that fits your area. Call up and talk to the public relations person.

Almost every idea you get will have a starting place—a name, an organization—and this one will lead you to others. All you have to do is ask the first few people you interview, "Who else would know about this?" Their answers will start you on an interviewing chain that will lead from source to source until your research is complete. A good way to show how this works is to describe such a chain.

The trigger for the idea was a *New York Times* story which reported that the Junior Chamber of Commerce of Hopkins, Minnesota, had given one of its members, Richard Tenneson, the job of preparing a scrapbook of the group's activities. This routine job was a milestone for Tenneson, the *Times* reported, because he was one of twenty-one US "turncoats" who had chosen to remain in Communist China after the Korean War ended. He got a job because the JC members believed Tenneson, who had since regretted his decision and returned to the US, "was on his way back to healthy citizenship."

The item was interesting because ever since the war, there had been a great deal of talk in the press about "brainwashing"—making it a kind of mysterious rite akin to voodoo—and much national breast-beating about the number of US soldiers who had broken down and collaborated with the enemy or given up and died in captivity. This showed, said the breast-beaters—usually among the authoritarian right wing—that the younger generation was weak-minded and lacking in moral fiber.

This seemed to me to be nonsense. I'd read about brainwashing in books by Arthur Koestler and Joost Van Meerloo, and there was nothing mysterious about it. It was simply a clever, persistent attack on a person's psyche. It was an extension of the police method of questioning a suspect that I'd seen as a reporter. Further, I'd become convinced that no one could withstand the process if it were properly planned and continued long enough; anyone could be made to tell what he knew. The French underground, one of the toughest resistance movements in World War II, had known this so well that when one of their members was captured, that person was required to remain silent for only twenty-four hours, to give other members of the unit time to disappear. They knew no one could hold out very long under Gestapo methods. Finally, it seemed illogical that young men who had behaved so courageously in World War II, just six or seven years before, could become so weak so soon. Generations don't change that fast.

But I was working for *Redbook* at the time, and what had all this to do with our readers? How was their self-interest involved? First, Tenneson was twenty-five, married, and had a small daughter, which meant that our young adult audience could identify with him. (While most *Redbook* readers were women, we were then trying to attract young men, too). Second, many of our readers were Korean veterans, and the attack was on them; indeed, since the attack was on a generation, it impugned *all* our young readers. A defense, we reasoned, would be a service that we could and should render them. A way to do it would be to write Tenneson's story, showing what had broken him down and how and why he had ultimately rejected the Communist way. The story should explain the general methods of "brainwashing" so that readers would understand the process and by demonstrating that anyone could be broken, it would help remove the stigma from a generation.

All this made sense in editorial terms, but many questions remained. Had Tenneson's experience as a captive been representative of what others had gone through? Was he intelligent enough to understand what had happened to him and articulate enough to explain it, or had he been simply a straw blown about by different winds? How reliable was he? The Communist ideology, I knew, justified any deceit in furtherance of its goals; could you believe anything he said? Finally, was he the kind of man the magazine wanted to support—because the overall effect of an article about him would be an espousal of his story. Certainly the research on this one was going to require much cross-checking, plus a deeper knowledge of what had happened to US soldiers captured in the war.

Obviously the first thing to do was to talk to Tenneson and see what kind of man he was. I had to go to Honolulu on another story, and I stopped in Minneapolis to see him. (Hopkins, where he lived, is only a few miles from Minneapolis.) I jotted down a list of things I wanted to find out:

"Childhood? When married? Wife's reaction to past? Why didn't appreciate kind of life this country can give you? What kind of picture of US did early life give? What experience in the army? Any trouble getting jobs after came back? Any social pressure? What happened in captivity?"

When I got to Minneapolis I called Tenneson and told him we were thinking of doing a story on his experience as a way of explaining to everyone what it had been like in the prison camps. I asked to see him; he jumped at the chance and offered to come to my hotel.

Tenneson was a slight, highly nervous young man with dark short hair and large blue eyes with a semiglazed look that sometimes seems to come from thoughtfulness and suffering. But he laughed a lot as he talked. And he talked eagerly, continuously, the way some people do as a way to release inner tension. He seemed intelligent and highly volatile, either because of emotional instability or immaturity. As he told his story, I detected a good deal of self-justification (which meant I'd have to do a lot of checking), and many hints that, deep down, he felt he wasn't worth much (one of the first things he said, with an embarrassed laugh, was "My father was a bootlegger").

He left after two hours, and on the plane to Honolulu I tried to decide whether his story would do the job we wanted done. His childhood had been unstable; his mother and father had been divorced when he was a year old, and for seven years he'd lived with grandparents who, he said, were over-indulgent. At eight he went to live with his mother and her new husband, who tried to give him some discipline and teach him good work habits. But the discipline had been harsh at times, and the boy resented it. He ran away from home several times, and, though he was intelligent, did badly in school. When he was fifteen he'd gone to live with an aunt. In the middle of the school year he'd run away and wound up in jail for car theft in Nebraska, but said he was later exonerated (was he?).

He'd joined the army at seventeen, without finishing high school, and had botched up his career there. He'd been sent to Korea only a few months after induction and had never really become a part of any outfit. He'd been in combat twice, and both times his regiment had retreated. Only two months after he'd landed in Korea, when he was still seventeen, he'd been captured.

He had not been physically mistreated by the Chinese, and he didn't understand the psychological conditioning they were subjecting him to. Either through clever planning or by coincidence, the treatment the Chinese gave him had appealed to some of his deepest emotional needs.

The story seemed to have a happy ending: he had rejected communism (had he really?) and seemed to be making a strong effort to rehabilitate himself as a citizen (was he? what forces were working pro and con?).

I decided the story was a good gamble and my editors agreed. I went back to Minneapolis some weeks later with a list of people to be seen and facts to be checked. I also had a long list of questions for Tenneson. I've found that such a list, prepared in advance, serves two purposes; it ensures that you don't overlook some areas of inquiry that you might forget during the heat of the interview, and it gives you a ready question to throw in at those times when, concentrating on taking notes or comprehending what the man has just said, you don't think ahead to the next question.

The first person I interviewed was Don Pobuda, head of the Junior Chamber of Commerce (I got his name from the original *New York Times* story). From him I learned about Tenneson's activities in the JC, and how and why he was accepted as a member in the first place. As I always do, especially in the early interviews for a new story, I asked Pobuda for the names of other people who were involved with Tenneson as employers or friends or co-workers. He gave me the names of two of Tenneson's employers, as well as a couple of friends. I interviewed them to find out what kind of employee he'd been, what his friends thought of him.

Since Tenneson had told me about his arrest in Nebraska, I thought I ought to check and see if he had any other police record. I called a Minneapolis detective I'd worked with on a previous story, told him what I was doing, and asked if he'd check with both the local and state police to see if there was a record. A few days later he called back to say there was not.

Next I had a long interview with Tenneson in which I took him back over his whole life, with great detail as to names, dates, army career. I got him only as far as his capture and arranged another interview later.

During the interviewing with some of my other sources I'd heard about an incident in a bar a few months before in which a soldier had grabbed Tenneson, called him "a Communist son-of-a-bitch," and worked him over a little before Tenneson's friends had pulled the man off. As far as I could tell, it had been the only incident of its kind since Tenneson had come back. So I talked to two men and a woman who had been there, to get the story straight.

These contacts gave me the names of other people who knew both Tenneson and his wife, and I later talked with several of them. Obviously I had to talk to Tenneson's mother who, I learned, was living on a farm some miles from Minneapolis. I called and made a date to visit her. Then I interviewed Tenneson again for several hours, not only getting more details of his experience, but questioning him specifically about "brainwashing" techniques I'd noted down from books on the subject.

The next day, I drove through the cold, barren, snowy country to see his mother. Again in detail, I took her through Tenneson's childhood, his arrest in Nebraska (and got the name of the lawyer who had defended him), her own trip to Japan to try to talk her son out of joining the Chinese Communists, and the long period after his return when he stayed with her and her husband. She also gave me the name of a doctor, Philip Bloemsma, in Washington, DC, who had himself been a prisoner of the Japanese during World War II and had subsequently made a study of the psychological effects of prison life on soldiers.

Back at the hotel that night I called the lawyer in Nebraska and got his story of Tenneson's arrest, time in jail, and subsequent release. He said Tenneson had been an innocent victim. I asked him if he'd send me copies of the court papers on the disposition of the case, because the only testimony I'd gotten had been interested—Tenneson's, his mother's, and the lawyer's. Later the lawyer sent the papers, and the stories checked out. Also that night I made another list of questions to be covered with Tenneson, his wife and friends, questions that had been raised in previous interviews.

The next day I talked with a young woman who was a close friend of both Tenneson and his wife and got an outsider's view of their person-alities and their marriage. I also talked with another man who had been present at the fracas in the bar. And then Tenneson again—this time mostly on his experience in China after the war, his decision to return home, and what happened thereafter. I also got a dates-and-places chro-nology of when he came to Hopkins, where he lived and worked, how he met his wife, got married, and so on. (I've learned that in a story like this the inteviewee tends to skip around in time, so that it's hard to put together a chronology later when you're assembling the story. But if you try to pin them down to specific dates and places at the time you're interviewing, it tends to stop the flow of talk. So I try to do the whole chronology later at one time.)

Next I had a long talk with Tenneson's wife, Jan. Obviously a man's wife is not an objective witness. But I've learned you can offset the bias somewhat by putting the proposition to her that you're trying to under-stand this man, to learn what goes on beneath the surface, and since she knows him better than anyone alive, she can help. Usually she'll try to level with you as best she can. You start by asking questions about specific incidents: What did your parents say when you told them you were going to marry Rick? What was his reaction to meeting your parents? And so on.

Then I had a final interview with Tenneson, in which I cleaned up loose ends and again checked things I'd learned from others.

Before I left Minneapolis I called the late S.L.A. Marshall, in Detroit, and asked if I could see him the next day, a Sunday. Marshall was a newspaperman, a reserve general, and one of the best military historians writing. I hadn't met him, but I'd read a couple of his books, knew he was deeply interested in what makes men fight—or not—and that he had been in Korea interviewing combat soldiers.

I had asked for an hour; we spent seven together, and it was one of those rare and wonderful times when two minds mesh—exciting, stimulating, and for me, at least, rich in new insights. He also gave me the names of some officers in Washington who had conducted with Korean War soldiers one of the most extensive investigations the army had ever run on why men fight or give up. Finally, he gave me the name and address of the general commanding Tenneson's division in Korea, which was to prove invaluable.

Marshall also advanced a reason why the army had supported the attack on a generation of soldiers as weaklings; the army knew perfectly well the techniques of "brainwashing" that would be used on captured soldiers ("Hell, we'd used most of them ourselves on Japanese prisoners in World War II") but had failed to train its own soldiers in what to expect if captured or give them any defenses against the psychological pressures they were sure to meet.

Then I flew to Washington and went to the Book and Magazine Branch of the Department of Defense in the Pentagon. I told them about the story I was doing and asked to see the official records of the regiment Tenneson had belonged to, in order to check his story of what had happened during the two battles he'd been in. After a couple of days word came back that I could not have them; they were still classified (despite the fact the war had been over for five years, and presumably the enemy knew what had happened). So I tried another tack: I made up a list of specific questions covering the major points of Tenneson's story and asked if they would check the records and give me the answers. (I received the answers some weeks later, after the story was written.)

I wrote the commanding general whose name Marshall had given me. This time I wrote exactly what Tenneson had told me about the battles (briefly), explained why I wanted to check the story, and asked his help. He replied immediately, told me what he knew himself, and said he was writing to the commanding officer of Tenneson's regiment for fuller details. Shortly I received a detailed reply from this officer as well. Both men were most appreciative that I'd written. Thus was it possible to get around Pentagon red tape.

One thing the Book and Magazine Branch did do that was most helpful was give me the name of a navy lieutenant who had been a prisoner of the

Chinese and who had successfully resisted their efforts at "brainwashing."
I found him not at all smug about his accomplishment. He was full of
knowledge about how the Chinese had worked (which checked with what
Tenneson and others had told me) and compassion for those men who had
not been able to withstand the pressure.

Next I talked to two officers—one a psychiatrist—who had conducted
the long investigation of the prisoners mentioned earlier. They added new
insights into the psychological pressures the Chinese had used and into
the different backgrounds, both in the army and before, of both the men
who had broken under the pressure and those who had not. They also
denied, as Marshall had, that there had been significantly more collabora-
tion with the enemy in Korea than in other wars.

Finally I went to see Dr. Philip Bloemsma, who had been in a prison
camp for three and a half years in Burma during World War II. He told me
that prisoners of war commonly experienced a definite psychological
sickness, which he called "the fence complex." This sickness, he said, had
been studied by Dutch and British doctors during World War II, and its
syndrome was explained to him when he headed a hospital in Bangkok
after the war. The symptoms of the sickness exactly fitted some of the
feelings and attitudes Tenneson said he'd had. They also jibed with things
the army men had told me.

(A year later I described the sickness to an expert on civilian prisons in
the US. He had never heard of it, but said it matched his own observa-
tions of what happens to long-term civilian prisoners. And thus another
story idea was born.)

That completed the research for the story. What does this rather
lengthy process demonstrate?

That writers shouldn't panic when they start on a story and don't know
where the parts to it are coming from. Almost always there's one source at
the beginning (Tenneson, Pobuda), and if you ask questions, this one leads
to others until you have a long and complete chain.

That you usually start in a library, getting background information so
you know what your sources are talking about.

That you check things a source has said against documentary records
whenever there's a chance that his or her self-interest might lead you
astray. And do it anyway if such records exist.

That while you're researching you keep alert for other names, other
sources that will add new facets to the story—and follow them up.

That you don't take an official no for an answer. Find another path to the information.

That you prepare a list of questions that your reader would want answered before you start, and draw up other, more specific lists before you go into each interview.

That you go there, see your sources in their native habitat, if possible see where the action took place. (Once I drove 160 miles to visit a diner where a murder took place so I could describe it in the story.)

That research takes a great deal of time if the story is to have any depth. Once I spent a full day in research to get one line in a story; often a two-hour interview will yield only one colorful, felicitous phrase, but it is still worth it.

That you keep interviewing until your sources begin to repeat each other. This accomplishes two purposes, and possibly a third. If two or three experts, with differing points of view, agree on a fact or a principle, you can be pretty sure it is accepted in their discipline. Second, the agreement tends to offset personal bias by any individual source. The third? It has been my experience that when your sources are no longer telling you anything new, your research is about finished.

One of the pitfalls of this kind of writing is that you can over-research. The chief reason, I think, is that it's easier to interview people than it is, finally, to sit down alone before that terrible blank sheet of paper and start writing. But the loss of time from over-researching is only the lightest penalty that writers pay. The serious one is that they can get so much material that they lose sight of the story line, wallow in confusion for days trying to recapture it, and sometimes never do. When that happens the story fails.

But beginning writers are more inclined to do too little, rather than too much research. So the final rule is, interview, observe, and keep at it.

5

Interviewing

*T*here's an ancient gag in the newspaper business that goes: "So this guy wanted to be a reporter, but he couldn't because nobody would tell him anything."

Like most one-liners that survive long enough to become ancient, this one has truth in it. One of the most persistent failings of unskilled reporters is that they don't see enough people about a particular story, don't ask the right questions and thus don't get the right answers. The art of interviewing breaks down into two parts: how do you get to see people, and how do you get them to tell you the things that will make a story pertinent, lively, readable?

In solving the first problem it is important to understand what you have going for you. It is not difficult to get to see most people for an interview, because essentially what you're doing is asking for their opinion or their expertise. And asking people their opinion is flattering. Most of us spend our lives being told things—by our colleagues, our bosses, our husbands, or our wives—and have to fight to give posterity our own special wisdoms. So when somebody comes along and asks us to tell them what we know or what we think, especially if it's going to be published so the whole world will benefit from our advice, we are delighted to agree. Thus, in many cases, the only thing a reporter has to do to see a person is call up and ask.

But, particularly in depth stories and magazine articles, many of the people you want to interview have days and nights already full of requirements imposed by their jobs, their families, their own interests or ambitions. You have to break into their schedules—which is troublesome for them—and to do it you have to convince them it will be to their self-interest to take the trouble. There are various types of leverage you can summon to help.

The late Dan Mich, one of the great editors of his time, made a basic point a few years ago when he was talking to his writers:

Before starting out on . . . interviews, I would read every available word on the personality or situation involved. I would make notes on what I read. When I reached the point of asking questions, I would know what questions to ask. Instead of boring my source of information with dull routine, I would be able to make the interview challenging and interesting for him.

The last few words are the operative ones, both in getting to see your source and after you are in her office. You accomplish this, as Mich said, by preliminary reading, but also by thinking about the coming interview from her point of view. Not yours, *hers*. What's in it for her to give you time from her busy schedule? Will it help get her a promotion? Will it enhance her reputation? Will it help her defeat a rival? Will it increase the profits of her business? Will it help her solve a problem? Will it help get her votes, or a larger audience for her next show, or more readers for her book?

Once you've figured out what her self-interest is, make your pitch on that basis when you call to ask for an interview. Say, "I'm doing an article for *Reader's Digest* on the increase in crime, and, based on your statement in the *Times* a couple months ago, you disagree with the attorney general and many others about the causes for the increase. I'd like to talk to you further about this; can I come and see you?"

This does several things for you. It tells her you are not some unknown hopeful, but a writer good enough to have an assignment from a well-known publication. It tells her you have done your homework and know enough about the subject to know her position and the attorney general's and thus won't waste her time with a lot of uninformed questions. It gives her an opportunity to attack or answer or defeat her professional rivals—in an influential medium. And it suggests that you will do all this for her with the least possible inconvenience to her—by coming to her office at a time she sets. She'd be a fool to refuse.

But suppose you don't have an assignment from the *Digest* and thus don't have the prestige of the magazine's name to increase your leverage. This happens often, not only with beginning writers, but also with established journalists who are doing the preliminary research necessary to validate—or knock down—an idea before they present it to an editor for approval. You can't count on your name being known to the person, even if you've published a hundred magazine articles, because people rarely pay attention to writers' by lines. But you can use other kinds of leverage, and one is flattery.

It is difficult to overestimate the average person's capacity for flattery. For years I have used the most blatant kind: "I'm working on an article on air pollution, and I understand there isn't anyone in the country better informed on it than you. Can I come to see you?" Usually I do have decency enough to say the last part in a half-kidding way, but it is surprising how many people aren't bothered at all by the exaggeration. Usually they say, delightedly, "Oh, I don't know about that—but sure, I'll see you." Or if you can't bring yourself to be this obvious, you can say with complete sincerity: "I'm trying to get a true picture of air pollution in this country. I've talked to people on all sides of the question, and certainly I can't do a complete job without talking to you." This has the advantages of being both true and consistent with the best journalistic ethics.

Or you can use a variation of the old reporter's hook: "I've got Joe's side of the story, what's yours?" In this one you play one person's self-interest off against another's. If you want to talk to the Republican county chairman about politics in court appointments, you tell him you have talked to the Democrats (if you have) and now want to talk to him. Or you tell a union leader you've already seen the management people and want to get her side. Once I wanted to see an expert on juvenile delinquency who had just gotten a top appointment in Washington and was extraordinarily busy. From background reading I knew he disagreed violently with parts of a study done by Sheldon and Eleanor Glueck of Harvard, which was what I was writing about. I simply told him I was doing a piece on the Glueck study, knew he didn't agree with parts of it, and wanted to talk to him about it. It worked. And it also added depth and balance to the final article.

I learned one of the most unexpected and effective hooks some years ago. I'd read in the paper that a sociologist at Ohio University at Bowling Green, Samuel Harmon Lowrie, had done the survey of dating habits mentioned in Chapter 2, which showed that the kids who had the most dates got the best marks. Obviously I needed to spend a good deal of time with Professor Lowrie to learn about his study. I called and asked for an appointment; he was not interested.

I suggested that publication of my article would broadcast his findings; he didn't want this, at least at the moment, because he wanted to have his study published in a professional journal first. Besides, he said, he was highly dubious about the popular press, and thought it too sensational. Although he was too polite to say so, I got the idea he thought I would cheapen his study. I tried to tell him I was not a sensationalist (how do you convince a stranger you're an honest man?) but wasn't getting very far. Over the phone I could feel his resolve not to see me hardening, and I grew desperate. Finally I said, "Look, you've got an answer here that will help thousands of kids. Most parents think dating hurts their youngsters in school. You've demonstrated the opposite; if we can convince parents of this, we'll not only be removing a source of family friction, but we'll be improving the kind of education thousands of kids will get."

It did the trick. The appeal to his altruism, the suggestion that he could help others, was strong enough to overcome his perfectly legitimate reservations. Since that experience, I've learned that this appeal to a person's altruism is one of the strongest arguments you can use. It has won me access even to convicted criminals in jail, who were going to stay in jail no matter what I wrote, and even though the basis of the appeal was insulting: "If you talk to me maybe it will prevent some other guy from becoming a bum like you." (Of course it was never phrased that way, but the implication was there.)

Another very simple, and often overlooked, device is to put your body in the man's office. You ask to see him. He's busy. Okay, you say, I'll wait. So you sit. What's he going to do with you, throw you out? That would be pretty drastic, especially since all you want to do is ask his opinion about something. You may wait two or three hours, but almost inevitably you'll get to see him.

For one thing your presence puts pressure on the receptionist. She starts out by resenting you for not leaving the way you were supposed to when she turned you away. But the longer you sit there being polite and pleasant and silently importunate, the more sympathetic she gets. After all, you just want to see the man and what is he, some kind of god that he hasn't a couple of minutes to talk to a perfectly nice writer? So she starts working for you, phoning in at intervals and saying, "That writer is still waiting for you." Pause. "I know you did, but he won't leave." And pretty soon you get in.

A similar kind of pressure can be put on the man's secretary, who is paid to keep you from seeing him. You do it with phone calls. First call, she says he's not in, which may or may not be true. So you tell her who you are and what you want to see him about. (Secretaries are usually more impressed by writers than their bosses are.) Ask what time he'll be in; if she says eleven o'clock, call back at about 11:15. Now she's on the defensive: she can't tell you he's not there without some explanation, because it makes her look as though she doesn't know her job. Further more, if he is there, she resents having to lie for him when you have done exactly what she told you to. Don't push her; be amiable, flexible, and politely ask when he's likely to be in. You want to build the feeling that you understand her problem and that you and she are working together toward a common goal—to talk to the man. Keep repeating the process and sooner or later, you'll get to talk to him.

Maybe on the first call she says she doesn't know when he'll be back, but she'll have him call you. Don't do it. Say, "Well, I'll be moving around town, so I'd better call him." Then call in about two hours. Keep on calling at intervals for the next day or two; you are putting on the same kind of pressure as when you sit in the office. Most times you'll get to talk to the man before too long.

You have to be imaginative in adapting your techniques for getting to see a source to the particular situation. Writers have come up with dozens of different devices, and here are a couple that I've run across that apply leverage in particular situations.

Once I was in Hollywood to do a story for *Redbook* on Red Skelton. I'd spent two or three days at CBS talking with his producer and director, his writers, some of the people who worked on the show with him, to a couple of vice-presidents, and to the public relations people. Now I was ready to talk to Skelton, but his public relations man wouldn't make an appointment for me. I tried for a day or two, meanwhile talking to friends and other associates and continuing to call the PR man. He gave me nothing but excuses. There was no way to bypass him and go directly to Skelton, because his estate is fenced and its gates locked and he won't talk on the telephone to strangers.

I didn't know what to do. One afternoon I was griping to an editor at CBS, who finally said, "I don't know if it will work, but why don't you try this? Get people to send telegrams to the PR man. We'll send him one saying you've finished your work with us, and we know he wants to cooperate by getting you to Skelton as soon as possible. I'll get our vice president to send him one. Get Skelton's business manager to send one. Get your editor in New York to send one, and anybody else you can think of."

I did. Most of them arrived the next morning. At eleven o'clock the PR man called me to say I had a date with Skelton for that afternoon.

Mort Weisinger once told the members of the Society of Magazine Writers about a hook he used to reach VIPs by phone that worked "nine out of ten times.""—at least for out-of-towners. From a public phone booth, he said, he would place a long-distance, person-to-person call to the celebrity at his office. "When I reach him, the operator invariably says, 'I have your party. Please deposit $3.25.' Then I go into my ritual of inserting 13 quarters. If I had phoned him from my home phone, he might curtly tell me he's busy and to send him a letter. But when he knows I've shelled out hard cash, a fact which has registered on him via the tolling of the coins, he is sympathetic, helpful, and most cooperative."

Telephones are fine for making appointments; they are no good for the actual interview, unless you have no time or simply want to check a point you forgot in an earlier face-to-face interview. (Everybody forgets sometimes.) They're no good because they don't let you see what your source looks like or watch the expressions and mannerisms which help reveal his or her character; because they're always hurried and you need time for depth interviews; because they don't let you see the person's home or office; and because they're a barrier to the interplay of your two personalities. And this is important, as we'll see in a minute, in getting you the kind of detail and color that creative writing requires.

Most important of all, they're bad because they're inaccurate. While working for a master's degree at Stanford University, Fred C. Berry, Jr., made a study of accuracy in three San Francisco area newspapers. He did it by sending copies of 270 news stories to the people mentioned in them for comment, and he found that 46 percent of them were completely accurate. But, he found, "the most frequently used sources of information were not the most accurate sources. Personal interviews produced about one and a half times as many accurate stories as telephone interviews." (*Journalism Quarterly,* Autumn 1967, p. 482)

One of the wisest things ever said about accuracy is a remark made by a British official to a reporter: "You think," he said, "that we lie. We don't, really we don't. But if you count on that, you make an even bigger mistake: you think we tell you the truth."

Once you get in to your sources, how do you get them to talk? Many people are happy to talk forever about things they want to talk about, but creative journalism requires that they talk about the things you want, that they reveal themselves in many ways—perhaps their deepest inner conflicts, their opinions on touchy situations that they prefer to conceal, their emotions, sometimes even things they have done that will get them in trouble with the law or colleagues or friends. Often you have to carry their thinking on a problem further than they ever have before, by presenting it from an angle they've never considered.

Once, for example, I had to get a young woman to tell me, step by step, about a mental breakdown she'd had, about her feelings and experiences during nine months in a mental hospital, about her adjustments and deceptions in fighting her way back into normal life. Another time I had to induce the mother of a man who had murdered three people in a week to tell me about his childhood troubles with the law and even the things she and her husband had done that had damaged his personality.

It helps in this kind of depth interviewing if you understand the dimensions of the problem you are facing. In their book *The Dynamics of Interviewing*, Robert L. Kahn and Charles F. Cannell, of the Survey Research Center at the University of Michigan, list the barriers we all build against communicating with each other:

Under the continuous impact of sales pitches in newspaper and magazine, radio and TV advertising, we build a tidy skepticism of the things people tell us. We learn to disbelieve as a form of self-protection. This carries over into all our daily conversations but makes us especially careful when we're talking to a journalist whose obvious motive—to get us on record, in print—may be entirely consistent with our own best interests.

We build defenses against another's ill opinion of us. We don't want to appear in a bad light, especially to a reporter. This is a hurdle public opinion pollsters have had to learn to get over. For example, an early survey, trying to find out what features in newspapers people liked best, startled everyone by showing that most readers turned to the editorials first. This, of course, was nonsense. It took a while for the pollsters to realize that people were saying this because it was intellectually classy.

We don't listen to what the other person is saying. We pick up the key words or phrases, then assume we know what the rest of the sentence is going to be. At that point we tune them out and start thinking about what our answer will be.

Our memories are selective. Many of us have psychological reasons for not being able to remember something or remember it accurately. Often the conclusions we draw from a set of facts lead us to change the facts themselves. This is not intentional, but it is nearly universal—which is why good reporters always must check things they're told against documents or other evidence.

Kahn and Cannell write, "The way each of us sees the world or anything in it depends in part upon external objective reality, and for the rest on our individual needs, goals, motives and past experiences." Someone who is paid $50,000 a year as a publicist for an automobile company is unlikely to give you an unbiased version of the safety of American cars.

Most of us aren't very articulate. Kahn and Cannell say the average person knows fewer than 10 percent of the half million words in the English language. So even when someone is trying hard to explain something to you, he or she may not have the words to do so. Further, most of us have particular habits of speech resulting from our backgrounds, our jobs, our hobbies. This is especially pronounced, in our compartmentalized world, among various kinds of experts; a sociologist talks an entirely different kind of language from a jazz musician. A reporter, interviewing either, must first learn the lingo.

To overcome these barriers to communication, "the interviewer," write Kahn and Cannell, "must create and maintain an atmosphere in which the respondent feels he is fully understood and it is safe to communicate fully without fear of being judged or criticized. . . . An interviewer focuses on *content*, and the respondent is encouraged to explore fully and frankly his own position."

Psychologists list three qualities that produce good interview results:

1. Warmth and responsiveness. This shows you're interested in and accept the person. The interview should resemble a conversation, not a grilling.

2. Permissiveness in letting respondents express their feelings. Give them the idea they can say anything at all without penalty; maintain that attitude whether you agree with them or not. You almost never argue with a source; if you must disagree with something they say, quote an authority—a book, an article, an expert you've interviewed earlier—and ask for a comment on that. This lets you off the hook; *you* aren't attacking them; you're simply asking them to explain an inconsistency. (Sometimes it is valuable to argue but only if you want to make the person mad enough to say something he shouldn't. In thirty years of interviewing, I've done this perhaps half a dozen times.)

3. The atmosphere you want to set up is: "We're a couple of responsible people exploring this issue together."

Beyond the general atmosphere of the interview, there are a number of specific techniques that have worked out for me. For example, when you first walk into a person's office, there usually is some small talk to ease your strangeness with each other. You can make this work for you by taking a quick look around the office and spotting something your source is interested in. It may be a golf trophy on a file cabinet; say, "You must be a pretty good golfer." It may be pictures of children on her desk; as, "Are those your youngsters?" Giving a person a chance to talk about something she's interested in warms her up and also gives you insights into her personality and some facts about her nonbusiness life.

When the small talk is finished, outline the basic idea you're working on so the interviewee knows specifically what areas you want to talk about. Very often the idea involves a problem or public issue; outlining it invokes the impulse, widely shared by Americans, to try to solve problems. It also gives the person a creative role consistent with point number three, above: she can bring her own knowledge to bear in a way that may help solve the problem.

Then you proceed to explore the problem together, with you being the interested, intelligent, but uninformed student who wants to learn from this expert. Don't hesitate to ask her to explain further if you don't fully understand part of what she tells you. And use your prepared list of questions to lead her into other dimensions of the problem. Don't argue, discuss, and bring your own background knowledge to bear: "I saw a report from the Council on Family Relations the other day that shows——. How does that bear on what you just said?"

Having the facts is excellent leverage for prying out information the person is reluctant to reveal. Once I was doing a story on sweatshops in New York City. It was built around the experiences of a young man named Francisco Mangual, who had courage enough to fight against both the labor union and the company management that were exploiting him and his co-workers. He led a walkout one day in defiance of both and was promptly fired. He took his case to the State Labor Board and, after a hearing, the employer was ordered to rehire him. I had, of course, read the record of the hearing before I interviewed the employer.

He was unfriendly. He didn't want an article written about sweatshops generally and especially not about his own. I made it clear to him, politely, that the article was going to be written anyway and asked him why he had fired Mangual. "Oh," he said, "he was no good. He was a lousy worker, always goofing off, and several times the girls in the shop complained to me that he'd been bothering them. Which," he added virtuously, "was a damn shame, considering that nice little wife of his." (The Labor Board had considered and rejected these same charges.)

"Then why did the State Labor Board order you to rehire him?"

"Oh, you know about that, eh?" Pause. "Well, you know how these labor boards are, a bunch of bureaucrats who don't know anything about business. Besides, they're all run by the unions."

Obviously the employer had no specific rebuttal to Mangual's story and, since the Labor Board had confirmed it, I could assume it was true. But of course it had been necessary to give the employer a chance to knock it down.

It also pays off if you take the time to frame very carefully, in advance, the tough questions you are going to have to ask in an interview. This not only helps you pin down precisely what you want to find out, but also enables you to build in psychological hooks which will help guarantee an answer—and many people, particularly politicians, are adept at evading tough questions.

One key to these psychological hooks is self-interest. Think carefully what your respondent can get out of the interview, and make sure your question suggests it. For example, I was doing a story on John F. Kennedy while he was still in the Senate. It was obvious he was preparing to run for the presidency, and when he did his Catholicism was going to be an issue. I wanted to get him on record on the subject. The night before the interview I spent more than an hour wording the question. It went:

"Senator, before I could vote for you, I'd have to have the answer to one question. If the dictates of your church conflicted with the demands of your public office, which would you follow?"

The "before I could vote for you" bit was the self-interest hook; all politicians want votes. I debated this, because the senator ran from Massachusetts and I lived in New York; it opened the door to a quibble on his part. But I figured he was intent enough on the presidency, where I would be eligible to vote, to overlook it. The word "dictates" took a lot of thought. It was a nasty word for a Catholic, suggesting his church was a dictatorship. Yet I knew many non-Catholics felt this way about the church, and I finally decided that the nastiness would work for me; it would irritate him and thus might provoke him to answer seriously instead of evading.

It worked. The first thing he said was, "In the first place my church doesn't dictate to me." Then he went on and answered the question, saying much the same things he said a few years later when he was actually campaigning for the presidency. But my article was the first that put him on record on the subject.

During the whole interview listen actively. Reporters can't afford to listen like normal people; they must work at it. You recognize that most people aren't very articulate, that their words are a screen that often shadows or distorts information which is very clear in their own minds. You have to penetrate this screen and see the idea as clearly as your source does. It takes work.

You must concentrate hard on each word the person says, probing for the precise meaning behind it. You watch his face, his gestures, the movements of his body, the expressions in his eyes. You follow his thoughts and complete them for him. You pin him down, but not aggressively: "I don't understand. You said ———." "But how does that work in this situation?"

And let the man know you're listening to him; it flatters him and makes him try harder. Quote himself back at him: "You said a minute ago that — ——. Does that mean ————?" Keep your eyes on him so he knows you're paying attention. Encourage him to continue talking by making neutral comments that show you're with him. Things like, "Boy, I'll bet that hurt." "What happened next?" "How did that work out?" Should you let your man wander off the subject? Not if you're pressed for time or if you need only specific, factual information from him. But if you have time and need depth, I've found that often when a person gets comfortable with the subject and starts to wander, he gives you not only unexpected information but also new insights into his personality and viewpoint. And it is precisely these nuggets that make your story broader and deeper than the usual newspaper or television interview.

Of course you do have to keep some kind of control over the interview, otherwise you won't get what you came for. This is especially important if you're interviewing a glib PR man who wants to fill you up with commercials about his company, or a political wheelhorse who learned long ago how to evade a question by snowing you under with a blizzard of unresponsive words. You know the type.

REPORTER: Senator, we all know how bad the drought has been in your state, with farmers having to buy water to keep their cattle from dying, with crops dried up in the fields, and families facing the loss of all their savings and perhaps even of their farms. Since this is so, Senator, why did you vote against disaster crop loans for your state?

SENATOR: Miss Marsh, I want you to know that nobody knows better than I the plight of farmers in my state. Why, I grew up on a farm, and I've put in my days pitching had and milking the cows. I venture to say, without being immodest, that I know as much about the problems of farmers as anyone on Capitol Hill. And I respect them. The farmers are the backbone of this country. We have the situation of this great industrial country with its 230 million people all depending for their very lives on the work and skill and faithfulness of only about a million dedicated farmers. No, ma'am, there's nobody who knows better than I how important our tillers of God's soil are to all of us.

REPORTER: Then why, Senator, did you vote against the bill?

SENATOR: Vote against it? Where did you get that idea?

REPORTER: Each week the *New York Times* publishes the voting record of Congress on important bills. That's where I got it.

SENATOR: Now, Miss Marsh, I'm not going to be put in the position of criticizing the *Times*. To my mind it is one of the great—I'd even go so far as to say the greatest—though I'm not criticizing the papers we have in my state, mind: some of the finest journalism in America is being practiced in the papers of my state. No ma'am, I will stand up for the rights of a free press and especially the record of the papers of my state against all comers. I'm not afraid, ma'am, to take a stand!

REPORTER: But Senator—

SENATOR: Now, Miss Marsh, I've got to run along; I've got a very important committee meeting that started ten minutes ago, and I can't shirk my duty to my constituents. I've enjoyed talking to you, and I want you to know that anytime you've got any questions you just come right along to me. My door is always open.

What's a reporter to do? This is one time when I'd stop being polite. The senator was obviously caught and was trying to weasel out; further, he was showing contempt for the reporter's intelligence. Along about the middle of his second peroration, I think I'd have broken in with a polite remark like, "Senator, cut the crap!" Respect is due high office, but not when its holder demeans it. Another option is to print a transcript of the interview, as I did above, to show readers how unresponsive your subject was.

But usually you can control the interview in less drastic ways. You can be sure the interviewee is watching you. If she wanders too far from the subject, you can often call her back simply by leaning back in your chair and looking out the window in obvious boredom. You can exert many degrees of influence by the way you take notes. Normally the subject will watch what you write down and what you don't. This serves as a guide to her; she wants to say things that will make you take notes and once she sees what you write down and what you ignore, she'll try to feed you more of the significant material. You can use this: when she wanders, simply stop taking notes. She'll get the message. If she doesn't, I've sometimes gone so far as to close my notebook and toss it disdainfully on the desk. That rocks her.

The way you take notes can have other important effects on the interview. Every experienced reporter knows you can't take down everything the interviewee says; it takes too long and stops the flow of talk. It keeps you so occupied you haven't time for the other two important jobs you should be doing—watching and evaluating the person and thinking up the next question. You make notes on the operative words and phrases, on names and dates and addresses and figures. You remember the rest, and you have to train your memory to do it.

It's not as difficult as it seems. For one thing, a good part of the interview is commonly spent in inconsequential talk. For another, if you're concentrating on the interview as you should be, the person's words are deeply imprinted in your brain, and you recall them automatically later on. And it will not be much later; as soon as a noteless interview is finished, I have gone somewhere nearby—a library, a restaurant, my hotel room—and written down the entire interview in detail. Sometimes this takes almost as long as the interview itself, but it's worth it. You may not be writing the story for a couple of weeks and you won't remember the details that long, especially since you'll be doing other interviews in the interim.

Finally, there is another truth that I learned from Chester Barnard, then head of the Rockefeller Foundation and one of the most brilliant men I've ever met. Barnard had come up through the Bell Telephone Company and at one point had been one of the youngest presidents of a phone company—Pennsylvania's—in company history. On this job he had to visit offices and installations all over the state, then write reports on what he'd learned. He told me later that at first he was scared he'd forget something important and would take extensive notes on every visit, every interview. But after a while, he said, he discovered that the facts and figures that ultimately ended up in his report were those he remembered without consulting his notes. From then on he took only the sparsest of notes.

After he told me this, I reexamined my own experience and discovered the same thing. The points, the quotes, the anecdotes that wound up in the finished article had come full-blown into my mind when I was writing. Almost invariably when I checked them against my notes, I found I had remembered them accurately. (In spite of this, of course, I was never quite sure enough of myself to take no notes at all.)

Why should you ever attempt a noteless interview? Because sometimes your notebook scares the interviewee so badly that he or she never relaxes and talks freely. This usually happens with people who have never dealt with a reporter before, but sometimes notebooks create discomfort even in those who are used to journalists. When I was doing the story on Red Skelton mentioned earlier, I assumed that a man who had been in show business as long as he had—since the age of ten—and had been interviewed as many times as a star has, would be perfectly at ease in the situation. So when the first interview started I hauled out my notebook and went to work.

After about fifteen minutes it began to dawn on me that things weren't going well, and I took a good look at Skelton. He was sitting in his chair with his feet together and his arms pressed to his sides, as still as a department store mannequin. I couldn't believe it, but it was obvious the man was scared. So I ostentatiously closed my notebook, put it in my briefcase, and pushed it aside. And we just talked. Slowly he began to relax, and after about ten minutes he was at ease and talking freely. For the next five hours we had a marvelous time, and I learned a good deal about the man and his world. That was one of the times when I made the notes back at the hotel before I went to sleep.

What about tape recorders? The jury is still out on this one. They have definite advantages: you get the full interview, with all of the man's individual ways of saying things and many more details than you could possibly take down in notes. You also get complete accuracy: if there is ever any question that you have misquoted him, you have a record to prove your case. You are freed from the job of taking notes and can concentrate wholly on drawing the man out.

They also have disadvantages: every time we have used them we have found they inhibited the interviewees. They were always conscious of the recorders. Maybe this is not true of all interviewees, especially those who are interviewed often. There's a certain amount of bother; you have to stop the interview to change tapes. One of the biggest difficulties is that when you are ready to refer back to the interview for a quote or an anecdote, you have to play the whole tape, which takes as long as the original interview. When you make notes, you edit and take down only the important stuff; it is much easier and quicker to find the exact quote you want later on.

Also, there are built-in mechanical difficulties: We've found recorders to be useless when you're interviewing someone over lunch; the machine picks up so much background noise the words are often lost. And a recorder can fail in the middle of an interview without your knowing it. When you get home you discover you have nothing. One television reporter we know solves this by using the recorder *and* taking notes. This seems a little elaborate.

But there is no doubt at all about one aspect of recorders: if you use one you must let your source know about it. It is highly unethical and in some states illegal to tape an interview secretly.

One interviewing problem that every writer we know has difficulty with is getting good anecdotes. An anecdote is a little story that makes a point—like the one about interviewing Jack Kennedy. They are absolutely essential in mass media nonfiction because they explain or illustrate a point in specific, concrete terms instead of in abstract generalities—and most readers aren't accustomed to handling abstractions. They are also convincing to readers because they evoke emotions, making them say, "Yes, that could happen to me." Because they are what makes the piece readable, one of the most frequent instructions of editors is, "Get some more anecdotes into it." They are also hard to get.

When being interviewed most persons tend to get pretentious. After all, their own words are here being recorded in deathless prose for all future generations to delight over. They talk in broad generalities and profound philosophies, most of which have been said earlier and better by someone else. It's our job to bring them down to earth, to make them talk like people instead of books, to lead them to reveal their uniqueness of thought and experience.

The major problem is that the person you're interviewing is not thinking in terms of specific stories, case histories, experiences, and so when you ask him for a story, he or she can't bring it to mind. The other night a television reporter was interviewing a man who was retiring after forty-two years as sheriff. The reporter said, "There must have been many humorous things that happened during your long experience." The sheriff answered, "Oh, there were. Many" Pause. Smile. "But I can't think of any right now." The reporter's job is to trigger the man's mind so he will remember.

One of the best ways to do this is to tell an anecdote yourself. This not only gets his mind working in the right direction and defines for him the kind of thing you want but also provokes his old competitive urges to top your story. The stock reporter's question designed to produce anecdotes is, "What was the funniest thing that ever happened to you as a life-guard?" But this usually doesn't work very well because it requires the man not only to cast his mind back over a long series of experiences, which he can't remember very well, but also asks him to consider many and select one as the all-time great. That's asking too much all at once.

It's much more effective to narrow the area for him. For example, when I was doing the sweatshop story mentioned earlier, it seemed to me the people who worked in them lived in a constant miasma of fear. Everything in the society preyed upon them—employers, unions, the police, land-lords, criminals. I was talking to my man's wife, an extraordinarily beautiful young woman. I mentioned the police lock on the front door of their apartment and asked why they had it. Because of the danger, she said. What danger? Men. Banditos. Dope "addicks." Had they ever bothered her? Oh, yes. When? Lots of times. She thought a moment. "But it's not as bad here as in the project where we used to live." What happened there? Then she told me the anecdote. Once when she had got on the elevator to go up to her apartment, a man was already inside, and on the way up he tried to rape her. She had fought him off, and when they reached her floor she ran to her apartment, yanked open her window, and screamed to her husband, Francisco, who was sitting on a bench outside, what had happened. Francisco ran in when the elevator came down, he caught the man and beat him.

There was a story; now it was just a question of taking her back over it and getting the detail that would make it come alive for the reader. Had the man raped her? No. What did he look like? How was he dressed? When did he attack her—as soon as the doors closed? What had he done—had he wrestled her to the floor? What had she done to fight back? And so on. What you must do is keep questioning about even the most minute details—what color were the walls, what furniture was in the room—until you get a clear mental picture of the scene and the action. Only then can you recreate it so the reader will see it too.

S. L. A. Marshall, the late military historian, told me about an interviewing technique he had used with success when he was writing *Pork Chop Hill*, a detailed report of a single patrol action in the Korean War. He had gotten all the men together immediately after the patrol and taken them over the action minute by minute. Where were you at that moment? What did you do? Did you see Smith? In this way, he said, the men checked on each others' memories of the events, and he got an unusually complete and accurate account of everything that happened to each of them.

I tried it later and found it worked very well. But it took hours to do because the individuals sometimes argued about whether Tim had done exactly that at that moment, and you had to let them resolve it before you could go on. And there may be another weakness: for the method to work, I think the members of the group have to trust each other. I tried it again with a group of people who did not, and the session wound up in a cat fight, with individuals attacking each other, working out their hostilities and gripes instead of telling the story.

Often it helps to get anecdotes if you apply the subject under discussion to the interviewee's own life. Have you had this problem? How did you handle it? Have any of your friends faced it? What did they do?

Also, of course, official records are full of case histories—police, court decisions, social agencies, congressional hearings. From them you get the main lines of the story, then you flesh it out by talking to the individuals involved. Officials can help you locate anecdotes if you simply ask for case histories to illustrate specific points in the story. And they speed the process, because their own experience has included many such stories; once you get them thinking in these terms, they remember the outstanding ones.

Public relations people can do the same thing for you. But, of course, you have to remember that their job is to build a favorable image for their organization, and you must check whatever they tell you with others who are involved. PR people can help you in another way, too: If you tell them the idea you are working on, they can pinpoint the people in their organizations who would be most helpful and arrange appointments for you. Of course they will select the people who will give the positive picture; if you rely on them alone, your story will be unbalanced. Only the very best PR people, knowing a reporter's need for balance, will give you both favorable and unfavorable facts about their organizations.

The requirement for balance in a story is, of course, one of the cardinal rules of ethical journalism. It is also good practice. If your story is too one-sided you sacrifice credibility. Readers are not dopes; they know that every question has two sides, that ointments come equipped with flies, that no human being is all sweetness and light. If you give them only one side, they think you're trying to gull them and they stop believing in you. The moment that happens you're out of the communications business.

Further, by interviewing the other side, you often get material you could get no other way. Whenever I've been doing a piece that was going to hurt someone, I've had to walk around the block five times before I could get up courage enough to go in and see that person. There's an awful temptation to skip it, figuring you've got all you need anyway, and why put yourself through what is bound to be an unpleasant scene. But you can't afford to give in—and not only because if you give the person a chance to tell his or her side you'll be in an infinitely stronger position if the person sues you for libel.

Once Lester Velie, one of the country's best reporters, was doing a story on Artie Samesh, a lobbyist in California. The title, "The Secret Boss of California," gives the idea; Samesh had built up so much power in the state legislature that he could have it pass almost any law that would favor one of his clients. Velie had spent weeks digging up evidence to prove this, and the time came to see Samesh himself. Velie walked up to his house in what four-syllable writers call trepidation.

Samesh met him with a big smile: "Come in, come in. Sit down. Have a drink."

After the niceties were over, Velie brought up a case of influence-buying and asked Samesh about it. Samesh verified every item Velie had dug up and went on to add some details Velie did not have. It went on like that in case after case, so that by the time it was over Velie had facts and figures that no one else could have given him. Indeed, Samesh was so cooperative that he even allowed a photographer to pose a ventriloquist's dummy, with "The State of California" written across its chest, on Samesh's knee and shoot the picture.

Velie's story cost Samesh his influence with the legislature and probably helped send him to jail. Why was he so cooperative in his own destruction? The only reason Velie could figure out, he said later, was that while Samesh had this tremendous power, he felt neglected because nobody knew it. He wanted a little public appreciation of all his hard work.

6

Evaluating the Research

*E*valuation is the heart of the interpretive writing process. It is also the most difficult part for the writer, for it is here that we must finally make a judgment, here we must identify truth. It is not only a rigorous intellectual exercise, it is the core of the creative part of this kind of writing. For this is the period of chaos, mentioned earlier in Cathy Covert's definition of creativity.

At this point, when you have finished your research, you must summon to your mind the huge mass of facts, figures, statistics, expert opinions, conflicting viewpoints, anecdotes, tangential information, the motives and emotions of the individuals in your story—summon all these to mind and make a judgment about where the truth lies. This judgment will be the "something new" that is the end product of creativity. And you must do this, not as an omniscient and impartial god, but as a fallible human being, complete with faulty logic, prejudices, opinions, intellectual hobbies, emotional bents. All these must be surmounted, as best you can, for you're going on record with your judgment, and your work, in turn, will be judged by it.

Consider the dilemma of the writer. He or she—let's say he—starts out with an idea for a story, an approach to a set of facts. He has validated the idea in his preliminary research. Yet he knows that a cardinal sin of journalism is to collect only those facts and opinions which support his original idea. So he does a thorough research job, amassing all facts, both pro and con. Inevitably he discovers that his original idea has changed under the impact of the research. Now what does he do? Does he hew to the line and forget the inconvenient facts? He knows this is dishonest journalism, so he can't. But how much is the original idea changed? Where? This is what he must decide, and this is where his personal integrity enters the picture.

As always, integrity has a heavy price. Sometimes the price may be the loss of the story and the necessity of explaining to your editor that you were wrong: the idea you worked so hard to sell him is not supported by the facts. This is a particularly unhappy spot for a writer, because not only does his ego take a fall, but there is always the suspicion that if he had worked a little harder, seen more people, been more successful in eliciting the required information from them, the story would have come through. The temptation is almost irresistible to fudge the facts and save the story.

Once, for example, I went to India on assignment for *Reader's Digest*. One of the stories I was working on was about a missionary-agronomist from Massachusetts who, in twenty years of work in one of the country's worst famine areas, had introduced modern farming methods and enormously increased crop yields—a major success in a country that was chronically unable to feed its population. I had gotten the basic facts of the story from the church official in charge of Indian mission activities, and one of the main points was that the agronomist had introduced new methods of rice growing that had doubled or tripled harvests. Since rice was a staple in the diet of millions of Indians, this was vastly important.

But when I got to the mission station, I discovered the agronomist had not introduced the new rice-growing methods: the church official had been wrong. The agronomist had taught the Indian farmers many other modern methods—irrigation, terracing of fields, crop rotation, better plowing methods, use of pesticides—which had increased yields, but not rice culture. It was not a rice-growing area.

Normally I would immediately have called the editors and told them what I'd learned, but I was 8,000 miles away, there were no telephones, and letters would have taken too long. So I went ahead and gathered all the information on the other things the agronomist had accomplished. The story failed. The editors bought it because they were responsible people, but they never published it.

I think the reason it failed was that there was nothing in it quite so dramatic as the rice-yield increase, nothing as significant in terms of the country's overall food-production problem. I recognized it when I was in India, and when we discussed my findings after I got back and before I wrote the story, this was the point the editors instantly fastened on.

Editors are not stupid; if a story has a factual weakness they can spot it immediately. Thus to the ethical argument against fudging facts is added a very practical one: it doesn't work.

What does the writer do in this situation? Two things: he tries to find a replacement story while he's in the field—either a completely new story or a new approach to the present one that is factually sound. If he can't do either, he immediately phones the editor, explains that the story has failed, and comes home. If he has found a replacement, he explains this to the editor, tells why it was necessary and hopes the editor agrees to let him go ahead on it. The whole process is traumatic, and it indicates the stark, objective questioning the writer must apply to his own work, even while he is subjectively involved in it.

It seems to us there is a parallel between this process and the scientific method. One of the best descriptions of the scientific method, especially as applied to the social sciences, is in Stuart Chase's book, *The Proper Study of Mankind*. He lists ten elements of the method:

1. A problem to be solved . . . maybe cosmic rays, maybe juvenile delinquency.

2. Gathering the available facts about it, searching the literature.

3. A theory to explain the problem, a pattern sketched.

4. Rigorous verification of the theory by other scientists. Emotion and bias ruled out.

5. A stubborn atmosphere of doubt. The cheerful ability to say, "I was wrong."

6. Prediction in terms of probabilities, not absolutes.

7. Thinking more in terms of process than of linear cause and effects.

8. Thinking in terms of *structure*. How things are related to one another; the order in which they come—the structure of a skyscraper, a corporation, a community, a conference, an argument, an agenda.

9. No closed solutions; room always for new data which may give a closer fit.

10. No secrets, no monopolies, no pay-offs.

This is a pretty good definition of the process of interpretive journalism. It demonstrates that in journalism, as in scientific research, the place for objectivity is in the mind of the writer. In the old "just the facts, Ma'am" kind of journalism, reporters discharged their obligation to objectivity by presenting all sides of a question, without drawing any obvious conclusions. But, as we have seen, this approach is inadequate in today's complex world. On the other hand, if you throw out the ideal of objectivity, reporters become mere propagandists. So the ideal is retained, but inside the mind and conscience of the reporter, and it comes into play when he or she is evaluating the facts the research has turned up.

Erwin Canham, the great editor of *The Christian Science Monitor*, pinpointed it: "Background, motives, surrounding circumstances, related events, and issues all need to be understood and appraised as well as the immediate event. . . . But interpretation requires integrity and knowledge and understanding and balance and detachment."

To achieve complete objectivity when you are evaluating your research is obviously impossible. We are human beings, with prejudices, preconceptions, and opinions, and, as journalists, we usually feel strongly about public questions. Yet while the ideal is impossible of achievement, we are all obliged to come as close to it as we possibly can. Checking your research to make sure your facts *are* facts is the most obvious way. But an attitude of consuming skepticism also helps. So does noninvolvement.

Federal Judge Learned Hand made it a rule never to join any organization—political, economic, civic, even social, like a country club—because he never knew when some member of the organization might come before him to be judged. He said it was hard enough to be objective in passing judgment under the best circumstances, and being a member of the same organization might lead him to be either too lenient or too severe on the individual before him. The rule may well apply to journalists, too.

We think it helps, too, to remember that you have prejudices and consciously to try to offset them when you're making judgments. Are you a political liberal? Then when doing a political story, make sure you spend at least mas much time getting the conservative side as the one you naturally lean to. Do you believe the blacks have been exploited by the whites? Then do as much research discovering and understanding the white point of view as the black before you commit yourself to the main line of your story.

This is not only ethical journalism, it is self-protection. You will be judged by editors, other writers, and the public by what you write—not by whether you are a good parent or have soulful eyes. You will be forgiven some mistakes and some sins of omission. You will not be forgiven sins of commission.

The thing that makes this evaluation process so difficult is that you have to *think*. You are forced to analyze your facts and decide what they mean, what pattern they shape. That takes thinking. You have to compare conflicting bits of evidence and decide which is overriding. That takes thinking. You have to weigh the pros and cons of a situation and decide which is dominant. And that takes thinking. Finally, you have to decide what truth the dominant facts add up to. What's my story here? What am I saying in this piece?

I have spent a full week on this process, and all the while I appeared to be doing nothing. During it I might have scribbled a few sentences or paragraphs on copy paper—most of which were thrown away.

For me this was the hardest, most frustrating, most infuriating, most demanding part of the whole job—much harder than actually putting the words on paper. What I was trying to do was to write one sentence, one sentence that would give the main point, the message that all the research added up to. It had to be a sentence that encompassed all the findings and that contradicted no solid fact. It had to be short and not diluted by qualifications. It might end up as the title; surely the title would encompass its idea. But only after that sentence was written did I have the main theme of the piece, and only with the main theme before me could I go ahead and organize the bits and pieces that would make the final article. Without the sentence the article would have no unifying theme, no focus, and hence no single, compelling message. It would sprawl. Instead of hitting the reader with the force of a jet from a fire hose, it would have the impact of a lawn sprinkler.

Some other devices can aid the process. When they have finished their research, many writers I know spend a day or two retyping all their notes. They make little or no attempt to organize or expand them; they simply retype. This, they say, does two things—it makes them put everything they've learned through their minds again, and it gives them material *on paper*, which they can then cut up, rearrange, expand, or throw away. It is laborious, but they say it helps.

Because I'm congenitally lazy, I don't do this, but I do go through all my notes at one time and mark in red the nuggets that seem too good to leave out of the finished piece. One advantage this shares with the other process is that by reviewing at one time bits of information you may have collected three weeks or two months ago, you can see patterns and relationships you might otherwise miss.

Here's another trick: without referring to my notes, sometimes I simply sit down and recall those things in my research which stick in my mind and jot down, in no particular order, a few key words that identify each. (The things you recall immediately probably have some universal appeal that made them stick in your mind; if they impressed you, they'll impress your reader.) Then after I had organized and outlined the piece, I checked the outline against the list to see if it omitted anything important; if it did, the outline was probably faulty.

The business of distilling out the essential message from the mass of your research serves a double purpose. It not only gets you to the truth about the facts, but it also helps to shape the story, for only after you have written the single sentence can you decide what among your research supports the message and what doesn't. And only then can you decide the most effective way to get the message into the reader's mind and emotions. Probably the best way to illustrate this process is to describe a case.

When I was at *Redbook* the newspapers carried a story about Charles Kelly, who had won the Congressional Medal of Honor for his heroism in World War II. Ten years later, Kelly had just come out of the hospital, where he had nearly died from a burst appendix and ensuing peritonitis. The story revealed he had been down on his luck for years; he was living in a municipal housing project in Louisville, Kentucky, and had had a long run of joblessness. And there had been sickness too, not only for himself, but for his six young children. He had come to New York to be on one of the television giveaway shows that were edifying the soap opera set in those years, and the editors suggested I go see him. We had no definite idea for a story, but he was in our readers' age group, and we thought we might do a piece somewhat along the lines of how a hero readjusts to normal life.

The show was being produced at one of the midtown theaters, and Kelly was on when I arrived, so I stood in the wings and watched. The more I saw, the madder I got. They were humiliating him. Kelly was a proud, independent man who had fought his way out of the back alleys of Pittsburgh, and he had to tell the story of his own failures. In return, they showered money and gifts on him. But the jolly master of ceremonies, in "intellectual" black-framed glasses, let his contempt for Kelly's failure show. I suppose it made a good show, something like a public hanging, but it infuriated me to see a man who had won the nation's highest honor for valor exploited for the purpose of selling more deodorants, or whatever.

Kelly was a small, wiry, thin-faced guy with a nose like the blade of a hunting knife, and he'd lost so much weight in the hospital that his out-of-style suit hung on him in folds. When he came off the stage I was shocked to see he had tears in his eyes. I talked to him for only a couple of minutes—partly because he was obviously on the thin edge of control, and also because I didn't want to commit the magazine to doing a story until we were surer. But all the way back to the office I was telling off—in my head of course—the wise-guy master of ceremonies, the producer, the director, the network, the sponsors, and the whole television industry. It was pretty devastating.

I suppose it was anger as much as anything that made me decide to do the story—on the idea that this is what happens to a hero when the war's over—and the editors agreed to go along.

I dug up Kelly's service record and got the commendations for his Medal of Honor and other medals. They were impressive; obviously here was a man who, in a crisis, could act fast and effectively and with great courage.

I picked up the story, as usual, in bits and pieces—in Louisville and St. Louis, where Kelly was working on the new job he'd gotten after the publicity about his plight. Here are my notes on the story. While they may seem voluminous, they are about average for an article. My own comments, written at the time, are in brackets. Following the notes is the article I wrote from them. Comparing the two illustrates part of the writing process. You can see how disjointed the information is as you get it, and how it still must be assembled to make a readable piece. You can see how much of what you get never ends up in the article. Most important, by going through the "chaos" process with one writer, you can see how identifying the underlying theme of the story can give direction, movement, and unity.

FIRST INTERVIEW, AT TV SHOW: Chas. Kelly, 36, 137 lbs., first wife died of cancer '51—I watched her die for three years. Was chauffeur for Attorney General of Pennsylvania . . . married second wife '52, she from Louisville . . . couldn't make living Pittsburgh—$125 month for apartment, $40 month gas, $7 electricity . . . Clothes burned up in construction shack Frankfort . . . Baby to hospital with pneumonia; wife to hospital for sixth kid . . . her doc had emergency operation; his replacement delivered her . . . she in Tues., out Fri. . . . I ruptured appendix Sat-Sun, given three days to live, lost 28 lbs. Got Louisville job $1.25 hour, pick & shovel—furniture in storage, bill $350, couldn't raise; had save 3-4 weeks. [He should never have sent furniture; can't plan.] When baby in hospital—no insurance—cost $97—knocked on ass again.

Moved form Pittsburgh because couldn't make ends meet.

Watched first wife die cancer three years, giving increasing doses morphine.

Couldn't collect unemployment insurance since operation because not fired, not laid off. No workmen's compensation because not hurt on job. [If this isn't true it doesn't make any difference because he *thought* it true.]

[This is the story of the little man—limited, unsure of himself, with all the fears and limitations—but the man who perseveres, who is indomitable at last. He has courage and warmth and he survives.]

Used to say marriage was 50-50; well, today it's 75-25—75 for wife and 25 for man. I get up at night when kids cry; my wife needs her sleep. She has a bum ear, sleeps on the good one. But that's good. When I was sick I tried to get up but couldn't make it . . . shook her. She told me, "Why you not wake me? Kids my job." But they mine too.

[Chews tobacco and is self-conscious about it.]

KENTUCKY UNEMPLOYMENT INSURANCE DIVISION: Kelly unemployed "through no fault of own." Can't draw while unable to work and can't get workmen's compensation unless hurt on job.

BETTY (KELLY'S WIFE): Met Ft. Knox in '45 . . . Married Jefferson-ville, Ind., in '52, November . . . first wife died '51 . . . Children: Virginia, 10; Charles, Jr., 9; Michael, 5 [Mrs. K's by early marriage—divorced]; Lee, 3; Wm. Bennett, 1; Jerrie Lynn.

[Kelly's] father died '41, mother, '55 . . . worked in gas station for year after leaving Army in '45 . . . Worked four years as "investigator" for Pa. Attorney General, the late Chas. J. Margiotti, then four years as painter . . . to Louisville March '55.

June '55 Army sent him Bronze Star and second Silver Star; has about 10 medals . . . Here May '55 [housing project] he worked till Nov. '55, drew $14 unemployment from Pennsylvania; not here long enough for Kentucky.

[Betty's] uncle, the foreman, told Chuck would work that winter, but partnership [in company he worked for]splitting up; expected work again in Dec. No call. Decided wait until Jan. 1. No call. He told Kelly he didn't know when would reopen business. Kelly got odd jobs—not much paint-ing; the previous year he was off 2–4 months because of bad weather. In June he went to work as a painter . . . from Jan. to June mother, friends, neighbors kept us in food; Harry Holt [an insurance agent and friend] kept Kelly in spending money . . . William [called Bennie] got bronchial pneumonia in June '55, shortly after Kelly's mother died . . . When Kelly had appendix flare-up in August he wouldn't complain—he never does. Saturday night he crawled from living room couch into bedroom and asked me for the pain tablets; they in cabinet over kitchen sink; he crawled in but couldn't stand up to reach them . . . next morning he so white, said he couldn't move . . . Holt had said he had appendix the night before . . . I called Henry [Holt] and asked him to call the Veteran's Administration Hospital because a Medal of Honor winner can get in anytime. Henry came over and argued with Kelly an hour and 15 minutes before he'd agree to go. Left here Sunday morning at 9:30 . . . I alone; mother was in the country . . . Harry back at 5:30 with Kelly's clothes, they had operated . . . 8:30 I called hospital, talked to nurse, she said he fine . . . I saw him on Monday, 4:30 to 9:30 . . . He under dope for three days . . .

Sunday night I was in the kitchen from 12:30 to 3:30 praying, crying, smoking . . . I went to the hospital every day for 3–4 hours; he was unconscious . . . he came out of it Thursday, got no food until Friday . . . He in hospital 12–15 days. He in hospital 10:30 A.M., they didn't operate until 4:30 P.M.—thought he didn't have busted appendix; when operated found peritonitis had started. He put ice packs on belly Saturday night.

When he came home why they give him keys to the city? That won't feed us; give him a job. It has been 12 years since he came home from the war, now after 12 years they want you to come home to go to work . . . At breakfast you sit down and give the kids cereal; they want more; no more to give . . . My uncle took Virginia for the summer; mother took Chuckie; this was a big help.

The story of Kelly's sickness was on the wires—AP, UPI, the *Courier-Journal*, the New York papers . . . I flabbergasted; nothing like this had ever happened to me before . . . Kelly was scared to death to go on TV . . . He was going to have to tell a story he didn't want to tell. It took a lot of courage to do it.

People are wonderful; it makes tears come to your eyes . . . the kids are upset; photographers here all the time . . . wake the baby up . . . we both lost 10 lbs. over it.

In Pittsburgh I had to pawn a diamond engagement ring for $34, and couldn't redeem it. Got another when Kelly working in Frankfort; had to pawn it just before the baby was born and couldn't redeem that, either. I never want another.

"When a baby is born you can well understand who makes it; there's only One Person who could."

When Kelly working Frankfort he come home Saturday and couldn't wait to wake the kids up from their naps, take outside and romp with them for a couple of hours . . . He shows affection by cleaning the house, taking care of the kids while I go to the show a couple of nights a week. I'll go play cards with a couple of girl friends; he puts the kids to bed. He's older, he had his running around, so he lets me have mine. That's the way he shows love.

What do I want? A home with enough ground so that I know I can put the children out safely, that some other kid won't walk up and beat the kids up or take their toys . . . What does Kelly want? To be left alone.

After all the publicity we got a letter from an old lady in an old ladies' home; she enclosed a dime . . . One woman brought that couch, that chair, those two lamps; another gave us a youth bed, two hats and some clothes for Virginia . . . St. Vincent de Paul brought groceries and notified the welfare department; welfare paid the rent and gave us $20 a week until late September.

Name: Betty Dugzinski, born Michigan. From Mt. Vernon, Ky., 120 mi. from here. Came Louisville '49. Florida State University Fall '49. Got married '50, back Louisville '50. First husband's name; don't use. Got job photo studio in '50; worked two years, married Chuck '52.

Had met Kelly when about 14 when he on bond drive, asked autograph. He said cute kid, gave me nickel, told call when grew up. Here again on Veteran's for Eisenhower campaign in '52; friend was entertaining one night, asked me over. I said, you owe me another nickel; phone calls cost a dime now. "What?!" He didn't remember; we talked all evening, he kept calling me later.

Mother: Mrs. Robert Cummings, works Louisville. Father, Michael D., Detroit. Grandfather in Lily, Ky., Ed Newland. He sends food canned stuff from garden. Uncle, B. H. Hall, Corbin, Ky., stayed with him when K. in Frankfort. Met K. Oct. '52, married six weeks later. She stayed here. In March, convention in N.Y.C., she there, then marriage announced.

Sends two oldest children to Hazelwood Baptist Church. His first wife was Catholic, had kids in Catholic boarding school. She wants small farm. Has twin sister, 15, Margaret and Mary. Mary helps care for children. Diamond engagement ring $275, pawned in Pittsburgh when broke for $37. Got second one cost $150, pawned for $11. Kelly offered a total of seven jobs [after publicity about his illness] from $40 to $75 a week. Gov. Chandler made him a Kentucky colonel, offered him a highway job; he refused. Offered lifetime membership in Moose. Betty, 24.

Saturday night in kitchen [day K. went in for operation] 12:30 to 3:30, saw him before me. Was like he said, "Betty, take my hand." I started cry and I never prayed so hard in my life. Sat there smoking and crying and praying until 3:30.

[Quote her saying he scared to death to go on TV and he having no education, wanting her with him, but show wouldn't pay her expenses. He had to tell a story he didn't want to tell. Tears in eyes when came off.]

KELLY (in St. Louis where he working): First wife May Frances Boish, married '45 in Phoenix City, Ala., stationed at Fort Benning. About '48 had two children. She had backaches, took to doc—family—he sent us to a specialist, Dr. Shubb, Pittsburgh. He examined, Medical Arts Bldg., called me aside, said wife has cancer, like to have her in hospital, tomorrow? Fine. Walked out, in elevator wife: "What he say?" "Said you have cancer." She didn't cry, say anything.

Didn't bother her until later. Had hopes could beat it in hospital. After hospital said, "We can keep her alive a few years." It in womb. She only 25. She died '51. We living home, 713 Annandale St. She kept working until about '50, taking X-ray and radium treatments. Then 1–2 day's work, she felt pretty good; she danced, went to card parties. Later '50, couldn't walk up the stairs, had to carry. Went to see Ed Sullivan show, felt fine, but I had to carry her up the stairs.

Each day it got worse, Doc giving her shots; nurse, friend, came in to do it. I bathe her, feed her, massage her. Weighed 118 lbs., at death weighed 45. She had cravings—strawberries, ice cream. I get them for her, sometimes in middle night. I took the kids to her sister's home, Betty

Fullerton; Virginia about 3, Chuckie 2. This about two months before her death. Before, I took care of kids, gave her morphine shots; doc showed me how. Used to buy it by the bottle. Shots every four hours, then increased amount morphine, then shots closer; finally 1–½–2 grains every hour; every 45 minutes at end.

She'd ask to see the kids, then say, no, don't want them to see me like this. I catching a sandwich when I could, got very little sleep. Slept in chair by bed. We had a cocker spaniel, Cindy, got killed. She said get another—a mutt—about year before she died.

I working from 9 to 6–7 at night, sometimes later. Sometimes out of town for a couple of days, maybe a week. She died April '51, buried Westview Cemetery.

Sold house, lived hotel; children went to brother Edward, Westview. He crippled, worked in post office, has two girls younger than Chuckie. He next to youngest brother. Every time I saw the kids they wanted to come with me. Mostly on weekends, sometimes not on Sunday because working.

Fall '52 Jim Duff had appointed Attorney General Charles J. Margiotti (died '56). Duff in Senate. Had campaigned for Duff when ran for governor. Clarence Adams, Veterans for Ike, in Chicago. He invited me to GOP convention in June—parades and stuff. Started traveling through 17 states [67 speeches] for Ike. Did some traveling before 17-state tour.

Met Betty first in '44 when on bond tour. She 14. Gave nickel, said call when grow up. Called her every night for 3 weeks from whatever town I was in. Married Nov. Indiana. She back to Louisville. I in Pittsburgh, she met the kids. Had had to sell all furniture to pay bills for May's sickness and death. So no furniture, nothing except clothes and two kids. Now a wife and three kids. Had sent money to Betty, to brother Ed for the kids— about $50 a month for kids; I had to buy clothes and live myself. In Jan. '53 Betty came up, we picked up the kids—Virginia was in boarding school and the headmistress called Betty. Chuckie was with Ed. We picked up both and brought to a hotel. Betty and kids slept in bed, I in a chair. Next day I left, she took them back to Louisville. She had 4-room apartment on West Market St. Two bedrooms, living room, kitchen. The lady downstairs had been taking care of Mike [Betty's son]. Betty quit her job. I sent her money. Once I flew down to see and couldn't leave—stayed three days. I looking for furnished apartment. As fast as I'd save money, she'd want to come here or want me to come down. Fare $43 round trip.

In December they came to Pittsburgh. I borrowed a car, drove down, loaded all her belongings, all the kids, including a playpen, and drove back, 800 miles, no sleep. A guy promised to rent me his apartment—he, wife split. They made up; no apartment. We stayed at my mother's a three-room apartment. Mother slept on the couch, the kids in the bed, I on the floor. There about two weeks.

Found a 2–½ room apartment, furnished. Bedroom, kitchen, alcove with a couch, for $12 a week. Were there couple months. Found a furnished apartment for $125 a month. Two bedrooms, living room, kitchen, bath, sunporch. Had own furnace—gas—hot water heat. Water wouldn't circulate. Gas bills were $40 a month or more. Later moved down to a basement apartment—two bedrooms, living room, kitchen, bath. It was warm, had a backyard. $100 month.

I quit Margiotti in Spring '53. worked as a painter, P. A. Freyvogel, painting contractor and joined the union. I had belonged before and it cost $100 plus dues of about $12.50 every three months. Now it costs $150 plus dues. I making $2.95 an hour minus 10 cents an hour insurance. Making $114 a week, take home about $100. I worked nights, worked six hours and paid for eight. My wife scared be alone at night. I worked Saturdays, then she got pregnant and I had to cut down overtime.

There was a strike—out two months in the summer—I stayed home, had no money and borrowed. I laid off three weeks before Christmas, but all the presents had been bought so we had a good Christmas. I picked up a job painting an apartment next door. But I was out of work four months. Some guys will work overtime for straight time pay; they'd get the winter work. I was a foremen. Had been a wall-washer before the war and became a foreman. After I quit Margiotti I started at the bottom and became a foreman again. We painting five and dime stores. We had stool pigeons. We took half an hour for lunch; you take five minutes more and they told the boss. They told that I letting the men smoke—a man smokes all his life, how's he going to stop? We finished on job, I told the guys if they finished in eight hours we'd be paid for eleven. We finished in seven, I called it eight. I got chewed out for it and from then on I was on the outs. Got bad jobs. This in Fall '54. Betty kept wanting to go back to Louisville. One Friday night just before Christmas, she had a suitcase packed and train tickets. We went on Saturday, said she had a place; her mother had called. I'd had no job because the weather was too bad for nearly three weeks. We stayed with her mother, who worked. I stayed with the kids and when the twins came home I'd go look for a job.

Her uncle, J. C. Newland, was superintendent of a construction gang. I got a job with him as laborer on the roads at $1.25 an hour; dug ditches. In two weeks I was raised to $1.45 and when the weather got better, to $1.60. Owner, G. D. Davies, Frankfort, Fuller & Davies. I painted his house—a new house. By then the road was done, Newland went to Greenville,

Ohio, on a road job. I went along as labor foreman. We were raising manholes and catch basins two inches and black topping over brick. I was raised to $2.25. Worked about a month, then operated a gravel machine filling ditches at $2.50 an hour. We were there two more weeks, then back to Kentucky to the airport at Frankfort. I in charge of heavy equipment, laying rock and so on. I was next to Newland, who in charge of job.

A month after I started work Betty and the kids came down from Pittsburgh. [He was confused; Betty and kids already in Louisville.] Had bought furniture in '54. I had the money to bring them down, but not the furniture. One outfit would move the furniture down and put it in storage—which didn't cost anything then. Betty flew down—Lee had chickenpox and she was pregnant. She stayed with her mother for about six weeks and had the baby. Right after that we got in the [housing] project but couldn't get our furniture. We'd been delayed about three months getting into the project because we had to wait until somebody moved out. Her mother said it was okay to stay with her, but it wasn't—with all of us, it was too much for her. They talk about when a girl marries her mother doesn't lose a daughter, she gains a son. Well, she sure was getting a daughter.

I had to pay a hospital bill of $105 for Benny. I paid the doctor off for Benny, and Jerrie at about the first of October '56. We owed $300 for the furniture; I borrowed it from my boss and paid two months rent—$82. Furniture bill was $360; Betty borrowed $60. There was much missing—clothes, tools. But we finally got into the project and everything was pretty good.

I was now working in Frankfort, in a cabin with six men in three rooms—two bedrooms and a kitchen. I worked steady at $2.50 an hour, knocked off for rain, averaged $85–90 a week. So things were pretty good. Benny got bronchial pneumonia in the fall of '55. Had to go into the hospital for about a week. In one hospital, didn't like it; the baby would cry and nobody would care for him—at $11 a day. Baby was 4–5 months old. Took to another hospital where they had specialists—Benny's windpipe would close. After that the roof fell in.

I had all my clothes in Frankfort. On weekends when I came home I brought nothing but the clothes I wore. Monday morning I brought some jeans and a work shirt, walked in to get my work shoes and the cabin was gone—burned. Everything was gone, my medals, clothes, razor, shoes. Only thing I found was a pair of pliers. I had $5 to last me the week. The cabin owner had no insurance and neither had I. He said we'd have a place to stay, so four of us slept in a trailer. I lived in it for a month. No heat. Washing in a gas station, took baths at the airport.

About two weeks before Christmas the job folded—bad weather. The boss said the company was dissolving; as soon as it was settled up we'd be called back. I waited about two months for the weather to break. The boss didn't have enough work. I went back to $1.25 an hour putting in driveways and such. I went around to the factories trying to get a job— Dupont, Ford, Naval Ordnance—nothing. Drawing $14 a week unemployment from Pennsylvania. In the spring I got two houses to paint and we had enough to live on—with everybody helping out.

I got a job working for Leroy Heighbaugh—$1.45 an hour for a nine-hour day, 7–4:30, and five hours on Saturday. 50 hours a week. We were maintenance men. He owned houses, apartment houses, and we'd paint. Worked there 5 weeks. Betty went into the hospital to have Jerrie, in on Tuesday, out on Friday. I had to borrow $97.20 to get her out. She felt lousy; her doctor was in the hospital when she called Monday; she called a replacement, and he was in the hospital. She called all day Monday for a doc and finally got one. She went in Tuesday, baby born Wednesday and her doc not there when baby started.

Friday night she took sleeping pills. I felt lousy Saturday and didn't go to work. The pain kept getting worse; I was at Harry Holt's house and we thought it was my appendix. I went back home. Harry and I walked up the street for a Coke; I was full of pain. I bought an ice pack; the pain was worse. I filled the ice pack and put it on my belly while guests were there. Harry said go to the doctor. No; too many bills. He said we better leave. I went in and lay down; I had the ice pack, a towel wrapped around the ice trays from the refrigerator and a water bottle frozen solid on my belly. After everybody went to bed, it got worse so I crawled into the bedroom to get the phenobarbital—I couldn't walk and Betty wouldn't wake up, she'd had a pill too. After she did she said it was in the cupboard over the sink in the kitchen. I crawled back, but couldn't pull myself up to reach it. I lay on the floor. After about half an hour the pain left. I went into the living room and sat in a chair with the ice packs. She came out at 8, asked, do you want breakfast? No. She called Harry. He came. I couldn't get up—weak. Finally got dressed; Harry took me to the VA hospital; they examined me—blood counts and so on. Said no appendix. After other reports came in they decided to operate. I didn't know anything until Tuesday. I had peritonitis; I think it broke about 2 A.M. Sunday. They operated about 4:30 P.M. In hospital 12 days until about Aug. 15.

How he met Betty [this by Betty]. Friend called, said having K. and others over for supper. I hunted up my nickel and went over. He out walking dog. Came in, I up and said, owe another nickel. What? Do I know you? You gave me a nickel to call you when I grew up, but now it costs a dime. Later he called me from St. Louis, Washington, Detroit, Massachusetts.

Kelly won Congressional Medal of Honor, Silver Star, Bronze Star, Italian Cross of Valor, British medal for bravery—can't remember name. First story (of their trouble) broke when Jerrie born. *Saga* had story, N. Y. *Post* called, *Louisville Courier-Journal*. All told he got about 100 job offers—Texas, Utah, Calif., Fla., Pa., Mo., N. Y., Ky. "Strike It Rich" paid $500; got $100 from hotel chain. Pittsburgh City Commissioner John Walker announced a Kelly Fund be started in Mellon Bank; about $2800 in it—from all over.

Started St. Louis job Oct. 12. Betty to hospital for operation about Oct. 1—complications resulting from babies—cyst. When the *St Louis Dispatch* had the story Jerry Cataldi came to see me and offered the job. Was going to form a corporation and make K. part of it; Betty checked the corporation. Now making about twice as much as before; also will move family up here.

Facing the enemy was easier than the terrible six months. In battle you have a job, you know it, can do it. The other way, hands tied; you have a thing to do, can't do it. Go ask a man for a job; he says no; turn around and walk out. You walk 3–4 miles and they say the same thing. I'd have 50 cents in my pocket, no cigarettes or chewing tobacco. I'd go see men 3–4 times, then have go home and face wife. She: do any good? Naw. Next day, same thing.

You sit and try to think what can I do. You can't talk. You get so many no's. She sees this, says let's talk out. There's nothing you can grasp. You are asking for a job, you don't know if you can do it. Never had a high school education. Don't know much. But will try; every job I had I ended up on top of it. Seems every time I have to start at the bottom. Would walk out of house with a bus ticket and 15 cents for chewing tobacco. Sometimes I didn't have enough to get a room, so I'd sleep in a truck instead of borrow off the men. I just don't like to borrow.

The most important thing in my life is kids and wife. I took my bumps from when I was a kid. I want them not to make the same mistakes I did. Chuckie wants to go to West Point; I help as I can. I'm not brilliant, but I do what I can. Sons of Medal of Honor winners can get a special appointment to the Point, but must meet the same qualifications as anyone else.

I want to get my wife and family into a home of our own. At "Strike It Rich" I was scared because of no education. They said tell what you want: 1. job; 2. operation for Betty; 3. a sewing machine.

I try to help others. I've raised money for Red Cross, Salvation Army, war bonds; they use my name for fund drives and so on. I did practically nothing else for two years except go around and help raise money. It cost me money; I got $6 a day and transportation. $3 for a hotel and $1 for meals. So it cost me; I never had a hotel for less than $6 and sometimes up to $14. Nothing for cleaning, I had to buy own clothes, take care of tips. I used up all my Army pay and had to dig down for other money.

My notes ended there. Of course they are fragmentary, mere triggers to make your memory supply the full sound and flavor of what they said. For example, Kelly's account of the night he had the appendicitis attack was a long story with many more details; the notes merely give the progression of the action. the rest was so colorful and moving that it was deeply imprinted on my mind; after years, I can still see and hear him as he described it.

And now back home, the evaluation process started. What did all these bits and pieces add up to—what did they say, what single message could be drawn from them that would be important to our readers? What self-interest of theirs would be piqued so they would say, "Yeah, that could happen to me"? What emotions would the story evoke, so readers would not find it a dry recital of another's experiences with no real pertinence to their own lives? How should the story be constructed—what should come first, what next? What should be used, what left out? What would the story *say?*

I thought about Kelly, that cocky, vulnerable little man with the wad of chewing tobacco tucked in his cheek. I remembered the way his voice deepened with self-importance when he talked about the parades he'd been in, his visits to the White House, the obvious relish with which he described the cheering crowds that surrounded his car during the war bond tours. I recalled the big cigar he had that day at lunch in St. Louis, and how he talked importantly about forming a corporation, when he obviously didn't have an inkling of what a corporation was or entailed. I thought he was being used for his publicity value, and when that died away he would be eased out onto the streets again—and he didn't know it. I thought, the guy is a phony; he was really taken in by all the public relations razzle-dazzle; he believed what the press agents said about him (which is fatal). And I thought, why should we add to this? The man is not worth doing a story on; he's hollow.

And then I remembered the tears in his eyes at the TV show; they, by God, were no press agent's gimmick. And I remembered that he had known he was going to be humiliated at the show and had gone anyway. Why? Because he needed the money, because his family needed the money. I remembered Betty saying that when he was working in Frankfort and came home weekends, he was so anxious to see the kids he'd wake them up and take them outside to romp. I remembered that during the bad times, he must have known that all he had to do to start the golden shower of money and jobs was to go to the newspapers with his story. And he'd had too much pride and independence to do it. I remembered his face, blank with concealing his emotions, as he said, "When you give the kids a bowl of cereal for breakfast and they ask for more and there isn't any more, you don't feel like much of a man."

I thought, he may have been taken in by the razzle-dazzle, but there are damn few men who wouldn't be, and he has shown that he's a tough man, he keeps on fighting. Is that what the story says—that a man ought to keep fighting? Big deal, who *hasn't* said that before?

Is Kelly the kind of man we want to do a story on? Look at all the mistakes he made, like paying $275 for an engagement ring for Betty when he should have known that kind of money was way out of his class— and then having to pawn it a few months later for $34. Yeah, but look at it another way: maybe he *did* know it was out of his class and bought it anyway because that was way of showing his love for Betty. Or take that marvelous little story about Betty and the nickel and the way they met. He was being lionized—the big hero accepting the homage of the natives. So why did he take time out from being lionized to walk his hostess's dog? Doesn't this show a kind of simple helpfulness so strong in him that it overrode his vanity?

Or take the time when the doctor told him May had cancer and advised him not to tell her about it. Kelly told her immediately, before they even got out of the building. Wasn't this callousness? Maybe. But also maybe it was a kind of faith in her—faith that she was strong enough to take whatever she had to take. Certainly the business of sitting by her bed for three weeks, giving her morphine injections every hour, grabbing a sandwich when he could, catching naps in the chair, going out for strawberries at 1:00 A.M.—all that didn't indicate callousness. Probably the man was speaking the literal truth when he said his kids and wife were the most important things in his life. Maybe this is a love story, a man's love for his family. *That* certainly would be pertinent to our readers' lives.

And so the process goes on—weighing, evaluating, analyzing. I spent two or three days at it. Once I went out into the backyard and walked back and forth for three or four hours thinking, "This has obviously got to be a narrative; how in hell am I going to get narrative into it? What's the problem to be solved? What are the conflicts and suspense in it?" And suddenly it began to come clear that this was a story of courage, of two kinds of courage—the kind that enables a man to win the nation's highest honor for valor and the kind that sustains a man through the grinding attrition of day-to-day living, running a marriage, raising kids, meeting the bills, coping with sickness and emergencies, keeping the whole shebang going against the slings and arrows of outrageous fortune. Remember how Kelly himself had said that just living was harder? That business about when you are in battle you have a job to do, you know it, and know you can do it; but the other way your hands are tied—you have a thing to do and can't do it. That was it.

I went into the house and scribbled on a sheet of paper: "We're showing that it takes more courage to live an everyday life, raise a family, and take on all the things life can throw at you than it does to win a Medal of Honor." And I wrote the title: "A Hero Is Many Men." (Later the editors changed it and rightly so. The title was ambiguous I knew what it meant, but the reader wouldn't.) The story was, it turned out, a simple straightforward piece.

At that point, I could start to organize the story, to select and assemble those bits and pieces that would get the message across to the reader, that would make the narrative flow, evoke the readers' emotions so they would see themselves in Kelly's struggles. I'm not very happy with the result—I think in many places I failed to make it as strong and compelling as I should have, and I didn't make Kelly as rounded a character as he really was—but here it is:

A Man's Fight for His Family

"Commando" Kelly had earned the Medal of Honor, but when misfortune struck his home, he needed even more courage— just to live from day to day.

The door to the office opened, and the doctor appeared with May at his side. He told her to take a seat for a few moments, then looked at Chuck Kelly and said, "Will you come in, please?" Kelly knew instantly that it was bad, but he didn't say anything as he walked in and sat down in the chair next to the desk.

The doctor's face was solemn. "I'm afraid I have very bad news for you, Mr. Kelly. Your wife has cancer; I believe she has only a few years to live."

Kelly blinked, but his voice was level, almost uninterested. "Wouldn't an operation stop it? What about X-ray treatment?"

The doctor shook his head. "You can try them, of course. An exploratory operation would show how bad it is, but I think we already know that. I doubt that X-rays would help. I haven't told your wife—I think it would be better not to."

Kelly didn't say anything more. On the way down in the elevator May asked what the doctor had said. Kelly, who believes that people can take what they have to take, answered, "He says you have cancer." May didn't say anything, didn't cry or do anything at all. They walked out of the Medical Arts Building and went home to their two children and their house on Annandale Street in Pittsburgh.

Probably you have heard of Charles Kelly. A few years before that day at the doctor's he had become one of the 15 living Americans to receive the Congressional Medal of Honor, the nation's highest decoration for courage.

Kelly was 22 at the time, a slim, tough kid who'd grown up in a back alley in Pittsburgh and learned a cocky independence from his blacksmith father, from earning his own way as soon as he finished grade school, from being able to handle himself in street fights.

He went in on the beaches at Salerno, Italy, in September 1943, and in two days of furious fighting around Altavilla, he led volunteer patrols against entrenched German machine gun positions and wiped them out and took another patrol through two miles of enemy-held territory under constant sniper, mortar and artillery fire. When his company was surrounded in a house, Kelly ranged from window to window pouring a torrent of fire into the enemy. In a few hours he burned out nearly half a dozen Browning automatic rifles and then used, in succession, a Thompson submachine gun, Garand and Springfield rifles, carbines, a 37 mm. anti-tank gun and a bazooka. Once he repelled a German assault by picking up 60 mm. mortar shells, pulling the safety pins and hurling them like hand grenades.

Later Kelly led 44 men across the bloody Rapido River and brought eight back. Three time his outfit was in the line at Cassino—for 15, 43, and 36 days at a time, under fire so terrible that once Kelly, a sergeant, was the highest-ranking officer left alive.

Kelly's exploits won him the nickname "Commando" and constitute a record of courage that seldom—if ever—had been surpassed in U. S. history. But is the kind of brilliant courage that carries a man to the peaks in a flashing moment of war the same kind that sustains him in the slow, grinding attrition of everyday troubles that so many heads of families must endure?

In the five years after his date with the doctor, Kelly was to find out—was to have his courage tested to the utmost. For there is nothing in the world that is more important to Chuck Kelly than his wife and kids—not his job, not his war record, not even his own well-being.

At first the cancer didn't interfere with May's activities much, and Kelly stayed at home at night to look after Virginia and young Chuckie in order that May might go to the movies or play cards with her friends. But increasingly, before the movie or card game ended, the pain would hit her. After a while she gave up the nights out. About a year before she died she couldn't walk upstairs any more; Kelly carried her. And sometimes she'd get great cravings; Kelly went out and hunted the city for strawberries or ice cream.

After she became so weak she had to stay in bed most of the time, Kelly hired a nurse to come in and bathe, massage and feed her—and give her the morphine shots that were steadily increasing in size and frequency. Finally May got so thin and was in such pain, she didn't want the children to see her; they were sent to her sister's to live. But she never cried.

At this time Kelly was working as bodyguard and chauffeur for the late Charles J. Margiotti, then attorney general of Pennsylvania. He was making a fair wage, but long sickness can devour any income. When the money ran low, the doctor taught Kelly how to give the injections. May required almost constant attention now—injections every 45 minutes—and Kelly's boss let him stay at home all the time during the last weeks.

He often slept in a chair and grabbed a sandwich when he could. The rest of the time he sat with his wife, talking to her, holding her hand, watching her die. Finally death came, in April 1951.

Kelly had to sell the house and furniture to pay the bills. He moved to a hotel and his brother Ed, who worked in the post office, took the two children. Kelly's job kept him out of town a lot, but he visited the kids as often as possible. Every time he left, they wanted so badly to come with him that he felt like a criminal.

The following year, Kelly was asked to help campaign for General Eisenhower's first term as a "Veteran for Ike." While in Louisville, Kentucky, he met Betty Dugzinski.

He had met her once before, during the war when he was on tour trying to boost War Bond sales and she was a star-struck kid of 14. She'd come up for his autograph, a cute, blonde youngster, and he'd whistled to make her feel good and pulled out a nickel. "Here," he'd said, "call me when you grow up."

Now he was in Louisville with the campaign troupe, and she was running a photography studio there. A friend called her, said she was having the veterans over for dinner and would Betty come to help entertain them? Betty hadn't forgotten Kelly. She went home, dug out the nickel and was at the friend's house when he walked in the door.

"You owe me another nickel," she said.

"What!"

"You owe me another nickel. Telephone calls cost a dime now."

"What? Who are . . . Do I know you?"

Then Betty explained.

Before the evening was over, Kelly told her seriously, "I'm going to marry you." Betty didn't believe him, of course. The next night the troupe was in St. Louis; he called Betty and talked for half an hour. He called next from Detroit, then Worcester, Massachusetts, then Washington, D.C. Six weeks after they met they were married in Jeffersonville, Indiana.

But they couldn't be together right away. Kelly had to find a place to live and save money for furniture. So Betty went back to her job in Louisville, and he stayed in Pittsburgh. Kelly looked for a furnished apartment big enough for three kids—his own two and Mike, Betty's son by a previous marriage. Finally he found one that was big enough, but it cost $125 a month and had a gas furnace which cost $40 a month to run during the winter and even then didn't heat the place.

To get more money, Kelly quit working for Margiotti and went back to his old trade—house painting. He was bringing home about $100 a week, but he had to work at night to do it. Being alone frightened Betty so that after a while Kelly switched to day work, even though it meant a cut in take-home pay.

There was a strike that summer which meant no pay for two months, and Kelly was laid off three weeks before Christmas when the weather turned bad. Still, since they'd already bought the kids' presents, Christmas was all right that year. Weather kept Kelly out of work four months that winter— about average for painters—and although he managed to pick up some jobs on his own, there was barely enough money to go around.

Prices kept going up. Lee was born in the spring, and Kelly started having trouble with his boss. A misunderstanding arose and Kelly started losing good assignments. Finally he had to pawn the diamond engagement ring he'd given Betty. He got $34 for it.

One night Betty said it seemed to her they weren't making any headway; they couldn't keep going into debt. She thought they could do better in Louisville where her uncle, who was superintendent of a highway con-struction crew, could help Kelly get a job. She also counted on finding a much cheaper apartment in a municipal housing project.

They went to Louisville, Kelly did get the job and—eventually—they moved into the housing project. Kelly started as a pick-and-shovel man at $1.25 an hour and worked his way up to foreman in charge of the heavy machinery, just under Betty's uncle.

The job was at the airport in Frankfort, Kentucky, about 50 miles from Louisville. Kelly was living in a cabin near a gas station down the road from the airport and coming home only on weekends. He missed the kids so much

Republican precinct worker who had become Kelly's closest friend, helped out most of all. He hired Kelly to paint his house, which really didn't need it, and paid well for the job.

Kelly found another house-painting job and then in June he finally went to work as a painter-maintenance man for a real estate operator. He made $1.45 an hour and worked 50 hours a week.

Five weeks after he got the job, Betty went into the hospital to have their sixth child. The bill was $97.20, which Kelly had to borrow to get her out of the hospital.

The next day Kelly had a sharp pain in his stomach and didn't go to work. As it grew worse, he decided it was not his appendix. That afternoon, when Harry Holt came over, they walked to the drug store and Kelly bought an ice bag. Harry told him to go to a doctor, but Kelly, thinking of the bills, refused.

Betty went to bed and Kelly stayed in a chair in the living room. The pain was getting intense, and pretty soon Kelly had the ice bag, a water bottle that was frozen solid and three ice trays wrapped in towel, all on his abdomen. There weren't enough. He remembered that Betty had some sleeping pills for her own post-childbirth pain. He started to go for them found he couldn't walk. He crawled into the dark bedroom and had a terrible time waking Betty, who had taken some pills herself. She mumbled that they were in one of the kitchen cabinets, but she didn't wake up enough to comprehend Chuck's agony.

He crawled into the kitchen, but couldn't hoist himself up high enough to reach the pills. He lay on the floor, drowning in the pain; then he blacked out.

Later the pain broke. He looked across and there was the familiar living room chair under the cone of light from the lamp. In his abdomen now was only a dull ache. He got up and lurched over to the chair and sat down and dozed.

At eight o'clock Betty came in, took one look at his drawn, white face and went downstairs to phone Harry Holt. Harry came over and took Kelly to the VA hospital. They checked in at 10:30 in the morning and Kelly told the doctors he thought his appendix had burst the night before. They took tests and operated at 4:30 that afternoon; by then peritonitis had set in.

Betty couldn't sleep that night. Harry had come by and told her about the operation and said Kelly was fine, but something about his manner kept her from believing him. Finally at about 12:30 she went into the kitchen for a drink of water. She was standing by the sink looking out the window at nothing when suddenly,

"I saw Chuck," she said, "and I could feel him there in the room. He was reaching out to me, and I knew something was terribly wrong.

"I started to cry and I don't think I ever prayed so hard in my life as I did right then. I stayed in the kitchen for three hours praying and crying and smoking cigarettes."

The next morning, Monday, she insisted on going out to the hospital, although it was not yet seven days since she'd had the baby. Kelly was unconscious and stayed that way until Thursday. Each day Betty was beside his bed for the full four hours that visitors were allowed.

Kelly was in the hospital 12 days and lost 28 pounds. When he came out, the nation had heard of his trouble; Harry Holt told the newspapers when he went into the hospital. Then the golden shower began as the American people poured out their generosity on a family that needed help. One woman brought a chair, a couch and two lamps; another brought a bed; another gave clothes. After Kelly appeared on TV, letters with money poured into the Mellon Bank in Pittsburgh until the total reached $2,800. The most touching letter came from a woman in an old ladies' home; she wished the Kellys well and enclosed a dime.

Kelly received more than 100 job offers from all over the country, and the Governor made him a Kentucky colonel. The tiny Kelly apartment was swamped with reporters, photographers and broadcasters. President Eisenhower sent Kelly a telegram and later invited him to take part, on TV, in one of the question-and-answer shows that were a part of his campaign for reelection.

But the golden shower was not without its dark clouds. Kelly was invited to appear on the "Strike It Rich" television show, and it was this appearance that swelled the money and job offers into a flood. But it was also an ordeal.

"He was scared to death," Betty said. "He knew he couldn't answer the questions they'd ask him, because he never forgets that he didn't even go to high school. And he had to go up there before all those people and tell a story about himself that he didn't want to tell. He's an independent man and he was ashamed.

"He hated it, yet felt he couldn't refuse to go because we needed the money so badly. He very much wanted me to go with him, but the people wouldn't pay my fare and we had no money of our own. So Chuck went alone and it took a lot of courage. I watched the show; at the end I could see he had tears in his eyes."

One day last fall Kelly was talking about courage. I asked him which took more—to face the Germans that day at Altavilla, or to live through the past few years. He answered instantly:

"The past years took much more. When you're in combat you have a job to do, you know how to do it and you know you can do it. So you just go ahead. Besides, when you're in a fight, you get so hopped up you don't even think about the danger.

"But these years have been rough. Your hands are tied. You have a thing to do, but you can't do it. You go in and ask a man for a job. It's a job you never had before and you're asking for it, but you don't know if you can do it. And you get so many 'No's.'

"Then there's your family. You give the kids cereal in the morning and they ask for more and there isn't any more. When you tell them, you don't feel like much of a man.

"But you just have to keep on and do what you can."

This article, of course, is flawed. There are minor failures, such as not noting that it was after midnight the time he went out for the strawberries for May, not realizing that most readers think of housepainting as an outdoor, daytime job and that I should have explained that Kelly was painting the interiors of apartments at night. I should have used the date of the summer strike, and I should have noted that it was wintertime when he slept in the unheated trailer. But the greatest failure was that I didn't present the side of Kelly that was seduced by the razzle-dazzle, didn't show his vanity, his self-importance. In the evaluation process I decided this wasn't as important as other things he did and was, and left it out in order to hew to the stronger line. Since then I've read better journalists than I who found ways to include this kind of material without destroying the main theme of the story and thus produced a finer, deeper, truer piece.

7

Organization

Most of the textbooks on writing that we've read have sections on organization, and most didn't help us when we faced the actual job. Most start by saying organization is vital to good writing, which is true, then go on to talk about jotting down sections of the piece on 3×5 cards and arranging them in order, or scrawling ideas, quotes, and facts on butcher paper and tacking them up all around the room, or similar mechanistic approaches. None dealt with the basic problem: how to assemble all these bits and pieces into a compelling article?

Perhaps one reason for this is that each part of a piece is different—the material you have, the feel of the story, your objective in writing it. Good organization must reflect all these, must grow inevitably out of the story itself, and while the manipulation of pieces of paper or cards might help, it doesn't get to the heart of the problem. For while organization *is* part mechanics, it can also be where the writer's creativity shines through to make a collection of facts glow with a special warmth.

When you're writing a typical news report, organization follows a pattern, and it takes place more or less automatically in your mind. But when you face a longer piece like a depth story or a magazine article, the familiar system doesn't work. You have many more facts to contend with, some of them contradictory. You have abstract ideas, suggested by the facts, to be distilled out and stated clearly. You have to sustain reader interest over a longer period. All this means that you have to analyze and plan—consciously.

This is creativity. For writers who are very good, talent dominates the organization process, and they may come up with something so new and effective that people still remember it years later. But most of us aren't that talented—or that talented every day—and as journalists we have to keep writing. So when inspiration fails, craftsmanship can move in to fill the gap. Your piece may not be brilliant, but it will be sound.

The heart of the organization process is first to refine out the single theme or idea that the facts indicate, as we discussed in the Kelly story in Chapter 6. Once you have this, the job is to summon all the material—statistics, quotes from experts, anecdotes—that support the single message. Everything in the piece should support or relate to it; anything that does not should be left out, no matter how attractive it is in itself. But how do you arrange the material? What comes first, what next?

All our training in linear thinking and logic pushes us to arrange a story chronologically. Are you writing history? You start at the beginning of a century and work through to the end. In recounting a series of events you report what happened first, then next and next until the story is ended. One of the best examples of chronological organization is in Jim Bishop's "day" books. In the first, and perhaps best, of these, *The Day Lincoln Was Shot*, Bishop started his story twenty-four hours before Lincoln's death, then carried through hour by hour until the end. This gave the whole series of events immediacy and allowed him to build an unusual tension as characters and events moved toward the climax of the assassination in Ford's Theater.

But the book also illustrates the weakness of chronological organization. In order to let the reader understand the motivation of his characters, Bishop had to break chronology and go back in years to report the events that shaped their lives. For example, Bishop had to go back almost to John Wilkes Booth's childhood to explain Booth's frustration and bitterness. These excursions broke the tight chronology and, though Bishop handled them well, tended to relax the tension of the book.

This same problem was illustrated much more concisely in an excellent little piece in the *New York Times*. Here it is:

Little Man Has Day in Night Court

By Bill Kovach

He was a small man, the plaintiff, and standing before the bench looking up at the judge, he seemed even smaller. His hands trembled as they darted from his black rimmed glasses to his silver hair and back again.

It was not just the courtroom, wood paneled and large, that emphasized the smallness of Isaac Spira, but also his adversaries. Mr. Spira, the owner of a small cleaning establishment, was challenging the New York Telephone

Company, with its attorney and battery of experts holding folders of wonderfully detailed technical information.

Like many of those who have been using Night Court in steadily increasing numbers to try to right what they consider wrongs, Mr. Spira was unlearned in the law.

Armed with only his complaint, he jumped to the attack, pouring out a torrent of words. "They cost me business, Your Honor," he argued. "I was without phone service for three weeks because they cut off my phone at my old place—I even had to go next door to a neighbor's to make my calls and my customers told me they tried to call and couldn't get me—and when they put it in at the new place it rang in the old place, too. It was from July 26 to Aug. 14 before I had decent phone service, Your Honor."

Patiently, Judge Andrew R. Tyler let Mr. Spira make his complaint in his own words, not allowing technical details of legal procedures to interfere with his telling of the story.

Isaac Spira, who was born in Germany and spent more than five years in German concentration camps, was having his day in Night Court.

Each year thousands of New Yorkers like Mr. Spira go from the streets and the marketplaces into court with their arguments. It is in this courtroom on the ground floor of the Civil Courts building at 111 Centre Street, in lower Manhattan, that literally thousands—the total last year was 65,000—get their first experience in court.

The night sessions of Small Claims Court, a part of the Civil Court, were organized in 1957 by Judge Daniel Gutman. Realizing that a man suing for $100 (which was the limit of the court in 1957, but is now $300) could probably not afford a day off from work or business to press his claim, Judge Gutman struck upon the plan for a night court.

The success of the court has generated widespread sentiment to raise the maximum claim to $500 or even $1,000. For $2.91 to pay for a summons, anyone can bring suit for civil damages. There are no other costs.

Neither is there a need for an individual to bring a lawyer.

"This is simply a people's court," Judge Tyler said. "Many come here as a matter of principle. We let them tell their story in their own way—all we are after is the truth, and we let each side tell that as best they can and as best they see it."

Judge Tyler is one of the regular judges of the Small Claims Court, which meets on each weekday. Each judge, on a rotating basis, sits for a week in Night Court.

Similar Night Court operations are maintained across the street in the Criminal Courts for those accused on criminal charges.

Many Get There Early

Night Court convenes at 6:30 P.M. A hand-lettered sign notes that that means "6:30 sharp." But, many plaintiffs and defendants arrive early. They stand about, their voices subdued and small in the marble and glass expanse of the two-floor lobby.

If the weather is nice, some wait on benches outdoors, employees head for home, or go across to the Court View Bar for a quick drink.

As they gather, most of them segregate themselves into little groups: here a plaintiff and some friends; there a defendant casting sullen glances at his accuser.

Sometimes they are friendly. One night recently, a typical night at the court, one of the 60 new cases docketed that night was settled in a friendly discussion in the lobby. A store owner, sued by a customer for a defective air conditioner, met her as she went into court.

He had explained he "could do nothing personally" about the machine, but her suit had brought in the manufacturer. On this night a representative of the manufacturer was present and in a conference in the lobby, agreed to send the machine back to the factory for service and repairs.

Satisfied with the arrangement, the three left, no longer needing the services of the court.

How the Court Works

Promptly at 6:30 Joseph Hyland, clerk of the court, opened the doors to begin the preliminaries before Judge Tyler assumed the bench.

"What we try to do," Mr. Hyland explained to a hundred or so people, most of whom had never seen the inside of a courtroom, "is to expedite your cases. We have two choices available to you. If both sides agree, your case can be handled quickly by arbitration. If you cannot agree to arbitration, we can try the case before the judge."

The distinction, he went on, is that arbitration—conducted by an attorney with the same qualifications as a judge—is final. There is no appeal. At trial, a transcript is kept and an appeal is possible, although with a maximum claim of $300 the cost of an appeal is generally prohibitive.

Mrs. Shirley Eisner, a Manhattan housewife, considered the alternatives. Carrying her evidence—a blue and white suit coat, marred, she said, by her cleaner—she hoped to avoid a trial.

"I still do business with him. I don't want to have to go through that," she said. "Maybe we can settle this."

Mrs. Eisner and her cleaner ("Let's leave his name out of this," she said. "It couldn't be helped and we still get along") agreed to arbitration. She settled for less than the $509 she originally sought, and the two left, apparently pleased with the results.

Most of the litigants agreed to arbitration, but the few who insisted upon a trial presented for Judge Tyler a series of problems.

One woman sought a postponement: "I had all my evidence in my pocketbook," she told the judge, "and I changed pocketbooks to come down here and left them in the other one."

He put the case over to October 16.

Another, an elderly woman who appeared confused by the proceedings, presented the judge with a fistful of papers—42 in all.

"If you'll read these," she said, "you'll understand my case."

Quietly and patiently, Judge Tyler waded through the documents, some of them handwritten.

"Don't you have an attorney?" he asked the woman, the defendant in the case.

After a moment she answered: "My attorney could not come. He is a lovely old man and he is in the hospital dying of cancer."

Both Sides Are Ready

Over the protests of the other side, Judge Tyler ordered the case set over: "She cannot handle this alone," he said, "I'm not going to let this case go to trial in this manner."

By the time Judge Tyler came to the case of Isaac Spira, doing business as Jac-Le-Valet, vs. the New York Telephone Company, the docket had almost been cleared.

Both sides were ready in this one, and the issue was joined immediately. Accustomed to a more formal procedure, the company's attorney began on several occasions to rise and object to the statements of Mr. Spira. A calm wave of Judge Tyler's hand, however, kept him in his seat.

"Just let him tell his story," the judge said quietly.

And when he was through, the judge similarly overlooked Mr. Spira's dramatics in his cross-examination of defense witnesses.

In the end, the court reserved judgment. "We never give a final decision the night the case is in court," explained the clerk. "They've had their opportunity to present the case and they will call back later for a decision."

Few are disappointed, he said, no matter how the decision goes.

It's the Principle

"Most of these people are in here as a matter of principle." he explained. "It is not so much the money involved, but their right to sue anyone they believe has wronged them. But, in the heat of a courtroom argument—when they are re-enacting the wrong they feel done them—tempers can build. We don't add to that by ruling for one side or the other the same night. It seems to work very well; we have very few complaints."

A janitor was sweeping away cigarette butts in the hallway at 11:30 this night when Night Court ended. He paused for a minute, leaning on his broom, and shook his head with a smile. Mr. Spira, who moments before condemned every phase of the telephone company's operation, was walking out with the company attorney.

"Sure," he was saying, "I understand your problem. Come on, I'll take you home in my car, your place is not far from where I live."

Here Kovach uses a kind of chronological organization. He starts by showing Isaac Spira in action, pleading his case before the judge. He gives readers a single man to identify with and evokes their underdog sympathies—the little man versus the giant corporation. But after seven paragraphs, he must depart from the Spira story to sketch the larger significance of his piece—what the night court is and how it works. Then he goes back to the chronology again, under the subhead "Many Get There Early," by picking up the story as the court opens. He follows through with succeeding cases and finally winds up with the rest of the Spira story and the closing of the court.

If our training pushes us to chronological organization and the requirements of comprehension prohibit it, how does the writer solve the dilemma? I got the first glimpse of the answer from an editor with whom I worked. I had done a piece and while he liked the idea and the research, he didn't like the way it was put together. He was trying to tell me what was wrong with it. "You've got to organize it by concepts," he said.

"What do you mean? I don't understand."

"Well, look: You make certain points here—or the facts you report do. But they're not clear; they're not stated clearly and then each point driven home with facts, supporting evidence. That's the way you put a story together; you make a point—tell the reader what it is—then prove it with evidence. Then you go on to the next point and do the same thing."

To make this new approach penetrate my dim brain, he had to take the manuscript and point out specific instances of what he meant. Finally I got it and ever since when faced with the problem of organizing a piece, I have gone back to his formula for guidance. It works. It works for all kinds of stories; it is almost infinitely flexible. Even stories that seem to be put together chronologically are in fact organized conceptually. Like the Kovach piece, above.

The first six paragraphs are the lead in which Kovach catches the reader's interest and presents, by illustration, the theme or idea; here's a way little people who feel they have been wronged can get justice. Then he goes from the specific to the general to point out the significance of the court and, briefly, its history. After three paragraphs he makes his first point: "Neither is there need for an individual to bring a lawyer." He nails this down with a quote from Judge Tyler, then gives two more paragraphs of background explanation.

Under the subhead "Many Get There Early," he goes back to chronology and makes another point: some cases are settled in the lobby outside court. This one is not stated explicitly, but is implicit in the reporting and in the last paragraph:

"Satisfied with the arrangement, the three left, no longer needing the services of the court."

The next point—claimants have two choices—is made in the next three paragraphs and driven home with the anecdote about Mrs. Shirley Eisner. The next—Judge Tyler has to handle many human problems—is made in the paragraph starting, "Most of the litigants agreed . . . ," which does double duty by also carrying the chronology forward. Then he goes back to the Spira case and, in reporting it, makes the point that the judge won't let legalisms overwhelm a lawyerless claimant nor let an emotional claimant subvert the law. His final point is made by the night clerk: "Most of these people are in here as a matter of principle."

The chronology is ended with the last two paragraphs, which also restate the theme that little people can get justice by showing Spira satisfied and friendly.

The skeleton of a piece that is organized conceptually, then, can be simply stated:

* Lead—to hook the readers in, get them emotionally involved.

* Statement of the theme/idea what the story is about and why the reader should read it. Answer reader's question, "What's in it for me?"

* Point number 1 to prove theme/idea, supported with evidence: facts, quotes, anecdotes.

* Points number 2, 3, 4, etc., similarly supported.

* Ending—summary, wrap-up anecdote, snapper, or restatement of theme/idea.

After you have used this formula a few times you'll begin to get disgusted with it; it will seem too simple, mechanical. You'll think, "Hell! I've got more artistry than that," and you'll be right. So start experimenting with it; put in your supporting evidence before you state your point and let the evidence lead up to the point; let one of your characters make the point, as Kovach did, if you have a suitable quote. Try other variations (some are noted later on). You don't have to be a slave to your outline, but be very cautious in departing from the formula; it can be clothed in many different styles and types of writing, but basically it is sound and will produce for you a solid, compelling piece.

Howard Whitman, who was to become one of the country's outstanding magazine writers, talked about this when he was just making the switch from newspaper to magazine writing. We were talking about organization, and I asked him if he outlined his stories before he wrote them. He said yes, always. Why? "Well," he said, "I don't have much confidence that I'm a genius. I think my writing is OK, but not great. But when I organize and outline a piece carefully I know that at least it will have everything in it it ought to have—the editor won't be able to fault me on that."

("Look, Ma, No Hands" Department: the paragraph above is an example of a variation. It does three things: I am about to move to a section on outlining; this introduces the idea. It validates the idea of outlining by quoting the experience of a good writer. It breaks the impersonality of the chapter by getting people into it.)

I hadn't written many magazine articles when Whitman said this; later, when I was writing full-time, I stole his idea and always outlined a piece before I wrote it. I still do. The word "outline," incidentally, has two distinct meanings in the magazine business. The first is what an editor asks you to prepare when he or she interested in one of your ideas; this is a two or three page item designed to sell the editor on the idea. It's also called a query. The second meaning is what we're talking about here—the skeleton of your piece. Nobody else ever sees it; it's a memo from you to you. The memo can take almost any form; it need not be the kind of thing you English teacher taught you in the fifth grade, though some writers do follow this form. Others simply jot down notes on the lead, the theme/idea, the points with supporting evidence, the ending.

There's a reason in addition to Whitman's that outlining is valuable. It breaks the writing process down into two parts. In the first you distill out your theme/idea and the various points you're going to make in the article. You arrange them in order and decide what facts, quotes, and anecdotes you're going to select to make each one convincing. Once this is finished you know you've touched all bases, you know what you're trying to say. Then when you start to write you don't have to think of any of these things, but are free to concentrate on putting the right words on paper in the right order. This freedom lets you get more pace, drive, flow in the writing; you can concentrate on the effects you want to create and on building clear, concise sentences and paragraphs.

Of course, once you get the story moving you may find you want to depart from the strict outline. Go ahead. But remember the outline represents your cool, logical judgment of what ought to be in the piece; in the heat of creation, when you're really rolling on a section, some item in the outline may seem inconsequential. Leave it out and keep going. But later, after the whole piece is written and the creative drive has been spent, go back to the outline and reconsider. That way you get the best of both worlds: the ecstasy of creation and the coolness of deliberation.

One of the troubles with talking about outlines is that the talk is too general, while in trying to put a story together you're dealing with very specific and often intransigent facts. So it may be helpful to use the journalist's trick of illustrating the general with the specific.

The following article, which appeared in *Reader's Digest*, does several of the things articles should do. It personalizes a major problem facing the country. It involves the readers' emotions, by showing how the farm crisis has affected a small group of people. And, it is clearly organized and written. The writers used the conceptual organization mentioned earlier in this chapter.

Hard Times in America's Heartland

by Carl T. Rowan and David M. Mazie

Some evenings, Dennis Tangeman, 34, looks out his window at the corn and soybean fields that he—and his father and grandfather before him—used to farm in northwestern Iowa. "They've taken farming from me," he says softly. "They've taken farming from my kids."

Mike Mahlendorf, 36, spends anguished evenings too. He's president of the Sibley State Bank and must decide whether area farmers will get money for operating expenses. "You sit in the office and tell people they're facing severe financial problems, and then you go home. You can't forget it," he says.

Sibley, the seat of Osceola County, Iowa, is not the bustling town it once was. Its main street isn't filled with shoppers these days. "For Sale" signs are common in store windows and on front lawns of the tree-lined residential streets. Merchants are worried. "Right now, living in rural America is not the American dream," says supermarket owner Steve Davidson.

For much of rural America, the dream has indeed been shattered by the worst economic crisis to hit the heartland since the Great Depression. It has made once-proud farmers angry and despondent, and threatened them with the loss of land that their fathers and grandfathers farmed and that they in turn had hoped to pass on to sons and daughters.

Family farms and rural towns have been bulwarks of American life for generations, a treasured part of our heritage that not only has fed this nation abundantly but has personified its social and cultural values. Now many of these communities are fighting for survival.

The crisis has reached beyond fields and barns—to those nearby small towns where hardware, clothing, implement stores are hurting, banks are squeezed, schools are consolidating, homes are up for sale; and to larger cities where farm-machinery manufacturers are laying off workers. It has created divisions and distrust—but at the same time brought people closer together to battle adversity.

The seeds of this bitter harvest were sown in the 1970s when America's agricultural exports quintupled, commodity prices hit historic highs, and farmers were urged by government, bankers and agricultural experts to expand their operations. To do this they had to borrow at skyrocketing interest rates, but with the price of land shooting upward, farmers simply used that as collateral. And lenders—whether local banks, cooperatives such as the Production Credit Association (PCA), or government agencies like the Farmers Home Administration (FmHA)—were more than willing to loan money. A farmer might ask the bank for $500 and be told no. "Better take $1000." Farm debts soared from $53 billion in 1970 to $216 billion in 1983.

Feelings of Frustration.

Those golden years finally ended in the early 1980s, when the grain embargo against the Soviet Union crippled the export market, new nations entered as sellers of agricultural products, and the strong dollar made U.S. commodities more expensive. The value of Iowa's agricultural exports plummeted from $3.76 billion in 1981 to $2.85 billion in 1983. At home, commodity prices tumbled. So did land values; an acre of Iowa farm land that sold for an average of $2147 in 1981 was going for barely half that in 1985.

Net farm income declined 50 percent between 1981 and 1983. Suddenly, many farmers found it difficult to earn enough to live on, let alone repay debts.

One of those was Dennis Tangeman, who lives with his wife, Beckie, and sons, Matt and Josh, in a mobile home on his father's farm, ten miles southeast of Sibley. For 52 years the Tangeman family had farmed the same 160 acres. Each spring, like most of his neighbors, Dennis would borrow money to buy seed, fertilizer, fuel and other supplies to plant crops and raise hogs; each autumn he would pay it back. The profits were not great, but the family got by and loved living on the land.

Then, in 1983, with crushing, 18-percent interest rates adding to his expenses, Tangeman barely broke even. He sold some of his hogs to pay off FmHA and other loans, but debts still piled up, and crop prices continued to fall. In June 1984, at the FmHA's insistence, he sold all his machinery. The sale brought only about one-fourth of the $96,000 Tangeman owed. Then a few months later the bank took possession of his breeder pigs, and shut off his credit line. Last December he filed for bankruptcy.

Feelings of frustration, bitterness, confusion fill the Tangeman home. "It's a real slap in the face to have the farm taken away," says Dennis. "Everything I did, I did with approval of the FmHA and the bank."

While a few farmers went overboard during the expansion of the 1970s, many of those who are in trouble were considered among the best farmers— young, college-trained and innovative. "They started playing under our set of rules," says Richard Haack, PCA loan officer," and the rules simply changed on them."

But that's little comfort to families like the Tangemans. Today Beckie is a secretary for a fertilizer dealer and has swallowed her pride to accept free cheese offered to families in need. Dennis, who has had two part-time jobs off the farm, is deeply bothered by having to tell merchants he has known all his life, "Hey, I can't pay you." However, he intends to repay everyone. "It will take me a while, but they're gonna get paid."

25 Cents on the Dollar

Actual bankruptcy and foreclosure are still relatively rare. Iowa State University reported last spring that only four percent of Iowa's farms were insolvent, with more debts than assets. But another 28 percent had a debt-to-asset ratio greater than 40 percent, considered serious. A Des Moines *Register and*

Tribune Iowa Poll found that one out of six farm operators reported having sold off assets during the previous two years. Only 32 percent said they were making a comfortable living or prospering.

Of all the hardships, probably the most agonizing for these farm families is the feeling of having broken faith with generations past and future—the continuity upon which family farms are built. In many cases, fathers borrowed money in the 1970s to help sons and sons-in-law get started, or they bought a piece of land next door to their own to bring children into the operation. Sometimes grandparents co-signed on the notes, and suddenly three generations were dragged down.

Besides financial problems, the agricultural recession is wreaking emotional havoc. Requests for help have risen 40 percent at the Northwest Iowa Mental Health Center in Spencer. "Children as well as adults feel a great anxiety about the future," says Pete Zevenbergen, former director of the center.

The suicide rate in some farm counties has climbed to twice the national average. In one town in west-central Iowa, three farmers killed themselves in an 18-month period. A few weeks after losing his farm near Sibley, Dayton Monier suffered a fatal heart attack. "They say he died of heart failure," observes one of Monier's neighbors. "I know it was a broken heart."

The tension also has eroded some of the friendliness of rural America. Many families have become more withdrawn. "We just don't neighbor as much as we used to," lamented one Osceola County farm wife. In some cases, neighborliness has given way to hostility and distrust—most of it directed at the lenders, "That tears at a community," says the Rev. Durwood Clauson of Trinity Lutheran Church in Sibley, who senses feelings of discomfort when a farm family share a pew with someone they owe money to.

Not every farmer is the sworn enemy of his banker. "They've got their problems too. I'd hate to be in their shoes now," says one farmer. But many feel that bankers could have handled them with greater respect and understanding.

Actually, farmers and business people are in this crisis together. Larry Swanson, an economist formerly with the University of Nebraska, calculates that for every seven farms that close, one commercial business goes under.

Oliver Leu, who's been selling farm equipment in Sibley for 31 years, got only 25 cents on the dollar at an auction sale he held to get rid of his inventory. "It was either sell low or pay interest for another two years," explained Leu.

Hotline

Sibley's two banks also have serious problems. Reports published last April show that their troubled debts (those more than 90 days past due) significantly exceeded their capital—an indicator of potential danger. As a result, bankers like Mike Mahlendorf feel "caught in the middle." On one side is pressure from the bank's owners and federal examiners, who are worried about too many shaky loans; on the other side pressure from farmers who desperately need money to keep going. But Mahlendorf and other lenders insist they are doing all they can to help farmers. "We spend hours trying to find a way to make it work," he says. "My goal is to get them through these hard times in any way we can. Survival is what we're aiming for."

There are others working to help farmers survive. In recent months several states have stepped in with actions such as a moratorium on farm repossessions, training farmers in finance and law, and loosening rules that govern eligibility for certain financial assistance.

Iowa has been among the most active. It set up the Rural Concern Hotline for farmers and communities to use if they have financial or emotional problems. Last year, project ASSIST was initiated to inform local leaders about farm problems, provide individual financial counseling to farmers, and help communities marshal their resources.

One of the most significant efforts in Iowa is a network of peer counselors organized by the Northwest Iowa Mental Health Center. Farmers generally are stoic people who don't talk easily about their problems. But support groups are attracting more and more participants. "We can't save their farms," explains clinic caseworker Joan Blundall, "But at least we help ease the pain and depression."

Difficult Decisions

Despite all its damage, the farm crisis may have positive effects. Both townspeople and farmers show a new awareness of their interdependency. A farm wife who admitted she had not been very concerned when four businesses left in three months now grants that "Main Street is important to the entire economy." Although on the brink of financial collapse himself, Sibley fuel dealer Frank Leu extended credit to one struggling farm family. They eventually pulled through and now feel much closer to Leu and others in town who stuck with them.

Sibley's business and professional leaders have organized a development corporation to find ways of bringing new industry and jobs to their town. Says grocer Steve Davidson, "If we work together, we can save the small-town way of life. Everyone is ready to do something. Trouble is, no one is sure exactly *what* to do.

That same dilemma is evident in Washington. Many policy-makers have argued against any new government subsidies on the ground that farming is a business like any other. Why, they ask, does Uncle Sam have any greater responsibility to save family farms in Iowa than, say, steel mills in Pennsylvania?

For one thing, comes the reply, the government helped to create the problem with past policies and misguided advice. Also, despite bumper crops this year, there is no assurance that agriculture's troubles are over. Moreover, it is argued, family farming is *not* like other businesses.

The Administration, Congress and the states must give high priority to resolving these arguments. Short-term help is needed to get hard-hit farms and communities through the current crisis. At the same time, difficult decisions must be made about a long-term agriculture policy that would serve both rural America and the national economy. One suggestion is to target subsidies to struggling family farms, not to large agricultural enterprises.

Most of the crops are harvested now, but many of the farmers working in the fields in Oxceola County on chill autumn days are not sure they will be driving tractors through them again next spring. Yet for all the pain and sorrow they've endured, these farmers and townspeople are determined to fight for their cherished way of life—and for their futures.

It's possible to outline this article in a way similar to that described on page 88. Such an outline would look like this:

Possible Outline

Bam-bam-bam lead (see Chapter 10) shows the dimensions of the problem.

Theme statement: "The worst crisis to hit the heartland since the Great Depression." Effects summarized in a sort of road map to the article.

Point 1. How the crisis arose. Figures on decline in exports, commodity prices, farm income, land prices. Tangeman anecdote and government quote.

Balance paragraph: Bankruptcy is rare.

Point 2. Broken faith with past. Three generations hit. Emotional costs. Suicide rate.

Point 3. Community damaged. "We don't neighbor." Clauson quote. Farmers and businessmen in it together. Swanson quote. Leu quote. Mahlendorf quote.

Point 4. States help, moratoria on repossessions, training farmers, easing financial assistance. Iowa's Rural Hotline, peer counselors, Blundall quote.

Point 5. Positive effects. Recognize interdependence, Sibley Development Corps.

Point 6. Washington's role. Some oppose help, others say farmers special and government helped create problem.

Point 7. What can be done. Needed: short-term help, long-term policy.

End: Back to Osceola County.

8

Presenting Your Findings

*I*t is a comforting conceit of writers and teachers to pretend that ideas and processes flow in neat and logical order—for instance, that in putting together a magazine article you first get the idea, then do the research, then evaluate the research, then plan the organization, and last, figure out exactly how you are going to write up your findings. Trouble is, it doesn't work that way in real life. Things happen simultaneously: you are often evaluating your research while you're doing it, you plan the *kind* of article it's going to be while doing the organizing, and so on.

What do I mean—*kind?* Well, after a good many years of writing I learned that it helped in shaping a piece if I thought, "Yeah, this is going to be *that* kind of story." Once I identified the kind, I knew pretty well what it should contain and how it should be shaped. So I made up a list of categories. Of course, it's only one man's opinion, but here it is:

Here's Something New Stories

A new piece of information, a new idea, a new process. An obvious story of this type might be about a new medical discovery or a new way that educators have discovered to help disabled children learn. Newness is important to editors, and there are many more "new" articles in magazines than there are discoveries to justify them (new ways to lose weight, to make your marriage work, to advance your career, stop smoking). So when a writer comes up with a genuine new discovery that affects the lives of millions, he or she has a world-beater. The "What Makes Kids Popular?" story, in chapter 2, is this kind of piece. In developing such an article, the points to be covered are obvious: Here's what it is. Here's why it's important. Here's how it affects you. Here's how it works.

Adventure Stories

These use the old fiction writer's plots: man against nature, man against man. (A good many of these stories are about women, of course.) The outdoor magazines are full of man-against-nature stories—the man-with-gun against a 1200 lb. grizzly bear, or man-with-fly-rod aginst the wily old brown trout. But other magazines use them too: stories about how an island family survived a cataclysmic hurricane; how a woman lived and worked alone for months in the African bush in order to study chimpanzees; how a town fought a flood.

Man-against-man stories are even more varied. Most detective stories are in this category, from true crime yarns to pieces about a special prosecutor's fight against the Mafia. Many business and political stories fit here, too—pieces about how a man battled his competitors to establish a new firm, or fought the establishment over a better way of running things. The Fort Lee airfield story, described in chapter 1, is such an article. Even love stories sometimes fit into the group: boy gets girl, or vice versa. And husband vs. wife pieces on marital relations. Self-improvement pieces also fit because man vs. man includes man vs. himself.

These stories are dramatic narratives that make full use of characterization, conflict, suspense. We'll talk more about this later, in the chapter on dramatic writing.

Problem Stories

In a sense, of course, all articles are problem stories, but this category refers to public issues or broad social problems. The piece may be about how a concerned group saved a Florida river from destruction by the army engineers or a power company, about cash-register justice in traffic courts and what to do to eliminate it, about the millions of youths who are out of school and can't get a job and how they can be helped.

Essentially the points this kind of story makes are: here's a problem that affects you; here's how it affects you; here's what it's about; here's what can be done about it. You start by defining and dramatizing the problem, go on to explore its dimensions in terms of people, then suggest possible solutions.

A subsection here is the *microcosm* story—in which you focus on a particular situation to illuminate a larger one—which you see over and

over again in newspapers and magazines. It is discussed further in chapter
15.

How to Do It Stories

This is another big category that includes everything from how to build
a backyard pool to how to win a guerrilla war. These pieces are used by the
hundreds in business journals—how to save money on materials handling,
how to train new salespeople; the women's magazines—how to stay slim,
how to make your eyes sexy; the men's magazines—how to stay slim, how
to dress sexy; shelter books—how to add space to your closet; sports
books—how to perfect your golf swing, how to navigate in a sports car
rally; and general magazines—how to recruit better cops, how to communicate in a marriage. This book is a how-to book.

Mostly they're unfancy, factual, and follow a simple step-by-step organization plan. "First you buy the lumber: twelve two-by-fours eight feet
long, twenty-four three-quarter-inch common pine boards in ten-foot
lengths. . . ." You must be specific and always give prices. You illustrate
ways to overcome obstacles by telling how someone actually did it. You
assume the readers already know why it's important to do what you're
telling them to do, so you don't have to waste much time selling the idea,
though you do include some of the rewards of the process, usually in
anecdotal form. When you have finished describing the last step of the
process, you stop.

Personality Pieces

These, obviously, are stories about people who are important to the
reader for some reason. When they are the familiar puff pieces about
television or movie or sports stars, they satiate the reader's curiosity and
help sell magazines. But the better ones are written on two levels;
ostensibly they're about a personality, while actually they illuminate a
human dilemma, impart some new information, explore some aspect of
the common condition. If they do this well, the personality does not have
to be well known; reader identification is satisfied by the other aspects of
the story.

To me these have always seemed the hardest of all stories to write. The reason is that you are trying to put on paper the true essence of the person with all his or her variety, contradictions, complex motives, neuroticisms, failures, and aspirations. Yet, as in every other kind of article, the piece must also have a single underlying idea. Satisfying the second requirement, however, sometimes tends to make your subject a two-dimensional, cardboard character. Preventing this is a major challenge to the writer's artistry.

In addition to the *kind* of article, it helps if you identify the *story* elements in the piece you're going to write. Is it a detective story, which presents your readers with a crime, then takes them, with the detective, through mystery after mystery until the criminal is caught? Is it a narrative, in which a woman has an objective and overcomes obstacle after obstacle until she achieves it? Is it a love story, in which two people slowly lose their loneliness in each other's trust? The characteristics of several of these stories will be discussed in the later chapters on kinds of writing.

Though each of these types of articles has its own approach and content, there are techniques of good writing that apply to all.

Number One: write about people. The newspaper reporter covering an event doesn't have to worry about this; there's no way to avoid it. But the interpretive journalist and the magazine writer often start out with an idea instead of an event and, being intellectuals, tend to write directly about the idea. That's OK if they're writing for *Harper's* or *The Annals of the American Academy of Political and Social Science*. But it's not for the mass media.

What you do is translate your idea into a report on people doing things by thinking how it affects them. What kinds of people? People over sixty-five? Vacationers? Homeowners? And how does it affect them? Go and ask them. When you've talked to enough of all the different kinds affected, you've got your story. Write it in terms of what happened to them. The story on Chuck Kelly in chapter 6 is an example; so is the one in chapter 4 on the soldier who was brainwashed in Korea.

Number Two: use specific details. For years fiction writers have said there are no new plots in the world; after years of work, nonfiction writers *know* there are only a limited number of basic ideas about the human condition. What makes a story fresh and new and colorful are the details. People have struggled for courage to meet adversity for centuries; what makes *this* story different is the way *this* unique individual struggles to overcome *this* particular kind of adversity. So the good creative writer spends hours and thought and effort to get details that demonstrate the person's uniqueness.

Further, it is the specific detail that convinces the reader that you know what you're talking about. You don't write, "Income tax returns were filed by millions of Americans this year." You write, "Income tax returns were filed this year by 67,327,000 Americans, one of every three men, women, and children now alive." And you don't fake the details; you do the research necessary to get them accurate.

Once I did a three-part story on the number of kids who are out of school and out of work. It was titled, "We Waste a Million Kids a Year," and I wanted to make the point that a nation's young people are its most valuable resource. Writing it just that way would have been true enough, but pallid. So I spent a day going through an exhaustive study of the distribution of talent among the various socioeconomic groups that make up our population. At the end of the day I was able to write this one line: "Among them [the million] are 50,000 of the finest minds in the country." I thought the day well spent.

Number Three: be precise in the words you use. There was a professor at Amherst who made a big thing of this in his freshman English classes. He'd get the class to define a simple word like "door." After wrestling with it for a while they'd come up with something like, "a door is what you use to enter a room." So the next time they met, the prof would climb in through the window and say, "I just came in the door."

"No, that's a window."

"Okay, then what *is* a door?"

It would go on like this until they had a definition that was completely unambiguous. Sometimes a week's homework assignment would consist of writing one sentence; then each student would have to defend every word in it from attack by the rest of the class. What the professor was teaching was precision in using words.

The late John Ciardi, speaking before the American Society of Journalists and Authors, emphasized the value of using just the right word this way. He'd been working with some original manuscripts of John Keats's poems, and he picked these lines from "The Eve of St. Agnes."

> Anon his heart revives: her vespers done,
> Of all its wreathed pearls her hair she frees;
> Unclasps her warmed jewels one by one;
> Loosens her fragrant bodice; by degrees
> Her rich attire creeps rustling to her knees. . . .

The girl, Madeline, was undressing while Porphyro peeked from the wings. The fourth line was originally written, "Loosens her bursting bodice . . .," but Keats had wanted to preserve a tone of purity in the scene. "Bursting" had been crossed out, Ciardi said, and "fragrant" inserted instead. You can see the different impression the change accomplished.

If this kind of precision is effective for Keats, it's just as important for you and me. Gay Talese once said in an interview that he rewrites sentences up to eighteen times before he is satisfied with them. His craftsmanship shows, as the Talese lead in chapter 10 proves.

There's an adjunct to this rule of precise word use that's made especially well in that little classic, *The Elements of Style*, by William Strunk, Jr., and E. B. White: "Write with nouns and verbs, not with adjectives and adverbs. The adjective hasn't been built that can pull a weak or inaccurate noun out of a tight place."

An adjective is defined as a "modifier" of a noun, and that's exactly what it does—modifies. It detracts, takes away the word's strength, reduces it. Adjectives are the lazy writer's out. Of course, they're necessary, but most of us use them as crutches. Once when I was trying to learn to write, I decided I wouldn't use a single adjective in anything I wrote for a month. It made the job about twice as hard, and everything I wrote took two or three times as long, but I think the exercise was worth it. Once you do it you find that your prejudice against adjectives carries over, and you use them sparingly ever after. Your writing improves as a result.

Number Four: take advantage of the connotations of words. Even the simplest words trigger different pictures or impressions in different people's minds. Psychologists who give word association tests see this every day. The word "color," for instance, will make many men think "red," many women think "blue" or "green." Skilled writers use these connotations to get their meaning implanted in the reader's mind.

In her book *Saying What One Means*, Freya Stark says it about as well as anyone:

Accuracy is the basis of style. Words dress our thoughts and should fit; and should fit not only in their utterances, but in their implications, their sequences, and their silences, just as in architecture the empty spaces are as important as those that are filled. The problem of all writing is the same as that presented by the composition of a telegram, one has to convey a meaning with the use of few and always inadequate words, and eke it out with what the reader, drawing upon his own reserves, will understand. The number of words that even the most profuse writer will dare to use is always insufficient for a complete impression, but the reserves he can draw upon in the reader's mind are lavish indeed. The whole generalship of writing is in the summoning and marshaling of these unseen auxiliaries.

Number Five: don't use gobbledygook. Every book on good writing says this at some point, and who needs to be left out of the parade? Besides, the gobbledygookers seem to be winning out over us purists. The reason, we suppose, is the increasing specialization of our society and the determination of every woolly-thinking "expert" to protect the barricades of his or her specialty by using language that mere humans can't understand. Writers who interview the specialists must, of course, become acquainted with the jargon, and after you've spent a week interviewing, say, social psychologists, phrases like "interpersonal valences" or "negative reinforcement" fall trippingly off the tongue, but you should never let them fall onto the page.

When Malcolm Baldridge was named Commerce Secretary, he decided to weed out some of the jargon that littered the department's letters, memorandums, and reports. Among the words he barred were *finalize, interface, parameter, prioritize, optimize, impact* (as a verb), *specificity,* and *utilize.* As writers aiming at the general public, we must also edit out such pompous, confusing, and even silly terms. We do not interpersonally communicate with one another—we talk.

We don't know why people use such words. Some of it, of course, is pure snobbery; when you first learn a lot of big words, you want to use them to show the world how educated you are. But after a while you realize that a better test of your education is whether you can communicate with people so they can understand. That's when you grow a little alarm bell in your brain that pings every time you use a word with more than three syllables. At each ping you stop short, go back, figure out exactly what you're trying to say, and find a way to say it simply and directly.

We think the two most important rules for good writing are: be simple; be clear. They are also, of course, the two hardest to apply, because it takes a great deal of hard thought to say a complex thing simply. And it takes a long devoted love affair with the English language to be able to use words with precisely the right meaning and connotation so they convey to your readers what you want them to know and feel. To get an idea across clearly and forcefully, nothing has ever been invented that beats the simple declarative sentence.

Hemingway understood this. He could load more meaning onto simple, short words than they had any right to carry, and I think he could do it because he was so very precise in using them. I think writers ought to study how he does it. For years I have reread *The Old Man and the Sea* because I think that, for technical brilliance, this is the capstone of his work.

A friend who knew him told me years ago that Winston Churchill had a rule about word use. He thought that the old Anglo-Saxon words had more power and guts than latinized words, and he tried to use them as much as he could. Consider, for instance, the raw sock of, "I have nothing to offer but blood, toil, tears and sweat."

Most books on writing say you ought to vary the length of your sentences and paragraphs, which, of course, is true. It keeps the reader awake. It's like the difference between driving on a narrow country road—where you have to contend with sharp curves, hillocks and dips, small-town speed limits, and straight open stretches—and driving on a super-highway, where you can pass anytime you like, where curves and hills are long and gentle, where you can maintain an unvarying fifty-five miles per hour, and where the monotony makes you fall asleep—or almost.

Figures of speech are one of the most useful tools a writer has to explain complex ideas or inventions, to marshal reader identification, to brighten dull explanations. In hack journalism most metaphors are clichés. Everybody wants to avoid them, but studying clichés can tell you something about how a successful metaphor is made. (After all it wouldn't have become a cliché if it hadn't been so apt.)

Take "cold as a dog's nose." A dog's nose isn't really cold at all, but it seems cold because we expect it to be warm like the rest of the animal, and when we touch it we get a shock. So a metaphor must be used on a common and memorable experience. How about "cold as the bathroom floor on your bare feet"? That's a common experience, but it's not much of a metaphor because it requires too much qualification: "cold as a bathroom floor" doesn't do it.

So you need shock, and conciseness in addition to common experience. Often you can get it by reaching halfway to Boston for your figure of speech. Raymond Chandler was master of the colorful metaphor. Once he wrote, "She had a voice you could use to split stove wood," thus using an image of physical action to describe a sound. Another time he wrote, "He was a big man, but not more than six feet five inches tall and not wider than a beer truck." The first part isn't so good, because it makes the reader do a mental computation—"Let's see, I'm 5'10" so he must have been . . ."—which drains the instant impact. But the second half is good;

a beer truck summons up exactly the effect Chandler wanted—massive, irresistible, and slightly disreputable.

In his play, *The Real Thing*, Tom Stoppard has one character, a playwright, refuse to help another playwright, Brodie, improve his work because of Brodie's insensitivity to the power of words.

[Words are] innocent, neutral, precise, standing for this, describing that, meaning the other, so *if* you look after them you can build bridges across incomprehension and chaos. But when they get their corners knocked off, they're no good any more, and Brodie knocks the corners off without knowing he's doing it. So everything he builds is jerry-built. It's rubbish. An intelligent child could push it over. I don't think writers are sacred, but words are. They deserve respect. If you get the right ones in the right order, you can nudge the world a little or make a poem which children will speak for you when you're dead.

9

The Uses of Indirection

Several years ago I visited several air force and navy training bases to get material for an article about a new citizenship training program that the armed forces had developed. It taught me a basic lesson about creative journalism.

I was at Lackland Air Force base, in San Antonio, Texas, watching an instructor teach a class in something called the "Rule of Law." He gave no lecture; instead he gave each man a printed sheet on which was this story:

There is a thief in the barracks. Of this there can be little doubt. For the last week the men have been missing small items such as cigarettes, candy bars, and razors. Then yesterday Jim Brown had his wallet stolen while he was in the shower. All efforts to trace down the thefts have failed. The men are angry and sullen. Every man is suspicious of every other man.

Today the men return to the barracks from drill five minutes early. Jim Brown is the first man in the door. Upon entering he sees Tom Baker, who was excused from drill because of blisters, taking a pack of cigarettes from another man's footlocker.

"Here's the thief, men," Jim Hollers. "I caught him in the act. Let's give it to him."

Jim drops his rifle on the floor, clenches his fists and, with his right hand cocked, moves in on Tom. Several men join Jim. The others watch intently.

After they'd discussed this story for ten minutes or so in small groups, the men were asked whether they would help give Tom a licking. The men said yes in various ways. One said you should have a kangaroo court, another said you should report it to the flight chief and let him handle Tom. But most disagreed and said a good beating would teach Tom a better lesson than any flight chief could.

Then a slight, dark-haired youth in glasses stood up and said, "But this is mob violence!" in a surprised tone and sat down again.

The discussion continued, but once the idea had been presented it began to grow. At first every third or fourth speaker would say something like, "Well, you ought to let a court martial handle it." As the argument continued this idea crept in more and more, and finally a rangy, ginger-haired man in the back stood up.

"I saw mob action once," he said. "A man and a woman had been murdered—robbed, I guess. And here comes a couple kids down a dark alley—they didn't have nothing to do with it, but they were kind of tough kids and they came down this alley. So the crowd saw them and right away decided they were the murderers." He took a deep breath and let it out. "They strung 'em up right there. Two weeks later they found the murderer."

In the silence the instructor said, "I've got a film here I'd like to show you." The film was MGM's *The Ox-Bow Incident*, cut to twenty-eight minutes. It tells of a posse that hanged three innocent men for a crime the members of the posse only thought had been committed. It had the wallop of a Missouri mule; when it ended the class was dismissed.

You know how when a class breaks up, in a high school or a training base, there's always a great clatter of shifting chairs, of talking, yelling, and whistling. When this one broke up there was a hush in the room. A few men talked, but their tones were subdued; they walked out carefully, not hitting the chairs, and in single file. As he reached the door one man said, "It makes you want to spit!"

Another time at the end of this class, a recruit came up to S. Sgt. John Oliver, the instructor, and said, "You know, we got a G.I. shower planned for a guy in our flight tonight. This guy is a real sourball—he never takes a bath and you can't stand to sit next to him." (In a G.I. shower a gang of men strip the victim, hold him under the shower, and scrub him vigorously with stiff brushes, usually taking off a layer of hide. Occasionally the victim ends up in the hospital.)

"That so?" said Oliver indifferently. "Well look, you're probably going to be down in this section tomorrow. I wish you'd stop around and tell us what happened."

The next day when the man came back Oliver asked him how it had gone. "The whole thing was forgotten," the recruit said. "The man who'd been the leader just never started it."

The new kind of instruction was devised by Dr. James E. Russell, of Teachers College, Columbia University, and called "Hours on Freedom." Later he explained why this session worked. The real message, he said, was in the movie. "But if you just showed that, the men would all go to sleep—they're usually so tired they'd sleep through a sex movie. It's the barracks situation that keeps them awake—by a kind of reverse psychology: they almost always end their discussion by agreeing you shouldn't beat up the crook, but down underneath nearly every man knows that he would. That hidden guilt feeling keeps him interested—and also helps give the movie its terrific impact."

But Russell did more than provoke a psychological reaction in his audience. The story of the barracks thief was chosen so that his particular audience would identify with the situation. Had he been dealing with college students, it would have been a dormitory thief; with industrial workers he would have used a locker-room thief. Of course, like a fiction writer, he could change the story to fit the audience; a journalist must go out and find a true story to do the job.

Russell was voicing a principle of good teaching. Since responsible journalism is a blend of teaching and entertainment, his method was also a good description of effective writing.

The modern interpretive piece does not preach as a sermon does. It doesn't tell people, "Do this." It identifies and explains a problem by demonstration, then demonstrates a solution, sometimes by quoting experts, more often by showing people working out their own solution. It reports the actions, emotions, thoughts of the actors. It convinces by demonstration and by reader identification, not by exhortation.

One morning I started work by rereading a piece I had written the day before. As I read the day got colder and grayer and bleaker. I dropped the last page on the desk and said, "You *stupid* jerk!"

I grabbed a piece of paper and in large black capitals printed:

DON'T TELL IT—SHOW IT HAPPENING!

I thumbtacked it on the wall above the typewriter, where I could see it every time I looked up. It stayed there for almost a year and may even have done some good.

The point is, you want your reader to become involved with your story and its characters. When you tell about them you interpose yourself, the Almighty, Invisible (hah!) Omniscience, between the people in your story and your readers. So the reader gets everything second hand. What you ought to be doing, instead, is showing the readers a movie of the characters acting and talking and struggling with their problem as they truly did. Then they get the message firsthand and, of course, it is more compelling. Gay Talese has talked of moving his "camera" from one scene to the next, to show the reader what Talese thinks is important.

In *Client-Centered Therapy,* the noted psychologist Carl Rogers wrote: "In order for behavior to change, a change in preception must be *experienced.* Intellectual knowledge cannot substitute for this." A writer wants readers to change, if only by understanding something they didn't know before. So by allowing the readers to live through a situation along with the characters involved, the writer follows Rogers' precept.

Recreating scenes of action puts quite a burden on your research ability because in order to do it, you must first see it in your own head in all its color, action, sound, and conflict. The only way to accomplish that is to take the people involved in it back over it in meticulous detail, getting the scene, the thoughts, motives, aims of the each individual. If possible you have to interview *all* the people involved so that they can check each other's memory of the incident.

Truman Capote made this point in an interview with George Plimpton at the time *In Cold Blood* was published. Plimpton asked if Capote didn't sometimes give way to the temptation to fictionalize parts of the story. Capote's answer:

No. . . . One doesn't spend almost six years on a book, the point of which is factual accuracy, and then give way to minor distortions. People are so suspicious. They ask, "How can you reconstruct the conversation of a dead girl, Nancy Clutter, without fictionalizing?" If they read the book carefully, they can see readily enough how it's done. It's a silly question. Each time Nancy appears in the narrative, there are witnesses to what she is saying and doing—phone calls, conversations being overheard. When she walks the horse up from the river in the twilight, the hired man is a witness and talked to her then. The last time we see her, in her bedroom, Perry and Dick themselves were the witnesses, and told me what she had said. What is reported of her, even in the narrative form, is as accurate as many hours of questioning, over and over again, can make it. All of it is reconstructed from the evidence of witnesses.

In the same interview Capote talked about another way in which indirection is used in first-class nonfiction. The question is, if I, the reporter, keep out of the story, how do I express my own judgments on the situation? Many journalists believe it should be done directly; their idea is, "I've done all the research and become an expert on the subject, so I should give my opinions." But they want things too simple; good nonfiction has more artistry, as Capote knew:

Of course it's by the selection of what you choose to tell. I believe Perry did what he did for the reasons he himself states—that his life was a constant accumulation of disillusionments and reverses and he suddenly found himself [in the Clutter house that night] in a psychological cul-de-sac. The Clutters were such a perfect set of symbols for every frustration of his life. As Perry himself said, "I didn't have anything against them, and they never did anything wrong to me—the way other people have all my life. Maybe they're just the ones who had to pay for it." Now in that particular section where Perry talks about the reason for the murders, I could have included other views. But Perry's happens to be the one I believe is the right one, and it's the one that Dr. Satten at the Menninger Clinic arrived at quite independently, never having done any interviews with Perry.

I could have added many other opinions. But that would have confused the issue, and indeed the book. I had to make up my mind, and move towards that one view, always. You can say that the reportage was incomplete. But then it has to be. It's a question of selection, you wouldn't get anywhere if it wasn't for that. I've often thought of the book as being like something reduced to a seed. Instead of presenting the reader with a full plant, with all the foliage, a seed is planted in the soil of his mind. . . . I make my own comment by what I choose to tell and how I choose to tell it. It is true that an author is more in control of fictional characters because he can do anything he wants with them as long as they stay credible. But in the nonfiction novel one can also manipulate: If I put something in which I don't agree about I can always set it in a context of qualifications without having to step into the story myself to set the reader straight.

Capote, of course, was a novelist before he wrote nonfiction, but good journalists who have never written novels know and use the same technique. Bob Greene, for example, used selection to make several points in a story about two fifteen-year-old boys spending a day at a shopping mall.

American Beat

By Bob Greene

"This would be excellent, to go in the ocean with this thing," says Dave Gembutis, fifteen.

He is looking at a $170 Sea Cruiser raft.

"G - says his companion, Dan Holmes, also fifteen.

This ⌐ a Herman's World of Sporting Goods, in the middle of the Woodfield Mall in Schaumburg, Illinois.

The two of them keep staring at the raft. It is unlikely that they will purchase it. For one thing, Dan has only twenty dollars in his pocket, Dave five dollars. For another thing—ocean voyages aside—neither of them is even old enough to drive. Dave's older sister, Kim, has dropped them off at the mall. They will be taking the bus home.

Fifteen. What a weird age to be male. Most of us have forgotten about it, or have idealized it. But when you are fifteen . . . well, things tend to be less than perfect.

You can't drive. You are only a freshman in high school. The girls your age look older than you and go out with upperclassmen who have cars. You probably don't shave. You have nothing to do on the weekends.

So how do you spend your time? In 1982, most likely at a mall. Woodfield is an enclosed shopping center sprawling over 2.25 million square feet in northern Illinois. There are 230 stores at Woodfield, and on a given Saturday those stores are cruised in and out of by thousands of teenagers killing time. Today two of those teenagers are Dave Gembutis and Dan Holmes.

Dave is wearing a purple Rolling Meadows High School Mustangs wind-breaker over a gray MASH T-shirt, jeans, and Nike running shoes. He has a red plastic spoon in his mouth, and will keep it there for most of the afternoon. Dan is wearing a white Ohio State Buckeyes T-shirt, jeans, and Nike running shoes.

We are in the Video Forum store. Paul Simon and Art Garfunkel are singing "Wake Up Little Susie" from their Central Park concert on four television screens. Dave and Dan have already been wandering around Woodfield for an hour.

"There's not too much to do at my house," Dan says to me.

"Here we can at least look around," Dave says. "At home I don't know what we'd do."

"Play catch or something," Dan says. "Here there's lots to see."

"See some girls or something, start talking." Dave says.

I ask them how they would start a conversation with girls they had never met.

"Ask them what school they're from," Dan says. "Then if they say Arlington Heights High School or something, you can say, "Oh, I know somebody from there."

I ask them how important meeting girls is to their lives.

"About forty-five percent," Dan says.

"About half your life," Dave says.

"Half is girls," Dan says. "Half is going out for sports."

An hour later, Dave and Dan have yet to meet any girls. They have seen a girl from their own class at Rolling Meadows High, but she is walking with an older boy, holding his hand. Now we are in the Woodfield McDonald's. Dave is eating a McRib sandwich, a small fries, and a small Coke. Dan is eating a cheeseburger, a small fries, and a medium root beer.

In here, the dilemma is obvious. The McDonald's is filled with girls who are precisely as old as Dave and Dan. The girls are wearing eye shadow, are fully developed, and generally look as if they could be dating the Green Bay Packers. Dave and Dan, on the other hand . . . well, when you're a 15-year-old boy, you look like a 15-year-old boy.

"They go with the older guys who have the cars," Dan says.

"It makes them more popular," Dave says.

"My ex-girlfriend is seeing a junior," Dan says.

I ask him what happened.

"Well, I was in Florida over spring vacation," he says. "And when I got back I heard that she was at Cinderella Rockefella one night, and she was dancing with this guy, and she liked him, and he drove her home and stuff."

"She two-timed him," Dave says.

"The guy's on the basketball team," Dan says.

I ask Dan what he did about it.

"I broke up with her," he says, as if I had asked the stupidest question in the world.

I asked him how he did it.

"Well, she was at her locker," he says. "She was working the combination. And I said, 'Hey, Linda, I want to break up.' And she was opening her locker door and she just nodded her head yes. And I said, 'I hear you had a good time while I was gone, but I had a better time in Florida.' "

I ask him if he feels bad about it.

"Well, I feel bad," he says. "But a lot of guys told me, 'I heard you broke up with her. Way to be.' "

"It's too bad the Puppy Palace isn't open," Dan says.

"They're remodeling," Dave says.

We are walking around the upper level of Woodfield. I ask them why they would want to go to the Puppy Palace.

"The dogs are real cute and you feel sorry for them," Dan says.

We are in a fast-food restaurant called the Orange Bowl. Dave is eating a frozen concoction called an O-Joy. They still have not met any girls.

"I feel like I'd be wasting my time if I sat at home," Dan says. "If it's Friday or Saturday and you sit home, it's considered . . . low."

"Coming to the mall is about all there is," Dave says. "Until we can drive."

"Then I'll cruise," Dan says. "Look for action a little farther away from my house, instead of just riding my bike around."

"When you're sixteen, you can do anything," Dave says. "You can go all the way across town."

"When you have to ride your bike . . ." Dan says. "When it rains, it ruins everything."

In the J. C. Penny store, the Penney Fashion Carnival is under way. Wally the Clown is handing out favors to children, but Dave and Dan are watching the young female models parade onto a stage in bathing suits.

"Just looking is enough for me," Dan says.

Dave suggests that they head back into the mall and pick out some girls to wave to. I ask why.

"Well, see, even if they don't wave back, you might see them later in the day," Dan says. "And then they might remember that you waved at them, and you can meet them."

We are at the Cookie Factory. These guys eat—approximately every twenty minutes.

It is clear that Dan is attracted to the girl behind the counter. He walks up, and his voice is slower and about half an octave lower than before.

The tone of voice is going to have to carry the day, because the words are not all that romantic:

"Can I have a chocolate-chip cookie?"

The girl does not even look up as she wraps the cookie in tissue paper.

Dan persists. The voice might be Clark Gable's.

"What do they cost?"

The girl is still looking down.

"Forty-seven," she says and takes his money, still looking away, and we move on.

Dave and Dan tell me that there are lots of girls at Woodfield's indoor ice-skating rink. It costs money to get inside, but they lead me to an exit door, and when a woman walks out we slip into the rink. It is chilly in here, but only three people are on the ice.

"It's not time for open skating yet," Dan says. "This is all private lessons."

"Not much in here," Dave says.

We sit on benches. I ask them if they wish they were older.

"Well," Dan says, "when you get there, you look back and you remember. Like I'm glad that I'm not in the fourth or fifth grade now. But I'm glad I'm not twenty-five, either."

"Once in a while I'm sorry I'm not twenty-one," Dave says. "I want to save up for a dirt bike."

"Right now, being fifteen is starting to bother me a little bit," Dave says. "Like when you have to get your parents to drive you to Homecoming with a girl."

I ask him how that works.

"Well, your mom is in the front seat driving," he says. "And you're in the back seat with your date."

I ask him how he feels about that.

"It's embarrassing," he says. "Your date understands that there's nothing you can do about it, but it's still embarrassing."

Dave says he wants to go to Pet World.

"I think they closed it down," Dan says, but we head in that direction anyway.

I ask them what the difference is between Pet World and the Puppy Palace.

"They've got snakes and fish and another assortment of dogs," Dan says. "But not as much as the Puppy Palace."

When we arrive, Pet World is, indeed, boarded up.

We are on the upper level of the mall. Dave and Dan have spotted two girls sitting on a bench below them, on the mall's main floor.

"Whistle," Dan says. Dave whistles, but the girls keep talking.

"Dave, wave to them and see if they look," Dan says.

"They aren't looking," Dave says.

"There's another one over there," Dan says.

"Where?" Dave says.

"Oh, that's a mother," Dan says. "She's got her kid with her."

They return their attention to the two downstairs.

Dan calls to them: "Would you girls get the dollar I just dropped?"

The girls look up.

"Just kidding," Dan says.

The girls resume their conversation.

"I think they're laughing," Dan says.

"What are you going to do when the dumb girls won't respond," Dave says.

"At least we tried," Dan says.

I ask him what response would have satisfied.

"The way we would have known that we succeeded," he says, "they'd have looked up here and started laughing."

The boys keep staring at the two girls.

"Ask her to look up," Dan says. "Ask her what school they go to."

"I did," Dave says. "I did."

The two boys lean over the railing.

"Bye, girls," Dave yells.

"See you later," Dan yells.

The girls do not look up.

"Too hard," Dan says. "Some girls are stuck on themselves, if you know what I mean by that."

We go to a store called the Foot Locker, where all the salespeople are dressed in striped referee's shirts.

"Dave!" Dan says. "Look at this! Seventy bucks!" He holds up a pair of New Balance running shoes. Both boys shake their heads.

We move on to a store called Passage to China. A huge stuffed tiger is placed by the doorway. There is a PLEASE DO NOT TOUCH sign attached to it. Dan rubs his hand over the tiger's back. "This would look so great in my room," he says.

We head over to Alan's TV and Stereo. Two salesmen ask the boys if they are interested in buying anything, so they go back outside and look at the store's window. A color television set is tuned to a baseball game between the Chicago Cubs and the Pittsburgh Pirates.

They watch for five minutes. The sound is muted, so they cannot hear the announcers.

"I wish they'd show the score," Dave says.

They watch for five minutes more.

"Hey, Dave," Dan says, "You want to go home?"

"I guess so," Dave says.

They do. We wave goodbye. I watch them walk out of the mall toward the bus stop. I wish them girls, dirt bikes, puppies, and happiness.

How better could Greene have showed us what it is like to be fifteen and male? And he did it almost entirely indirectly, by showing us what Dan and Dave look like, how they behave, how they talk, and what they talk about. With the exception of two paragraphs near the start, where Greene comments on fifteen-year-old boys, and the last paragraph, the piece depends entirely upon Greene's ability to select from among the things the boys have said and done to create a believable picture of the two, and, by extension, of all fifteen-year-old boys. He shows them dreaming of toys they cannot afford; imprisoned in their homes where there's "not too much to do"; saddened by the loss of a girlfriend but too proud to play second fiddle; yearning for the day when a driver's license will set them free; caring about the animals cooped up in a pet store; and trying ineptly to meet girls.

Selection is used to accomplish other purposes, too—indirectly. Once I did a piece on the General Accounting Office, which is an arm of the U.S. Congress whose job it is to investigate the entire executive branch of the federal government. It sends its accountants and investigators out into the field to see what Uncle Sam is getting for the millions he spends on crop support programs or submarines or embassies abroad. I proposed, and *Reader's Digest* editors agreed, that it should be written as a series of little detective stories about the most important investigations the agency had run.

But it was also important to select the stories to make other points too. One was to show the vast scope and diversity of the investigations. Another was to show how the GAO ran a typical investigation, including the kinds of specialists it used. Neither of these points was stated directly; the stories themselves made them, without any comment by the writer.

The story on farms in chapter 7 is an example of a microcosm story, which is, by its nature, indirect. You tell a particular story about particular people, which gets the reader emotionally involved in them and their struggle. But in the people you pick to write about and in the things you select to say about them, you are exploring a larger, more universal issue.

The very best journalists use indirection in a similar but more sophisticated way than that. They write a story on two levels; they tell one story, but do it in such a way that they are also telling another. One of the best examples of this is a piece by Joan Didion that appears in her book *Slouching Towards Bethlehem*.

The piece, titled "Some Dreamers of the Golden Dream," is the story of a California woman, Lucille Marie Maxwell Miller, who was convicted of murdering her husband by burning him in the family Volkswagen. It reports in detail her actions, the situations that led up to it, her trial, and the trial's aftermath, so it gives full coverage to the murder. But it is much more than that; it also has an underlying message, which is that the superficial values of the mass media world—happiness is everything, buy lots of things to get status in society—lead to disillusion and death.

Didion starts by describing the San Bernardino Valley where it happened, then states her basic message:

> Here is where the hot wind blows and the old ways do not seem relevant, where the divorce rate is double the national average and where one person in every 38 lives in a trailer. Here is the last stop for all those who come from somewhere else, for all those who drifted away from the cold and the past and the old ways. Here is where they are trying to find a new life style, trying to find it in the only places they

know to look: the movies and the newspapers. The case of Lucille Marie
Maxwell Miller is a tabloid monument to that new life style.

Indirection is also used to present the very idea of a story. Mass
magazines must be read by millions of people or go out of business.
Millions of people will not read the kind of intellectual exposition of an
idea or a social or economic problem that *The New Republic* or the *New
York Times* might print. So mass magazine writers must find ways to
explore social problems in a way that will get read; usually that means
making the point indirectly.

An editor of *Good Housekeeping* told how this worked while visiting a
journalism class at Syracuse University. A graduate student asked him
why the magazine didn't do more socially responsible articles on the huge
problems the country faces, like race relations. The editor answered that
the magazine had done thirty-five articles on race problems in the past
eight years. But, he said, they were not preachments, saying white people
ought to get over their prejudices, or black people ought to stop trying to
make a separate society. Nobody would read those. Instead the articles
made their points indirectly.

One, for example, was called, "The Pride of Five Women." It consisted
of the stories of five black women who had fought their way out of poverty
by their own efforts. The reader had a personal narrative to identify with,
but the underlying message of the piece, aimed at white women, was that
black women had as much courage, perseverance, and drive for independence as anyone else and were thus deserving of respect.

This kind of indirection is probably one of the least understood aspects
of the mass media. Nobody can force magazine readers to read anything,
and it is very easy for them to turn a page. Mass media writers and editors
know that they must make readers *want* to read whatever it is they're
trying to tell them; hence the message usually is wrapped in some kind of
emotional, universal, self-interest appeal. When this is skillfully done
readers gets the message, often without realizing it.

10

Leads and Endings

*M*any writers I know say they can't get to work on a piece until they've written the lead exactly as they want it to be. I've always heard these confessions with the smug warmth of superiority because I don't work that way, and obviously the way I do work is not only better, but more sophisticated, intelligent, and creative. But when I was thinking about this lead, a flash of objectivity showed me that my complacency, as often before, was phony. In fact I *do* write the lead first—not on a typewriter and not in its entirety, but I know what it's going to be and I can see it and feel its dimensions in my mind.

The reason for this grows out of the nature of a lead. It has two jobs: to start the reader reading and to state, either directly or indirectly, the underlying idea of the story. Obviously you can't accomplish the second job until you've reviewed all your research and decided what it says. In reviewing it, you've run through your mind all the possible candidates for the lead—and consciously or unconsciously evaluated the reader appeal of each. Thus, as is usual in artistry, your mind has been doing several things at once—often without your being aware of it.

Different kinds of leads do these two jobs in different ways. The anecdotal lead is probably used more frequently than any other in the mass media. The chief reason is that it is the strongest in the "hook the reader in" department. Instantly, it gives the reader people to identify with, action to watch, a problem to worry about. It's the kind Bob Greene used in the story about the fifteen-year-olds quoted in the last chapter. Both movies and television have borrowed the idea of this kind of lead in the way they start the action of a story and present at least part of its problem before they give you the title and credits.

This kind of lead can be adapted to a great variety of stories. Greene used it to introduce us to his subjects; here's an anecdotal lead that started a quite different kind of story by Claire Safran. It appeared in *Woman's*

Day and dealt with a group of parents fighting to protect their children from the effects of toxic wastes, and encountering along the way a great deal of opposition from the government officials the parents thought would protect them.

There's an empty room in the tidy red ranch house at the east end of Woburn, Massachusetts. The little boy who once slept there was just twelve years old when he died in 1981. Add his name, Jimmy Anderson, to the list of victims of the modern-day plague we call toxic waste.

Add little Robbie Robbins's name, too. Indeed, add the names of twenty-two Woburn children who have been stricken with leukemia, all but five of them now dead. Then figure in the names of their anguished parents, their grieving brothers and sisters, their terrified neighbors living with the fear that it could happen to their children as well.

It is sad to hear Jimmy's mother, Anne Anderson, tell her story. It hurts to look into her eyes, bruised with pain. "Why Jimmy?" she asked at first. "Why any child?" she asked later on. Because Anne Anderson and other parents insisted on answers, the children of Woburn are safer today than they once were. Because they are still asking questions, still demanding answers, children in other cities and towns may be safer too.

Like this one, all good anecdotal leads tell indirectly what the story is about. But a good anecdotal lead goes further and demonstrates the crux of the idea in the most dramatic terms possible. Certainly, the deaths and illnesses of the children of Woburn were the most compelling aspect of the story.

This "crux" idea is a good guide to selecting which among the many anecdotes your research has turned up is the best for the lead. If the story is about a conflict between individuals, the moment of confrontation between them is the one to use. For example, once I did a piece about a man, Dr. Earle Reynolds, who challenged the right of the U.S. government to test nuclear bombs in the atmosphere and to block off sections of the Pacific Ocean to do so. To test the law, he violated it by sailing his boat into the forbidden area while tests were going on, thus risking his own and his family's health to prove his point. The lead was a two-page report of exactly what happened when Reynolds and his family were arrested on the high seas by the U.S. Coast Guard—the moment of physical confrontation between him and the government. Why? Because the basic story was of the conflict between a man and his government and the place to start it was obviously the moment of confrontation.

Very good journalists select an anecdotal lead that expresses the mood of the story's underlying idea, though it may not report the problem or crux in overt terms. Gay Talese used this type of lead on a piece about Joe DiMaggio's life after the death of his ex-wife, Marilyn Monroe. (The piece originally appeared in *Esquire,* and was reprinted in Talese's book, *Fame and Obscurity.*

It was not quite spring, the silent season before the search for salmon, and the old fishermen of San Francisco were either painting their boats or repairing their nets along the pier or sitting in the sun talking quietly among themselves, watching the tourists come and go, and smiling, now, as a pretty girl paused to take their picture. She was about twenty-five, healthy and blue-eyed and wearing a red turtleneck sweater, and she had long, flowing blonde hair that she brushed back a few times before clicking her camera. The fishermen, looking at her, made admiring comments but she did not understand because they spoke a Sicilian dialect, nor did she notice the tall gray-haired man in a dark suit who stood watching her from behind a big bay window on the second floor of DiMaggio's restaurant that overlooks the pier.

He watched until she left, lost in the crowd of newly arrived tourists that had just come down the hill by cable car. Then he sat down again at the table in the restaurant, finishing his tea and lighting another cigarette—his fifth in the last half-hour. None of the other tables was occupied, and the only sounds came from the bar where a liquor salesman was laughing at something the headwaiter had said. But then the salesman, his briefcase under his arm, headed for the door, stopping briefly to peek into the dining room and call out, "See you later, Joe." Joe DiMaggio turned and waved at the salesman. Then the room was quiet again.

Here Talese has said a great deal about what will be the essential message of his story. The girl, of course, is a symbol for the dead Marilyn, the fishermen, for DiMaggio, who came from a family of fishermen. The gulf between them is suggested both by the fact that she is a tourist, taking their picture and that they speak a dialect she cannot understand. Joe, watching from behind a window suggests the distance of his loss of her.

The next paragraph tells about his loneliness, his tension—his fifth cigarette in a half hour—his reserve, his prominence, and the adulation he still gets as a former athlete. Quite a bit to get into two paragraphs.

The summary lead is exactly what its name says it is. It summarizes, as succinctly as possible, exactly what the article is about. Writers try to make them as dramatic and provocative as possible, but the main purpose is to tell the reader what he or she will get in the story. In this they are similar to the traditional newspaper lead which tells who, what, when, where, why, and maybe how. Here's the lead of a profile of Babe Ruth written by Roger Kahn and included in his book, *How the Weather Was*.

In his time and in his way, George Herman Ruth was a holy sinner. He was a man of measureless lust, selfishness and appetites, but he was also a man undyingly faithful, in a manner, to both his public and his game. Tradition, which always distorts, remolded Ruth as extensively in a quarter-century as it remolded Abraham Lincoln in a hundred years. Just twenty-five years after his death and thirty-eight years after his last disastrous season, only the image of holiness remains.

Kahn then goes on with a penetrating portrait of America's greatest sports legend.

Here's another summary lead, this one by Garry Wills.

For a teenaged pacifist, she did a lot of fighting. She quit her first newspaper job, on the socialist *Call*, after being reprimanded by an editor for slapping an incoherent radical at a public affair. Jailed with suffragists, she bit the notorious warden of the Occoquan workhouse and kicked two guards in the shins as they wrestled her down. It was always clear that she would leave her mark on the world; but it must have seemed, in 1917, that the mark she would leave would be a bloody one. No one could have guessed—least of all Dorothy Day herself—that she would become, with Gandhi and Dr. King, one of the principal exponents of nonviolence in our time.

Summary leads are usually short, because you figure that while you may provoke the readers' interest with your general statements, you'd better quickly get down to specific cases and people for them to become interested in. After the lead in the Ruth piece, Kahn immediately gives the reader an anecdote that occurred at Ruth's funeral, and Wills follows his lead by bringing the reader face-to-face with Dorothy Day.

Closely related to the summary lead is the one that contains a striking or shocking statement concerning something that is of immediate self-interest to millions of readers. For example, a piece I did for *Reader's Digest* on traffic courts had this lead:

Each year more than 30 million motorists are summoned into traffic courts throughout the United States. For nine out of ten of these citizens, their day in court will be the only opportunity they ever have to observe American justice in operation. But instead of a true court of justice, the man accused of a traffic violation will too often face a mere fine-collection agency. He will probably have to wait hours in a crowded, noisy courtroom, only to appear finally before a bored, unpatient judge who is more interested in disposing of his case than in safeguarding his legal rights.

"These courts," wrote a former U.S. Supreme Court justice, Charles E. Whittaker, "are so poorly housed, staffed and equipped, the proceedings so lacking in dignity and their judgments so perfunctory, that they actually create disrespect, if not contempt for all law and all courts."

This one is very close to a summary lead, but it does not suggest all the dimensions of the story, and the emphasis is on the shock value of the statements—something you can't achieve in all summary leads. Other shocking statement leads don't even try to sum up the story idea.

Here's one that William Barry Forlong put in a story he did for *Good Housekeeping*:

It was a pleasant summer day-warm with just a hint that it would grow hot and humid later on. Doctors moved quietly among a score of patients at the Jewish Chronic Disease Hospital in Brooklyn, giving them injections under the skin of one thigh. It was just a test of their immunity, the patients had been told. There was no real danger, though they "might feel a little discomfort and perhaps see a lump for a while." But there was one thing the patients weren't told: that the injections contained live cancer cells.

This one is close to an anecdotal lead, but is so short that the anecdote is not fully realized, and constructed so that the shock comes in the last few words. (Part of the shock, incidentally, derives from Furlong's artistry in setting up a contrast: a felicitous summer day, doctors moving quietly among patients seemingly in a situation of trust and healing.)

The fourth kind of lead is one which, for want of a fancier name, we call "bam-bam-bam." In this one, you try to hook the reader in with three telescoped anecdotes, the diversity of which illustrate the scope of the story. For instance, Randy Fitzgerald started a *Reader's Digest* piece on food-stamp fraud with the following lead:

In Kentucky undercover policemen discover that federal food stamps are being traded for automobiles, drugs and automatic weapons. Among 30 suspects arrested is a 62-year-old man convicted of selling the sexual services of a 14-year-old boy for $6000 in food stamps and $1000 in cash.

In Chicago a 34-year-old woman is convicted of defrauding food-stamp and related welfare programs of $92,000 over eight years. A Justice Department official estimates food stamp fraud in the Chicago area totals $36 million annually.

In New York City five members of a family are sentenced to prison for participation in a conspiracy involving the theft of between $4 million and $5 million in food stamps, and laundering them through meat markets.

The purpose here was to catch the reader's interest with the amount of fraud, and also to demonstrate how widespread the fraud had become.

That second point—scope—is important when you're writing for national media. Most magazine writers live around New York City; the media circulate nationwide. So writers must demonstrate that the things they're writing about apply all over the country to all kinds of people. The simplistic way of doing this is with trite phrases like "from Maine to California," but professional self-respect demands a little more than that. So you select your illustrative material from different geographical—or vocational or ethnic—areas.

The trouble with the three-part lead is that it uses up, in minimal space, good anecdotal material, which is usually scarce. The three food-stamp fraud cases cited above in three paragraphs could easily have been expanded to a page or so each, and used to illustrate later points in the article. So you only use this kind of lead when you have an abundance of good anecdotes.

Writers use a descriptive lead when they think the mood of the story is of primary importance and should be established immediately. Well done, this kind of lead gets the reader emotionally involved instantly. A secondary purpose is that it locates the story geographically. The first paragraph of Joan Didion's story "Some Dreamers of the Golden Dream" in *Slouching Towards Bethlehem* accomplished this:

> This is a story about love and death in the golden land, and begins with the country. The San Bernardino Valley lies only an hour east of Los Angeles by the San Bernardino Freeway but is in certain ways an alien place: not the coastal California of the subtropical twilights and the soft westerlies off the Pacific, but a harsher California, haunted by the Mojave just beyond the mountains, devastated by the hot dry Santa Ana wind that comes down through the passes at 100 miles an hour and whines through the eucalyptus windbreaks and works on the nerves. October is the bad month for the wind, the month when breathing is difficult and the hills blaze up spontaneously. It is the season of suicide and divorce and prickly dread, whenever the wind blows.

Descriptive leads do not always present a countryside; sometimes they present people, as in a piece journalist and biographer Barbara Gelb did for the *New York Times Magazine* on director and producer Mike Nichols.

> Mike Nichols sits erect, arms folded, at a trestle table in a large-windowed, bare-floored rehearsal room, where he is directing a new play by David Rabe. Rabe sits slumped in a chair nearby, ready to leap protectively to the defense of any seeming slight to his precious words. The actors clutch their scripts—insecure, groping, desperate to please—watching Nichols for a sign of approval. Nichols, who is in a position more or less to have his pick of scripts and stars, has experienced both the joys of taking creative chances and the pitfalls of playing safe. He has been nominated for an Antoinette Perry Award for his direction of Tom Stoppard's "The Real Thing;" if he wins next Sunday, it will be his sixth Tony. And now—as he intermittently feels compelled to do, he has chosen to try a risky play.

Here, Gelb uses the description to show Nichols at work. She also shows the tension under which he is operating, and the esteem in which he is held by the actors, who watch him, seeking a nod of approval.

The "you" lead is the kind in which the writer talks directly to the readers in an attempt to convince them that their self-interest is intensely involved in this piece. It has the advantage of being as direct as a face-to-face conversation; it has the disadvantage that the reader may respond to the "you" with a "not me, Buster"—which he'd be too polite to do if you were face-to-face, but which he's quite free to do when he's alone with a magazine.

I used this kind of lead in the "What Makes Kids Popular?" piece in chapter 2. I haven't used one lately; they seem to be somehow simplistic and perhaps too manipulative.

Like all categorization, this list of kinds of leads is too clear-cut. As must already be apparent from the examples given, many leads, perhaps most, are combinations. Sometimes this is deliberate; more often it results because the writer tries to work in the most compelling material possible to get the reader started. For example, the following lead from a Ken Auletta profile that appeared in *Esquire* contains elements of the descriptive, anecdotal, and shocking-statement leads.

Snow pelted the late-model Plymouth Volare as it slid out of the city of Oswego, New York, on its way along Route 57 to Syracuse, forty miles south. Harnessed in the front seat by a three-point seat belt was the guest speaker at the State University at Oswego that night, accompanied by three undergraduates who had volunteered to drive him to his hotel, near the airport.

The four-door Plymouth barreled along at about thirty-five miles an hour, lashed by heavy winds that shoved it left and right, pounded by the thickest snowfall of the year. Suddenly, just after midnight, the car skidded out of control, spinning perpendicular to the highway, its momentum carrying it forward, slicing through knee-deep drifts, scraping and jumping a wall of ice, and coming to a halt at a forty-five-degree angle at the bottom of a ditch dividing the four lane highway.

While the car spun, the passenger in the front seat said nothing. He sat calmly holding a giant manila accordion file folder containing brochures in his lap, wrapped in the same black raincoat, gray baggy suit, and blue oxford shirt he had worn to give five college speeches in thirty hours. While the car spun, the passengers in the back seat anxiously turned to check that another automobile would not plow into the Plymouth, that the car would not skid to the right, where a steep plunge menaced. All the while, the passenger in the front seat fixed his dark, intense eyes on the feet of the driver, never wavering throughout. When the car finally jolted to a halt, the passenger cooly complimented the student who was driving, Michael Murray of New City, New York, for having kept his foot off the brake. The car might have flipped over had Murray hit the brakes. "That was a classic case of a hydroplane landing," marveled Ralph Nader.

Two types of leads used by inexperienced writers usually fail: quotations and questions. The quotation lead is generally ineffective because most quotations need explanation to be understood, and explanatory material can slow down the lead. Besides, any writer who can't write better than most people speak, is in the wrong field. Having said all that, we should point out that we have used as examples in this book two excellent stories that start with quotations: in writing all rules are made to be broken. As for questions, a good rule to follow is that a writer's job is to answer them, not to ask them.

Every cub reporter learns what a lead is the first week on the job, but nobody ever tells you anything about endings. You can spend years in the newspaper business—the great training ground for journalists—and never hear a word about endings. Probably this because the old inverted pyramid structure, used so often in news stories, written with the least important material at the end so that when the make-up editor chopped off the last couple of paragraphs to make the piece fit the hole that was left on the page, nothing much was lost. So traditional news stories went out with a whimper, but creative journalism demands that stories end with a bang—or at least a snap.

Since we seem to be hooked on categorization in this chapter, we suppose we should list the kinds of endings. Trouble is, there are only three, as far as we can see. One is the summary; another, the snapper; and the third is, well, the third kind.

The summary is a kind of retread of the lead. It's the Q.E.D. kind of thing, like your old high school geometry theorems. In the lead you make some promises to the readers—here's what I'm going to tell you about; in the summary ending you tell them you have kept the promises—here's what I have told you about.

Claire Safran used a summary ending on her piece about toxic wastes in Woburn.

The children of Woburn and Reading are safer today that little Jimmy and Robbie were. The danger has been reduced, but more needs to be done and more needs to be known about the causes. The bond of trust between people and government has been broken, and the sense of communal safety is gone. As a parent, Rev. Young is still worried. His own family lives in a different neighborhood, where he's been told that the water is "fine." Still, as he says, "When one of my children feels tired or ill, I don't think of a cold or flu. I rush the child to the doctor and hold my breath until the laboratory tests are done."

Nevertheless, he and his family stay put. So do most of the families. This is where they live, where their friends, churches and schools are. This is their home, and their major family investment. "If I knew for certain it was dangerous, I would sell my house," says Judy. "But if we knew for certain, who would ever buy it?"

For Anne Anderson, there is another question: "Where would we go?" She recalls the case of the families who were moved out of dioxin-contaminated Times Beach, Missouri, only to find themselves on another site contaminated by the same deadly chemical. "There is no place to hide from this problem," says Anne. "We will stay and fight it here."

This ending summarizes the main theme of the piece indirectly. It also returns the reader to the characters and events mentioned in the lead, giving the reader the feeling that the story has come full circle. Like all good summary endings, it wraps up the piece in a neat package.

Snapper endings are artistic, fun to write, and they fulfill an old, sound, show-business maxim, "always leave them laughing"—or crying. The snapper is usually a pointed anecdote or incident or quote that characterizes your main theme much the way anecdotal leads do. It is crisp, short, often wry, usually witty. The trouble is that when you come across an item that fills that prescription, it's usually so good you use it early in the piece. To save it for the ending requires the kind of self-restraint and foresight many writers, ourselves included, can't muster more than once every five years. Sometimes, though, you have such a wealth of colorful material that you can save a good one for a snapper. An example is the ending of a profile of Dr. Herbert R. Axelrod that Robert Boyle once wrote for *Sports Illustrated*. For thirty-five long paragraphs, Boyle had told his readers what a prodigious man Axelrod was. He was an explorer, scientist, friend of kings, writer, publisher, millionaire. Boyle then ended the piece with this paragraph:

But for all the fish, all the Mongolian gerbils, and for all the money rolling in, Dr. Herbert R. Axelrod occasionally sinks into gloom. "I'd be happy to be a pauper," he says, "if I could play the fiddle as well as Jascha Heifetz."

Simply reprinting the ending this way does not demonstrate its full impact; to get that you have to read the whole article. When you do that you don't believe Axelrod's statement, because Boyle has so thoroughly documented the man's energy and determination in making his millions that you know such a man would never be satisfied to be merely a great violinist. This is only one of the nuances that gives the ending its kick.

This kind of ending must be planned and the material held aside when the story is being outlined. This is a nice idea, but writers are not often that foresighted. What usually happens is the third kind of ending. This is the one that grows out of the story itself, naturally. It doesn't fit in any category; it evolves from the type of material you're using, the kind of story it is, and the point you're at when you finish the body of the piece and realize that now you've got to put an ending on it.

For example, take the Commando Kelly story, back in chapter 6. The whole point of the story was the two kinds of courage—the kind required to win a Medal of Honor versus that needed to survive the trials of everyday living. Partly as a suspense device, and partly because you can't expect the average reader to hold still for this kind of abstract disquisition, I merely laid the groundwork for the comparison right after the lead, then said nothing more about it until the final two paragraphs. By that time, I figured, the reader had all the facts which supported Kelly's final conclusion, so when it was given, he believed it. (I did sort of plan that one in advance.)

The third kind of ending is more a product of the writer's creativity than anything else. In a piece Norman Maclean wrote about retrievers for *Esquire,* he used such an ending. The piece actually dealt with much more than retrievers. It told of Maclean's relationship with his father. Near the end of the piece, Maclean tells of the death of his brother, and the crushing effect it had on his father, who adopted the brother's dog, and whose life was changed thereby. Maclean ended the piece this way:

The dog and my father were inseparable, whereas before my father cared to be with dogs only during the hunting season. As for the dog, I am sure there are other cases like this, but he was the only dog I ever saw that became another dog for love of another man. For my brother he had been a duck dog, and now for my father he became a fishing dog, if one can speak of such a species. He would sit all day in the boat on the seat next to my father and peer into the impenetrable water. He not only loved but admired my father greatly—I am sure he thought the whole fishing thing was completely under my father's control, as I did when I was the dog's age and believed my father could come up with a fish whenever he was so minded. After staring a respectable length of time into the water without seeing anything but pieces of sunlight, he would bark at my father, and when my father caught a fish, the dog would lick my father's whole face, though my father still needed part of it to see how to unhook the fish.

To the others in my family, the dog was something of a sacred object that had prolonged my father's life and helped to steady the rest of us. He was a fine dog, and after him, my father had no other dog.

Although some endings defy classification, there are a couple of rules for the latter parts of stories. In mass magazines, the ending should be up-beat if possible. Even if your story is pretty negative, you try to end with some kind of a positive thought or idea. Very seldom do you leave the reader with a "down" feeling, but if you do it should be a beaut. If your story is a tragedy and there is not even a hope at the end then, like Shakespeare in *Hamlet*, you really ought to pile the stage with corpses.

With personality pieces you often end with a summary anecdote that restates the theme of the piece. In problem stories you almost invariably end with a "what can be done" section and a short wrap-up. In "how-to" stories you often end with a summary restatement of the advantages of building a backyard swimming pool out of old newspapers for $4.69.

One final item: when you have finished the piece, stop writing. Time after time I've kept on going for two or three more paragraphs after the story was really finished. Inertia, I guess.

One time I was watching an artist paint a portrait. It was really finished, but he was fussing around with a dab here, a brush stroke there.

Finally he threw down his brush in exasperation. "Every artist," he said, "should have a man stand behind him with a big wooden mallet, to hit him smartly on the head when the painting is finished."

Same goes for writers.

11

The Body of the Story

*I*t may be an egregious kind of mechanization to presume to write a chapter about what makes up the body of a story. All you have to do is read half a dozen good articles to see that the content varies enormously. Obviously, what goes into the body depends on the kind of story it is, the quality of material available, the audience to which it is addressed and, primarily, the artistry of the writer.

You can look back at the piece about the two fifteen-year-olds in chapter 9, and see how Bob Greene uses his ability as an observer and a writer to show us the boys in their adolescent confusion and vulnerability.

Another example is the following, taken from Barbara Gelb's profile of Mike Nichols, in which she shows how Nichols works and gives a glimpse of the effect Elia Kazan's work has had on him.

Nichols nibbles on a bran muffin, sips coffee, chain smokes (without inhaling) and nods encouragingly to William Hurt and Sigourney Weaver, who are about to rehearse a love scene. She is playing Darlene, a rootless woman, bruised by love, who has a vague career as a photographer. He is playing Eddie, a marginally successful Hollywood casting director with a drug habit. "Hurlyburly," which is scheduled to open Off Broadway at the Promenade Theater on June 21, is in an early phase of rehearsal and the two young actors, though they have practiced the love scene a few times, are still feeling their way into their roles, improvising.

"Eddie and Darlene are talking about how it's lucky they didn't meet a year ago," Nichols explains. "Because, Darlene says, 'A year ago I was *crazy.*' And Eddie says, 'Oh, a year ago I was *nuts.*' Then *she* says they have to keep their hearts open, and *he* says they need time and space and no guilts. It's sort of like incantation."

[Playwright David] Rabe's dialogue for the scene gives no hint of any accompanying action, and Eddie and Darlene could be sitting across a table from each other during their exchange. But Nichols wants to find a way to "physicalize" the "underneath," as his observation of Kazan taught him to do, "so that the cliches are heard in stronger contrast." And he has found his clue in the last line of the scene, a ribald—and in a family newspaper unprintable—suggestion from Eddie to Darlene that they immediately consummate their relationship.

"I felt what would make the Event of the scene—the joke, or the irony—clearest, would be to have them—while they're in the midst of these cliches about *space* and *open hearts* and *no guilts*—be undressing each other and beginning to make love."

Sigourney Weaver slithers into William Hurt's lap, straddling him. Hurt, slouched on the sofa, begins fondling her. She pulls her sweater off. "Once I'd decided it would be a good idea for them to partly undress each other and themselves, Sigourney said she wanted Darlene to be quite aggressive," Nichols says. "It was her idea to straddle Bill. And I said, well, if she was going to do *that*—and I liked it very much, why not do it on the line, I'm *scared?* At one point, Eddie says, 'We need *time.*' And Darlene says, 'There's no rush'—whipping off her belt."

In the actor's lap, the actress unbuckles her belt and flings it away.

"We worked it out very carefully," Nichols says, watching approvingly.

Weaver kicks off a boot. Hurt tugs off her other boot. In one swift motion, Weaver zips down her dress, wriggles out of it and drops it on the floor behind her. She finally is wearing nothing but silk panties and a thin, clinging, pink knit camisole.

Hurt hastily pulls open the buttons of his shirt and shrugs out of the sleeves, as Weaver yanks her camisole over head and tosses it into the air. Naked from the waist up, the two embrace fervidly.

Nichols smiles with delight at his own handiwork and at his actors' adventurousness.

Sigourney Weaver is getting dressed. Moved by her daring, William Hurt says quietly, "You're very brave."

"You're brave too," Nichols tells the actor, smiling one of his ferociously protective smiles.

The anecdote is unusual, since Nichols, one of the characters, is commenting on the action as it occurs. But Gelb clearly recognized that by placing the quotes within the description of the actors' work, she could show readers what Nichols believes about direction, and how he helps his actors reach the goals he has set. Had she been less perceptive, the point would not have been made so well.

In addition to the artistry of the writer, this anecdote demonstrates another quality of first-class journalism: the writer must think deeply about his or her material, must have broad understanding of people, and must be perceptive enough to see the significance behind a fairly simple situation. These qualities probably cannot be taught or planned; they come from living and understanding.

So the body of a story cannot be compiled like a grocery list. But when you have read hundreds of interpretive pieces and written several score, you begin to see that there are some elements which many of the good ones share. Isolating them out helps you to ensure that the next piece you do will have at least some of the requisites of good work.

One is what, for want of a more perceptive name, we usually call the significance section. This is a paragraph or two, usually right after the lead, which tells readers why it is important to read this piece. It draws the broader significance of the story, perhaps by showing that it affects people all over the country, perhaps by showing that it touches deeply the lives of millions, perhaps by saying here is something new and important. It attempts to answer the reader's inveterate, unspoken question, "What's in this for me?" It may be a summary of all the points that will be made in the story and thus be a kind of road map of where the story is going; this helps orient the reader and, by defining precisely what is and is not going to be covered, sharpens the focus of the piece. It may be a general definition of a problem that the piece will explore specifically in terms of one person, one group, one city.

In the Gelb piece, for example, the significance section begins with a brief overview of Nichols's enormously successful career, then moves on to this:

> To watch Nichols at work is to perceive something about the making of a play that will never be discerned by its audience. To hear him talk about his work, as he did recently in full candor, is to perceive something about the making of a director and the sources of his creativity—in Nichols's case, a blend of life experiences that he applies to every project, whether a genial comedy like "The Odd Couple," or a tragicomedy, like "Hurlyburly."

Gelb is telling her readers that the story will show them something they have never seen before—how a great director works. If they read the story, she is saying, they will learn a great deal about a man whose work most of them have seen.

A different kind of "significance section" was included in the article "What Makes Kids Popular?" which we discussed in chapter 2. The piece has a "you" lead designed to make readers identify with story. The eighth, ninth, and tenth paragraphs are the significance section, which is supposed to tell readers why this is important, and to nail down their self-interest in reading it.

In the piece on toxic waste mentioned in the preceding chapter, Claire Safran moves the reader from a focus on the children and parents of Woburn, like Jimmy and Anne Anderson, to a focus on the problem as it affects the entire country.

When little Jimmy first became sick, no one wanted to listen to Anne's questions. City and state officials dismissed her as "an emotional mother." The tragic news had not yet broken about Love Canal, the Niagara Falls, New York, neighborhood built on a landfill that had leached out its toxic chemicals. Few people were aware of how the by-products of civilization could poison our air, our water, our land and our children.

The danger is now all too familiar. Each day, a new group of parents wakes to the nightmare Anne Anderson lived with for years. From across the country come reports of children becoming ill because of asbestos in a school's ceilings, deadly dioxin in industrial-waste oil sprinkled on a dusty road or other potentially lethal chemicals seeping into drinking water. In Woburn, as in so many other places, the cleanup is not yet even begun. The answers Anne found are not final ones—but they are a beginning and they point the way for other concerned parents to follow.

Safran here is clearly telling her readers that while her story is about one city in Massachusetts, the problem exists nationwide, and reading the story will help them if ever they have to face it. It is a clear appeal to the reader's self-interest.

The food-stamp-fraud story mentioned in the preceding chapter featured a similar theme statement. The lead comprised three anecdotes about fraud. It was followed by this:

The food-stamp program has been one of the fastest-growing of all federal programs—escalating from a $30.5-million budget and 367,000 recipients in 1964 to $11.3 billion and 22.5 million recipients today. It is also one of the most fraud-ridden and poorly run programs. Federal investigators calculate that up to $1.6 billion a year is wasted as a result of recipient fraud, administrative error, and organized theft and counterfeiting. In many parts of the country, food stamps have literally become a second currency, used to support a thriving black market in stolen and illicit goods. Says Sen. William L. Armstrong (R. Colo.), "Theft, abuse and error in the program are not just a rip-off of taxpayers; they are a crime against the poor."

The writer, Randy Fitzgerald, is clearly telling readers that the three incidents mentioned in the lead are not exceptional, that more than one-tenth of all money in the program is wasted, and that the problem is one they should read about and understand.

Since most writers are not authorities, but reporters, they have to seek out various experts and put their knowledge at the service of the reader. The way writers do this is another of the definable elements that characterize a sound article.

In the first place, the person you are quoting about a subject has to be a genuine authority on that subject. Just having an M.D. degree, for instance, doesn't make someone an expert on everything from heart disease to cystic fibrosis; if you need a medical authority, quote a doctor on the area in which he or she has special knowledge—maybe kidney ailments, maybe new ideas in family practice. And don't be deluded by the epidemic of degree-itis that currently afflicts the country. Someone can be an expert without having a Ph.D. or even a college education.

Suppose, for instance, that you were doing a story on dishonest mechanics who gyp people on auto repairs. To prove a particular mechanic had mistreated a car, you'd have to have an honest, expert mechanic who could diagnose what was really wrong with the car, what should have been done to fix it, and how much it should have cost. He might have no higher education at all, but if he knew autos from radiator to tail pipe, he would be a legitimate expert.

When you first quote your expert in an article, you must include his or her qualifications in order to convince the reader your source *is* an expert. Usually it's easy; the person's title is often enough—the secretary of state is obviously an expert for an article on U.S. foreign policy. Sometimes you must give a title plus the person's particular expertise.

Once when I did an article on a mass murderer named Francis Bloeth, it was necessary to go back into his childhood to discover the origins of his aberration. His mother was an expert on that. But then I wanted to show that some of the things that had happened to him as a child were probably the cause of his later behavior, so I needed an authority on the causes of childhood crime. Here's the way it went:

In 1943 [Bloeth] was pronounced "a delinquent child" in Queens County Children's Court. What made him such? His mother recalls that when he was six he jumped 30 feet out of a tree, got a concussion of the brain, and after that "really started to get in trouble." But the exhaustive studies of delinquent children made by Drs. Sheldon and Eleanor Glueck of Harvard University would point to other factors in his case.

The Gluecks have found five main characteristics that separate delinquents from normal youngsters. They made up tables to predict which children would become delinquent, and the New York City Youth Board has found them to be accurate indicators. Applied retrospectively to Bloeth's life, the tables give him less than a ten per cent chance of *not* becoming delinquent.

Then the story went on to cite specific areas of parent-child relations— like discipline—that the Gluecks had found to be decisive and reported that each had been present in young Bloeth's experience.

Here the Gluecks were cited and qualified as experts and their expertise further validated in the specific areas needed by the testing program of the youth board. And this little excerpt illustrated (minimally) another technique that works well in this kind of writing. It's in the first paragraph, where I quoted Bloeth's mother on the fall from the tree as a cause of his trouble, then immediately demolished that explanation with the citation of the Glueck's study.

What we're getting into here is a problem in both credibility and ethics. Take ethics first. When you write an interpretive piece, you are really making an argument for a particular point of view. You have arrived at this point of view after going through the tough evaluative process described in chapter 6, and it represents the objective truth of the situation as nearly as you can achieve it. When you write the piece you use all the skill at your command to convince the reader that it is the truth, so your writing is *not* objective. However, while it's highly unlikely, it's just possible that your "truth" is wrong—or wrong in part. So fairness and a decent humility require that you present more than one side to a question. Thus you present the other side briefly, then counter it with stronger evidence.

A major virtue of this technique is that it makes the piece—and your argument—much more believable for the reader because what you're saying, in effect, is, "Look, I've done a thorough research job on this situation, I know all the arguments, pro and con, and I've decided the pro is the strongest."

In his book *Attitude Change and Social Influence*, Arthur R. Cohen lists other reasons for giving both sides of a story. You should do it, he says, when the audience will be exposed to the other side later on; when the audience initially disagrees with your point of view; when all the facts on both sides of the question are well known; when the opposing argument and its defenders are better known than yours.

Finally, we don't have any scientific proof of it, but we do have a strong conviction that you are more persuasive when you level with readers. Your readers may lack information, but they are not stupid. Particularly in areas where they have first-hand experience or a strong self-interest, they cannot be fooled. Try it and their most likely reaction will be, "This guy doesn't know what he's talking about!"—and they turn the page. When that happens you're out of the communications business.

There are times when leveling is not only good practice, it's the only thing you can do. Your experts disagree on some essential point and try as you will, you can't find an overwhelming weight of evidence on one side or the other. One thing you can do is tell the reader there is no agreement, quote experts, with their qualifications, on both—or all—sides of the conflict, and let the reader decide. (I've always felt, though, that this was skimping on the job, that if I just kept researching, I'd be able to make a judgment. Many times this has proved to be true. But not always.)

Sometimes when you have trouble arriving at a judgment because of conflicting expert testimony, it is because you haven't thought deeply enough about the question—or about precisely what aspect of the question is pertinent to your line of argument. This happened when I did the story on Richard Tenneson, one of the twenty-one American turncoats, mentioned in chapter 4. Tenneson gave me his version of what had happened to him in battle, but the official accounts of the battles flatly contradicted Tenneson's version. Who was right?

There didn't seem a way in the world to resolve the differences, but the more I thought about it, the more two additional elements gained importance: (1) A battlefield is impossibly confused, and what is true of the overall situation as seen from divisional headquarters may not be true at all for the individual rifleman in a foxhole; and (2) What was important in determining Tenneson's future actions was not so much the objective truth, but his truth—what he *thought* had happened. This is what would form his feelings of belonging to a larger entity and of loyalty to the army and, beyond it, the country.

So I reported the two conflicting versions of the battles, then made the above two points.

There may also come a time when, as you move merrily through the research process, you discover a fact that demolishes the argument you had planned to make. If you find such a fact, you cannot ethically ignore it. You may even have to admit that your point of view is wrong, and forget about the article. That has happened to countless writers, so if it happens to you, take comfort in knowing that you are in good company.

Probably the most important single element in the body of a story for mass audiences is anecdotes—how many you use and how well. If there's one warning editors have given me more than any other, it is, "Be sure to get plenty of anecdotes into it." There are two reasons: the specific anecdote takes a general statement and shows it to the reader in its concrete application, making it easier to grasp; secondly, in anecdotes you are writing about people doing things, so readers can see them, feel with them, see themselves in the same situation—*if* they're well done.

Writing good anecdotes demands as much logical analysis and as much creative talent as anything a writer does. They must make the general point they're supposed to make, and while this sounds obvious, it is surprising how often they do not—and the writer fails to see it. They must convince the reader that these are real people in real situations, which means they cannot be made up. Many beginning writers try this kind of fiction when they can't get real anecdotes, but every experienced editor can spot a phony at ten paces; perhaps the reason is that the writer does not have much skill at writing fiction.

Anecdotes are really miniature stories with all the appurtenances of same. They must lay the groundwork so the reader can follow the action. They must introduce characters with clear objectives, then show the characters striving toward those objectives. They usually have conflict. They move toward a climax, then usually have a denouement, just like a short story. And they have to be structured; the raw material from which they're built is seldom in final form when you get it. Warning: "Structuring" does not mean changing facts, it means perhaps rearranging their order, cutting nonessentials, emphasizing the quotes or actions that drive home the point.

For example, here are two versions of apocryphal story, the first composed by a beginning writer, the second by an experienced one:

The late Bernard Baruch was witness to a scene in New York's Central Park: A middle-aged man sat down next to a pretty young woman and propositioned her to the tune of $25. Finally his bid was accepted for four times that amount. And as the couple rose to leave the park, Baruch heard the man utter to himself, "Now that we have established the principle, it's just a matter of degree."

At a dinner party Winston Churchill was seated next to the pretty young wife of one of his top administrators. He turned to her and said, "My dear, would you spend the weekend with me for £10,000?" The woman looked shocked, hesitated, then said, "Would my husband find out?"

"Of course not," Churchill said. "I'll send him to Iceland."

"Very well," the woman said.

"Would you do it," Churchill asked, "for £10?"

"Sir! Do you take me for a harlot?"

"The principle," Churchill said, "has been established. We are now haggling over the price."

Certainly the second makes the point better. Why? Some reasons are obvious. In version one the famous character is a witness, in version two, a participant, so reader interest is heightened. In the second story you see the little drama actually being played, with direct quotes; in the first it is summarized and therefore less vivid. In version one, the punch line is not clearly related to the conflict preceding it; in version two it is. Most important, in the first story the bidder starts low and ends up high, and the story won't work that way. You've got to start high and end up low in order to set up the situation for the punch line. Finally the quote at the end is weak; "it's just a matter of degree" is much less pointed than "We are now haggling over the price."

There is also a minor element that I put into the second version for the purpose of the comparison. When I heard the original story, it did not include the business about "would my husband find out?" and the next sentence. I put these in because it seemed to me that in this situation a woman would take a little time to make her decision, and I wanted to allow her that time in the progression of the action. Of course such fictionalizing is barred in good journalism—and if you pick your anecdotes carefully it isn't needed.

Dan Greenburg is remarkably adept at handling anecdotes, as he proved in a piece called "The Ninth Precinct Blues," which appeared in the *New York Times Magazine*. The piece told of the difficulties of being a policeman in a New York city area that Greenburg calls "ugly and terrify-

ing." Greenburg rode with the police of the Ninth Precinct, and told the
story almost entirely through anecdotes and quotations. Here's an example:

One night while I am riding with Chris Reisman and Barry Noxon, two
anticrime cops, in their battered sedan, a "job" comes over the radio—a
"jumper." Chris floors the accelerator and we tear around the corner
and over to the block, where two radio cars have pulled up with dome
lights flashing. The uniformed cops are out of their vehicles, gazing
upward. Six stories above us, a young man, either drunk or freaked out
on drugs, dangles dangerously over the parapet, shouting incoherently
about how terrible he has been to his wife.

Chris and Barry confirm that the uniformed cops have already called
for Emergency Services to come with a net, and then they make a break
for the front door of the building, with me following close behind. They
yell for me to hug the building so I won't get hit by the man if he jumps.

The front door of the building is locked. Chris and Barry bang on the
nearest window, yelling: "Police emergency! Open up!" The superintendent of the building sleepily appears and lets us into the hall. Barry,
Chris and I leap up six flights of stairs in 30 seconds. At roof level, Barry
gets down on his hands and knees, quietly opens the door to the roof
and creeps out onto the tar paper, with Chris and me right behind him.
Barry inches up to the parapet and crawls back to us.

"He's on a ledge about seven feet down," Barry whispers. He's going
to see me and jump before I can grab him, unless somebody on the
street distracts his attention."

Chris calls to the cops on the street on his walkie-talkie, *sotto voce*,
tells them to engage the jumper in conversation and to shine a powerful
light in his eyes. The cops on the street start yelling. A searchlight is
turned on. Barry goes over the parapet. The jumper sees Barry a
moment too late and moves to leap off the ledge. Barry reaches out and
graps him. They scuffle briefly, teetering over the ledge, then Barry
yanks him to safety and it is all over. The jumper curses Barry for saving
his life.

Before I know it, we are back on the street. Nobody gives Barry so
much as a pat on the back for rescuing the guy and nearly losing his life
in the process. It is 2:30 A.M.; less than 15 minutes have elapsed since
we first rolled up on the scene. On "Police Story" they'd have stretched
it out to fill an hour.

Two *Daily News* photographers are firing off flashguns in the
jumper's face and the just-arrived Emergency Services team is pouring
out of its van. As we head for our car, an Emergency Services man

passes Barry. "Thanks for doing our job, Fella," he says with mock sarcasm. Clearly, nobody is going to acknowledge Barry's bravery. I figure it's up to me. "Barry," I say, "you're a goddam hero. You know that?"

Barry shrugs. "If my timing had been a fraction of a second off," he says, "then I'd be a yo-yo."

The elements of the anecdote are the classic ones. The two cops are introduced, and, with the call about the "jumper," given their objective: to save the man. Conflict is introduced when the objective is blocked by the locked door, the slow-moving superintendent, the six flights of stairs, and the jumper's ability to spot Noxon from the ledge. But the two overcome all of the obstacles, and save the jumper; this is the climax. The denouement is the by-play that follows.

But there's much more to the story than structure: Greenberg points up the elements that show what it is like to be a Ninth Precinct cop. He never flatly states the points that he wants the anecdote to make, but he tells the story so that the reader gets them anyway.

At the beginning of the anecdote he mentions the radio call that tells Noxon and Reisman of a "job," a relatively bland term for what the two will be called upon to do. The fact that the pair use the term indicates that incidents like this are commonplace, as does the fact that the word "jumper" immediately tells them what they will face when they arrive at the scene.

He reinforces this idea with his dry description of the scene when they arrive. He shows Noxon and Reisman quickly deciding what action to take, and taking it. They seem cool, professional, and unsurprised by an event that most of us would find shocking and frightening.

Next, as they race to the door, both cops warn Greenburg to hug the building, so he will not be hit by the man if he jumps. Wouldn't that be a bizarre way to die? But one of Greenburg's points is that the bizarre and the dangerous make up a great deal of the life of a Ninth Precinct police officer.

The courage of the men becomes evident as Noxon risks his life to save a man who doesn't want to be saved. And the thanklessness of their job is driven home by the reaction to Noxon's heroism. The man Noxon has just saved curses him, the other policemen ignore him or joke about it, and when Greenburg finally tells Noxon that he is a hero, Noxon turns the compliment off with a self-deprecating smart crack.

That's quite a lot for one anecdote to do.

Good anecdotes are intensely *human* stories, stories of people doing things, overcoming obstacles, solving problems, changing, battling other people, helping them, loving them, hating them. They tell readers that the abstract idea you are presenting has very real effects on their own and other people's lives. By demonstrating those effects, in the dramas of people interacting with others, you help readers understand the situation—often their own—and help them identify with your characters and their situation. It's hardly a new technique. The Bible uses it, and the anecdotes are called parables.

What *is* relatively new—merely about twenty-five years old—is its use in journalism to add impact to the informational message. And it requires of the nonfiction writer the artistry of the fiction writer. So if you want to do it well, where do you look for your models? The fiction writers. And I've also found that the analysis of jokes helps. Jokes, after all, are short human stories with a very sharp point. Jokes evoke emotion, though only one—laughter. And jokes don't just happen, somebody writes them. So by taking them apart and seeing how they make their point, you can learn a good deal about structure and effectiveness. For example:

A man is speeding along the freeway in the pouring rain. He passes one of those ten-wheel, tractor-trailer trucks stopped on the side of the road and, out of the corner of his eye as he passes, he spots the truck driver kneeling down in front of the truck doing something with a little white kitten. Intrigued, he stops, backs up, and goes up to the truck driver in the rain. The driver has some string and is making a harness for the kitten and hitching it to the front bumper of the truck.

"Trouble?" the man says.

"Yeah. Truck broke down."

"Well, what are you doing with the kitten?"

"I'm going to get him to pull me into town."

"You think that little bitty kitten is going to pull that great big truck?"

"Sure. Why not? I got a whip."

Here the writer sets up the situation, a familiar one that any motorist can identify with, quickly in the first few sentences. Then he introduces the problem—how to get the truck to town—and builds it with the dialogue. The climax comes in the last line; there is no denouement.

But what makes it funny is the misdirection. Like a stage magician who makes sure your eyes are elsewhere when he drops in the chemical that will turn the pitcher of water into "wine," the writer sets your mind thinking along a certain direction—the stalled truck, the rain, the kitten, the harness. Then in the last line he flips your mind around to a completely new viewpoint. It startles you and makes you laugh, partly at the unexpectedness of it and partly at the truck driver's stupidity.

You can use misdirection in serious stories, too, to build up the point, heighten the impact.

Study television commercials. The good ones can set up and resolve a human situation in fifteen seconds, sometimes five. Of course they have added props of visual action and sound to help get the effect, but their basic techniques can be adapted. They have enormous compression of action; they deal only with the very nub of the situation, which is good technique in any kind of anecdote.

Getting good anecdotes is a major problem for writers. The first step toward its solution, I think, is to recognize that you must have them, and to keep researching until you have enough. The second is to use the old reporter's trick of getting a story by telling one. This does a couple of things: the story you tell outlines for your interviewees the *kind* of thing you're looking for; it starts them thinking along the lines you want; it challenges them to top your story with one of their own. I've also had good luck with the trick of taking the general subject you're talking about right down to the interviewee's own life. For instance, if I've been interviewing a social psychologist, say, on some aspect of parent-child relations, I might ask him how he handles his own children. Immediately his mind switches from dealing with broad, perhaps theoretical, considerations to the warm, personal area of his own kids. And usually, I've gotten good stories that illustrated some point that needed making; after all, he is an expert, and he's likely to have applied his expertise to his personal problems in trying to bring up decent, healthy children.

Finally, it's helpful if you keep in mind what good anecdotes are— stories about people doing things. In much of your interviewing you are dealing with abstract ideas, broad intellectual concepts; if you are constantly trying to bring these down to specific applications in the lives of people, and trying to make your interviewee do the same, you'll see the possibility of anecdotes in many of the things he or she says. Then you go after them by asking specific questions about the specific situation.

12

Dramatic Writing

*H*ere are two ways of handling the same story.

Houston, Jan. 24—An explosion sent sheets of flame roaring across waterfronts streets last night, setting fire to four houses on Avenue O and badly burning three boys.

The explosion came when high-octane gasoline, which had leaked out of a storage tank on Avenue O, suddenly burst into flame about 7 P.M. The three boys, Edward Von Kamp, 14, his brother Robert, 11, and a friend, Herman Holcombe, 12, had been in the Von Kamp home across the street from the tank when the explosion came. They rushed outside and were instantly engulfed in flames. The two Von Kamp boys were taken to the Texas Children's Hospital with third-degree burns and were on the critical list today. The Holcombe boy was taken to South Side Hospital where his condition was listed as good.

"After the second explosion, I ran out of my house and looked down Avenue O," a neighbor of the Von Kamps said. "About 50 yards away I saw a ball of fire moving toward me. Then I looked closer and saw that the ball of fire was a boy!

The neighbor grabbed the boy, Bobby Von Kamp, and rolled him on the road to smother the flames. Then he tore off the boy's charred clothing. As he worked, he could hear the clang of approaching fire engines and ambulance sirens.

Bobby Von Kamp, two weeks away from his 11th birthday, lived across the street from a gasoline storage tank on the Houston, Texas, waterfront. At 7 P.M. on January 24, 1961, he was watching television with his 14-year-old brother Edward and a 12-year-old friend, Herman Holcombe. His father, a seaman, was on a ship off the coast of Florida, his mother had just gone to the grocery store and his two older brothers were out for the evening.

As the Bugs Bunny cartoon was going off the air, the boys smelled gas. High-octane gasoline had been leaking out of the storage tank across the street. Suddenly the vapors exploded. Clouds of flame boiled through the air, licked through the open windows. The three boys dashed for the front door. Eddie held open the screen door as another explosion shook the street. He caught a burst of flames on his back. Part of the screening in the door simply melted into nothing.

The boys ran. Eddie slipped and fell. Herman said, "I'll stay," and knelt by his friend. Bobby yelled, "I'll get help!" He ran down the street with the flames streaming from his clothing.

As soon as ambulances arrived, Bobby and Eddie were sped to the Texas Children's Hospital. Herman, the least burned, was taken to another hospital.

The difference between these two stories is the difference between straight news and interpretive writing. The second, the lead of an article entitled "A Boy's Trial by Fire" by Joseph P. Blank, published in *Reader's Digest*, is also an excellent example of creative, dramatic writing.

The first story, like most news stories, focuses on the event and gives you the people only as they are affected by it. It is objective, factual, uninvolved—and leaves the reader the same way. The second focuses on the people affected by the event; it shows a little newsreel, letting you see the people acting out the event. It is also objective in that the writer takes no position, pleads no cause; it is factual—has even more facts than the first. But it is not uninvolved, and does not leave the reader that way. With its wealth of specific detail, it makes you see and identify with the boys and go with them through their surprise and shock, terror, and humanity as they help each other.

The structure of the story adds to the drama. We defy anyone to read the first paragraph and then stop: it pulls at too many basic emotions. The ball of fire rolling down the street intrigues with its mystery and evokes the primordial fear of fire out of control. The third sentence flips our minds to an entirely new understanding of the threat, then immediately triggers our sympathy for and need to protect our children.

This, of course, is the climax of Blank's little story, and he uses it as a lead to hook the reader's interest. In the next paragraph he finishes, briefly, that bit of action, then in a flashback technique, focuses on the minutes before the explosion and lets us live through it with the three boys. This is constructed, of course, as a chronological narrative and the wealth of detail—the Bugs Bunny cartoon, the screen in the door melting—allows us to experience it first hand. It builds back to the climax, skips it, and goes on to the denouement—the boys in the hospitals.

But basic to the whole story is the ancient universal drama of it. It is a story of someone fighting for life against one of humanity's great, natural enemies—fire. Because we all are unconsciously sensitive to this threat, we identify immediately with the boys' crisis. In fact, Blank has built his whole article around this universal identification. The article is about a new treatment for severe burns. "Dr. Miller found that [Bobby] was burned over 98 per cent of his body. . . . Only the soles of his feet had escaped the flames. . . . Few people have survived 50 per cent third-degree burns." To describe the new treatment, Blank takes Bobby step by step through the long process in the hospital, so that you are reading not simply about a medical advance, but about a boy's fight to live against overwhelming odds—which is the unspoken emotional agenda of the piece.

This is the essence of dramatic writing, for all drama is conflict. The deep, ancient conflicts are few and simple: man against nature; man against man; man against himself.

In the first category you get the adventure stories like those mentioned in Chapter 8. Probably included in this group are the stories of men and women struggling against the unknown, the occult, the mysteries of space—which helps explain the world's fascination with the explorations of space as well as stories of persons pushing forward the frontiers of knowledge in scientific discoveries.

The conflict of man against man lies behind many sports stories as well as political or corporation stories in which people battle one another for power and position. And, of course, it includes many men and women fighting evil, since evil is so often perpetrated or represented by other people.

But some of the latter are man against himself pieces, since "evil" may be a man's own weaknessess—fear, despair—or his primitive rages—for revenge, to conquer, to destroy. The story about the army colonel caught in a dilemma at Fort Lee, Virginia, outlined in Chapter 1, would be man against himself. Once I wrote a piece about a poor Rhode Island youth with a grade-school education who went blind as a result of an accident when he was twenty-one. In a year of rampant self-pity he went to pieces, then picked up his courage and entered a high school for the blind in Massachusetts. He graduated, went to Boston Law School, graduated second in his class, and today is a state supreme court judge. Basically it was a story of his victory over his own despair, brought on by a crippling handicap.

We are often our own enemies. A wise psychiatrist at the University of Maryland taught me this when I was doing an article on what makes people panic. "Fear of losing control of ourselves," he said, "is one of the most powerful, primitive anxieties we have." This insight not only helped me to structure the article itself, but enabled me to see the underlying drama in other human situations I wrote about later.

If you can spot the dramatic conflict in a situation that you're to write about, you can plot the article so that the dramatic story will carry your readers' interest, while its details give them the information you want them to have. We'll talk more about plotting in chapter 14.

Most writers do not make a distinction between the *story* and the *article*. Slowly, over the years of writing, they perfect their own understanding of what makes a good story, though most never consciously categorize or analyze its elements. They simply know. I never did until I started to teach and had to analyze what I'd been doing all those years. But it helps new writers, I think, if they can consciously understand the difference and the qualities that make a story. It helps in spotting those ideas which will be most likely to result in successful articles; it helps in planning the kind of material you will be seeking in your research; it helps in shaping the article after the research is finished.

Universal human conflicts are what make magazine articles timeless. Usually, within them, there is a section that is of its time, but the underlying story is ageless—like the one coming up.

Bonnie Remsberg, an excellent freelance writer, wrote it for *Family Circle*. It won the Outstanding Article Award of the American Society of Journalists and Authors in 1984. On the surface, the article is about the cancer that the nuclear weapons testing of the 1950s has brought to a small Utah town. But beneath the surface, the story deals with some of the most basic human themes and values. It is a story about fear and love, patriotism and loss. It is a story of hope betrayed, of courage and faith.

Beneath the Cloud

By Bonnie Remsberg

Utah is so beautiful, it's hard to believe that it's part of the real world. But a deadly cloud lurks over that lovely land.

Irene Houston McEwen knows that cloud well. From her white house on Main Street, in the pretty little mountain town of Panguitch, Utah, she has tracked it—and its victims—for more than 30 years. She can tell you about its beginnings and its seemingly relentless course. She can also recite the names on the casualty list—those who have sickened and died and those who have sickened and *not* died, but who live in fear for their futures and the futures of their children—born and unborn. It began at dawn on a glorious wind-swept day in January 1951, when a vast mushroom shaped orange cloud burst from the Nevada desert, 150 miles away, and floated over the valley below Panguitch and the mountains above it.

Irene McEwen watched the first explosion—and the next, and the next. She has lost track of how many detonations she actually witnessed, but she does remember that the bombs were released in series of three or four, at intervals of about three months, for twelve years.

In 1963, by our agreement with the USSR and England, all above-ground nuclear testing was abandoned. But by that time, the damage had already been done. The mushroom clouds were gone, but their legacy of cancer remained. It has meant sickness and death to an appalling number of Irene's friends and neighbors. "We didn't know," Irene says. "We couldn't have known." Indeed, in those early years of the Atomic Age, few people knew about the effects of atomic fallout. But Panguitch knows now, and so does Irene McEwen. They found out in the worst way possible.

The Panguitch Valley is a scenic pocket in the Henry Mountains, close to Bryce Canyon and the spectacular Zion National Park. In 1852, it was deemed, by a party of Mormon explorers, "a suitable place" for families to settle. Among the original settlers was a family named Houston.

Generations later, by the time Irene Houston—the oldest of five brothers and seven sisters—was born, the town was a thriving lumber, cattle and tourist center. Growing up, Irene remembers a good life, the warmth of church, family activities and weekly dances where "your father danced with you, your brothers danced with you and then, eventually, you just all paired off."

When it came her turn, Irene paired off with Clem McEwen, who, like herself, had been born in a small house near Main Street. "When we were growing up," she explains, "many people never left Panguitch. I was just lucky that Clem, who would be such a marvelous husband for me, was from one of the few families in town I wasn't related to!"

From the time she was a small, pert, pretty schoolgirl, Irene knew that she wanted to be a teacher. She studied for degrees in English, music, physical education and business, "so I would always have a job." When she was 20, she was accepted as an English and gym teacher by her home-town school system. At Panguitch High School, Irene would eventually teach all her brothers and sisters, her own children and most of the town's other young people.

Every summer, Irene took on the job of producing a community pageant. Its theme was always patriotism, and it always featured the flag. "That's the way we are here," she says. "We love our country and we schedule our lives around what's important to it." Mormon policy dictates such involvement. We're honestly more concerned with what news commentators have to say than with movie stars," Irene says.

Love of country peaked during the Second World War. "As each boy was inducted," Irene remembers, "we gave a party for him at the social hall. The next morning, everyone in town went to the bus to see him off."

Panguitch boys, including Clem, served all over the world. "One was a bombardier," she recalls, "one a tail gunner. One was in Spain and toured the castles of the Inquisition." When each one came home on furlough, Irene invited him to school to talk about what he'd seen and done. "But not all of them came back," she says. "We lost our share." (Actually, they lost more than their share. According to a town history, Panguitch's casualties, per population, were the heaviest in the state.)

Everyone in town was listening to the radio when the atomic bomb was dropped on Hiroshima. They were listening, too, three days later, when the second bomb was dropped on Nagasaki. The devastation was so great, so total, the town sensed instantly that victory had been won. "Now," Irene remembers thinking, "our boys can come home. No more will be lost."

Her first inkling of the hideous after-effects of the bomb came by way of a literary masterpiece. A year after Hiroshima, John Hersey published his classic account of events of that historic day. When his book, *Hiroshima*, appeared, Irene, a conscientious English teacher, ordered it from the library and, for three days, read it aloud to her juniors and seniors. Passages from it remain in her mind to this day.

"He wrote about how the bomb was silent," she recalls, "how you didn't hear it drop." She remembers the vivid picture of "point zero," where the bomb hit. She was particularly struck, and so were her students, with Hersey's descriptions of radiation poisoning. "I could think of nothing else," she says, "except how terrible it would be to live through."

And then the boys came home, and life resumed its normal flow.   ·

When the United States government began testing atomic bombs on Bikini Island, in the South Pacific, Irene read about it. Later she remembers reading that those tests had become too expensive and that further tests would take place within the U.S., on the large, flat, sparsely populated Nevada desert, in what looked on a map like the middle of nowhere.

January 27, 1951, the day of the first official mainland atomic test, dawned cold. Farther down the mountains, the people went out and sat on the hillsides to watch history being made. But up high in Panguitch, where it was too chilly to sit outside at 5 A.M., Irene gathered her family and a group of students in front of her living room window for the event. "There were no leaves on the trees," she remembers, "so we had an unobstructed view. I thought how wonderful it was that we could sit in Utah and see what was going on in Nevada. I couldn't wait to get to school to tell those who didn't get up to watch what they'd missed."

It came up like an orange mushroom, then turned white on the edges as it spread. Irene and her friends saw it dissipate into the air. It floated out and out.

There was nothing else. Nothing you could see, or feel, or smell, or hear. The next morning, Clem's brother-in-law came to visit with a new "toy" he had acquired for rock hunting. It was a Geiger counter. Standing on the McEwen's porch, he flipped it on and watched the needle jump to the far edge of the gauge. "See," he said, "we've got radiation here. That's how you can tell."

Still, no one added it up. There was, simply, trust.

During those years, Irene was occupied with work, family and church. Her parents lived in the house next door. Her daughter, Melanie, and son, Clem Jr., were bright, active children. As the town grew, her husband built and managed motels. Theirs was a full life.

Once she made a routine visit to the town doctor and learned from him that lately he'd been seeing an unusual number of miscarriages. She thought it odd, but dismissed it.

Then, a year and a half after the first tests, something strange began to happen to the men of Panguitch—those strong, healthy outdoorsmen who herded sheep and cut wood, who drank the clear water and breathed mountain air. They began to get sick. And what they were getting sick with was cancer.

The first case, in August 1952, was the McEwen's neighbor across the street. He had never in his life been out of Panguitch. As he slowly sickened and then died, his sons took sick, too. "There were five cases of cancer in that family," Irene recalls. "We couldn't understand it." Later Clem's brother-in-law developed cancer. "He died a horrible death, inch by inch," Irene says.

Mormons keep detailed family histories. The dates and circumstances of births, deaths and important events are call carefully recorded. As the town's English teacher, Irene was charged with the task of proofreading those histories. It was this that made her realize that what was happening was without precedent. There was no history of cancer in Panguitch's families. "Our ancestors died of other things," she observes, "diabetes, strokes, ruptured appendices. Women used to die in childbirth, and children of pneumonia. And some folks died of snakebite. But by and large, we were a healthy people. We just didn't have cancer."

Indeed, because Mormons have traditionally had a far lower rate of cancer than the general population, their life-style has long been studied for clues to cancer prevention. They do not smoke or drink or ingest other unhealthy chemicals. They have a low-stress environment and eat a balanced diet.

In addition to the health histories Irene had an even more dramatic look at what was happening in her town. As the community musician, she played the church organ for all funerals. At Mormon funerals, friends tell stories about the life of the deceased. The cause of death is announced. Irene heard the same story, again and again.

And then the epidemic struck home.

Irene and Clem were standing on her parents' porch one day in 1964, when Clem remarked to Irene's father that he had a sore on his tongue that had bothered him for a week. "You must go for help immediately," Mr. Houston said, and picked up the phone to make arrangements. During a long, hot trip across the Nevada desert, Clem and Irene talked about other men they knew who had developed throat cancer. Some were dead. Several others had lost their voices. Clem was lucky. Surgery took half his tongue, but he recovered and after months of arduous therapy, he learned to speak clearly again.

Irene had only begun to recover from that scare when she began hearing tragic tales about her girls, the beautiful, proud, strong girls of the Panguitch Drum and Bugle Corps.

At around the time the atomic testing had begun, a state law had made physical education mandatory for all students. Irene, who was teaching girls' gym at the time, found herself with a huge class. Since the boys' class had expanded too, there wasn't enough room inside the school to accommodate both groups. The solution was to take turns indoors and out. In order to find something for the girls to do, Irene organized a drum and bugle corps. But since the schoolyard had not yet been landscaped, maneuvers had to be held on the surrounding streets. It was there that Irene led her girls through their paces, not only during the regular gym periods, but early in the morning before school opened.

Money for bugles, drums, cymbals, batons, flags and music was contributed by the Lion's Club. "But the girls," Irene remembers, "furnished the blue and white satin for the uniforms. Three of the mothers sewed them. I'll never forget how they stood them all up in a line and pin-tucked the hems so they'd be exactly the same length."

They got so good that they entered contests and even traveled to Provo to take part in parades. "It was an exciting time," Irene remembers. Still, she felt a vague unease. She could not shake her memories of John Hersey's words. The effects of radiation, he had said, could be experienced 250 miles from the center of the bomb blast. The Nevada test site was 150 miles from Panguitch. On the mornings when the bomb went off, Irene worried about taking her girls outside. She remembers one occasion in particular: "I went into our principal's office and asked him, 'Do we have to go outside today?' He said, 'Well, it's the boys' turn inside. Where would you go? And what's wrong?' I felt almost silly when I said, 'They detonated a bomb this morning.' He was very supportive, very understanding. He said, 'I'll go with you to show you there isn't anything to worry about.' "

Looking back, Irene shudders at the memory. By the end of 1955, the principal was dead from cancer. "He was such a good guy," Irene says. "A wonderful man. I'll always remember him."

Later, the boys basketball coach also developed cancer and died.

By that time, most of the young men of the drum and bugle corps had married and started families. When the first of her girls died, Irene was deeply shocked. Then, she heard about another cancer case. Then another. One day, in 1975, a cancer screening clinic for women was announced in church. Just that morning, Irene had discovered a lump in her breast.

She remembers attending the clinic in the basement of the church. Women of the town in paper dresses. Afterwards, women crying. She remembers the cheerful, smiling face of Rama Yardley, one of the stalwarts of the Corps. By then, Rama was married, a mother. "She was blonde, very attractive," Irene says. "A capable, efficient person. She had just been told she had cancer, but that day, she was her usual optimistic self."

Within five years, Rama would be dead.

Irene herself took the advice of the clinic's doctor and went immediately to Salt Lake City, where she had a radical mastectomy. Afterward she could no longer play the piano; but she managed, once more, to play hymns on the organ. That Christmas, Clem surprised her with an organ just like the one in church.

There continued to be excessive demand for her playing. The president of a nearby college, who was the son of a highly admired local historian, died of leukemia. The doctor's wife succumbed to liver cancer. Another Drum and Bugle girl learned she had it.

In a drive around town, Irene illustrates the overwhelming cumulative effect of all this. "There isn't a block where it hasn't hit," she says, pointing. House after house, street after street. Over and over again. "It strikes—and keeps on striking," she says.

Last year, in 1982, Irene's brother had part of his intestines removed.

Clem's uncle is battling cancer now, undergoing long, debilitating treatments in Las Vegas.

There is no doubt now about what is causing it, and the courts are clogged with lawsuits. One set of suits concerns servicemen involved in the bombings and the tests. Another covers ranchers whose sheep died by the thousands from throat cancer as a result of the radiation.

Although not litigious, the McEwens have joined hundreds of other Utah residents in a lawsuit which they hope will bring the problem to public attention. They have little optimism, however, that much will change.

True, the tests have now been moved underground, but Clem and Irene are not reassured. Says she, "Now the question is, how much radiation is being released underground and seeping into the earth? How fast is it traveling?"

When maroon clouds gather over St. George, where Melanie and Clem, Jr., live with their families, and where the senior McEwens now spend their winters, Irene says, "We go out and gather the little ones in like a bunch of old settin' hens. All up and down the valley, mothers now bring in the children whenever the air looks bad."

But she bridles at the suggestion that they move away from Utah. "Our roots are here," she says. "This is our heritage, the land of our fathers. Our grandparents died for our right to be here, to live in peace and worship God the way we wanted to." Patriotism tangles her tongue as she adds, "I never dreamed that our government would do this to its own. It shreds you on the inside to realize that it not only did, but continues to do it."

Irene keeps a file, for the use of her family, of the best treatment centers for different kinds of cancer. And she tries not to worry.

When she lets herself think about the young casualties, Irene weeps first for Edna Beth Talbott.

Edna Beth was president of her seventh grade class, and one of Irene's favorites. She married another of Irene's students. When she was 27 and pregnant with her fourth child, she was told she had lung cancer. One day she came over to Irene's house and told her that 10 doctors had been called in as consultants on her case. Five had recommended an abortion; five had recommended against it. Edna Beth was left with the decision.

"My baby has the right to live," she told Irene. As the tortured young woman spoke, Irene remembers thinking, "She's telling me this because she can't face telling her own mother." Then, with a shock, the truth struck her: Edna Beth was telling her the story so that Irene could tell it at her funeral.

Edna Beth gave birth to a baby, a girl named Stormy. Then she died.

"If people could see what I saw that day at the church when they brought her casket down the aisle, with her young husband following it, those three little children hanging to his knees, that tiny baby he was carrying, that heartbroken mother and father . . . it was the saddest sight I've ever seen."

Irene *did* tell Edna Beth's story at her funeral. She astonished herself that she could remain composed. "But then," she says, "when they lowered her body into the grave, I collapsed." Since Edna Beth died in 1975, both her parents have developed cancer.

Neither Clem nor Irene likes, or wants, to come across a "cancer cripple." Indeed, they both appear healthy, vibrant and alive. Still, they live under a cloud. It casts a shadow on their lives and the lives of everyone they love. Their Melanie is pregnant now. They are all praying. Each pregnancy is a gamble; each normal birth, a triumph.

Irene knows that people in other parts of the country are beginning to be afraid of nuclear devastation. She has heard them speculate that in another war, it could reach America.

She wants them to know that it not only could. It has.

The first five paragraphs are a species of summary lead. They set the locale, introduce Irene, who will be the spokesperson and symbol of the town, establish the conflict—man against death—and set the quiet, almost elegaic, tone of the piece and the initial innocence of the people. The last two sentences state the threat and thus start the suspense that keeps you reading.

Remsberg sketches the town's characteristics, which will make the coming tragedy more poignant: "the good life, the warmth of church, family activities"; Irene even marries the boy next door. She tells us enough about Irene's actions and goals so that she will be real and important to us. Irene, and the whole village, represent the traditional values of the American small town, so we realize the story is not just about one isolated group of people, but about all of us.

Then Remsburg emphasizes the people's love of country—"we schedule our lives around what's important to it"—and this is verified by the sacrifices they make for it during World War II. It is important to show this, for it is this patriotism that will be the foil for the government's actions that produce the tragedy. This section ends with the irony of the promise they saw in the dropping of the first atomic bomb at Hiroshima.

The disillusionment begins with the reading of John Hersey's *Hiroshima;* Irene, perhaps alone in town, realizes its importance enough to read it to her classes. Still, the soldiers come home and life resumes its peaceful ways. And this one-sentence paragraph is another sign of Remsberg's artistry, for it forms one side of the contrast which make the following sections so powerful.

Quietly, with no polemics, Remsberg tells us that the atomic testing was moved to the mainland because safer testing in the Pacific was "too expensive." And the people greeted the first test as a kind of celebration, an affirmation of their country's power. This ends with the two-sentence paragraph, "There was nothing else. Nothing you could see, or feel, or smell, or hear." What makes these two quiet sentences heavy with omen is the reader's knowledge of the silent death that first test exploded into the air; Remsberg knew this and was artist enough to let us see it and understand it, too.

Then comes the paragraph about the Geiger counter and the almost gleeful, "See, we've got radiation here," as though this gave the isolated town a part in an important national adventure. And this, of course, emphasizes the innocence of the people and the time.

Remsberg creates suspense with the doctor's statement that he had been seeing an unusual number of miscarriages, then builds it with the report of the healthy outdoorsmen who are getting cancer. The paragraph on the Mormon custom of keeping family histories is necessary both to prove to the reader that there is factual support for the unusual incidence of cancer and to explain why Irene would be the most aware of the creeping plague.

Now the disease strikes home and Remsberg reports it by telling the details: Clem's tongue cancer, the cases of the girls in the Drum and Bugle Corps. To help the reader understand how heavily this plague has hit, it is necessary to describe the town's involvement with the Corps; a detail like standing the girls in a line and pinning their skirts so all will be the same length makes the picture come alive. The anecdote about the principal overcoming Irene's objections to taking the girls outside particularizes the threat, then drives it home with "by the end of 1955 the principal was dead from cancer."

Now Remsberg begins to build the action by reporting the increasing number of deaths and including the lump in Irene's own breast. One dramatic device that Remsberg uses several times here is ending a paragraph, or an anecdote, with a blockbuster statement. Rama Yardley, for example: "she was her usual optimistic self" is followed immediately by "Within five years, Rama would be dead." Note, too, that in such cases Remsberg uses no adjectives; her prose is simple, factual. This unquestionably heightens its impact; the emotional content of the statement is so strong that any attempt to heighten it with dramatic language would be too much and the statement would lose effectiveness.

Then Remsberg summarizes the devastating effects of the epidemic and builds the suspense with the paragraph describing the drive around town. Note how much more effective this description of people doing something is, than would be a simple statement of the statistics of the deaths.

Honest journalism requires that Remsberg report the growing lawsuits against the government, even though this fact undercuts the mood of patriotism and innocence that she has been building. She ascribes it to the townspeople's hope that it "will bring the problem to public attention"— which some may find questionable. And, knowing what her ending is going to be, Remsberg has a loose end to clear up: the tests have moved underground, but Clem and Irene are not reassured.

Then comes the only direct attack by Irene on the government which has allowed this tragedy to hit: "I never dreamed that our government would do this to its own." Even this is muted, and probably more effective because of it.

Remsberg presents the climax of her story with the account of Edna Beth. Because it is the climax, she must go into some detail about the relationship between Irene and Edna Beth, such as the talk they had about Edna Beth's possible abortion and the description of her funeral.

Remsberg has now all but completed her story; there remains the need to mention what the future will likely bring and to emphasize the significance of this little story by showing the broader picture. She does it with the next-to-last paragraph. Then she writes the final two sentences, which are clearly Remsberg speaking, but, consistent with the focus of the entire piece on Irene, she attributes the sentiment to her. The restraint of these two sentences unquestionably heightens their impact.

13

What Does It Look Like? How Does It Smell?

Salina, Kan.—The short, winding streets of Schilling Manor are silent in the early darkness of an autumn evening.

Homework and the chill p ⸱rie wind have imprisoned the children in the neat, one-story duplexes and small single-family homes of the development two miles west of Salina. But everywhere are reminders of their presence—an overturned tricycle silhouetted in the gathering gloom, a forgotten football nestled in a patch of brown lawn.

Dinner time is near and the lights of the tiny community are beacons of warmth and welcome. But inside the homes, the women fussing in kitchens, setting tables, urging grimy youngsters to try soap on their hands this time, have tired eyes.

Not the ordinary workaday tired eyes of too much housework, too active children and a fallen cake in the oven. The tired eyes of absence, responsibility and frequently of a fear painfully unspoken.

For in the streets of Schilling Manor there is no rush of weary husband traffic. And in the houses there is no before-dinner moment for unburdening math problems and football furstrations, no martini ritual to soothe household anxieties. The husbands of Schilling Manor are career servicemen and they are gone—most of them to Vietnam. (Douglas E. Kneeland, "Lonely G.I. Wives," *New York Times*)

*H*ere Kneeland brings his scene and his people alive by using specific details: "an overturned tricycle silhouetted in the gathering gloom," "women fussing in kitchens, setting tables," "and a fallen cake in the over." The mood is one of quiet and desperation.

Other writers have set similiar scenes many times, but this has a uniqueness that makes it stand out for the reader as something new. And that's what every writer is after when putting together a description. For there really is almost nothing that hasn't been written about before, yet creative writers are constantly presenting us with scenes and people that seem new. They do it by giving us the particular and significant details of the particular place or person. And it works because, while few situations are new, *this* situation of *this* person has some qualities that are individual and unique.

To accomplish this happy result, writers must train themselves to observe. Simple? Not so simple. The average person doesn't see a room, a landscape, a meeting, a person with much attention to detail. Unless we train ourselves to do otherwise, we get an overall impression of color, shapes, dominant emotions, an aura that serves very well for normal purposes. But as writers we must do more; we have to be able to re-create the scene for our readers, which means we must experience its overall impression, then go on to analyze it and make notes of those details that distinguish this scene or action from all others.

You do it by focusing down on details of a scene, then trying, while you're looking at them, to put together the precise words that will convey their unique flavor. For example, once I was walking around the backyard of my house in the snow while trying to think through the organization of an article. I wasn't seeing much; my mind was turned inward, wrestling with the problem. I stopped before a large azalea bush, looking at it but not seeing it. Suddenly a film seemed to drop from my eyes (I think it was really the mind's old trick of finding anything at all to interrupt hard work), and I began to see the bush. I saw that each branch ended in a little cluster of four or five twigs, and caught within their black prongs was a tiny cone of snow. The whole bush was a skeleton globe decorated with the little cones, like the whipped cream rosettes on a birthday cake. Not an earth-shaking perception, of course, but merely another of those realized pictures that a writer constantly files away to pull out and use sometime. Like now.

It seems to us that writing, which for the reader seems to flow so smoothly and fast, is the laborious putting on paper of these thousands of perceptions that have been built up one by one over the years, that a writer is working twenty-four hours a day, perceiving, analyzing, putting into words, filing away bits of reality like this. We learn to do it by doing it. And the only initial step it takes, we think, is to make an adjustment in your mind so that you not only look at things, you see them and tell yourself what they look like—or sound, or smell, or taste or feel like.

This is both the curse and the blessing of writers. A curse because once you get your mind trained to do it, it never stops and there's always a cool, detached little figure sitting up there in the back of your mind with a notebook taking down what you are experiencing. He never stops and the price you pay for him is that you never again become involved in an experience wholly, with nothing held back. The blessing is that, with the scales gone from your eyes, you perceive in vivid colors the richness and variety of the world each of us rents for a lifetime.

Writers share this ability with visual artists. His canvas before him, the painter wants to re-create the sky and water before him. The water, of course, is blue—or green or black or silver. Suppose it is blue, what color blue? What colors will he choose from his palette to reproduce the precise blue of the water? To decide he must analyze and experiment: a little cerulean blue, some white, a touch of green perhaps, some umber? When you see the finished picture you get little shock of recognition—yes, that's it, that's it—but you never know the thought and trial and failure that has gone into it.

How do you get started on the process? Well, what words would you use to describe the cry of a sea gull? Shrill? Raucous? Lonely? Strident? Happy? Angry? Resonant—with a feeling of space? Or what does a new car smell like? Exciting? Oil? Plastic? Spicy? Leather? Rubber? Paint? A combination of which of these? You can spend ten or fifteen minutes thinking about each of these, refining out the precise words that recreate the feeling you get from the experience. And this is precisely what a writer does in describing something. The description you read in five seconds probably took the writer an hour to get on paper.

Here, for example, is a description of an animal with which we are all familiar, but which we see anew through the eyes of the writer, Alexander Theroux, whose article "How Curious the Camel," appeared in *Reader's Digest*.

A camel has been described as a horse planned by committee. It has a comic munch of a face—loony, serene and disgusted all at once—with liquid eyes that shine bottle-green at night. Its eyelashes are as long as Ann Sheridan's. Its large nostrils can close against blowing sand. A ruminant, it chews its cud, and its floppy lips, seemingly insensitive to thorny plants, cover teeth long enough to eat an apple through a picket fence. You can almost chin yourself on its bad breath.

It is a large creature, reaching lengths of ten feet and standing about seven feet at the shoulder. Its smooth padfeet, each with two toes united at the sole by a web of skin, serve long, pistonlike legs able to gallop at up to 15 m.p.h. (though it much prefers to walk). It can live 40 years, spits, can travel untold miles of waterless desert. Its stomach contains a wet cud—the half-chewed slop that the animal sucks back up to its mouth with a slobbering sound as it plods along, all the while gurgling as if to remind the rider of the liquid inside its body.

There's another dimension to this business, though. The details you see and choose to write must be not only true, but significant. They must convey more in perception or emotion than they do in words. In *The Content of Writing*, Richard B. Sewall of Yale has an apt illustration—"the tailored woman down for the weekend from Smith, who forgot to clean her fingernails."

Here's another example, from "Country Boy Makes Pretty Good," a profile of Tom Brokaw written by Lynn Darling for *Esquire*.

Yankton, South Dakota, lies on a bluff overlooking the Missouri River, a low-slung town of pickup trucks parked diagonally on broad empty streets, a place where both the Sunday morning sermon and the Saturday night saloon can count on collecting a crowd. The former territorial capital of the Dakotas, Yankton was the last stop on the riverboats' run, a jumping-off point, a town that understood the language of the last chance. It was also the place where outlaw Jack McCall was hanged for shooting Wild Bill Hickok, but that was as hot as it ever got here in Tom Brokaw's hometown.

In just over 100 words, Darling has taken her readers to Brokaw's hometown, and let them see and feel what it is like to be there. We see this "low-slung town of pickup trucks parked diagonally on broad empty streets" where "both the Sunday morning sermon and the Saturday night saloon" draw crowds—and presumably nothing else does for the rest of the week.

In his article on Ralph Nader, the lead of which is reproduced in chapter 10, Ken Auletta used different types of details to show Nader's austere style of living.

One sees Nader's persistence in his shoes. They are low-cut black Army dress shoes with worn, slanted heels. When he served as a cook in the Army in 1959, Nader says, he purchased twelve pairs of low-cuts for six dollars apiece at the PX. He now wears the eleventh pair, and he says that to buy new heels would cost more than he paid for the shoes. Nader has not purchased a pair of dress shoes since, and he boasts of the one new pair waiting in the closet of his one-room efficiency apartment in

Washington, just off Dupont Circle. Nor has Nader purchased a pair of socks since selecting four dozen calf-length cotton-and-wool socks for thirty-five cents a pair at the PX. "I only regret that I didn't buy two dozen more," he says.

Auletta obviously obtained much of that material from an interview, but his reporter's attentiveness to detail was what made him ask Nader about the shoes in the first place. It also enabled him to write the following:

Recently, Nader accepted a tuna fish sandwich only after quizzing the activist who picked him up at the Boston airport, "Is this today's tuna?"; he grilled two different students about whether the grape punch served at Salem State College was real grape; at Oswego, he was thirsty but would not allow the red punch to touch his lips, wondered why the fish served at dinner was fried, and was shocked that anyone would touch the roast beef, saying, "Did you see how red that meat was?" Although Nader can laugh at himself, he says he eats only 14 pounds of red meat a year, can tell you how many teaspoons of sugar are in a can of Coke (nine), and has in the past referred to cigarette smokers as being "weak" in character.

While Auletta is describing behavior, rather than a town or a street, he uses the same techniques as the writers whose work we looked at above. (We'll have more to say about bringing characters to life in chapter 15.)

It's selection again. You make note of the details of the experience, then select those that evoke a common experience or present a larger reality. Perceiving the hidden glories and understanding the larger realities of a situation are what add depth to a writer's work—and, not at all incidentally, to his or her life.

One Memorial Day weekend a friend asked me to crew on his magnificent Herreshoff sloop in a race from Larchmont, around Block Island, and back. It was a slow, man-killer of a race. The breeze was so slight that you had to adjust the sails constantly, repeatedly take down one jib and put up another to catch each cupful of wind; twice we had to anchor to keep from going backward in a foul tide. In the first night and day we got virtually no sleep.

By the second night we had been becalmed off Montauk Point for nine hours. I caught a couple of hour's sleep below and came on deck to relieve the skipper at the helm at about 3 A.M. He sat in the cockpit with me for ten or fifteen minutes, then went below for some sleep, and I was alone with the ship.

I was cold. It was the first of June, and I was wearing woolen socks, chinos, foul-weather pants, a Swedish fisherman's shirt, a woolen shirt, a sweater, foul-weather jacket, wool cap and gloves; I stood behind the wheel and shivered.

I was lonely. The sea is an alien place, not warm like the land, but cold, impersonal, heaving with massive power, and in its depths lurks terror. There was not another boat in sight, and the only light symbolizing other humans was the automatic aero beacon on Block Island that swept the sky in ominous mechanical exactness and made me think of *Wuthering Heights*.

I was scared. I'd managed to get the boat moving on a drift of air out of the northeast, but I wasn't sure where I was going. The light on the binnacle was so dim and the compass card so yellow that I couldn't read it as I stood behind the wheel. I was coming up on Block Island but didn't know exactly where it was. I'd sailed enough to know there's a loom off the land that makes a line in the water, but it isn't the shoreline. Many a man has sailed his boat up onto the beach—or the rocks—deceived by that line. I was not at all anxious to do this, because the skipper didn't think much more of the boat than he did of his right arm, and because there were five people below, sleeping in trust of me.

It went on like that for almost three hours. Then the light began in the east and after a while the tip of the sun came up out of the ocean off the starboard bow. And suddenly I could see Block Island and knew where I was. Off to the north were three or four other boats, warm with company. And the sun began to warm me. A little later, when I was relieved, I was so grateful I went forward, stripped to the waist, and rolled in the sunlight like a cat.

Weeks later, thinking about it, I suddenly knew how primitive humans must have felt when the rising sun drove off the terrors of the night. And I knew why sun worship played a part in so many religions. I understood why the rising of the sun was the miracle of creation.

Much better writers than this one have used their awareness of larger realities to add dimension to their description. Bruce Catton, for instance, in *A Stillness at Appomattox*:

It was the fourth day of May, and beyond the dark river there was a forest with the shadow of death under its low branches and the dogwood blossoms were floating in the air like lost flecks of sunlight, as if life were as important as death; and for the Army of the Potomac this was the last bright morning, with youth and strength and hope ranked under starred flags, bugle calls riding down the wind, and invisible doors swinging open on the other shore. The regiments fell into line, and great white-topped wagons creaked along the roads, and the spring sunlight glinted off the polished muskets and the brass of the guns, and the young men came down to the valley while the bands played. A German regiment was singing "John Brown's Body."

Beside the roads the violets were in bloom, and the bush honeysuckle was out, and the day and the year had a fragile light that the endless columns would soon trample to fragments. The last campaign had begun, and a staff officer sat on a bank overlooking the Rapidan and had a curious thought: how odd it would be if every man who was to die in the days just ahead had to wear a big badge today, so that a man watching by the river could identify all those who were never coming back!

Even historians, writing nearly a hundred years after the event, by using acute observation, careful selection, and an understanding of larger realities, can write a description that lets you *be* there.

14

Mobilizing the Reader's Experience

*E*ven back in the days of "just the facts" journalism there were
emotional writers. They were called sob sisters—but many were
men—and they slapped it on with a shovel. Other reporters, smug in
their rationalism, scorned them. But particularly in the innocence of the
twenties and in the more garish tabloids, they were stars in the eyes of the
circulation manager. They dealt mostly in primary emotions: sexual titilla-
tion; pity; maudlin sentimentality; bathos. There are still a few of them
around in the more backward newspapers.

But even while they were still the darlings of those editors who hadn't
changed their judgment of news values in half a century, the slow evolution of more sophisticated interpretive writers was showing them their
age. Today the best creative journalists evoke the emotions of their readers
with the deftness of a Tolstoy.

It was inevitable. Emotions play far too large a part in all our lives to be
ignored, as they were by journalistic devotees of the age of reason. The
mass of people perceive things far more convincingly with their emotions
than with their minds, and no serious journalist could afford to ignore this
weapon in the arsenal of communication. As Freya Stark said, the whole
generalship of writing is in the marshalling of the reader's reserves of
understanding and experience.

If you want to get philosophical about it, this development is probably
the journalist's application of the ideas of existentialism. Perhaps it started
with a theory that Hemingway developed in his early days in Paris. In *A
Moveable Feast* he wrote: "It was a very simple story called 'Out of Season'
and I had omitted the real end of it which was that the old man hanged
himself. This was omitted on my new theory that you could omit anything
if you knew what you omitted and the omitted part would strengthen the
story and make people feel something more than they understood."

When he developed this theory he was writing a story called "Big Two-hearted River." It was about a man who takes a camping-fishing trip alone in Michigan, and he is obsessed that everything he does must be done exactly right. So you know he is trying to put some structure back into his life after some experience which has shaken him to the core. Of it, Hemingway wrote, "The story was about coming back from the war but there was no mention of the war in it." I had thought the cataclysm that had struck the man was a divorce; war never occurred to me. Thus I drew on my own feelings for an understanding of the situation, and to me the man's motivation was just as valid as the one Hemingway had in mind. This is the deepest kind of involvement by the reader, and it's what Marshall McLuhan meant when he called writing a "cool" medium.

So what has all this to do with existentialism? Webster says existentialism "regards human existence as not exhaustively describable or understandable in idealistic or scientific terms . . ." So if you can't describe human existence in scientific (read rational) terms, you convey understanding by reporting the human situation as it happened, with close attention to those aspects of it that will trigger emotional responses in your reader.

It is artistry, of course, that enables a writer to select and present the kind of material that will evoke an emotional response by the reader. But we think there are some identifiable techniques, too. One of them, surprisingly enough, is cool objectivity.

The *New York Times* uses this repeatedly when it reports, each year, its "100 Neediest Cases."

Eleanor C. is only 18, but for almost a year she has struggled single-handed to make a home for her brothers—Eric, 14, Johnny, 12, and Tommy, 9.

Two years ago the children's mother died of cancer. Last January, when their father died of a kidney ailment, Eleanor, a high school senior, immediately left school, determined to keep the family together. But she found it difficult to budget her father's veteran's benefits, and the unfamiliar household tasks were overwhelming. The boys, grieving for their parents, became unmanageable. Recently, despairing of her ability to keep going, Eleanor sought help from the agency.

An agency homemaker is now bringing order and stability into the home, and Eleanor, relieved of some of her burden, plans to complete her schooling and seek a secretarial job. A "Big Brother" has been assigned to Tommy, who seems most affected by his father's death. In the year ahead, Eleanor will need continued guidance in her valiant struggle to keep her orphaned brothers together.

There are really only two "emotional" adjectives in the piece: "valiant" and "orphaned," in the last sentence.

It seems to us that when you're dealing with material that has as much emotional dynamite as this, the impact is heightened by this kind of objective writing. If you tried to build up the effect with more adjectives and adverbs, you'd run the risk of becoming maudlin.

The strength such starkness creates was shown by a recent *Times* article by Andrew H. Malcolm. It began:

ROCHESTER—When the 69-year-old man entered the hospital here recently he thought he had only a back problem. When he left for home six days later he had chosen to die.

In between, he learned he had a fatal illness and had to make the decision confronting a growing number of aging Americans: whether to prolong his life aggressively with medical machines and modern technology or surrender to the natural dying process very soon. The patient—call him Robert Anderson, although that is not his real name— chose to give up.

'I Want to Go Home'

"I want to go home," he told Dr. Richard B. Freeman, a specialist he had met only recently.

Dr. Freeman leaned over the bed and asked, "You understand what this decision means?"

Mr. Anderson nodded, and then smiled. Dr. Freeman patted his patient's hands. And in a moment the two said farewell.

Notice the simplicity and starkness of Malcolm's prose, and the power it gives to the anecdote. A less-skilled writer might have loaded that section with adjectives and adverbs in an attempt to be sure that the reader got the point. But Malcolm knew that the story of a man's decision to die was powerful, and that the more simply it was told, the greater its effect would be.

He uses this stark writing style later in the piece, when he describes the meeting during which Dr. Freeman told Anderson that he had cancer. Malcolm is convinced that the doctor is a caring and concerned man, but again, Malcolm lets the doctor's actions prove the point.

Dr. Freeman had a cup of coffee before entering the patient's room that Wednesday morning, five days after meeting Mr. Anderson. "Hello," Dr. Freeman said, "How're you feeling?"

"I'm not off to a very good start today," said a pale Mr. Anderson. "My bones hurt a lot."

"Uh, huh," said the doctor. "Well, you've been poked and probed a good deal here."

"You'll have to speak up," said the patient. "My wife's hard of hearing—and so am I."

"That's right," said Mrs. Anderson. "Don't blame it all on me." And the trio chuckled.

Careful Choice of Words

Dr. Freeman raised the volume of his voice a notch. "I'll be as straightforward and honest as possible with you," he said. "You said you wanted that. I have a feeling you already know what's going on in your body, but let me tell you what we know and you can begin to think about what we do next."

The doctor chose his words carefully, using pauses and firm gazes to emphasize the seriousness of his words. He outlined Mr. Anderson's medical history, the back operation and the lethal calcium problem.

"Now, why did this happen?" asked the doctor. "There are many holes in your bones. Some of your ribs are broken. There are lumps on your kidneys and bladder and lungs. These are tumors. And they're spreading. You kind of thought that, didn't you?"

Mr. Anderson nodded.

"Can we do anything?" the doctor continued. "Maybe. We don't know yet what kind of tumors these are. There are hundreds of kinds. A few respond to treatment. Some go away." He paused. "Others we can't do much about."

He paused again. "We'll be very honest with you about the outlook," he went on. "But I won't have all the information for a day or so. Any questions?"

"No."

"You knew it?"

"Yup. Keep right on it, Doc."

"I will, but—are you a football fan?—well, it's fourth down, Mr. Anderson."

"Thank you very much, doctor."

"I don't know," the doctor said softly, "if 'thank you' is the right thing to say."

"What did you say, Doc?"

"Nothing," said Dr. Freeman, "I'll be back later."

Notes on a Chart

On the patient's chart Dr. Freeman noted the conversation and added: "Family and patient still have some hope. Pls do not give final negative prognosis yet. Perhaps tonite or tmw."

Again, Malcolm understands the power of his material. The writer who has a good story to tell should tell it simply. He needn't comment on it. The reader will get the point and feel the emotions if the story is told well, as this one was, from the beginning to the ending, which follows.

That evening when Dr. Freeman returned to Mr. Anderson's room to continue the grim prognosis, the patient was dozing. "Oh, good morning, doctor," said a glazed Mr. Anderson, "How are you today?"

"Nurse," said Dr. Freeman, "what have you got him on?" The answer was morphine; his pain had been too great. "So much for rational discussion this evening," said the doctor.

'The Two-Minute Warning'

The next morning Mr. Anderson was alert. "I've talked to the oncologist," the doctor said. "We can only treat some of this pain with radiation. That will raise the calcium. And then we can clean your blood every couple of days with an artificial kidney. But you might find this a miserable prolongation of things. I'm afraid things are not going to improve. The outlook is, uh, well, the two-minute warning is in."

"I understand," said the man. "We've talked about it. And I want to go home. I appreciate everything you all have done. It's been the greatest care in the world."

"I wish I could do more," said the doctor.

"Me too," said the man, smiling. "It's a very poor deal. But I'll try to put some more points on the board."

"I'm sure you will." And the doctor kissed the man's forehead.

"I'm sure I'll see you again," said the patient. But the doctor did not respond.

Outside the room he spoke to Mrs. Anderson. "I don't want to give you any false hopes," he said. "We're talking a few days to a week."

"I thought so," she said.

After arranging the immediate transfer back to the rural hospital and consulting Mr. Anderson's doctor there, a grim Dr. Freeman walked down the hall past some laughing visitors. "I don't know what's right," he said. "I just do my best."

That was Thursday noon. Sunday morning at the rural hospital, about three hours before dawn, Mr. Anderson's heart stopped. He and his wife had agreed to a Do Not Resuscitate order. When the alarm sounded, the nurses did nothing.

The death certificate said Robert Anderson died of "cardiopulmonary arrest."

The same kind of starkness was used with great effect by J. Anthony Lukas in his famous piece in the *New York Times*, "The Two Worlds of Linda Fitzpatrick." (The article is expanded and reprinted in Lukas's book, *Don't Shoot—We Are Your Children!*)

The underlying theme of Lukas's piece is that Linda Fitzpatrick's parents knew nothing at all about her "other" life, which included "crash pads, acid trips, freaking out, psychedelic art, witches and warlocks," and which ultimately led to her murder. For example, Lukas described the Fitzpatricks' decision to allow Linda to leave their luxurious Greenwich, Connecticut, home and live in Greenwich Village:

"She told us she was going to live at the Village Plaza Hotel, a very nice hotel on Washington Place, near the university, you know," her mother said.

"'I'll be perfectly safe, mother,' she kept saying. 'It's a perfectly nice place with a doorman and a television.' She said she'd be rooming with a girl named Paula Bush, a 22-year-old receptionist from a good family. That made us feel a lot better."

The Village Plaza, 79 Washington Place, has no doorman. A flaking sign by the tiny reception desk announces "Television for rental" amidst a forest of other signs: "No Refunds," "All Rents Must Be Paid in Advance," "No Checks Cashed," "No Outgoing Calls for Transients."

"Sure I remember Linda," said the stooped desk clerk. "But Paula Bush? There wasn't no Paula Bush. It was Paul Bush."

Ruffling through a pile of stained and thumb-marked cards, he came up with one that had Linda Fitzpatrick's name inked at the top in neat Greenwich Country Day School penmanship. Below it in pencil was written: "Paul Bush. Bob Brumberger."

"Yeh," the clerk said. "She moved in here on Sept. 4, Labor Day, with these two hippie guys, Bush and Brumberger. They had Room 504. She paid the full month's rent—$120—in advance. Of course, she had lots of other men up there all the time. Anybody off the street—the dirtiest bearded hippies she could find."

In my files I have a folder labeled "Humility Department"; it contains a dozen or so clippings that I sometimes read over when I begin to feel satisfied with my own work. One of them, from a book entitled *The Last Days of Sevastopol*, by a Russian journalist named Boris J. Voyetekhov, is one of the finest examples I know of delicacy and restraint in handling emotional material.

Sevastopol is on a peninsula sticking out into the Black Sea. In World War II the German armies sealed off the mouth of the peninsula and moved down toward its tip. One detachment of Soviet soldiers was ordered to remain to cover the withdrawal of the wounded "until the last man." A captain, commanding the group, gave Mr. Voyetekhov a letter to his wife; it concluded:

I know that when I am dead, for you I will continue to live, and that nobody will edge me away from your careful heart. I know this wound will never heal. But if it happens that you meet a man fine enough for your grief whom you will love a little, and if as a result of your love you have a new life and it is a son, then let him bear my name. Let him be my continuation, though I am dead and your new friend is alive. This would not punish him, for not everybody must die, and if he cannot understand and would not like it, then leave him without sorrow or tears or longings and let it be not his but our son; and when a new Sevastopol is built, come here, and somewhere on Chersonese, somewhere near the sea, plant poppies. They grow here very well. And that will be my grave. It may be that you will make a mistake. Maybe it won't be I but another who lies there. It doesn't matter. Some one else will think of her own and plant flowers above me. Nobody will be left out, for we shall lie close, and there will be no space to spare where we lie.

15

"Get Some Narrative Into it"

O ne of the most frequent directions that editors gave me when I was trying to learn to write magazine articles was, "Get some narrative into it." For a long time I couldn't figure out precisely what they meant. After all, my job as a journalist, I thought, was to inform, to explain, to illuminate a set of facts, a situation; what did narrative—telling a story— have to do with this? I wasn't writing fiction, I was reporting fact.

It finally dawned on me what they meant, and when it did I had— though I didn't realize it until long afterward—one of the key differences between interpretive writing and conventional newswriting: you present your information not as disembodied facts or ideas, but in terms of people acting out those facts and ideas. And since you're showing people doing things, your job, if you have any artistry at all, is to arrange it as a story, a narrative. Suppose you want to write a piece saying that millions of Americans don't get enough to eat each day. You do it by writing about the men and women and children who live with hunger and who must struggle to survive. This allows you not only to explain the reasons for the problem, but also to work in the human story of people fighting against almost overwhelming odds. It's the human story that holds your readers' interest because they, too, probably have had to struggle to survive at some point in their lives, and they want to know how somebody else made it—or didn't. They pick up the facts and explanations you've included almost without realizing it.

This has been said before in earlier chapters, but what we haven't explored is the range of techniques that help you do the job. Narrative is one of the things a good interpretive writer borrows from fiction writers. It is telling a story, building suspense, putting your characters (and the reader) into a situation, and then taking them through it—complete with emotional involvements—to a resolution. It's not changing facts, but arranging them. It is plotting.

The skeleton of a plot goes like this: You introduce a main character, who must be admirable so the reader identifies with him and starts pulling for him. You introduce the element of conflict in your story: you give your character an objective and show him trying to reach that objective and failing. Finally, by his own efforts—usually as a result of a change in himself—he reaches his objective and collects the rewards, or pays the price. Like all skeletons, this is spare and oversimplified, but understanding it both helps you recognize a good story when you hear one, and guides your questioning when you are building a story and interviewing the people who lived the situation.

For example, when I was doing the research on the Commando Kelly piece that we discussed back in chapter 6, I began to see it as the story of a brave man, whose wife and family meant more to him than anything else, struggling to survive in a world he was not very well equipped to cope with. So, applying the formula:

* Kelly, of course, was the main character, which meant the piece had to focus on him throughout.

* I had to show he was admirable, which meant I had to get enough details so, right at the beginning, I could show him winning the Medal of Honor.

* I had to show his dominant characteristic—his love for his family—so I went after incidents and anecdotes that illustrated this.

* I had to show him struggling to preserve his family against odds, which meant I had to go after the details of his jobs, his income (showing why it was not enough to cover expenses), his unemployment and search for another job, his illness and fight against it.

* Finally, I had to show him winning his fight, which in this case meant surviving his illness, getting help to pay his bills, getting a new and better job.

You get this kind of information from interviews, but one of the key concepts of narrative writing is that you don't always present it in exactly the way you got it. For example, I got the details for the lead of the piece—Kelly and his first wife finding out she had terminal cancer—from the only survivor, Kelly himself. But I didn't present it as a long quote from Kelly. Instead, using the details he gave me, I recreated the scene itself so the reader could watch it unfold, instead of getting someone's account of it, secondhand.

In the *New York Times* interview mentioned earlier, Truman Capote told how he did the same sort of thing when he was writing *In Cold Blood:*

On the other hand, in that same first part [of the book], there's a scene between the postmistress and her mother when the mother reports that the ambulances have gone to the Clutter [the murder victims'] house. That's a straight dramatic scene—with quotes, dialogue, action, everything. But it evolved out of interviews. . . . Except in this case I took what they had told me and transposed it into straight narrative terms. Of course, elsewhere in the book, very often it's direct observation, events I saw myself—the trial, the executions.

As Capote said, it is possible to achieve great accuracy for purposes of reconstruction by careful and assiduous interviewing. For example, I once did a story for *Redbook* about a man, Earle Reynolds, who thought the testing of atomic bombs in the atmosphere was a threat to the world's children. (The story about the children of Utah in chapter 12 would seem to indicate that he was right. And the continuing protests about nuclear weapons testing would seem to prove a point made earlier, that many magazine stories are, in essence, timeless.) The United States had scheduled a series of such tests in the western Pacific Ocean and had barred all shipping from the area. Reynolds decided to protest the testing by sailing his boat into the prohibited zone, getting arrested, and thus forcing the whole issue into courts for a ruling.

I wanted to start the piece with the scene of the actual confrontation between Reynolds and his government—the moment of his arrest by the Coast Guard. I had to be able to visualize the scene in order to reconstruct it.

First I went aboard Reynold's boat, the *Phoenix*, and looked it over in detail—size of the cockpit, location of main hatchway to cabin, which bunk each member of the family slept in, location of the radiotelephone, and so forth. Then I borrowed the group interview technique, mentioned in chapter 5, that S. L. A. Marshall had told me about. I got all those who had been aboard the boat that night into Reynold's apartment and spent hours going over with them exactly what had happened, minute by minute. They checked each other; where one's memory of what had happened proved faulty, another would point it out:

"Then I got up and went on deck. . . ."

"No, you didn't; not then. It was later. Because I was at the helm and the first one up was Earle; you came up a minute or two later."

"Oh yes, that's right. I remember now, I was awake, but I didn't get up right away. . . ."

After I had taken the group through the entire scene (as well as what happened in the next few days) I had one side of the story. I needed the other, so I went down to Pearl Harbor and went aboard the Coast Guard buoy tender *Planetree*, which had made the arrest, looked over the ship, and interviewed her captain. Again, I took him through the confrontation minute by minute. Then, having both versions of the same set of actions, I reconstructed the scene:

The first move came at about eleven P.M. when they were 19 days out of Honolulu. Ted Reynolds, a thin, very mature 19-year-old, was on watch. "It was perfect trade wind sailing," he said. "The seas were moderate— about four or five feet high—and *Phoenix* was slipping along beautifully. It was very dark and suddenly off to the southeast I saw a light, the first since Honolulu. I immediately called the skipper."

The skipper, Dr. Earle L. Reynolds, a noted scientist, swung out of his bunk just below the cockpit and came on deck. He flipped on *Phoenix's* masthead light and he and Ted watched the other light on the horizon. In a few minutes they could make out a green running light, too, so they knew it was a ship and was heading for them. Earle Reynolds went below and called to the ship on the radio, but got no answer. His calling aroused everybody else aboard the 50-foot *Phoenix*—Earle's wife, Barbara, Jessica, their daughter, 14, and Niichi Mikami, a Japanese friend. All crowded into the small cockpit aft and watched the other ship approach. She was the Coast Guard buoy tender *Planetree* returning from a four-month trip into the far Pacific, and her captain, Commander Armand J. Bush, had been ordered to intercept the *Phoenix*.

She came on, looking bigger and more ominous as she approached the little *Phoenix*. She kept coming until she was so close her tall sides cut off the wind from *Phoenix's* sails, and the little boat became unmanageable, unable to get out of the way. The Reynolds stopped breathing; they knew the heavy steel *Planetree* could crack their boat like a walnut.

Earle Reynolds went back to the radio and called again, "Please talk on the radio." No answer. (Commander Bush told me later he hadn't heard Reynolds. This seems unlikely, and Bush added, "Even if I had heard him I wanted to talk face to face. That way I knew who I was talking to.")

But *Planetree* didn't quite hit the *Phoenix*. Slowly she came to a stop beside and astern the wallowing ketch. Over the noise of the slapping sails, the wash of the seas and the rumble of *Planetree's* idling engines Bush called, "Are you all right?"

"We're fine, thanks," Reynolds replied.

Bush gave him their position, then gave him the position of the prohibited zone where the U.S. Atomic Energy Commission was testing nuclear bombs. He quoted the AEC regulation forbidding American citizens to enter the zone and said the area ahead was dangerous. Then he asked, "Are you going to enter the zone or go around?" "Enter," Reynolds called back. "Where?" "Fourteen degrees north." No more was said. The *Planetree* dropped astern for the rest of the night and followed at a distance of three or four miles.

Like many narratives, this story was written on two levels—the intellectual argument against nuclear testing and the human drama of a family risking their lives and freedom to protest a governmental act they believed to be wrong.

In putting the story together it was necessary to work on both levels. For example, in both I had to handle motivation: *why* did they do this? On the intellectual level I did it by reporting that Earle Reynolds, a noted physical anthropologist, had been sent by the National Academy of Sciences to Hiroshima to study the effects of atomic radiation on the growth and development of children; the deleterious effects he found helped explain why he made the protest. On the human level I tried to handle it by concentrating on Reynolds's wife, Barbara. She not only had an active social conscience, she was determined to hold her family together, and if Reynolds was to sail into the forbidden zone, she would go along.

It was also necessary to carry the narrative along on two levels—both climaxing in the decision to make the trip. I tried to handle the "intellectual" by showing Reynolds doing a research study of the effects of testing in the atomsphere, then bringing his findings home each night and talking them over with Barbara and the kids. In the process the case against testing was made by reporting the specific things Reynolds learned. On the "human" level I showed Barbara and Earle arguing out the decision on whether to take the children along on the protest voyage. In the course of the argument the danger becomes clear and suspense grows.

I think I didn't succeed very well. It's difficult to report the drama of a decision that somebody makes because it is an internal process; you have to get inside a person's mind and first understand, then try to show the battle of the pros and cons. Writing about thoughts doesn't make very sensational reading; about the best you can do is try to find actions that reflect the thoughts and write about them. In this case I tried to do it by showing Earle and Barbara talking out the pros and cons. Rereading it later, I saw that it slowed the narrative down and wasn't very convincing.

Another technique you use in narrative is to play it like an accordion. You can't possibly report everything that happened during the time span your story covers. You need to lay certain foundations for the story—like "qualifying" Earle as an expert on radiation effects or explaining Barbara's role. You must tell enough about your characters' backgrounds so readers feel they know them. Much of this material is purely factual and when it is, I think the thing to do is compress it into the shortest possible space. You pack your sentences full; this alone helps give a feeling of pace and movement. For example, in the section on Earle's background, I reported that both his parents were killed when he was in high school so he had to get a job and support himself; but he also took correspondence courses at the University of Chicago in an effort to get a college degree. Then this paragraph:

One June when he got back his examination paper in a course in anthropology from the University of Chicago, the professor had scribbled on it, "You better come up and see me." That autumn Earle and Barbara arrived in Chicago with no money and a determination to get Earle a degree. The professor helped get him a job on a research project and Barbara, who had graduated from Teacher's College, Columbia University, got a teaching job. This pattern of work and study marked their lives—except for time out for Barbara to have two of their three children (Tim and Ted)—for the next six years while Earle earned his bachelor's degree in anthropology from Chicago, then his master's and doctorate from the University of Wisconsin.

But your readers, I think, won't hold still for too much of this, so you have to get through it quickly, then give them a break by telling a story. And the stories must be given enough space so they can involve the reader's emotions. For example, after the "compression" section on their background, I got into the explanation of the relations—and conflicts— within the family. Because the piece was for *Redbook*, a women's magazine, I concentrated on Barbara. The situation was this: in Hiroshima, Earle had built a boat and decided to fulfill a lifelong dream of sailing around the world. Then this:

Barbara didn't want to go. She was afraid of the water—her father had drowned in a sailing accident while she was a child. But she also knew how determined Earle was. Sitting in the cockpit of the *Phoenix* at Honolulu a few weeks ago, she explained:

"I knew he was going to do it and if he did it would be an important experience in his life. Well, if a marriage is to be good, there ought to be as few important experiences as possible that haven't been shared by both partners. So I said I'd go along." She looked off toward the rugged black mountains of Oahu for a moment, then with a rueful smile, added: "I also thought if I sailed with him to Honolulu, I could get him to sell the boat and go back to normal living."

She couldn't. From Honolulu the family sailed around the world in the *Phoenix* and during the four years it took, they all had experiences that made their ultimate protest voyage both possible and likely.

If a family is to break with accepted behavior it must have great internal strength—and freedom. Thus the most important thing Barbara learned—and the hardest—was to cut her roots, to break with the idea that a family ought to have a home in one place, that children ought to be brought up in a particular place and have normal playmates and schooling, that there should be a steady income and insurance policies and money put aside for retirement. To break, too, with the many things that make up security for most women: her own furniture and dishes and silver, curtains at windows, the solidity of her home and her place in the community.

"Now," Barbara said, "our roots are in the family itself, not in any *place*. We are self-contained and self-nourishing. We have our fights and disagreements, but we have learned to know each other as individuals and to like each other. Ted and Jessica, for instance, are five years apart and had their own groups of friends ashore and had little contact with each other. But on the trip they found things in common and ways they could have good times together."

"We talked over everything—we were always short of money and we didn't hide it from the children. We all discussed things and decided together how much we'd spend and for what. And then of course we learned to work together for the safety of the ship, and learned what each could do so that we became an interdependent unit."

Five paragraphs on the "human" explanation; in the middle of it one "compression" paragraph on a voyage that covered four years. (That hurt; I had pages and pages of good material about that voyage, but of course it didn't belong in the story, so I had to forget it.)

How do you select the scenes to be expanded? They must be significant parts of the story. The lead of the piece was one such, and it was worth expanding because it showed the actual confrontation, which is what the story was all about. This last was another because it showed Barbara's motivation, her intelligence, and the strength of her self-discipline, all of which made her more real to the reader and more admirable, which a protagonist in a story ought to be.

This trick of personalizing an idea is used over and over again in all the mass media—newspapers, magazines, television documentaries, films.

It's what Remsberg did in the story about Utah, what Malcolm did in the story about the man's decision to die, what Lukas did in the Linda Fitzpatrick story. There is a definite procedure for writing these stories, which, for want of a better name, we call microcosm stories.

The idea comes in one of two ways: (1) You spot a trend or a problem or an issue that affects hundreds of thousands of people; (2) You spot an event that has deeper implications reflecting the same kind of widespread problem or issue. In either case your procedure is basically the same, though it varies in details. Take the first:

You've made an observation that *seems* true; the first thing you have to do is find out whether it really is true. For example, once I was talking with the director of a mental hospital in Connecticut, and at one point he wandered off the subject. The thing that drove him up the wall, he said, was what happened to his patients after they were released. Here we have people who have broken down under the pressure of too much stress, he said, we put them back together again, and then they go out and run into much more stress than they had before they came in. Why? Because they've been in a mental hospital, they're "crazy." Employers won't hire them, friends, family, and acquaintances treat them differently—either shun them completely, or go to the other extreme and treat them so gently that the patients know they're under suspicion. The trouble, he said, is that the public generally is afraid of mental illness and doesn't understand that a person can be cured after a mental breakdown just as surely as they can be cured of pneumonia.

This sounded logical, and I thought there might be an article in it. But first I had to find out whether the director knew what he was talking about. I checked around with other hospital directors, with psychiatrists, and other mental health experts, and they agreed the problem did exist pretty much as the Connecticut man had outlined. As we talked about it, there began to emerge a pattern of the specific kinds of things the released patients faced; getting a job was a major difficulty, because of employers' suspicions. Working out normal relations with other people was another, including for single persons the whole question of whether to marry, whether to tell the intended about the illness, and whether to have children (would they be mentally unstable?). Probably the biggest problem was the enormous blow to—perhaps the complete destruction of— the patient's self-confidence: "I've lost control of myself; it has been *proved* that I can't run my own life. How can I ever again believe that I can make it from here on out?"

This pattern of specific problems had to be the outline of the article; these were the major points that had to be dealt with. It seemed that the best way to do the piece would be through a personal narrative—find someone who had lived through the experience, who had dealt with the separate parts of the pattern, then write the story in terms of his or her experience. Since I was working on *Redbook*, the patient should be one with whom our readers could easily identify. It should be a young woman, preferably married with young children; in addition, of course, it would have to be a woman who was not afraid of being identified in print, who was willing to talk about her experience, and who was articulate.

How to find such a woman? You usually start the search by locating some person or organization or institution that has broad knowledge of the kind of people or situations you're interested in. In this case I went to the National Association of Mental Health, which had local chapters all over the country. I told the public relations director what I was trying to do and asked her if she would circularize their local chapters to find such a woman. She did. About a month later she came up with half a dozen candidates, plus a good deal of information about the experiences of each.

The one who seemed most promising was a young woman in San Francisco. She didn't fit our formula exactly—she was married, but had not been when she had her breakdown, and she had no children—but she was willing to talk, and her experiences illustrated the major points of the pattern. So I went to San Francisco and spent hours and hours interviewing her.

She was a brave woman. Going back over her initial breakdown, her experiences in the hospital, and her later fight to win back a place in the "normal" world was excruciatingly painful for her. She was often in tears and once was so shaky I was afraid she might have a relapse. But she was convinced that the story might help others in the same situation, and she found the courage to go through the ordeal. I didn't dare subject her to the additional stress of taking notes; after each interview—one lasted from 7 to 11 P.M.—I rushed back to the hotel and spent hours reconstructing the interview as nearly verbatim as possible.

I'll never forget one thing she said: "The thing that hit me the hardest was when they took away my keys in the hospital."

"Your *keys!* Why?

"Because your keys are your life. There's the key to the office, that's your job. Your key to the apartment, that's your home, your security. The key to your car, that's your freedom."

Once I finished the interviewing, it was simply a job of writing the narrative of her experience, using the skeleton plot mentioned earlier, and making sure that the major points covered in the story fitted the pattern of the overall problem.

The preliminary work on this kind of story often takes longer than the interviewing after you've found your person. In this case it took six or seven weeks; once it took a year and a half to find the right man. (Of course, I was doing other articles in the meantime.) But sometimes this kind of story works the other way: you turn up the personal story before you've identified the problem. As you explore the story, you begin to see the dimensions of the problem looming in the background. (If nothing looms, you have only a personal adventure story, which is much less significant and is not really an interpretive piece. It's a straight news story or feature.)

That's what happened with the story of Francis Bloeth, a mass killer. He killed three people, capriciously and at random, in a week. Long Island was terrorized; people were afraid to go out at night, all-night restaurants and gas stations closed down, people who had never had guns bought them. Then a few days after the last murder, police arrested Bloeth and a couple of days later he confessed. The papers gave complete coverage to all aspects of the affair and when it was over and Bloeth was in jail awaiting trial, the story seemed to be over.

I suppose it was the terror that made me think more about the incident, and the more I thought the more it seemed that there was a deeper story that needed to be told. Every institution our society has erected to protect itself from a man like this had had its hands on Bloeth and had let him go to kill three people. That became the underlying theme of the piece, and of course I had to verify the hypothesis by interviewing a flock of experts before I could be sure that it was sound. Once that was done, and I understood the deeper issues involved, I could write the story, using Bloeth's life as the narrative that carried the pattern of the problem.

There's a danger in this technique—a danger that you get so carried away by the human narrative that you rely too heavily on your own observation of the underlying problem. You don't check it out thoroughly enough with the experts who have a much broader and deeper view than you do, and you end up with a strained, or even false, article. Once I thought I spotted a good story idea—that the people who bought new homes at inflated suburban prices were paying more than their fair share of property taxes. The reasoning was that since they paid higher prices than had owners of older homes of equal size and value, their assessed valuations, based on the higher prices, would be greater and thus their taxes would, too.

It sounded reasonable and comparisons on the tax rolls seemed to bear it out. So did other information I gathered from a few, rather restricted, studies I was able to locate. I was about to start the search for two specific cases I could use in a comparison article when I interviewed a man at the

Census Bureau in Washington. I was working on another story, and when we finished that subject I mentioned the tax idea to him, to keep the conversation going. He said, "Yeah, I know it sounds logical, but it's not true." How did he know? "Well," he said, "we thought it was true, too, so we did a nationwide study. Found out it wasn't, that old houses get sold often enough so that they, too, reflect the inflated prices and so do their assessments." I took a look at the study, verified that it was a sound one, and watched my story go down the drain.

It was chastening, as it always is, to find that you're not as brilliant as you thought, but it's much better to find out at this stage than after you've gone roaring into print fat, dumb, happy—and dead wrong.

16

How To Handle Dull Stuff

O ne day when he was editor of *McCall's*, the late Dan Mich called and asked me if I'd like to do an article on varicose veins. This was not a subject that I'd been aching to cover for my whole life and Dan sensed it. Well, he said, I know it's not the most attractive idea in the world, but it is important; millions of women are afflicted by the ailment, hate it, and there have been some new medical developments in treatment. So how about it?

I didn't like the idea, but I respected Dan's judgment, and I'd learned that once you started research on a subject, however unlikely, your interest usually grew. So I said I'd do it.

I blew it. The research was sound and structurally the piece was OK, but it was about as interesting to read as a Pentagon memo. If I'd had any sense, I'd have called Dan when the research was finished and told him I couldn't handle it. But false pride plus the free lance's inveterate need for money kept me from doing it.

This was one of those times when you don't live up to your expectations for yourself so you don't talk about it, but the failure keeps nagging at you. Because of this, I think I finally figured out what I'd done wrong, and the more I thought about it, the more it seemed the mistake applied to more than this one incident.

Certain stories that journalists have to handle are about as interesting as a discarded beer can. They have to be written because they contain a good deal of information that is important to large numbers of people. Like the annual income tax story in April, the analyses of city or federal budgets, a new discovery in genetics, obituaries, or a revision of the city charter. Normally when you're assigned one of these, you approach it with resignation and, if you're a competent journalist, you do a competent job. You get all the information in, accurately, in some kind of logical order and as concisely as you can manage. So it's clear and complete and sound, but exciting it ain't.

We think you can do better. What it takes is a change in approach and, of course, imagination and the other attributes of creativity.

Your first triumph over the material comes in your attitude toward it. If you approach it as necessary drudgery, your story will be dull. If you look at it as a challenge, are determined to make it something special, and use your imagination to identify the special something, you'll probably start getting the ideas that will result in a fresh handling. And it will be rewarding because this kind of creativity always gives a glow of satisfaction.

Judith Crist clued me in on this. When she was first working on the old *New York Herald Tribune,* she, like most beginning reporters, was given obituaries to write. She hated it. She used the considerable force of her personality to try to convince the editor to give her something else to do and failed. So, she said, she took a new look at what she was doing. Suddenly, she said, she saw the job in a whole new light: here was a person's life spread out before her; it was finished and now could be looked at whole and evaluated for its direction, its accomplishments, its failures, and its drama. With this approach the material became not a dull recountal of facts, but a living document, the story of a human life. "Besides," she said, with a glint in her eye, "I realized that I had the last word."

Immediately her work began to take on color and movement.

What Crist had done for obituaries was to complete the first step in winning a victory over all dull material—to *think* about it, analyze it, try to relate it to other things in history or humanity, to figure out where it's going, its effect on the country, on people—if it's important it *must* affect many people—and on what kinds of people. Then go see some of those people and write the story of how and why it affects them.

But before you can convince your readers that the subject is important you must enable them to understand it. In his bestseller, *The Soul of a New Machine,* Tracy Kidder uses a familar analogy to describe one part of the workings of a computer:

". . . the main issue was the computer's storage system. Here, in packages of symbolic bits, are kept both information for the computer to manipulate and also many of the instructions that tell the computer what to do with that data. The system resembles that of a region's telephone system; phones are of no use unless they are distinct from one another, and an item in a computer's storage system is of no use unless it has its own "phone number," its own unique symbol, known as an address. A 16-bit machine can directly generate symbolic addresses only 16 bits long, which means that it can hand out to storage compartments only about 65,000 unique addresses. A true 32-bit machine, however, can directly address some 4.3 *billion* storage compartments."

Another example of making potentially dull material as interesting as possible comes from the *Manhattan, Inc.* piece by Peter Wilkinson, the outline of which we looked at in chapter 3.

Early in the piece, Wilkinson had to describe the kind of white-collar crime that pervaded the garment district of New York. The section could have been a plodding description, the kind often seen in newspaper stories, but Wilkinson used his talent as a writer to make it interesting.

Dirty, rambunctious, and overflowing with trucks, people, and push-carts, New York's garment center is a huge production machine fueled by the energies of hundreds of tiny, family-owned companies making everything from silk shirts to the hangers to display them on.

Accordingly, "making a living" in the garment center means playing by a unique set of rules. Competition, a desperate need for ready cash, and greed have left the area a playground for operators with muscle or a scam. Payoffs, funny loans, and sundry other shakedowns take place daily—all in the interest of keeping the machine humming at its own manic pace.

In this haven of the minor malfeasance, a more lucrative scam has been spawned on Fashion Avenue. Government agents call it "phony invoicing." It is a complicated game in which a businessman solicits bills for goods he doesn't want and never receives, pays them, and takes back up to 90 percent of what he paid, in cash, from a cooperative conspirator.

Folks on the street call it "buying green," and it is a fine way to raise business expenses, pay less tax, and fill pockets with wads of money— legitimately earned or, in some cases, creatively embezzled and begging to be laundered. The beauty of the plan is the paperwork— reassuring piles of official-looking documents to hoodwink nosy IRS agents. Dozens of apparel firms (some existing only on paper or as a name chiseled on a battered office door) are known to provide this "phony paper," taking commissions of 6 to 20 percent for their trouble.

The areas of science and technology are among the most important in today's society. Every day, major breakthroughs occur in the physical sciences, and seemingly every hour, they occur in the computer sciences. These advances often quickly have an effect on readers, so the job of a science writer is important. It is also difficult, because as important as scientific advances may be, they usually must be described in technical terms, and technical terms have a nasty habit of sending readers on to the next article.

To avoid that, the best science writers use all of the writer's weapons. They make their articles as interesting as they are important. Doing so requires hard work, but the result makes the work worthwhile. The following is an excerpt from a *Time* article about two pilots, Dick Rutan and Jeana Yeager, who had flown an experimental aircraft called *Voyager* for four and one-half days, and more than 11,600 miles without stopping for refueling, and who planned to fly the plane around the world nonstop. Writer Michael D. Lemonick began the article with an anecdote about the flight, but soon had to describe some of the unique technical qualities of the aircraft. The story could have become dull or confusing at this point, but Lemonick's writing glistens and carries the reader through the section.

But the mission's undisputed star was *Voyager*, a distinctive, almost ethereal craft, whose shell weighs only 938 lbs.; add engines and other equipment, and it is still shy of a ton—lighter than most small cars. The rest of its takeoff weight of nearly 6,200 lbs. (which will be closer to 12,000 lbs. for the around-the-world flight) is mostly fuel, distributed evenly in 17 tanks, located in the wings, fuselage and "outriggers" that flank the cabin.

Voyager began life in 1981 as a sketch on a napkin at the weather-beaten Mojave Inn, near the airport. The sketcher was Burt Rutan, 43, an engineer with an established reputation for building quirky-looking but aerodynamically ingenious planes. With his brother Dick and Jeana Yeager (no relation, believes Jeana, to famous Test Pilot Chuck), Rutan had decided to attempt the around-the-world flight.

The key to such a marathon would clearly be a lightweight, efficient, flying fuel tank. Eighteen months and many sketches later, when *Voyager* assumed its basic shape, it was a textbook example of feather-weight design and construction. The shell is made from quarter-inch-thick panels of Hexcel honeycomb, a resin-coated, paper-like polymer, covered with graphite fibers embedded in epoxy. The panels weigh just 4 oz. per sq. ft. but have remarkable tensile strength; the ends of the craft's thin, 110-ft. single wing can flex up and down as much as 35 ft. without breaking.

That section is a study in clarity and in making potentially dull material interesting. The reader never becomes bored or confused. Lemonick used words like "ethereal" and "quirky-looking," and mentions the napkin incident to give the piece a human tone.

One of the keys to making unfamiliar concepts understandable to the reader is simplicity. A reader will find it much easier to grasp "4.3 billion" than "4,300,000,000." In statistical stories it's always easier on the reader if you do the arithmetic—not, "this year's budget for the Department of Social Services was $68,474,387, up from last year's $44,674,256," but "this year's budget was $68 million, up a third from last year."

And it helps to reduce big numbers—there don't seem to be small ones anymore—to the smallest possible. Instead of writing "750,000 of the one million school children in the city are black," write, "three out of every four school children in the city are black"; it's even clearer than saying "75 percent are black."

When you have a number of concepts to get across in a complex story, you can provide a roadmap for the reader by numbering the paragraphs containing each. "There were four major reactions to the governor's proposal. 1——. 2——. 3——. 4——." Then later in the story when you want to refer back to one or the other, you use the numbers. This device helps clarify things for your readers: they see the four different viewpoints all at once, then can go on for fuller explanation in successive paragraphs if they want to. The trouble with this device is that it's too mechanical; as you switch from concept to concept without transitions, the flow of the story is wiped out. But there are stories so complex that clarity is a greater virtue than flow.

The same objection applies to the question-and-answer format, although it is used a great deal by people who want to get across much factual information quickly and concisely. It gives you great control over your material and saves the space taken by transitions. But it cannot be done successfully without deep and careful thought.

When we're reading "Q and A" pieces, our most frequent reaction is that they're not asking the questions we want answered. Many of the questions are set-ups—put there only to give the writer a chance to say something in the answer that he or she wants to say. We usually quit reading at that point. The key to successful use of the Q and A format is to think long and deeply about your readers' interests and to frame the questions they would want answers for.

We think "Q and A" is too clumsy a device to use in an interview—as *Playboy* uses it, for example. In an interview story your purpose is to give the reader an understanding of a person, his or her thinking, personality, experiences, and role in society. The "Q and A," while revealing, imposes a mechanical structure on what should be a human story. You can see how much the writers chafe under the *Playboy* formula when you notice that the answers get longer and longer, the questions fewer, so that the interviews become less like "Q and A"s and more like those in which the subjects reveal themselves by talking. This—allowing the subject to talk— was one of the devices introduced years ago by the *New Yorker* in their profiles, and it works beautifully when it's artistically done. (We'll talk more about that in the next chapter.)

17

How Do You Bring Them Alive?

Of all the kinds of interpretive writing, profiles may be the most interesting to do and the most difficult, both for the same reason—you're attempting to re-create a human being.

They're interesting because you are getting under the skin of another person (let's say a woman), learning to understand her with all her ambitions and hangups, the satisfactions of her successes, and joys at the unexpected beauties that have entered her life, her self-contempt at her failures, the contradictions of her personality, the drama of her conflicts, her courage and cowardices, the main direction of her life, the ultimate tragedy of her entrapment in her own inadequacies, or perhaps the inspiration of her ultimate victory over forces that should have been too strong for her.

And these are the same things that make writing a profile so difficult. For you must try to understand all these dimensions of your subject's personality and then encompass them in the pale, two-dimensional medium of words. There are never enough words within the length limits you cannot exceed. And to find the precise words to convey the color and contradictions of a person is a damnably difficult chore you never fully master. To do the job superlatively, which is what all writers want, all that is required of you is that you be a great artist.

Of course you never make it. But then, if you're any good as a writer, you're never satisfied with anything you do; that comes with the territory. (That also is what makes writing such a good way to spend your life; as your skills increase, the ceiling of your aspirations keeps getting higher. Probably the worst thing that can happen to you is to bump your head against the ceiling when you're halfway through life.)

So how do you arrange to come close? The job breaks down into two stages that, like many aspects of writing, go on simultaneously but must be explored one at a time. The first is the research—getting under the person's skin; the second is pulling it all together, figuring out what the

187

main thrust of her personality is and what, from among all the material you have, will best illustrate it.

The research job is shaped like a spiral; you start outside the person, go round and round her, getting closer all the time and finally finish at the center, with her. You start by reading. Has she written anything? Read it. Nobody can write anything without revealing herself. Has anybody written about her? Read that—with your notebook beside you, so you can note the questions that pop into your mind to ask her. Some writers also note the perceptions that they get about the person—not as final conclusions, but as impressions to be verified or denied as your understanding grows.

Then you start interviewing. You talk to the person's colleagues, her co-workers, her boss, her secretary, her employees. You talk to her family— her parents, her brothers, her children—recognizing always that they are biased by their emotional attachments to her. You talk to her friends— current friends and, if you can find them, friends during earlier stages of her life, when she was in school or starting her career. Then you talk to her enemies, to offset the bias of others and recognizing that they, too, are biased. You talk to people who can be objective about her—if there are any—either because enough time has passed to dim their emotional attachment, or because their relations with her were of the kind that required them to be objective—like a college professor who had her as a student.

During each interview you recognize that you are getting only one aspect of the woman's life, though, of course, you probe for as many aspects as each interviewee has been exposed to. You go after anecdotes, things the woman did in certain circumstances, because anecdotes are mostly what your story is going to be made up of. And after each interview you sit down and think about what has been said and note down questions that you will later ask another interviewee or the subject herself.

You may talk to twenty or two hundred people in this process, depending on how exhaustive your story is going to be and on whether you're doing one side of the person or a full, rounded portrait. That "one side" needs explanation: it does not mean you set out to do a biased picture, like a hatchet job. It does mean your original story idea may encompass only one aspect of the person's life. For example, let's say you're doing a piece on the particular style of acting of Robert Redford and you want to show how he developed it. Then, of course, you concentrate on that side, see the people who would have first-hand knowledge about it, and forget the rest. But even that kind of limited approach requires you to interview many more people than you expect.

Finally, you see Redford himself. You are armed with all the questions you have noted down after all the other interviews, plus those you thought of when you were reading books or articles about him. You spend as much time with him as he will allow—a day, a week. If possible you live with him, you meet him in the morning—paying due attention to what he's like before breakfast—go to work with him, eat with him, watch how he acts toward his co-workers, the director, his wife, his kids. You pay close attention to the way he dresses, the furniture in his office, and the pictures on the walls; you listen to the way he talks, catch the rhythms of his speech, his inflections, his individual phrasing and favorite expressions; you note the way he walks and skis; you describe to yourself the precise way he smiles and the expression his face wears in repose, the shape of his mouth and eyebrows and the way he moves his hands when he talks—or keeps them clenched in his lap or stiffly along his thighs; you watch his eyes and the way they change as emotions or thoughts filter through them; you open the shutter of your perceptions to catch the nuances of his relations with other people, the way he reacts to them and they to him; you try different gambits on him and watch how he reacts—flattery, argument, opposition, the put-down, agreement.

This is what Tom Wolfe calls "saturation reporting" when he talks about the "new journalism"; it is an essential in doing profiles, but new it isn't. Interpretive writers have been using it for more than a quarter of a century. Nevertheless, Wolfe and Breslin and Talese and several others use it beautifully, and some of the things they have written after using it have reached heights of sophistication and artistry that many earlier practitioners did not approach.

This is an almighty difficult process, and it is absolutely essential to work through it if your piece is to have any focus. Once in my early days of free-lancing, I was doing a profile of the late Chester I. Barnard, then head of the Rockefeller Foundation. I had read everything he'd written, most of it privately published and covering an enormous range of subjects. I had interviewed all the people, I had spent hours and hours with him, I had gathered all the facts of his career. It had been remarkable.

He'd been a poor boy in New England who had worked his way through Harvard by leading a jazz orchestra and had quit a couple of months shy of graduation because he thought he'd gotten all he could, and the degree didn't mean anything to him. He had joined the telephone company and shortly had become such a master of the complex mathematics of rate-making that he'd been on the government's wartime telephone board while still in his twenties.

He'd been the youngest president of a phone company in history. He

had a large library of music and was an accomplished pianist, so determined on perfection that he'd take out a piece of music and play it over
and over again until he felt he'd done it as well as he possibly could, then
go on to the next. He taught himself French by writing a dozen French
words and their English translations on three-by-five cards; he carried
them around in his pocket and pulled them out to study them while
waiting for a bus, riding home from the office, waiting for an appointment.
When he knew them all, he'd throw the card away and make another.

He'd written a book called *The Functions of the Executive*, which
revolutionized the theory of how to manage an organization so that it
accomplished its goals. He was an expert on Napoleon, the Catholic
Church, and on the foundation, development, and organization of Islam.
He was such a lousy golfer he'd quit in disgust at himself. During the
Great Depression, when food riots wracked city after city, he'd organized
one of the first government welfare operations in the country. He was an
accepted member of half a dozen conservative clubs of top executives, and
he'd gone to Russia and written a pamphlet on what he learned that shook
the clubs to their foundations and got him called communist. He'd been a
member of an ultra-select group of five men who had drawn up a plan for
the control and use of atomic energy, both national and international. It's
still being followed. He had been called "one of the six finest minds in the
world."

He was iconoclastic, witty, irreverent; talking to him about the problems of the day was like watching a brilliant beam of light played on a dark
roomful of writhing monsters. He was fascinating and so diverse that I
couldn't encompass him. After struggling for days to pin down the main
thrust of his life, I finally called for help. I went up to see Charley
Ferguson, the editor at *Reader's Digest* I was working with then, and
talked out the problem.

Fergie said, "Before you can start to write a profile you've got to
complete this sentence: John Smith is the man who ———."

So I went home and spent more tortured days trying to complete the
sentence. I finally did it, but not very well and the resulting piece was not
as sharply focused as it should have been. Fergie's sentence had clarified
the problem and given me a direction in which to work. I believe he was
right; you've got to complete it before you can start to write.

Once you've completed the sentence, how do you proceed? Very much
as you do in any other piece. The organizational structure can, but need
not, be the same conceptual pattern outlined in chapter 7. Because you're
writing about a person, your lead is usually an anecdote which illustrates
the point made when you completed the sentence, like the leads about
Joe DiMaggio and Mike Nichols in chapter 10.

Or you can use a summary lead, like the one Garry Wills used in his profile of Dorothy Day.

Then you go ahead and reveal the subject, let's say a man, mostly by showing him in action, point by point—with the points being those aspects of his life and personality that seem to you the most significant. It's a tough and delicate job of selection. You may or may not take him through his life chronologically—probably not, because the most illuminating anecdotes didn't happen chronologically. You usually end with an anecdote that sums up the man.

But one thing is absolutely essential; you've got to show his bad side as well as his good, his weaknesses as well as his strengths (or if the main thrust of your piece is negative, his strengths as well as his weaknesses). Without this, you're doing either a puff piece or a hatchet job, and in either case the reader doesn't believe you. Readers *know* nobody is perfect or all bad, and they figure if you make a man that way you're being dishonest.

Creating a balanced piece is not easy to do for two reasons: One is that by the time you've learned enough about your subject to understand him, you like him—because we think you almost always like those persons you really understand. The other is that it's difficult to find anyone who will be critical of your man—especially if he is a person of power, or a person who has accomplished things in his life—because people who have accomplished enough to be worthy of a profile usually have more positive than negative traits.

I had a terrible time with this when I did the piece on the late President Kennedy. For one thing he was a genuine golden boy. For another, I liked the guy. For a third, his public relations people had built one of the fanciest, gold-plated, stainless steel fences around him I'd ever tried to get through. This was while he was in the Senate, and about the only deleterious thing I could get about him was a crack a colleague had made to him one day: "What we'd like from you, Senator, is a little less profile and a little more courage." (Clever, but not quite fair, because I was convinced Kennedy had great courage.)

I went to Boston and talked to Republicans and to members of those wings of the Democratic party that were anti-Kennedy. I didn't get much, probably because the Democrats were afraid of his power and the Republicans were respectful of it, and most people who knew him liked him. Finally I went to Harvard and looked up some of his old professors. Most of them liked and admired him too, but they were more objective, and one or two of them had revealing insights into the sources of his ambition and the kinds of obstacles he'd had to struggle against in his early years. And that was a key.

If a man is truly admirable, if his life has been mostly positive, if he has had many more successes than failures, you can humanize him, make him believable to the reader, by identifying the things he had to fight to overcome and then by showing him doing it.

One of Kennedy's traits, for example, was his great need to win, implanted by his father ("My father was never interested," he said once, "if you came in second") and by his competition with his brothers. Honed since childhood, this need became a spartan self-discipline which drove him several times in his life to go beyond what should have been the limits of his physical endurance. Once at Harvard he was in the infirmary with grippe and fever when the trial heats for a coming swimming meet with Yale were announced; he sneaked out of the infirmary and took part in the trials. His health suffered for the rest of the term. When he campaigned for the Senate in 1952, he had an open wound in his back, the legacy of the PT-boat smash in World War II, and had to get about on crutches. Yet many times he'd address a late-night rally in one town, then get in the car and try to sleep as he was driven to the next town. There, at seven in the morning, he'd be at a factory gate to shake hands with the workers as they came in. Not once during the campaign, his aides told me, did he mention the pain. This kind of need to win may be a virtue or a vice in your personal lexicon, but showing a man coping with it can do nothing but humanize him.

Another technique for adding balance to a profile is to allow the person to reveal himself through quotes. In her profile of Mike Nichols, Barbara Gelb let Nichols tell of his attempts to get over his own vanity.

"Having fame is wonderful," Nichols says, if you can control its tendency "to make you feel like a baby."

The struggle with his baby feelings was at its most pronounced during Nichols's years as a performer, when, he says, his vanity all too often would take over and cause him to behave petulantly. "It's—you know—'I don't like the way the ads look,' or, 'One of the lights is out, I'm not being lit properly.' As a director, those things concern me for the *project*, not for *me*. When you're worried about it for *you*, that's something I'm very uncomfortable with."

In a *Rolling Stone* cover story, one of Glavin's former students, Rob Hoerburger, used good description ending in a quote to prove one of his major points about rock star Phil Collins. Hoerberger had earlier described Collins as rock's Cabbage Patch kid, an unlikely star, a plain, homely singer surrounded by MTV glitz. He also showed that Collins's style of living differed markedly from those of his fellow rock stars. He began that section by desribing Collins at home during a week in which his wife was away.

He looked a bit haggard, admitting that he didn't sleep well alone. The cats didn't get fed for three days, because Collins, who wasn't used to feeding them, kept forgetting to buy cat food. And with only a week to go before they moved into a new home, there wasn't a single gold record packed, not even a box in sight.

Collins did, however, air out the hot-tub room and start up one of two mountainous jukeboxes he had stocked with his favorite 45s, mostly vintage Beatles and Motown—although looking through the dusty glass that shielded the titles, he had some trouble remembering them. The house itself is small by rock-star proportions, really just an oversize cottage with a second floor. It would be hard to imagine Eddie and Valerie living there, for instance, but Collins, like the house, fits right in with the gentrified populace. Driving around Guildford on an unusually warm day in December, his fuzz face might have been the only thing to give away his identity—Guildford seemed a place where men shaved twice a day. Otherwise, in his cotton-checked trousers and argyle sweater, he was a natural, waving to an elderly bicycling couple who let him pass on the lane. This wasn't the typical MTV look, and Collins often feels less comfortable around his more chic pop peers. At the Band Aid taping, he found himself surrounded by photogenia—Sting, Duran Duran, Culture Club—as he sat behind the drums in his argyles. "I looked around and everyone had leather trousers on, jumpers with three-quarter sleeves that would have been girls' ten years ago. I'm so unfashionable, it's embarrassing."

The quote at the end of the section finishes it nicely, but the strength of the section lies in Hoerburger's description of Collins's life.

So while quotes gathered in interviews may reveal a great deal about people, their actions usually reveal more. In the Barbara Gelb article on Mike Nichols, Gelb starts one section with a quote from an interview, then uses an anecdote to show Nichols practicing what he preaches.

Nichols often makes things clear for his actors by illustrating bits of motivation with incidents from his own life. "Partly, I do this because it's all I *know,* and partly because I very much want to encourage them to pour *their* lives into what they're doing. I believe that the process can illuminate a scene and it also lets us learn a little more about each other, so that we can work together a little better."

In a scene, for example, where Eddie manifests blind jealousy over a fancied betrayal by Darlene, and Sigourney Weaver is at a loss how to react, Nichols asks her, "Have you ever been with an insanely jealous person?" He is thinking of a year in his own life, and just such a relationship.

"I know a great deal about that kind of jealousy," he says. "If, for instance, we were watching a movie together and there was a woman on the screen, I had to sit very, very still, or I would be excoriated for a long time afterward. It was a *scalding* experience, and I learned from it that jealousy is entirely the problem of the person *undergoing* it, and it's not really attached to *you* at all."

And he gives the actress a startling image to think about: "Being with an insanely jealous person is like being in the room with a *dead mammoth.*"

Here Gelb, like Hoerburger, does what the best writers always do. She makes the point by showing her subject in action.

Epilogue

*T*he life of the nonfiction writer is filled with defeats and victories, frustration and fascination, risks and rewards.

The writer works with his own ideas and his own opinions. He can use his power, which is literally the power of the press, to influence the attitudes of millions of persons. For centuries writers have helped alter the course of the country's history. In fact, the writings of Samuel Adams, Tom Paine, and others helped spark the fight for the country's independence. In the early part of this century, the muckrakers, including Lincoln Steffens, Ida M. Tarbell, Samuel Hopkins Adams, and Ray Stannard Baker wrote of corruption in government and abuses by business, and created a demand for the passage of laws that governed such things as child labor, the quality of food and drugs, and truth in advertising. During the seventies, Bob Woodward and Carl Bernstein of the *Washington Post* unearthed the facts behind the Watergate scandal, facts that eventually led to the resignation of President Nixon. Today, writers like Claire Safran and Bonnie Remsberg, whose work we have seen in earlier chapters, continue the tradition of informing Americans of abuses by business and government.

The muckrakers were investigative journalists, but many more writers perform a different job. They help people by giving them information they need. It may be information on ways to solve a particular problem, like how to deal with a dyslexic child. It may be the information that helps explain a complex issue that is important to their lives, like a new tax bill or the effects of air pollution. It may be information that enlarges their readers' lives, like the Barbara Gelb piece mentioned earlier, which broadens readers' appreciation of a play by demonstrating the thought, trial and error, hard work, and inspiration that go into its production.

But presenting this kind of information in ways that will penetrate the readers' normal defenses is extraordinarily hard work, most of which comes under the headings of self-discipline and self-knowledge. Self-discipline means not being satisfied with the first way you write a sentence, but working it over until it says *precisely* what you want it to say. It means forcing yourself to think, to analyse a body of recalcitrant material: what does all this information add up to? how do these facts fit together—and where don't they? what does this story *say?*

Self-discipline means learning to handle the fears that every writer has. The most frequent of these is: what if it doesn't work this time; what if I can't handle it well enough so it will be published? Such fears either swamp you or you surmount them; if they swamp you, you say you have writer's block. You surmount them by bringing them up and facing them—which requires some self-knowledge. Facing them, you analyze them: what am I really afraid of? suppose this comes true, what's the worst that can happen? if that happens, will I die? will I starve? Anything less usually seems manageable.

Such fear usually stifles your creativity, and preventing it is where self-knowledge comes in. Creativity is a product of your unconscious mind; knowing this often allows you to trigger that mind force. And this not only usually solves the problem you face, but also produces one of the great rewards of writing. Creativity is seeing familiar things in a new or different way, and this, in turn broadens both your own and your readers' understanding of life's predicaments.

There are other rewards. An early one is the ego-satisfaction at seeing your name in print. This is joyful—and transitory. Next you want to see it in print over something you consider good, and will consider good a year from now.

A big and lasting reward is knowing that you have helped people to understand and appreciate their own lives; that you have had influence enough to get a bill passed or to stop a bad one; that knowledge you have passed along will help someone suffering with a dread disease, perhaps even to save a life.

These are some of the reasons why, despite all the hard work, all the struggles and frustrations, most writers would have no other job.

INDEX

THE ART OF WRITING NONFICTION

was composed in 10-point Caledonia
and 9½ point Optima Light and leaded two points on a Linotron 202
by Coghill Book Typesetting Company;
printed by sheet-fed offset on 55-pound, acid free, Glatfelter Antique Cream,
Smyth sewn and bound over binder's boards in pre-printed Holliston Lexotone
by Maple-Vail Book Manufacturing Group, Inc.;
with pre-printed covers printed in two colors
by Frank A. West Company, Inc.;
designed by Will Underwood;
and published by

SYRACUSE UNIVERSITY PRESS
Syracuse, New York 13244-5160

INSTANT HEALING

INSTANT HEALING

Serge Kahili King, Ph. D.

RENAISSANCE BOOKS
Los Angeles

12/03

Library of Congress Cataloging-in-Publication Data
King, Serge.
    Instant healing / Serge Kahili King.
    p. cm.
    Includes index.
    ISBN 1-58063-159-2
    1. Mental healing. 2. Mind and body. 3. Shamanism—Hawaii. 4. Healing. I. Title.
RZ401.K535 2000
615.8'52—dc21   00-056014

10 9 8 7 6 5 4 3 2 1

Cover design by Lisa-Theresa Lenthall
Interior design and typesetting by Geoff Bock

Published by Renaissance Books
Distributed by St. Martin's Press
Manufactured in the United States of America
First Edition

L

*This book and all the good that may come from it
are dedicated to Chris, Pierre, and Dion.*

ACKNOWLEDGMENTS

Thanks to all the many teachers who shared their healing wisdom with me, and to the family members, friends, students, and clients who let me practice on them.

CONTENTS

INSTANT HEALING

My "Talk Story"

A s the title indicates, this is a book about drug-free instant healing, which I define as significant or even complete healing results for a variety of conditions—including the healing of broken bones—in less than an hour. The book discusses how instant healing works and how to do it using simple methods that anyone can apply. Some of the methods require you to think quite differently about mind-body relationships, but the potential results are well worth stretching your belief system for. Because instant healing is not feasible for all conditions under all circumstances, you will also find methods for rapid healing (less than one day) and fast healing (less than one week). The methods you will learn have been used successfully by myself, my family, and thousands of people whom I have taught. Some of the results may seem miraculous in view of current ideas about health and illness, but I am not writing about miracles. This book is about practical ideas and techniques that work. On the other hand, I make no claims that a given illness or condition can be instantly, rapidly, or quickly healed by any individual at any time. You, as the healer, are the critical factor, and I will explain what's happening when the system doesn't work.

For those of you who may be interested, the following is a brief account of the events that led to the writing of this book.

When I was very young I had quite a number of childhood diseases, and for most of them I received the standard treatment available in the 1940s. However, I recall that one time when I was lying in bed feeling quite miserable, my mother lay down next to me and, as she told me later, "willed" my illness into herself. I remember feeling better the next day while my mother lay in bed suffering with the same illness. She said she had learned this ancient way of healing from her mother who had come from Italy. It was many years later before I realized how unusual it was to have such a fast, drugless healing. I believe that this experience planted the first subconscious seed for my lifelong fascination with the relationship between the mind and the body, and my desire to explore different ways to accelerate the healing process.

If the experience with my mother planted seeds, then the experiences with my father planted saplings. He was what some people would call a health nut: an advocate of taking vitamins, eating fresh fruits and vegetables, and getting exercise. I recall clearly my disgust at having to drink large glasses of buttermilk and carrot juice whenever I traveled with him. My father was an M.D., and he knew a great deal about the function of the body, though he never practiced as far as I knew. He knew a great deal about the mind, as well. He encouraged my interest in science, taught me the rudiments of mind-to-mind communication, and practically forced me to develop my powers of observation and analysis. He even formed an organization of people dedicated to improving their bodies and minds, but he died before I was old enough to join it and I think it faded away without him. However, we did have three years of close contact in which he helped to strengthen my belief in the importance of individual responsibility for maintaining physical and mental fitness. In terms of healing, the most valuable thing he taught me was self-hypnosis and directed imagination.

My father died when I was seventeen and I was a lost soul for a while. Over the following year I met my future wife, although neither of us would be ready for anything but friendship for six more years. I graduated high school next to last in my class, somehow got accepted into a college, and failed my first year outstandingly.

I finally had the sense to join the Marine Corps. I was walking along a street in Pittsburgh, Pennsylvania, without a dime in my pocket and wondering what to do with my life. A sign in a post office window leapt out at me: "The Marine Corps Builds Men." Underweight, out of work, an academic failure, I didn't feel like a man. And I wanted to. I had so many negative attitudes, habits, and complexes that it seemed like I was encased in suffocating armor and didn't know how to get free. So I decided on the spot to use the Corps to strip my personality down to its bare essence and rebuild myself entirely. I had no idea at the time how good the Corps would be at helping me do that.

Boot camp was both tortuous and thrilling. I entered at a weak and skinny 140 pounds, and finished it three months later at a tough and muscular 170 (over forty years later I kind of miss that feeling). Not exactly instant healing, but not bad considering my state of mind and body at the time. With the help of the Corps I did rebuild myself completely over the next three years, learning at the same time the healing value of willpower and attitude.

I had had a very little bit of boxing experience as a youngster, and shortly after entering boot camp, I was selected to represent our company in a boxing match. Unfortunately, the boxers were matched by weight, so my out-of-shape 140 pounds were paired with the 140 pounds of a feisty little Mexican-American who was just about to graduate. At first I was smug because it was clear I could box rings around him. That lasted until the second round when my sixteen-ounce gloves refused to raise themselves any higher than my waist. My arms didn't feel tired—I didn't feel them at all. My opponent didn't know what to do, so he just kept hitting my nose. By exerting a tremendous effort of will, I could occasionally block a punch or tap him lightly on the cheek, but that was all. So I turned my will to staying on my feet. By the fourth round, when I had bled on everything and everyone in sight, my coach literally threw in the towel and stopped the fight. To my astonishment I was applauded. My weakness of body could have made me the laughingstock of the camp, but my strength of will kept me going and won me the respect of my colleagues. What I learned was that the will alone cannot make the body do what you want it to, but the will can make it do more than you might expect.

Years later, my Marine Corps company was doing a 20-mile hike in two columns along a road. The captain was heading one column and I was heading the other, wearing only a sidearm and strutting along in my best John Wayne style. About halfway along, the radioman collapsed. Since, apart from the captain, I had the lightest load, it was my privilege to take on the radioman's burden. It took a few minutes for me to strap on the fifty pounds of gear, and by then most of the company had passed me by. So I revved up my willpower, pulled on my John Wayne attitude like a uniform, and strutted back up to the head of the column. For the rest of the hike I walked as if I were still carrying only a sidearm. Once we had reached the barracks and were dismissed—and no one was looking—I let go of the will and the attitude and collapsed. I hadn't yet learned to maintain them during the cooling off period after intensive effort. My will had kept me going, but, more importantly, my attitude had instantly changed the capabilities of my physical body.

Under the Corps's system of rigorous physical and mental discipline, I blossomed into a different and better person (this is not a recruitment promotion. I would recommend joining the Corps only in time of great national or personal need—in my case it was desperation). However, much of what I was able to accomplish during that time was due to things I learned off the base with the help of a very special woman.

When my father was about the same age as I was when I joined the Marine Corps, he had been adopted by a Hawaiian man from Kauai and trained in a particular form of traditional knowledge. I had forgotten about this until six months into my term of service when I received a telephone call one evening from a woman who claimed to be my father's Hawaiian sister. She invited me to come visit her the following weekend to meet her father and "talk story," a Hawaiian term for sharing ideas and experiences. I was always glad of an opportunity to leave the base, so I accepted. The visit was another major turning point in my life. In a simple ceremony, the woman's father—my father's adoptive Hawaiian father—adopted me as a grandson and turned me over to his daughter, now my aunt, to be my teacher in the same tradition in which my father had been trained. There was mention of a brother, who would be my new uncle, but I wouldn't meet him for many more years.

Auntie Laka, as I called her, was a lovely Hawaiian about ten years older than me. She taught massage and meditation at an informal school, and I spent every available weekend for the next two and a half years under her tutelage. I learned everything I could about how the body responds to loving touch, emotional energy and mental symbols. I finally developed her teachings into a system of bodywork called *kahi loa*, which will be described in detail later in the book.

When I left the Corps I went back to finish college and took up first Russian and then Asian Studies. This was an opportunity to study the healing ideas of Eastern religions and to practice Yoga, Tai Chi Chuan, Taoism, and Zen. During this period I was exposed to many different ideas about mind, body, spirit, and life.

My next major acquisition of healing knowledge came to me in Africa, where I was managing socioeconomic development programs for an American voluntary agency. That whole story is another, unwritten, book, so I'll just mention some highlights from my seven-year stay. Here, I think, was the real beginning of my understanding of the links between beliefs and the body. I witnessed rituals that caused both illness and healing; I learned how zombies were created; I was given herbs that "instantly" cured snakebites and the wounds of poisoned arrows; I was taken to "energy springs" and "healing waters;" I learned "killing chants" and "curing songs." I participated in rituals and experiences that radically transformed my views of reality and possibility. In one of my most profound experiences, I lay dying of malaria in the sub-Saharan savanna when an African shaman came to me in a dream and told me to eat the liver of a freshly-killed antelope hanging outside my tent if I truly wanted to live. When I awoke I crawled out of my tent, asked my companions to prepare the liver for me, ate it, and lived. Again, not instant healing, but pretty darn rapid. In between all the magic and mystery, I became a specialist in community development, the art of helping people to help themselves, and in the process gained priceless knowledge about the secrets of human motivation.

About a year before leaving Africa, while on a trip back to the United States to take care of some family business, I encountered my Hawaiian uncle, William, who preferred to be called by his Hawaiian name, Wana. During intense but sporadic meetings in various places over the next seven years he guided me through deeper and deeper levels of shamanic healing practices.

On returning to the States for good I earned a master's degree in management. Based on many years of study and practice, I opened a hypnotherapy clinic and did energy research while working on my Ph.D. in psychology and continuing to work with my uncle. During this period I intensively explored the healing effects of words, imagination, energy fields, and body movement. Eventually I formed an organization to train healers and teachers, wrote a number of books, invented energy devices, and gave lots of workshops all over the world that added to my knowledge of healing.

Along the way, my wife and I raised three fine boys who helped me to refine many of the techniques and methods you will find in this book. Our household was reasonably normal except for the fact that in our home you would not find any bandages, cough syrups, aspirin, or other medicines. This was not due to philosophy or religion. It was because we didn't need them. Our kids had the usual complement of cuts and scratches, bumps and bruises, as well as a few serious ailments and injuries. We had no hesitation about seeing a medical doctor if necessary. It's just that the need for a doctor was so infrequent that none of us had an answer for the question, "Who is your family physician?" The most serious condition occurred when my oldest son and his friends decided to race their skateboards down a steep road. One boy's board clipped another's and, as a result, my son had to be evacuated to a hospital by helicopter. He was briefly in a coma and the X rays showed that he had a concussion. The official prognosis was that he would gradually recover most, if not all, of his faculties, and that he would have to take a particular type of medicine for the rest of his life. Well, I used some of the things I'll be teaching you in this book and within a week he was his normal self again, even getting back on his skateboard a day after leaving the hospital. It took him awhile to regain his full sense of smell, but he never did take the medicine and to this day, about twenty years later, he has never had any ill effects from that accident.

So now it's time to learn the reasoning behind the "instant healing" concept and, even more importantly, how to do it.

Ahuwale ka nane huna.
That which was hidden shall be revealed.
—Hawaiian proverb

PART ONE

Preparing the Way for Instant Healing

CHAPTER ONE

How Does Healing Happen?

The next time you stub your toe or smash your finger in a door, how would you like to be able to heal it yourself in less than five minutes with no pain and no bruises? What if you could heal a burn in the same way, or get rid of a cold in under an hour? Wouldn't it be great if long-term headaches, depression, stiffness, pain, and many other problems could disappear in an hour, a day, or even a week? Well, the ideas and techniques in this book can do just that for you, as they have for thousands of others around the world. They may not work for everyone all the time, but they will work so fast, so effectively, and so often that you will truly be amazed.

I was trained in the Hawaiian shaman system of healing, but in my life as a healer, I have explored the most advanced techniques of the Western world, the most primitive techniques of the undeveloped world, and the amazing techniques of the shamanic practitioners of Hawaii. One very significant thing I have noted is that no matter which system is used, some people are healed through it, some people are not healed through it, some people are healed without it, and some people are healed in spite of it.

Different people in different places and times have, naturally, come up with different ideas about the causes and cures for illness and other physical problems. Human creativity in the healing field is a wonderous thing to behold. The concepts and practices held dear by one culture may be scorned or laughed at by another.

A MYRIAD OF METHODS

The best way for you to get the results you want is to understand how healing works. So before you jump to Parts II and III where the healing exercises are described, let's look at some of the ways that are used around the world to heal the body. It is worth noting that many of these methods have often been used successfully for the same illnesses.

1. Physical methods—herbs, drugs, other medicines, diet and nutritional supplements, surgery and bone-setting, chiropractic and massage, exercise, deep breathing, enemas and colonics, fasting, electricity and magnetism.

2. Emotional methods—affection and attention, laughter and play, anger release, fear confrontation, forgiveness, color, aroma, and music.

3. Mental methods—placebos, hypnosis and self-hypnosis, talk therapy, guided imagery, visualization, positive thinking, affirmation, and meditation.

4. Spiritual/metaphysical methods—pyramids and crystals, aura cleansing and psychic surgery, therapeutic touch, homeopathy and flower remedies, acupuncture, acupressure and applied kinesiology, telepathy and radionics, prayer, faith, ritual, soul retrieval, and "spontaneous remission."

This is really amazing. If the body can be healed by all these different methods—and there are countless case histories to support the healing effects of each one—then it seems clear that each and every method is just a means by which one thing, the actual healing process, takes place. No one theory of the healing process can be considered adequate when another gets the same effect. Therefore, something else is happening instead of, or in addition to, what the theorists say.

Healing starts when there is a need for it. When a person gets into a state of disharmony (illness, disease, injury, and the like), the body responds by trying to recover on its own. Sometimes an individual consciously tries to help, with or without the aid of others. Sometimes others try to help the individual, with or without his conscious help. When the attempts at recovery and help are effective, the person gets better. As noted above, there are many varied ways to help. I'd like to look at a possible common thread that links all the different kinds of disharmony.

THE STRESS FACTOR

No matter what kind of disharmony one is talking about, no matter what the name is of the disease or illness that may be involved, and no matter whether the condition is primarily physical or mental, there is always some degree of physical tension present. It's common to think of tension as a result of illness, except where certain kinds of stress are thought to contribute to illness, but let's play with another idea. What if tension were not an effect of illness, but the cause? If this were so, then all one would have to do to promote healing would be to relieve the tension. Not surprisingly, that's the assumption this book is based on.

Before I discuss relieving tension, however, it will be useful to examine the ways in which tension builds up in the first place. I'll begin by looking at the source of tension itself, a thing called "stress."

According to *Merriam-Webster's Collegiate Dictionary*, tenth edition, stress is "a physical, chemical, or emotional factor that causes bodily or mental tension and may be a factor in disease causation" and "a state resulting from a stress; especially one of bodily or mental tension resulting from factors that tend to alter an existent equilibrium." In plain language, this means that different kinds of stress can cause tension in the mind and body, and that we can get "stressed" or tense from resistance to change.

In another part of the definition, I have substituted the word "thing" where Webster used "body or body part." This section says that stress is a "constraining force or influence, as a force exerted when one thing presses on, pulls on, pushes against, or tends to compress or twist another thing; especially the intensity of this mutual force [and] the deformation caused in a thing by such a force." The plain language translation is that stress is not only the action of pressing, pulling, pushing, compressing, or twisting; it is also the *reaction* of pressing, pulling, pushing, compressing, or twisting against the other force. Stress isn't stress unless there is resistance. It is the resistance that causes the tension, and the tension that causes the problems. Note also that a "constraining force or influence" can also come from a lack of something, such as food or water or love, and is not limited to something active.

Stress, in and of itself, isn't bad. It's vital for building muscles, moving, breathing, motivation, and a number of other things that are useful and necessary. But if you try to lift a heavy weight for too long, the muscles will break down instead of build up. If you eat so much healthy food that your stomach is ready to burst, you are doing yourself more harm than good. If you try to save the world by making people change, you'll be so stressed out that you'll accomplish very little. Examine your own experience and you will find that it is not just the ordinary stress of daily living, but excessive sudden stress (acute stress) or sustained excessive stress over a period of time (chronic stress) that causes the severe problems. Too much tension, one could say, although "too much" will differ among individuals and circumstances. From now on, when I talk about stress I mean the excessive kind.

What kinds of stresses would cause too much physical tension in the body?

The Physical Stress Factor

Physical stress is a relatively simple phenomenon to describe. After engaging in physical effort for a long time the body begins to resist the activity more and more until exhaustion or accident forces it to stop. I would point out, though, that the more enjoyable the effort seems to be, the longer you can continue it, because you are not resisting it as much. Less resistance means less tension, and less tension means less effect from the stress. If you love to play volleyball, you may be able to do it for hours and hours and end up pleasantly tired but exhilarated. If you hate to do housework or clean out the garage, however, you may end up exhausted and achy after a couple of hours.

Another kind of physical stress that produces tension occurs when you are poked or prodded with something sharp, hard, or excessively hot or cold. Although you don't think it's strange to be cut or bruised or burned by such contact, some people's injuries remain for a long time, while others are able to heal very quickly, and still others can walk on fire or get punctured by nails without harm. Having walked on extremely hot lava rocks barefoot without injury, and having healed broken bones, burns, and bruises of my own in under an hour many times, I can tell you that reducing tension as quickly as possible is a critical factor in the length of the healing process. In the Mindblower Technique described in Chapter 7, I'll tell you exactly how to do that.

Physical stress can also come from reactions to the environment. Allergies are so common that many people take them for granted, and some people are highly sensitive to trace amounts of natural and man-made chemicals and to electromagnetic radiation. The body tries to protect itself against such intrusions not only by internal chemical means, but also by creating a barrier of muscle tension (note that our internal organs and nerves are surrounded by muscle tissue). And then there is the stress caused by such things as hunger, thirst, and lack of movement. It isn't very hard to see how physical stress can cause physical tension.

The Emotional Stress Factor

Emotional stress is usually thought to be generated externally, in other words, created by what someone else is doing to you. This perception is so widespread that many people are paid compensation for the emotional stress that others have caused them. In fact, emotional stress happens only when you become afraid or angry or excited, and all of these are internally generated responses. It's easier, and sometimes financially profitable, to blame others for making you feel bad, but you really do it to yourself. One person may be bothered excessively by a situation that would be taken in stride by another. Your attitude toward what others do has more effect on you than what they do.

The emotions most likely to cause stress are fear, anger, and excitement. Of course, there are variations and levels of these emotions. Emotions related to fear are anxiety, panic, terror, and embarrassment. Some related to anger are jealousy, envy, sadness, depression, and grief. Excitement includes enthusiasm and positive anticipation.

In a state of fear, your body is trying to get away from what is fearful. It would actually run if it could. If you decide not to run, the impulse to do so is still there, and the conflict between the impulse to run and the decision not to causes physical tension. In extreme fear, the tension can become so great that fainting occurs or body functions are impaired.

In an angry state, your body is trying to push something away, forcefully change it, or hurt it, and any of these impulses causes tension, too, especially when they are suppressed. Fear and anger are used to resist people and situations, and that gets translated by our body into physical tension. Sustained excitement can lead to tension caused by the body's need to rest. Acute or chronic fear, anger, or excitement can be very stressful in terms of the physical tension they produce.

Of course, direct muscle tension is not the only physical response to emotional stress. Chemical changes occur as well which can produce stress effects on other systems of the body that lead indirectly to increased physical tension. In fact, emotional and physical responses are so interrelated that chemical changes in the body, either natural or caused by food, drugs, or herbs, can induce emotional stress and physical tension. Endorphins, caffeine, alcohol, heroin, and cocaine are some of the better known substances that can do this. However, I want to remind you that even something as serious as drug addiction has been cured by many very different methods.

The Mental Stress Factor

Your slightest thought causes a slight physical response. Your strongest thoughts cause strong physical responses. Remembering, imagining, planning, speculating, wondering, meditating, and any other form of mental activity have corresponding physical effects. That means your body automatically tries to carry out the physical equivalent of your thoughts by activating your nervous system, modifying your breathing pattern, altering your hormonal and other chemical output, and adjusting your muscle tension, among other things. If you remember waterskiing, the muscles you used when you did it twitch right now in resonance with the mental act of remembering. If you wish you could kick your boss in the rear, the muscles required to do that tense up in preparation for the act. The more abstract your thinking—that is, the less related your thinking is to any kind of physical action—the less response there is in your body. However, sustained abstract thinking accompanied by shallow breathing and an unchanging posture can result in unhealthy physical tension.

Criticism, denial, doubt, confusion, and conflicting beliefs or motivations all produce mental stress and can cause physical tension. Criticism, by itself, is similar to anger without the depth of emotion. When you criticize, you are experiencing an impulse to push, change, or hurt, and when the body tries to respond to the impulse, the effort produces physical tension. Denial is a mental version of fear, with the same impulse to move away from something and the same kind of tension that results. Doubt occurs when ideas are in conflict, and confusion occurs when choices are in conflict. When your stressful thoughts also generate stressful emotions, the effects of emotional stress are added to the effects of mental stress and physical tension is increased even more. I'll elaborate on ways to alleviate confusion in the Emotional Energy section of chapter 7.

The Spiritual Stress Factor

The main symptoms of what I call spiritual stress are apathy and the severe form of boredom called ennui, although headaches and other physical and behavioral symptoms can also be connected with spiritual stress.

Apathy comes from a habit of increasingly distancing oneself from surrounding values, emotions, and activities to the point where a person is less and less stirred or motivated by the things that affect and interest other people. Apathy could be called the spiritual version of anger, because it seems to be a coping response to a sense of being helpless or frustrated. Instead of feeling angry or depressed about being helpless or frustrated, some people simply suppress feeling. Unfortunately, the only way to do this is to keep muscles in a state of tension so that feelings can't be felt. And more unfortunately, if enough additional stress of any kind is added to the mix, the effort to hold back feelings may break down and allow an outburst of violence. It is quite common for people who suddenly break out in a frenzy of aggressive activity to be described by people who know them as "quiet and unobtrusive." I remember meeting a man who was very placid until someone did something he didn't like. Then he became quietly menacing. I'm glad that no one did anything to really upset him while I was around.

Ennui is the spiritual counterpart of denial. The state of ennui, however, is characterized by a denial of importance rather than existence. This is related to a sense of being unwanted or unloved. By this method of coping, a person tries to pretend that it doesn't matter. It's a variation on running away and therefore a version of fear. When this form of turning away from others and from the world becomes acute or chronic, it can also produce physical tension.

A curious form of spiritual stress comes from excessive fantasizing or meditation. The effect is something like the result of eating too much good food. These activities may be termed excessive when they result in physical tension. While the effect varies greatly among different individuals, the process is the same. When consciousness is "away" from the body for too long, there is an increase in physical tension, which may include symptoms such as headaches and anxiety or worse. This effect is aggravated when fantasizing or meditation is used as an escape from ordinary reality, but even "healthy" fantasizers and meditators may feel a more or less subtle sense of relaxation or relief when they come back to body awareness. To some, the physical response of returning to body awareness is so strong that it seems as if their spirit is "slamming" back into the body because there is often a significant shaking or jerking of the muscles. A close study of this phenomenon has convinced me that the actual effect is one of a sudden release of tension.

Holistic Tension

Many modern healing systems are often ineffective because they are overly exclusive. In other words, they tend to treat illness as being caused *only* by physical or emotional or mental or spiritual conditions and to reject some or all of the others as having no bearing on the problem. Yet tension can come from any of these realms and there is usually a combination of more than one in a particular symptom. Even something as simple as a smashed finger can be related to feelings of guilt, or confusion about a life direction, or to spiritual alienation, or to all three at once. If the finger is only treated at the physical level, the healing will be slowed down by the tension being maintained by one of the other conditions. A healer ignores any one of them at the peril of the healee. Frequently, dramatic improvement in mental health occurs through nutrition, tumors are removed with hypnosis, and emotional release cures spiritual apathy.

In my view of healing, excessive physical, emotional, mental, or spiritual stress, or any combination of these, cause the excessive tension that produces illness or disharmony. It follows, therefore, that reducing or removing the stress, either the external condition or the internal resistance, would allow a relaxation of the tension that would either result in a healing or greatly benefit the healing process.

THE HEALING FACTOR

Tension is the illness factor. What is the healing factor? As I've related above, it certainly isn't the method, because too many different methods can accomplish the same thing. Is there any component in every kind of healing that would start the process? I venture to say that there is one thing and that it has two aspects.

The one thing that seems to be present in every healing is intent. Obviously there has to be some intention or motivation on the part of the individual to get well or it wouldn't happen. The two aspects of intent are the intent of the body and the intent of the mind.

The Intent of the Body

It's unquestionable that there is a natural intention of the body to get well. In any case of illness or injury, the body immediately begins to repair itself to the best of its ability, and it uses signals such as pain or hunger to notify the conscious mind that it needs help in getting back to a state of wellness. You could call it an automatic intent. Tension interferes with the body's ability to heal itself, sometimes to the point of turning a healing response into a self-destructive act. Blood clotting, for example, is a healing response, but stress can cause it to happen at the wrong place and time. Still, there is no doubt that the body's intent to heal itself is a critical healing factor and anything we can do to assist that intent, such as relieving stress, is useful and good. The intent of the body to heal itself may also be called the subconscious intent.

The Intent of the Mind

The other aspect of intent is conscious intent, also known as motivation, will, or willpower. Although one can assume the existence of subconscious intent to heal as a given in all situations, the conscious intent is a variable factor. At first, it would seem that everyone would naturally want to be well. Some people, however, consciously use physical disharmony as a spiritual discipline, as a means of learning, as a means of manipulation, as a means of self-punishment, or as a way of diverting rage. In other words, people are capable of multiple, conflicting motivations that can either encourage or interfere with the body's will-to-wellness.

The ability to maintain conscious intent is another consideration. You often hear about near miraculous cures that were due to a person's strong will to live or to be well. When it is said that a person has strong willpower, what is really meant is that he or she can hold a focus without being easily diverted or discouraged, whereas a person with a weak will is one who gives up or switches focus easily. So whether you call it conscious intent, willpower, or sustained attention, this is an important part of the mental aspect of the healing factor.

While the body's intent to heal is supported by relieving tension, as well as by providing the supplies it needs for healing, such as nutrients and oxygen, the mind's intent to be well is supported by positive expectation, or the belief that to be well is good and possible. Often this expectation or belief comes from within the individual. Perhaps more often, however, it is something outside the individual that provides the expectation. This outside something can be called a placebo.

One day as I was browsing the Internet, my eye was caught by an excerpt from a paper presented at the 104th annual convention of the American Psychological Association on August 12 at the University of Connecticut. The presentation, called "Listening to Prozac but Hearing

Placebo," was made by Guy Sapirstein, Ph.D., and Irving Kirsch, Ph.D., and was at least partly based on an analysis of thirty-nine studies of depressed patients from 1974 to 1995 who received various antidepressant medications. Remarkably, the study concluded that only 27 percent of the response to medication was due to a true effect of the drug, while 50 percent was due to a placebo effect and 23 percent was due to other nonspecific factors. Dr. Sapirstein stated that "people benefiting from drugs are benefiting because they think that taking the antidepressant medicine is working. If we take these results and say that improvement is due to what the patients think, then how people think and its effect on how they feel are more powerful than the chemical substance."

Wow! That's such an important statement that it is worth repeating. The expectations people have about a drug may have a more powerful effect on them than the drug itself.

According to *Merriam-Webster's Collegiate Dictionary*, tenth edition, the placebo effect is an "improvement in the condition of a sick person that occurs in response to treatment but cannot be considered due to the specific treatment used." Well. If, as seems to be the case, the results of one form of treatment can be duplicated by another totally different form of treatment, and if the only difference is what the person thinks about the treatment, then the actual method used doesn't matter very much.

Whoa, there! How can this be? Am I saying that medicine and surgery and diet and exercise don't really work as healing agents? Not at all. Don't panic. I'm not trying to overthrow the whole current health-care system. I'm just suggesting that they work to the degree that the patient expects them to. Physical interventions such as medicine, surgery, diet, and exercise clearly affect the body, but for a healing to take place, it seems as though they have to affect the mind as well. What exactly is it that gives placebos such power to stimulate positive expectations in the mind and in the body? Here's my theory about it.

Subconscious Expectation

Usually, one thinks of an expectation as being a strictly mental thing, either consciously intended or learned as a habit, that has little to do with healing. Naturally, you can find many instances in which a person expected to get well from a particular treatment and it didn't work. What happened in such a case?

This type of event can be understood if the idea of an expectation includes the expectations of the body as well as the expectations of the mind. The expectations of the body would include subconscious expectations based on remembered experience, as well as expectations based on genetic memory, the memories of our ancestors that we all carry around with us in different combinations. This would offer an explanation as to why different people have different responses to the same treatment even when their conscious expectations are the same.

The more familiar a form is, the better the body will respond to it. Familiarity might come from the form's appearance (e.g., shaped like a pill), from its taste (sweet or vile), from its origins (a doctor's office or a shaman's hut), or anything else that is associated with a previous healing. The healing effect occurs to the degree that the familiarity makes the body feel secure, helps it to relax, and stimulates it to carry out the process of healing. If it does those things, then the form doesn't matter. Depending on your background, eating turtle eggs under a sacred tree, taking antibiotics, or analyzing your dreams could each have the same effect.

Conscious Expectation

Conscious expectation is based on authority. What I mean by that is the belief that something or someone is powerful or important. Authority, here the power to heal, can be placed in an object or substance, in a procedure, in a person, or in a desire.

A sugar pill doesn't work very well as a placebo unless it is given to you by an authority figure, such as a doctor or nurse, or if it is presented as a drug that already has a successful reputation. The better the reputation, the better the effect, and this is true for pills as well as magical amulets or the cartilage of a shark.

If you are afraid of a particular form of treatment, such as chemotherapy, hypnosis, occult ritual, or whatever, the resulting tension will certainly interfere with the intended effect. But if you are impressed with the form and possibilities of such a treatment and you can hardly wait to try it out, then the effects can be miraculous. The stronger your belief that a treatment method will work, the better the effects.

Shamans, doctors, therapists, faith healers, and other kinds of healers usually go out of their way to impress you with their healing ability, using things like costumes, confidence, special behavior and objects, environment, certificates, books, cost of treatment, and anything else that will convince you they can help. There's nothing wrong with that as long as it helps your healing. Sometimes, a healer doesn't do anything to impress people and it is reputation alone that gives him or her authority. There used to be a Brazilian healer named Arigo who was very unimpressive to look at and who did nothing to seek clients. He worked out of a dirty hut and used only his hands and a rusty knife to heal all sorts of conditions for hundreds of people a day. But he was very effective and eventually people from all over the world came to him for treatment. The stronger your belief that a person can help, the better the effects.

Finally there is the "authority of desire." This sounds odd at first, but I'm talking about the placebo effect of having a goal or a purpose. When you have a positive motivation or reason for getting well—a state of health that you want to achieve or an activity that you want to do, rather than a pain or illness that you want to get rid of—the goal takes on a kind of authority that helps to mobilize your conscious beliefs and strengthen your body's healing abilities. Most of the stories related to this effect are about athletes, probably because they are usually well trained to give goals a great deal of authority or importance.

HEALTH IS FEELING GOOD

Ultimately, the only sensible way to define health is by how good you feel. If your physical body is functioning properly, but you are emotionally or mentally miserable then you are not healthy, both because you don't feel good and because the misery is causing unnecessary physical tension. One could say that a person is physically healthy but mentally sick, or emotionally healthy and physically sick, but those distinctions imply a separateness that doesn't really exist in experience.

Some typical characteristics of the healthy state are effective functioning of the body, physical strength, perceived energy level, emotional pleasure, and positive attitude. But these are also just effects of feeling good, so for the purpose of this book the personal perception of feeling good will be the measure of health. This means, of course, that a particular individual might be very healthy according to this measure, although some of his or her parts are not functioning perfectly and other people might not agree with the individual's perception. And then, there is health and there is *health!* It amazes me how many people think of health only in terms of not being sick, when there is a great range of health beyond that. Perhaps it is because in English there are no words other than adjectives to describe varying states of health, and even those words are general (very healthy, outstandingly healthy, exceptionally healthy, and the like). Yet, you can observe vast differences in the "healthiness" of, for example, a top athlete and a desk clerk; or a charismatic leader and a farmhand, even though each of them might be considered physically, emotionally, mentally, and spiritually healthy. By observation and experience, you can tell that the common signs of increasing health are more energy and endurance, faster reflexes, greater mental clarity, faster healing, and more charisma. But the English language doesn't acknowledge this. Curious.

The conclusion is very simple. Healing happens because the body has the capability and the intent. Healing happens better when the subconscious intent is supported by the relaxation of tension and by conscious intent. In the next chapter, I'll present the roles played by memory and imagination in the healing process.

CHAPTER TWO

Memory, the Body, and Healing

The human body is a magnificent organization of elements that is capable of many wonderful accomplishments. But perhaps the body's most outstanding ability is that it memorizes, which means that it learns, and it remembers.

In the beginning of human life, a sperm and an egg get together and share memories. The initial result is the awe-inspiring formation of a human body from a single cell. As the cells divide they start to differentiate, meaning that different cells use different memories to become different parts of the body. In general, every human body forms in the same way because each one remembers the same basic pattern. Differences in human bodies derive from memories of variations in the basic pattern. Hair color, skin color, bone structure, sex ... these and many other characteristics can vary between humans because of differences in remembered ancestral experiences, but overall the basic pattern is the same. Most humans look pretty much human.

Remarkably, the individual parts of the body tend to remember their individual variations on the basic pattern. The skin, for instance, is constantly changing. Every day old cells die and drop off and new cells are born to replace them. Most of the dust in your house, in fact, is probably composed of old skin cells. In a period of about six weeks, your skin has completely renewed itself. The new cells remember not only what color they are supposed to be, but, even though skin is different on different parts of the body, the new cells remember what kind of skin they are supposed to be. This is true for virtually all the cells of your body, although various cells die and renew themselves at different rates. According to some estimates, you have the equivalent of a brand new body every seven months. Reincarnation is a fact of life.

HOW DO WE REMEMBER?

Memory is such an important aspect of healing that you need to have some understanding of how people remember. However, I must warn you that I am now crossing into very theoretical territory. (On the other hand, this whole book could be considered very theoretical territory, so what difference does it make?) Given that caution, here is the explanation of memory that I use in my healing work and classes.

Genetic memory is stored in the cells. Popular thinking supposes that memory resides in the brain, but I suggest that memory of personal experience is stored in the cells of the entire body, not in the brain alone. Specifically, it is stored in cells or groups of cells throughout the body, particularly muscle tissue, that are activated or sensitized at the moment an experience happens. The more actively involved certain cells are at that time, the more involved they are in recalling the memory.

Because experiences include many different forms of sensory stimulation (such as sight, sound, and touch) the whole memory of an experience may be stored in bits and pieces in several parts of the body.

Memories related to driving a car, for example, are stored in all the different parts of the body involved in the driving experience. When enough memories have accumulated, your body can drive easily while your mind is primarily engaged in conversation or thought.

When a memory is recalled, the brain acts as an information processor; it receives and transmits signals from and to the rest of the body. It may have its own experiential memory, but it is not the entire storehouse of personal memory. If a memory is requested by the body or the mind, the brain sends a message such as this: "Hey, we need a memory of how to ride a bicycle" or "Give us the memory of Maryann's party last November." The presence of an actual bicycle can stimulate a very rapid recovery of all the memories held by the various cells involved in bicycle riding. The recall of details from the party may take a little longer, typically starting with the most energetically intense part of the experience (for example, when you broke Maryann's favorite vase) and pulling in other memories around it.

In both cases the recall is associative, that is, memories are linked to each other by association, rather than in a linear sequence. Touching the handlebars of the bicycle will trigger recall of how to sit, which will trigger recall of how to pedal, which will trigger recall of how to keep your balance, and so on, so rapidly that you probably won't notice any delay. In remembering something such as a party, however, you usually get the most intense experience first, then events surrounding that experience (not necessarily in chronological order), then events of lesser intensity and their associations, and so on. Somewhere in the middle the association process might leap to, for example, the first time you met Maryann, when she still thought you were a nice person. And so, on its own the body remembers by associations of energy, similarity, symbolism, and the like without regard to time and space. The mind can impose an orderly sequence to remembering. One example of using a memory for healing any number of maladies is provided in the Intentional Reverie section of chapter 5.

Memory itself is stored as a pattern of movement on a very small scale, like a code. Basically, the cells have an experience that is translated into a miniscule bit of movement. To recall a memory the cells involved in various parts of the experience vibrate their code in unison and send a signal of their activity to the brain, which translates these signals into a recalled experience and gives other cells signals to take action as necessary. When you say the word "brain," for example, some cells in some part of your body begin to vibrate with the code for the sound "b," while others send the signal for the sound "r," and so on, and still others vibrate with the parts of an image of the brain you saw once, etc. Meanwhile, the brain puts all these signals together to give you the memory of a brain.

Of course, in such a system there has to be great redundancy. That is, there must be many groups of cells that encode the same experience at the same time, so that if the brain cannot access a memory from one group of cells for some reason (see Stress and the Body, later in this chapter), it may be able to access the same memory from another group. Nevertheless, my research indicates that most, if not all, of our memories are dependent on key groups of cells that have to be stimulated first for recall to happen.

Cute, you may say. Or fantastic. Or even absurd. But to my mind, a practical theory. Look, I don't really know if this is the way memory works, but neither does anyone else, in spite of what they may claim. However, I use this model because it seems to fit the experience people have with memory, it answers a lot of questions about memory, and it's extremely useful in the process of healing. So I'm going to treat the model as though it's true until I run across a better idea, because it's very practical to do so. Using this idea of memory to help explain motivation, expectation, energy, and stress as they relate to the body allows for the development of many workable healing techniques. And a fascinating variety of these techniques will be described in later chapters.

MOTIVATION AND THE BODY

The essential motivation of the body is to move toward pleasure and away from pain. The reason is very simple. Pleasure feels good and pain feels bad. The body remembers this, and so it loves the one and fears the other. In the case of specific experiences, the body will categorize them hierarchically according to their pleasure or pain components as it memorizes them. Then it will seek to repeat pleasurable experiences and avoid painful ones. Or, out of a choice of pleasurable experiences it will tend to seek the most pleasurable by its memorized standards, and out of a choice of painful experiences it will tend to seek out the least painful. Or, again, it will put up with a certain amount of pain to reach a pleasure high on the hierarchy. Of course, successive experiences may change the hierarchy as well as the categories. This is the simple explanation for most human behavior. It tells us why children prefer video games to homework, why people climb mountains, and why people put up with painful relationships.

Motivation and Learning

As you grow up, your body must learn how to cope with changing circumstances and new experiences, from eating and walking to potty-training and playing, to working and illness, and all the other events of life. How does motivation affect learning?

I'll use the example of a baby learning to walk. First, there has to be the desire to walk. It's important not to take this for granted. As I've mentioned in another book, my eldest son didn't walk for so long that we began to think he had a disability, until one day we picked him up from a child care center to find him running. The woman in charge said he had been crawling along quite happily and then saw older boys having such a good time running around that he got up and joined them. Before that he had been carried everywhere and felt no need to walk. Most children, however, first want to see something or reach something or do something that requires walking, and that's what motivates the attempt. For anything to be learned, there must be a benefit to the learning that provides the motivation to learn.

The process of learning involves motivation, experience, feedback, and selective memorizing. Observing a child learning how to walk is very interesting. In the beginning, the steps are tentative as the child tries out various combinations of body movement and balance. By an adroit use of biofeedback—in other words, by finding out whether a particular combination results in falling down or staying up—the child gradually remembers what works, forgets what doesn't work, and learns the skill of walking.

There you have it, the keys to learning new behavior and skills. Remember what works and forget what doesn't work. That's how a baby learns; that's how a child learns; that's how an adult learns. That's how you learn to be healthier, and that's how you learn to be sick.

Sickness Is Learned Behavior

Did I just say that the process of learning to walk is the same as the process of learning to be sick? And did I just say that sickness is a learned behavior? Yup.

Everything that humans do is learned behavior, whether it was learned first by ancestors and remembered by genes, or learned in a given lifetime and remembered by cells. Every kind of learning necessarily involves the body, and every experience that repeats itself is learned behavior whether you are talking about language or colds. You learn a language by means of repeating patterns of physical behavior to produce meaningful sounds because it's useful. You learn an illness by means of repeating patterns of physical behavior to produce meaningful symptoms because it's useful, too. The usefulness, or benefit, of illness comes from its value as a means of reducing stress. It's common for a person's subconscious to generate an illness when work becomes too painful to tolerate; or for the subconscious to use illness as a means of avoiding a painful emotional confrontation. Unfortunately, much of the benefit is lost because the illness also produces stress. If the physical, emotional, mental, or spiritual benefits of an illness outweigh the disadvantages according to the body's hierarchy of memory, however, it will keep repeating the illness until it learns a better means of obtaining the benefits.

BELIEFS AND THE BODY

A body belief is an expectation that a particular event or thing will lead to another particular event or thing. The body is not concerned with truth as an abstract concept, only with truth as an experience. Its idea of truth derives from memory associations and not from reasoning. And it is very gullible. It will believe virtually anything if you present it convincingly enough, i.e., often enough or intensely enough or with enough authority to overcome any previously held expectations.

At the same time, however, the body is rigorously logical. Once a belief has been accepted on the body's terms, it will follow the logical consequences to the end. So people "catch colds" when they get wet in the rain and not when they take a shower; they throw away their crutches and walk normally after drinking holy water, and they lay down and die when a doctor tells them they have an incurable disease.

Authority and the Body

Authority is of the utmost importance to the body. The acceptance of a belief, or an expectation, is basically a learning process (essentially a memorizing process), that is dependent on motivation for its success. The most fundamental motivation for the body is sensory stimulation and, as I've mentioned above, this can be divided into pleasure and pain. For the body, sensory stimulation is the ultimate authority motivating learning and memorizing. This makes the effects of intensity and repetition on learning quite understandable, but what about the acceptance of the words of other people? Why do people buy a particular deodorant because a famous athlete endorses it? Why do people get sick or get well because of what a doctor says? Why do people copy the behavior of well-known actors? Where is the sensory motivation?

I don't think most people actually say to themselves, "Oh, if this athlete uses this deodorant it must be good," or "Oh, the doctor knows all about this so I'd better die," or "If I act like the actor, people will think I'm as good as he or she is." Some people may have these thoughts, but I think the reason for these types of behaviors is much more basic. As far as our bodies are concerned, we are animals—unusual animals, but animals nevertheless. Not only that, but we are pack or tribal animals, like the other apes. For a tribal animal one of the worst pains is banishment, or separation from the tribe. And one of the greatest pleasures is acceptance by the tribe. The leader of the tribe is the one who has the power to accept or reject its members. So the leader's word, which carries the potential for pleasure or pain, is accepted as the authority derived from remembered or expected sensory stimulation of some kind.

In modern times our tribes have become nuclear families, gangs, clubs, teams, political parties, churches, networks, and all manner of other associations. Today we can belong to a whole bunch of tribes at the same time, each with their own kinds of authority and expectations. And in areas of life where there is no clear tribal authority, we tend to accept the word of anyone who acts like an authority. It takes an exceptional person to become his or her own authority, but if that can be done, and if the body can be convinced, then the body will happily accept you as its leader.

ENERGY AND THE BODY

Learning is much easier and longer-lasting in the presence of physical, emotional, or subtle energetic stimulation of some kind. Anything that helps the cells to move increases the ability to learn. Your body will always remember best your most physically active experiences (such as riding a bicycle), your most emotionally charged experiences (like your first crush), your most energetically powerful experiences (a flood, or a tornado, or a big waterfall), and your most repetitive experiences (such as your habits and skills). Your body remembers best anything that produces intense or repeated sensations. Energy is necessary to memorizing.

Energy is also necessary to the healing process. The energy available to the body determines to a large degree the effectiveness of its own healing activities and the speed of the healing. How much energy the body has available for all the things it has to do, including the handling of stress, plus growth and regrowth, repair and maintenance, and just plain physical activity, depends on a complex mix of glucose, oxygen, water, vitamins, minerals, hormones, and the like. Poor diet, lack of exercise, and excessive stress can deplete the body's energy reserves very quickly, although some people do amazingly well by doing everything wrong. Also, the body seems to be able to get energy from sources outside of itself by means other than those just mentioned. Some people are uncomfortable with the idea, but the energy fields of people, places, and things can amplify, stimulate, or add to a person's own energy.

STRESS AND THE BODY

Stress has the effect of causing tension in the body, and tension has the effect of inhibiting cellular movement. The inhibition of movement, in turn, inhibits the access to various kinds of memory, from how to function to the recollection of learned skills and information. As tension accumulates, your ability to remember things worsens. This can happen over a period of time and the effect can be so subtle that it is often attributed to a "natural" aging process. There is nothing natural about the body losing its functions, however.

As an example, at my age (sixty plus) I am "supposed" to be wearing glasses. That's considered natural. The fact is that 99 percent of the time I don't wear glasses because I don't need to, and the 1 percent of the time I do wear something (nonprescription magnifiers or pinholes), it's only because I haven't bothered to relax my eye muscles. One of the sure signs that my body, and particularly my eyes, are under stress is when my vision becomes less clear. (I'll tell you about the exercises I use for my eyes in the Mental Energy section of chapter 7.) In sum, many physical problems are due to the suppression of memory by accumulated tension.

Acute tension coming from a sudden stress or shock produces very clear and definite effects on the body. At about the same time, the muscles tense, glucose is released into the bloodstream, blood vessels dilate and fluid is spilled into surrounding muscle tissue (causing dehydration as one effect), the heart rate increases, the thymus gland contracts (suppressing white blood cell production), vitamins and minerals are rapidly used up, and memory is severely inhibited, as well as less serious effects. Depending on the degree of stress or shock, a person may forget his own name (scared witless), forget how to speak (scared speechless), forget how to breathe (scared stiff), experience general amnesia, become pale (loss of fluid in the blood vessels), or faint (both from a restriction of blood to the brain and as a possible escape mechanism from the danger). Generally, all of these symptoms subside as the body relaxes.

The body's natural reaction to stress is to stress back. Remember the "mutual force" mentioned in the first chapter? When the body experiences pressure, it tends to exert pressure back (this is what builds muscles in weightlifting). When it experiences pulling, it pulls back (this is why stretching can be beneficial). When it is twisted, it twists back (this is why physical therapy can be helpful).

When the body is lacking something, it tries to compensate. It would prefer to fill the void with what is lacking, but if that's not available it will use a substitute, either a physical alternative or symbolic alternative (this is why the body may draw calcium from one bone to try and assist another bone, why people get cravings for things like dirt and paint, and why people who crave love may eat too much). If the body, or a part of it, seems to be in danger of imminent injury, the body will attempt to withdraw from the danger if it can, or at least surround the endangered part with a protective coating or buffer zone (that's why we get calluses and blisters or excess fat and muscle tension). If something seems to be attacking the body from the inside, the body will send agents to attack it back (that's why you have white blood cells and antibodies).

Regardless of whether the source of a stress is an injury or a virus, the actual symptoms known as illness are produced by the body itself. This is evidenced by the fact that different individuals who encounter the same source of stress may either produce completely different symptoms or no symptoms at all. Not everyone exposed to so-called carcinogens gets cancer. Not everyone exposed to someone with a cold gets a cold. Not everyone exposed to AIDS gets AIDS. Not everyone who is cut with a knife gets a scar, nor do all exposures to fires produce burns. Why are there differences?

When your body encounters stress, it must react. How does it know what to do? The answer must be that it remembers what to do based on previous experience with similar stress. Where do those memories come from?

Stress and Genetic Memory

The first source of memory for coping with stress is genetic memory. In essence, the body asks itself, "What did my ancestors do in situations like this?" Then it scans the genes until it finds a pattern of behavior that seems to fit and uses it. Ancestral, or genetic, memory predisposes a person to act in a particular way under certain kinds of stress. This is obviously true in the case of diseases with a multitude of symptoms, such as influenza, where some sufferers will get fever, some stomach upsets, some stuffy or runny noses, some chills, some aches and pains, and some will experience all of the above. The role of genetic memory is particularly important where emotional stress is concerned. In different people, reactions to similar stressful situations may manifest as bronchial asthma, pneumonia, heart disease, or lung cancer.

Stress and Experiential Memory

The second source of memory for coping with stress is personal experience. "What did I do the last time I encountered stress like this?" Then the body consciousness scans personal memory to find an appropriate reaction pattern. Many headaches can be characterized as such reactions. The greater the hidden benefit a symptom has, the more likely it will be remembered and used again. This source of memory includes learned and practiced skills, as well. Some people learn skills such as meditation or hatha yoga to use under stress, others learn how to find the drug store or make a doctor's appointment.

Stress and Adopted Memory

The third source is the experience of other people. "What is everyone else doing about this kind of stress?" After scanning its memory of other peoples' behavior in a similar experience, the body copies their behavior. Typically, the body adopts the behavior of others as a last resort, when it does not have a genetic or personal memory to use. Note that in some circumstances the body may be subject to "mob behavior" and take on an illness out of empathy with others, such as when a husband undergoes birth pains while his wife is in labor. It is my personal opinion that one of the greatest problems of modern times is "teeveegenic" illness, brought on by television ads selling remedies for colds, headaches, flu, and assorted female disorders. On the other hand, it may be important for the economy.

Even though illness may be a distorted reaction to stress, it is still the body's best effort to cope based on what's possible at the moment. Therefore, one can say that all illness is an attempt on the part of the body to solve a problem related to stress. Healing is the effort to help the body do a better job of solving the problem.

CHAPTER THREE

Imagination, the Mind, and Healing

T he mind is an intangible entity. Of course, you know that it's there because you can experience its effects, but you can't hold it or smell it or see it. For some behavioral scientists, the phenomenon of the "mind" is produced by physical processes within the body. Their idea of the "mind-body effect" is not that the mind and the body interact, but that the mind is an effect of the body. However, if that's true, then what they say is only an effect of physical processes and you don't have to pay any attention to it. It might be more useful to think about the mind in terms of a metaphor and say it is like the ocean, with a lot of layers, a lot of currents, a lot of hidden places, a lot of open places, and host to a lot of useful and very weird stuff.

Many people have tried to determine what the essential characteristic of the mind is, and so have I. I believe that the essential characteristic of the mind is imagination. All of the talents associated with the mind, such as analysis, synthesis, reasoning, determination, decision-making, and creativity, derive from its ability to imagine. The mind can imagine what was, what is, and what will be. Even more wonderfully, it can imagine what wasn't, what isn't, and what never will be, and on occasion, has a hard time telling the difference.

Everything that the body can experience, the mind can imagine, and then some. It is as if the mind uses memory as a springboard to create brand new experiences, first as thoughts, then as fantasies, then as plans, then as directed activities, using imagination from beginning to end. As a matter of fact, the so-called third eye that is discussed in many spiritual teachings is really the eye of the imagination, the "mind's eye." It is not the pineal gland, although that organ may play an important role in the imaginative process. Traditionally, the "third eye" is located in the center of the forehead, the area of the frontal lobes of the brain, while the pineal gland is located straight back in from the tip of your nose. Interestingly, damage to or destruction of the frontal lobes, as by the ill-famed process called "lobotomy," seems to have the effect of inhibiting or eliminating the faculty of imagination—another example of the body affecting the mind as much as the mind affects the body.

MOTIVATION AND THE MIND

Like the body, the mind is motivated toward pleasure and away from pain. However, pleasure and pain for the mind are not directly connected to sensations. As far as the mind is concerned, pleasure consists in "rightness" and pain consists in "wrongness." The specifics of rightness and wrongness have to do with beliefs, which I'll address shortly, but generally the mind moves toward rightness and away from wrongness. These two qualities do not seem to be absolute. Every human society has different criteria for rightness and wrongness, and every human being in a society has his or her own peculiar variations on the criteria. On the whole, however, rightness is associated with conformity, effectiveness, meaningfulness, importance, and knowledge, while wrongness is associated with nonconformity, ineffectiveness, meaninglessness, unimportance, and ignorance. The mind is very clever, though. Nonconformity to one person can be conformity to an ideal or a purpose in another person; ineffectiveness in one person's view can be effectiveness in the view of someone who wants others to do things for him; meaninglessness can be meaningful to someone who writes about it; the unimportant can become important as a distraction from stress; and ignorance is sometimes bliss.

PROBLEM-SOLVING AND THE MIND

The pleasure that people get from solving problems is so potentially intense that mathematicians have been known to have physical orgasms when an equation works out. In order to solve a problem, there first has to be an idea that a problem exists. Problems for the body are very simple: is there enough food, air, water, shelter, or sex to satisfy me in this moment? If there is, fine; if there isn't, get some. Thanks to imagination, however, the mind is able to create problems to solve. The need for food turns into land use problems; the need for air turns into pollution problems; the need for water turns into problems of dam projects; the need for shelter turns into problems with the housing industry; and the need for sex turns into moral problems. And then, because that's not enough to be satisfied, the mind creates opportunities for solving problems that have nothing to do with bodily needs, such as football, chess, theoretical science, and computer games.

The unsolved problem is a source of pain for the mind. It is a wrongness that must be righted, even if it is only a wrongness because it is imagined to be. Many people spend sleepless nights trying to solve big problems, such as how to prevent a war, and even little problems, such as the name of the Professor on Gilligan's Island. If the wrongness cannot be righted for any reason, the mind will often displace the problem. That is, it will pick another problem that is easier to solve to represent the first one. Then it will busily solve the second problem while pretending (imagining) that the first one does not exist. It's similar to doing crossword puzzles instead of doing your taxes, except that some kinds of displacement (such as abuse, compulsions, and obsessions) may have even more severe effects.

What people call "mental illness" is also the mind's attempt to solve a problem. When ordinary methods of resolving a difficult life circumstance do not work and no acceptable alternatives are available, the mind must invent other methods. If one's everyday personality cannot manage a situation, some people develop a substitute personality who can, perhaps by borrowing one from fiction or memory or creatively mixing different bits and pieces of each. If self-criticism becomes overwhelming, some people become deeply depressed (to a degree that threatens self-integrity), then switch over to mania to compensate, then fall back into depression when the mania ceases to work, then . . . over and over. If criticism from others becomes overwhelming, some people retreat to an inner world where no one can touch them. Every form of mental illness can be seen as a problem-solving strategy. Some of them even work at times.

CURIOSITY AND THE MIND

Closely related to problem-solving as a source of pleasure for the mind is curiosity. Many animals have curiosity, of course. You can observe it easily in dogs, cats, cows, and birds, but that just tells you that they also have minds. However, this is a book about humans, so I'll leave animal minds to someone else.

Curiosity requires imagination. In order to be curious about something, you have to be able to imagine that there is something worth investigating. The pleasure is not in the curiosity itself, of course, but in satisfying the curiosity (or at least anticipating/imagining such satisfaction). This characteristic of the mind is what motivates many great adventurers, explorers, inventors, philosophers, scientists, and writers, who are usually followed by problem-solvers. The Curies were curious about radiation and discovered radium, then someone had to figure out what to do with it. Nicolas Tesla was curious about electricity and invented alternating current, then someone had to figure out how to make it the standard for the world. Jules Verne was curious about human adventure and speculated about travel to the moon, then someone had to figure out how to get there. Captain Cook was curious about what was over the horizon and "discovered" Hawaii, then someone had to figure out how to take it away from the Hawaiians. With curiosity, the wrongness is the unknown and the rightness is the knowing.

BELIEFS AND THE MIND

There are those who think that the highest form of mental activity is reasoning, or so-called rational thought. This is because they don't understand what the use of reason really is. Reasoning has to do with explaining or making logical sense out of something, and "rational" simply refers to the use of reasoning. But first there has to be an assumption on which to base the explanation or the logic. This means you have to make up (imagine) an opinion about something and call it true, which turns it into a belief. Or you can borrow someone else's opinions and call them true, which turns their opinions into your beliefs. When you no longer question a belief it is called a fact.

There are relatively few real facts in the world, in the sense of experiences that are common to everyone and that are not just interpretations of experience. Gravity is a fact, but explanations of gravity are just opinions. Pain is a fact, but ideas about what causes it are opinions. Illness is a fact, but causes and cures come from the realm of beliefs, which are unquestioned opinions. And even actual facts are subject to beliefs. There isn't a single fact that you could name that someone else would not sincerely contradict. And that's a fact.

When the mind comes up with an opinion and turns it into a belief by deciding not to question it, the body remembers it and stores it as a rule that governs any related behavior. If your mother told you that you would catch a cold if you got your feet wet with your shoes on, and you accepted that as a fact, your body would adopt that as a rule and make sure that you would get cold symptoms whenever you got your feet wet with shoes on. If you decide that you won't catch a cold if you get your feet wet while wearing certain kinds of shoes, such as reef walkers, and if you turn that into a belief by not questioning that decision, then your body will revise its remembered rule so that you can splash around on the reefs without getting a cold. Beliefs created (imagined) by the mind can even override genetic beliefs inherited by the body, which is what happens in the case of many so-called miraculous cures.

Back to reasoning. Once the mind accepts or makes an assumption, it delights in drawing logical conclusions from it to explain something, conclusions that seem to be consistent with the initial assumption. A good example of a currently popular one is the Big Bang Theory of the universe. The assumption is that the universe began with an explosion, which is a pretty big assumption since no one was there. Scientists and reporters typically speak of it as an unquestionable fact, and many different conclusions are drawn from it, all of which are very imaginative.

If you have a sense of humor, it's fun to watch the response when observable phenomena don't fit the facts. There is a scramble to try and interpret the phenomena to make them fit, or, if that can't be done, to alter the facts just enough to allow the phenomena in, or, as a last resort, to ignore the phenomena. An example of this is the widely held assumption that the only viable way to treat cancer is by surgery, radiation, and chemotherapy, in spite of abundant evidence to the contrary. Some doctors who accept this assumption try to find the physical mechanisms that allow healing methods such as prayer and affirmation to be effective; some expand their assumption to include the placebo effect; and some insist that the healing of cancer by another means indicates that there was a misdiagnosis in the first place.

Reasoning includes the use of deduction, which is the art of drawing a specific conclusion from a general assumption (since exposure to a flu virus causes flu, it follows that if you are exposed you will get the flu). It also includes the use of induction, the art of inferring a general assumption from a specific event (you have the flu, therefore you must have been exposed to a flu virus, and exposure to a flu virus must cause the flu). Both are ways that humans try to make sense out of life, to make sure everything happens for a reason, that it has meaning, because meaninglessness is so painful. Reasoning is a valuable skill, especially if you choose your assumptions very carefully. The mind gives great authority to well-presented logic. Absurd assumptions dressed in impeccable logic can get away with acceptance for a long time before most minds will even notice.

ABSTRACTION AND THE MIND

Abstraction is the ability to take an experience and abstract (like extract) the assumed essence of it from reality and discuss it as though it is real instead of just imagined. This is so common that you are usually not aware that you are doing it.

Health is an abstract. There is really no such thing as health, not even good health. There are healthy and unhealthy people, but once you start talking about health itself you are in the realm of imagination, because health, apart from something that is healthy, does not exist except as an idea. That's not necessarily bad. Sex is an abstract when it is a topic of conversation or study. There is sexual behavior and male and female sexes, but sex is just an idea. Illness, too, is an abstract idea. Particular illnesses cause suffering in particular people, but illness just sits there and doesn't do anything until we use it as a topic of discussion.

The value of an abstraction is that it allows us to talk about complex issues in simple terms, such as "What shall we do about health reform?" Big issues need big thinking, and abstraction helps us do that. The danger of abstraction is that it can cause you to lose sight of the trees because you are too focused on the forest. Forest, by the way, is also an abstraction. It's the mind's way of dealing with a piece of the environment instead of the whole confusing thing. In the same way, it is easier for the mind to deal with health as a limited abstraction rather than deal with all the possible factors such as society, family, and environment that may be involved in a particular person's health. When we get too involved in the abstraction, however, we tend to pay more attention to health and forget about healing.

FOCUSING AND THE MIND

Focusing is the ability to keep your attention on something whether it is present or not. Sustained focus may be called meditation, contemplation, or determination. Many people are concerned with the apparent inability of children or adults to keep their attention on their studies or their work, and they try out different ways of "motivating" people to hold their focus. The solution to this problem is extremely simple, although not necessarily easy to carry out. All you have to do is make what you want people to focus on either very important or very interesting to them. When I lived in Senegal, West Africa, an Italian educational company was given permission by the government to try a pilot project with the peanut growers to see how quickly they could be turned from uneducated peasants into educated farmers. Astoundingly, the growers reached the equivalent of a fifth grade school level in the French school system in only three months! The secret? All the teaching took place in the context of growing and selling peanuts. With children, you have to make the schooling important and interesting to them. With adults you have to make the training important and interesting to them.

In terms of healing, better results are achieved when the process is interesting and the benefits are important to the person involved. There was a time when I was involved in helping people to stop smoking with the use of hypnosis. Such a method is only effective when you can help a person to focus on a benefit of not smoking that is greater than any benefit of continuing to smoke. With all of the people that I helped, the least effective focus was better health, probably because it is too abstract. The most effective focus, curiously, was on smelling better for the sake of friends and lovers. By the way, it is interesting to note that I never once came across anyone who could not quit because of a physical addiction to nicotine, even among heavy smokers. Once they changed their focus, they had no trouble stopping. This technique will be discussed fully in the Secret of Self-Hypnosis section of chapter 4.

You can also expand your focus or narrow it, and this includes your ability to shift your focus from the trees to the forest and back. Or from the wood nymphs in the trees to the fairies in the forest. This ability to shift the focus of attention can be extremely useful in the healing process and some exceptionally powerful instant healing techniques are derived from it. When you narrow your focus of attention to a particular part of the body, the body responds to this attention with increased blood circulation to that area, increased warmth and expansion in the area, increased activity of the cells, and increased sensitivity to stimulation. This is often good for healing. (Exercises for instant healing by shifting focus are found in the *Pikopiko* Techniques of chapter 7.) But sometimes such a focus also increases tension and pain because the cells in that area are either under excessive stress or have been given the task of blocking sensitivity or function (as when suppressing memory, for example). In that case, a determined focus away from the site may produce the best relief.

With the power of focused imagination, you can force order on your memories and tell a story or write a novel with a plot that makes sense to the readers. More important in terms of healing, you can also use it to change your interpretation of events, change the content or structure of memories, or even create new memories as the basis for new habits of mind or body. (See the Interior Redecorating section of chapter 5 for exercises to help you reshape your memories.)

ENERGY AND THE MIND

Like the body, the mind is highly influenced by energy. In fact, every source of energy that affects the body also affects the mind—food, drugs, environment, the works. The effect may be quite different on the mind than on the body, however. Things that dull the body may sharpen the mind, and vice versa. There is a traditional Pacific Island drink made from the root of a plant that numbs the body and clears the mind. You can spend an evening drinking it with friends, being extra witty and brilliant, but when you decide that it's time to leave you won't be able to get up to go home. Your mind will be shouting at your body to get going, and your body will be totally tuned out.

Usually, apart from drugs, whatever energizes the body will also energize the mind, helping to make thinking sharper and imagination clearer. Too much energy, though, and any or all of those functions can go haywire. Drugs and alcohol commonly produce this effect, but so do other kinds of energy input. For example, positive ions in the air can be stimulating, but too many (meaning too many for a particular person at a particular time) can produce excessive stress reactions such as headaches or flu symptoms in the body and paranoid or aggressive symptoms in the mind. The effects of environmental, chemical, and other forms of energy may be beneficial or not, depending on the current state of stress of the individual.

STRESS AND THE MIND

Apart from stress due to chemicals generated by or introduced into the body and excessive energy from the environment, the mind can get stressed by stressing itself. The mind's most commonly used methods of stressing itself are obsessing and conflicting.

The Obsessing Mind

Obsessing is like getting stuck in a thought loop, which is similar to a movie loop where a certain section of film plays over and over again. A thought loop, however, is made of imagination: it is designed to keep out other thoughts perceived as dangerous or too difficult or painful to manage; it often includes compulsive behavior; and it always produces a lot of stress that interferes with the functions of both mind and body. I had a friend who was obsessed with order. Wherever we went he would be straightening things out, lining things up, spacing things at equal distances. It was bad enough that he did it with his own stuff, but he got to the point of trying to straighten out other people's stuff, too. Can you imagine how annoying it would be if you were dining at a restaurant and another diner kept coming over to your table to straighten out your silverware and line up your salt and pepper shakers? His problem, of course, was that he needed to make some potentially painful decisions about his life, to straighten it out, in fact, and the obsession gave him a way to covertly procrastinate.

The Conflicting Mind

Conflicting is like deciding not to decide about something that you've decided is important. The simple form is when you encounter two mutually exclusive ideas, such as whether to take pre-med or drama in college, and you keep putting off the choice even though you have to make it before you go. This type of situation can produce quite a bit of stress. I met someone once who had a unique solution to this. He wanted to take up several mutually exclusive careers, but couldn't decide on one, so he kept making plans for all of them while doing something completely different.

The more seriously stressful and long-term form of conflicting comes from continually asking yourself unanswerable questions about issues that you've decided are vitally important, but which have little or no effect on your life. In my counseling practice I have often encountered people who do this. They come to me with an obvious need for healing, and proceed to focus on questions that seem totally unrelated. Two of the most common questions that fit into this category are "Why am I here?" (along with its major variation, "Why is this happening to me?") and "Who am I?" (with its major variation, "Who is asking the question?"). While both issues are very effective in terms of long-term procrastination, they cause a lot of stress along the road of life. My favorite solution as a therapist has been to devise very logical answers to those questions based on what I can learn about the person's belief systems to help the client feel secure enough to get on with the healing.

Here are some general answers that have helped a lot of people. For the question, "Why am I here?" a practical answer is, "To use your talents to solve your problems with whatever help you can get." For the question, "Why is this happening to me?" a practical answer is "Because you haven't figured out how to change it yet." For the question, "Who am I?" a practical answer is, "You are who you decide to be." And for the question, "Who is asking the question?" a practical answer is, "If the universe is infinite, the center of the universe is everywhere, and therefore everyone is asking the question." If you are a therapist, then you get to ask the next question: "Now, what do you want?"

MIND AND BODY TOGETHER, OR NOT

The mind and the body work together all the time. Actually, it would be more accurate to say that they interact all the time, because some of their behavior could not be called togetherness. In the sections above, I have purposely avoided discussion of many interactive areas in order to talk about them here.

When the mind thinks a thought, the body responds. Every thought sets off neurochemical activity that corresponds to the nature of the thought. Here's a simple experiment: take a moment and imagine you are a beggar in medieval London. You have no money, so you dip your bowl in an open sewer and take a drink. Go ahead and smell it and taste it. Stop! I don't want you to gag all over the book. You probably didn't go through with it anyway. But even the thought of doing it would have initiated neurological, chemical, and even muscular activity in your body, even if all you did was set the book down in disgust. If you did go through with it, you may have tasted foul stuff in your mouth, experienced your body growing heavy or contracted, and felt unhappy.

Now, imagine yourself as the king or queen of Atlantis, sitting on your throne of gold and velvet while the ambassador of Lemuria presents you with a box made of amber and filled with rubies, diamonds, and emeralds. Hold the box and feel the jewels while all the court applauds your wise diplomacy. Stop when you want to, but don't forget you are reading a book. Whether you were thrilled, amused, or bored with the little story, it will still have induced physical changes in your body. You may have felt the sensation of the jewels, experienced pleasure, a sense of lightness and expansion, or other very physical effects.

If you imagine you are going to get sick, your body will scour its memory and begin to produce the physical reactions and substances to generate the appropriate symptoms. And if you imagine yourself getting well, the body will start the healing process. If you don't hold your focus for long enough, however, you will only get partial effects.

The body accepts the mind as an authority, but it also accepts memory, energy, and other people, too. I've seen many elderly people who are still slaves to their dead parents' wishes, and too many people with such low self-esteem that they don't even dare tell their bodies how to behave.

The Emotional Link

The link between the mind and the body is emotion. Emotions are waves of energy that carry messages. When the mind communicates with the body, the latter reacts according to the degree of emotion stimulated by the thought, while it carries elements of the thought along with it, similar to the way radio waves carry information. When the body communicates with the mind, it uses memory to get the same effect.

Emotions exist only as they are felt. They are not stored, any more than the waves of the ocean are. When you think a joyful thought or when an experience triggers a joyful memory, the body generates a joyful emotion. When you think an anxious thought or an experience triggers an anxious memory, the body generates an anxious emotion. The emotion occurs right there in the moment. When the stimulus of thought or experience is gone, then so is the emotion. Emotions are not stored; emotions are not suppressed; you do not walk around like a warehouse of old emotions; you do not breathe yesterday's air or surf yesterday's wave.

Well, if you aren't carrying suppressed emotions, why do emotions based on old events break out so strongly in a crisis? The answer has to do with a combination of stimulus response and tension energy. Tension is the body's way of suppressing the ideas it learned from the mind that would, if acknowledged, generate an unpleasant emotion. On its own, the body just expresses emotions as they come up, regardless of the consequences. But if the mind creates a belief that certain kinds of emotions are not to be expressed, or certain ideas or memories are not to be acknowledged because that would be painful or dangerous, the body will suppress them in the only way it can—by tensing muscles so that they can't move. If the cells can't move, the memories will not transmit and emotions won't exist. Think of this as setting up a barrier so the waves can't form in the first place, or as a mountain that blocks the north wind and leaves the southern ocean nice and calm. But mountains erode under the pressure of constant wind, and the body erodes under the pressure of constant tension. When the stimulus of additional, related ideas or experience becomes so strong that the body cannot produce enough additional tension to suppress a reaction, or when the amount of tension present is so great it cannot be held anymore, the result is an outburst of emotion amplified by the release of tension energy.

Emotions are the means by which the mind and body communicate with each other. When the mind experiences pleasure or pain, there is an emotional response in the body. When the body experiences pleasure or pain, there is an emotional response in the mind.

Every thought produces a disturbance or excitement in the body's physiology. Thoughts that don't relate to the important issues of pain or pleasure cause little disturbance or excitement and little in the way of behavioral change. The dates of the terms of office of U.S. presidents usually go in one ear and out the other unless a test grade is involved, and the moment that the test is over, they usually disappear. Thoughts that relate directly to mental or physical pain or pleasure may cause great disturbance or excitement, depending on the degree of potential pain or pleasure involved. Thoughts of a burglar being in the house or of picking up a grand prize that has been won may cause massive energetic and behavioral changes.

Likewise, every physiological change, however stimulated, produces a disturbance or excitement in the mind's thinking process. (Consider what goes on in the mind at puberty.) Accordingly, physiological changes that are not related to the mental pain or pleasure of most people (for example, cell division), may have no noticeable effect on the mind. On the other hand, behavior experienced or perceived that challenges or strongly reinforces cherished assumptions and rules of the mind (for example, being forced to do something against your will or hearing a political idea that you don't believe in), may cause massive thinking activity.

To summarize: you can use the mind to bring pleasure or pain to the body, and you can use the body to bring pleasure or pain to the mind. This also means that you can use either to help in healing the other. The rest of the book is about doing just that.

PART TWO

Walking the Path of Instant Healing

CHAPTER FOUR

Instant Healing with the Power of Words

A bracadabra! This is probably the most well known magical word in the world. It is based on the first four letters of the alphabet, plus a couple of extra syllables to give it rhythm, but it is supposed to produce instant results. Why do people believe in magical words? Why do they sometimes work, but not all the time? How can we make words produce magical instant healing? In this chapter you will learn the answers to all of these questions.

MAGICAL WORDS

If you enjoy fairy tales, if you read sword and sorcery novels, or if you like movies and television series with magicians and wizards, you know how important magical words are. They are the major component of magical spells. After all, anyone can gather a few newts' eyes and lizards' tongues, but if you don't know the right words to say you're nowhere. By the way, isn't it interesting that the word "spell" means a magical chant as well as the naming of the letters in a word? It's also part of magical tradition that spells have to be memorized or recited from books. In Western lore, at least, they are not part of an oral tradition.

In former times, cave paintings and petroglyphs were symbols of magical import with meanings that were known only to a select few. As these symbols became more abstract, less like pictures, they seemed to be endowed with even more power. A person with the secret knowledge of reading could look at scratches on a tablet, a papyrus, or a piece of paper and tell you about the battles of yesteryear, could "see" what lay hidden in the hold of a ship, could predict the coming of the seasons and even an eclipse. This was real clairvoyance! And other papers full of scratches with magical seals or signatures could even give orders that made people do things. Here was psychokinesis, or influence at a distance! Still others could reveal the intentions of the gods, or God. Magic of the highest degree. Small wonder that the written word, and the spoken word derived from it, were thought to have such magical power. The magic came from the mystery.

As writing became more popularized, it lost a lot of its mystery, and therefore its magic, though some poets and a very few novelists can still evoke it. But where there is mystery, there is still magic. The less well known a language is, the more magical power it is thought to have. Imagine a powerful magician with a pointy little beard wearing a black cloak with red lining. He raises his arms, lightning flashes from his fingers, and he says in a commanding voice, "Do what I want!" Not too exciting. But if he says "Alakazam!" Wow, impressive!

As shown by the above example, mystery grants authority. If someone speaks gobbledygook with confidence, people who don't know that it's gobbledygook will be impressed. A friend once gave me a tape recording of a man speaking on some esoteric subject. My friend thought I should listen to it because it was extremely good. Now, my vocabulary is fairly extensive and I studied logic in college. The man on the tape was a strong, confident speaker, but what he said was nonsense. It wasn't that

I didn't agree with him. There was nothing to agree or disagree with. Most of what he said was rampant, inconsistent nonsense, and he randomly threw in big words for their sound and not their meaning. As gently as possible I analyzed this man's talk for my friend, and he was amazed that he had been so gullible.

If words are said in a certain way or in a certain context, that can also give them more authority than their actual meaning would warrant. The words of a prayer or a political speech, or those of a doctor or a hypnotist may have an impact far beyond their meaning because of when and how and by whom they are spoken.

Fundamentally, words are sounds or arbitrary marks to which you give meaning, and languages are organizations of sounds and marks used by particular groups of people. That's all there is to it. Any power that words have is given to them by you. The more power you give them, the greater their effect on you, but the power comes from you and not the words. Speak the most powerful magical incantation in ancient Hebrew to a twelve-year-old Chinese schoolboy and you'll get puzzlement, not awe. And you won't be able to turn him into a frog, either.

With that said, words are still an incredibly useful tool for healing. The most powerful use they have, as long as you understand their meaning and/or give them authority, is to help you direct your attention, to assist you in sharpening and sustaining your focus. The more clearly and consistently you can focus your attention on a healing thought or intent, the more quickly and thoroughly the body will respond in a healing way. Now let's see how to use ordinary words to get magical effects.

HEALING BY INTERPRETATION

Once when I was teaching a class, a regular member of the group arrived late, quite breathless and very agitated. After a few moments she calmed down just enough to tell us of a near-accident she'd had on the way to the class. In considerable detail she described how a car had come out of a side street and had almost run right into her. If she hadn't slammed on the brakes as soon as she had, she would have been killed instantly. On and on she went about how she had almost been killed and she was in a state of great fear and stress. Suddenly I interrupted and said, "But you're here and alive, aren't you?" "What?" she said, with a startled look. I repeated my statement with an added touch. "I said, you survived, you're here with us now, and that's wonderful, isn't it?" After a momentary confusion, her body relaxed, she smiled and looked around, and said "You're right!" And she was happy for the rest of the evening.

This woman had been locked into an interpretation of the event as a near-death experience. The words she used kept reinforcing that interpretation and the resulting focus maintained and even exaggerated her fear and stress. Instead of a tranquilizer, however, all she needed was a shift of focus. A few words based on observable experience led her away from imagined pain and injury to the experiential reality of being alive and well. Her emotional trauma was healed in less than a minute.

> Look for the good in the past event or the present result and make that the center of attention.

Reinterpreting experience is one of the most powerful healing methods there is. It can heal emotional wounds as well as physical ones. And it's all based on a choice of words. I'll describe some variations in more detail.

The Positive Twist

The positive twist is the simplest variation. It's what I used with the woman mentioned above. All you do is look for the good in the past event or the present result and make that the center of attention. You don't try to deny any negative experience. You just make the positive aspect more important. To the degree you can do this, you will relieve a lot of stress that may have accumulated from dwelling on the negative side of whatever happened. The more quickly that stress can be relieved, the more quickly a healing will result. Even physical symptoms caused by such stress can disappear with amazing speed.

The Skinny Description

Very often the negative effects of negative events are sustained and aggravated by repeatedly using "loaded" words in describing the events. A "loaded" word is one that provokes a strong, negative emotional reaction in a particular individual. Frequently, such words are abstract. That is, they don't actually describe anything specific, but they do intensify feelings.

For example, I have been called upon to help a good number of people who experienced child abuse in various forms. Often the only good that can be found is the fact that they survived, and this may not be enough of a positive focus to effect a healing. If you cannot find a sufficiently strong positive focus, another approach is to weaken the negative focus. In every case I've found where the effect of child abuse is an ongoing problem, there is always an emotionally loaded recall of the event or events. Regardless of whether or not this may be justified, if it isn't helping the person to be healthier and happier then it doesn't need to be maintained.

In one typical case, a woman described her experience like this: "My father violated me. He destroyed my self-esteem with his abuse and then he abandoned me." Translated into a skinny description, it came out like this: "My father touched me when and where I didn't want him to. I didn't like it. He left and I never saw him again." The facts

> The facts are the same, but they are reduced to the bare essentials without the loaded words.

are the same, but they are reduced to the bare essentials without the loaded words. The new description may lack the charge of righteous anger, but, on the other hand, it doesn't keep increasing tension. By consistently using this new description of her experience, the woman in question soon (in less than a week) was able to change many habits that had prevented her from moving toward the success and happiness she wanted.

To translate something into a skinny description, first remove all the adjectives you can, then change any other emotionally stimulating words into their neutral equivalents while keeping the basic facts the same.

Creative Translation

My favorite definition of truth is this: "Truth is." If you assume that the universe is infinite, then anything you add to that statement would also be true, including anything you make up. Thus, each individual decides what is true and what is not, based on his or her own background, experience, habits, beliefs, and inclinations. A fact has been described as an opinion that two or more people agree on. Whenever something happens, it is interpreted, and often the interpretation is treated as a fact itself. You may say "The sky is blue." That seems obvious at first, but a scientist may say, "No, the sky is colorless and what you see is the blue end of the spectrum of refracted sunlight." And then a mystic may say, "There is no sky. That is an illusion." Anything can be interpreted in any way one chooses.

Where healing is concerned, interpretation can be critical, because the treatment of a symptom is usually determined by an interpretation of its cause. The value of an interpretation, for healing purposes, is in how well it aids the healing. You can interpret symptoms and conditions in any way you like, or you can go along with the interpretation of a trusted authority. However, from a very practical point of view, the most useful interpretation of unhealthy symptoms and conditions I have found is that they are all related to levels of internal stress—physical, emotional, mental, and spiritual. The advantage of this interpretation is that you can immediately start working on something by whatever means and with whatever help you have available. Additionally, it tends to relieve a lot fear and helplessness, and allows you to incorporate any form of treatment in the healing process. Whether you use this interpretation or not, remember that you can choose an interpretation that will make you feel helpless or you can choose one that will increase your effectiveness.

> The value of an interpretation, for healing purposes, is in how well it aids the healing. You can interpret symptoms and conditions in any way you like . . .

To cite a specific example, there was a time when I came down with what the doctor diagnosed as advanced pneumonia. I chose to interpret it as the result of severe internal stress. I still took the antibiotics he prescribed because I knew they would help me relieve the stress. I also used a lot of other approaches and techniques, but all with the intent to relieve the stress. The final effect was that in three weeks the pneumonia symptoms were completely gone and I felt better than I had in years.

HEALING BY AFFIRMATION

Affirmations are statements you make that sound like facts, but which may or may not be so in the present moment. The objective is to say them in such a way that they become facts, or to reinforce facts that are only weakly believed. Affirmations are often treated like magical spells, but they only have the same power as other words—they help to keep your attention focused on what you want.

A successful affirmation is one that is incorporated by your body as a belief. A very successful affirmation is one which helps your body to do what it knows how to do. The ones we are interested in now are those that help your body to heal itself.

Many affirmations fail because they are too abstract or intellectual. The body just can't relate to them. There is a world of difference in the effect of an affirmation such as this: "Universal energy is flowing through me now and my body is perfect in every way" and one such as this: "Every day in every way I'm feeling better and better." "Universal energy" and "perfect in every way" are not part of most people's experience, but the body understands "feeling better" very well.

A good affirmation calls on the body's memory to evoke or strengthen existing skills. "I am healthy" is too abstract unless the word "healthy" evokes a very specific memory. "I'm feeling as good as I did when I used to play basketball" is very good, especially if you did play basketball and did feel good while doing it. You can also make reinforcing affirmations: "My body knows how to get rid of cancer cells and it's doing so now," "My body remembers how to move this arm and it does it well."

> Affirmations . . . have the same power as other words—they help to keep your attention focused on what you want.

How many times do you do an affirmation? As many times as it takes to get an effect. An affirmation is not like taking vitamins once a day. It's more like developing a new habit of mind that translates into a new habit of the body. The more quickly you want the effect, the more often you need to focus on what you want. Some variations on basic affirmative statements follow.

Similes

Wonderful healing effects can come from using similes that call up familiar memories. "My mind is as calm as a mountain lake." "My body relaxes like a resting cat." "My skin is as clear as my Mom's glass table." The act of comparing such memories to effects that you want evokes a body response in the direction of simulating those effects. When you compare yourself to a resting cat, the body tries to relax like the cat. The better, stronger, or more pleasurable the memory, the better the response.

Metaphors

The body responds powerfully to imagery, and words are excellent tools for evoking images that will assist a healing. A metaphor is a phrase that describes a symbol, most effectively in the form of a memory enhanced by imagination, which likens one thing to another. A metaphor like this: "I am a tree, full of life and strength. My roots receive nourishment from the earth; my leaves receive energy from the sun. I am a tree, full of life and strength," can stimulate the body to start making itself the human equivalent of a strong and healthy tree. Anything that has qualities or characteristics that you admire can be used for metaphorical healing.

> "I am a tree, full of life and strength."

Rapidisms

A rapidism is a type of affirmation that consists of repeating a short word or phrase over and over again very rapidly until a change occurs. The first time I used this was on a chair lift at a ski resort when my hands were freezing. I imagined a fire in a fireplace and said to myself, "Myhandsarewarm—myhandsarewarm—myhandsarewarm—myhandsarewarm," for about five minutes and my hands got toasty warm. Since then I've used it for a lot of minor ailments as well as emotional states and mental qualities, and it works very well. In workshops I have people silently repeat "I'mfeelinggood" for one minute and they are always amazed at the results. I don't know how well it would work on major illnesses, but in theory it should help, and it certainly won't hurt.

Radical Affirmation

Radical affirmations take a lot of courage because you'll be saying something that is clearly not true. I first learned this from a man who used it for his asthma. He had tried every conventional and alternative approach available and nothing had helped him. Finally he got so frustrated he decided to tell himself "I do not have asthma! I never have had asthma! I never will have asthma!" He broke all the rules of "good affirmations." But he kept it up, every day, all day long, for six months, and at the end of that time his asthma was gone. You may notice that he used a negative in every sentence. Some people say that the subconscious doesn't hear negatives, which is silly because it hears everything. What they probably mean is that saying "I don't have asthma" is like saying "Don't think of a pink elephant." In order not to think of it you have to think of it. Maybe that's why it took six months for the man's body to get the message. Even so, the important thing is that, with intensive repetition, a "lie" became a truth.

That statement deserves a little more attention. Certain people have trouble with affirmations because they feel as though they are lying to themselves, even with the most simple kinds of statements. They may ask, "How can I say I'm feeling good when I'm not?" This is a problem with interpretation and intent. If you interpret an affirmation as a lie and think you are trying to trick your body into getting well, that's "bad" and it won't work. If you interpret healing affirmations as guidelines and think you are trying to help your body to get well, that's "good" and it will work.

> With intensive repetition, a "lie" became a truth.

HEALING BY DIRECTION

Directions are commands, orders, or instructions that you give to your body. In this case, instead of giving your body a statement, you tell it what to do and, in some cases, how to do it. You are probably already familiar with the idea if you've ever told yourself to "Relax!" or "Stay calm!" You could also say, "Heal!" or "Get well!" or "Feel Good!" The really amazing thing is that to the degree you give your directions with confident expectations and right at the onset of symptoms, your body will respond faster than you thought possible. Many times my body has started to produce cold symptoms, back pain, muscle pain or stiffness, nausea, or headache and all I've had to say is "Stop that!" or "Drop that!" and the symptoms have instantly gone away. One time my wife began to get serious flu symptoms and she said, "You stop that, body! I don't have time for that, so you just stay healthy!" And the symptoms disappeared

> Directions will work better if they evoke some kind of visual image. "Okay bod, I want you to jazz up the immune system. Get those lymphocytes in there . . . and clean out the rubbish."

instantly. Of course, my wife is a strong woman and I'm not surprised that her body obeyed without hesitation. I would have, too.

Short directions are fine, but you can be more creative than that. As with affirmations, directions will work better if they evoke some kind of visual image. "Okay, bod, I want you to jazz up the immune system. Get those lymphocytes in there (you can imagine them as vacuum cleaners or anything else) and clean out the rubbish, and make sure those antibodies clean up and keep out the invaders. I want an immune system that's in good working order. You know what to do. If you need any supplies just ask. Call on the brain for anything you need. Just get the job done. Thanks a mill." You don't have to be formal with your own body.

Indirect Directions

Indirect directions are simply pairs of words designed to direct your body's attention to memories or images that will help produce beneficial sensations and feelings. Examples are:

- water flowing

- rain dripping

- cool breezes

- warm sunshine

- ice melting

- snow falling

- birds singing

- lions roaring

They have the best effect when said slowly with a pause afterward, giving time for the image to form itself. If you like, you can add more imagery: "birds singing in a garden when the sun comes out after a rain." They are really just brief descriptions of evocative moments, and the body responds to them by creating the associated feelings and sensations. For more specific effects, focus the conscious attention on a particular part of the body while doing this. Think "ice melting," for instance, while you hold your attention on an area of tension in your body.

HEALING BY BLESSING

Blessings are words that have the effect of increasing one's focus of awareness or intent. They may take the form of affirmations or of directions, but they are not quite the same as either of those.

Affirmational Blessings

Affirmational blessings are like compliments. They can take the form of appreciation (thank you), acknowledgment (good job!), and admiration (you sure are a clever body). Both you and your body are motivated to repeat and improve behavior that brings pleasure, and compliments feel good. You can bless your body for regrowing cells, mending wounds, breathing, circulating blood, cleansing itself, cooperating with medicine or other intervention, and whatever you can acknowledge as a good action on its part. It may seem a bit strange at first to say "thank you" to your own body for doing something that is natural to it. However, a great deal of experience by a great many people has shown that the

> The more you consciously appreciate what your body does, the more it does of what you appreciate and the better it does it.

more you consciously appreciate what your body does, the more it does of what you appreciate and the better it does it. Essentially, you are rewarding good behavior, and this is always the best way to train animals and children, as well as bodies.

In showing appreciation, mentally or vocally, don't be afraid to be extravagant, either. "Hey! You lost two pounds. That's great, keep it up!" Praise is its own reward. I know it sounds peculiar, but your body really does like to be praised. To use this for healing, you praise every single, tiny, itsy bitsy movement in the direction of the healing that you want, and you rigorously refrain from ever, ever criticizing your body for not doing a good enough job. The results may or may not be immediately apparent, but over a period of time (determined by how often you do it) you will start to notice definite improvements.

You don't have to limit yourself to blessing your body. Just as your body responds to a metaphor, so it will respond to a blessing or compliment that you give to anyone or anything. It is as if your body takes every compliment you give personally, and feels better and does better because of it. In a variation I call "saturation blessing" you bless every good thing you can remember and every good thing around you without a break for as long as you can sustain it. If you do take a break you go back to the blessing as soon as you can. One man I introduced to this technique was able to rid himself of a long-time pattern of asthma in less than a week, and I used it for myself to heal a knee injury in less than fifteen minutes.

Can you use blessings for emotional healing? Yes, but in this case you show appreciation to your own mind for noticing any good in yourself, the world, or other people and for any positive displays of mental abilities or faculties. For example, "Hey mind, you solved that problem very well; thank you for noticing the beauty of those flowers; it's good that you're able to forgive that person at least a little bit," and so on. The effect of this is to lower mental stress, thereby making emotional conflicts easier to resolve. This might even seem stranger than talking to your body, but it works, even if you never figure out who's doing the blessing.

Directional Blessing

Directional blessing can be compared to wishing someone well. "Bon Voyage!" is a directional blessing, as is "Bon appetit" and "Enjoy!" "May the wind be always at your back" is part of an Irish blessing for good fortune on a journey, and "get well" cards are a form of directional blessing for health.

> Tell your body or mind what you want it to do, and then give it a good reason for doing it.

To apply this kind of blessing for self-healing in the most effective way, you use the form "do this . . . so that . . . ." To your body you might say, "Take this medicine and use it to help strengthen our immune system so that we can feel stronger and enjoy a walk in the woods." To your mind you might say, "Settle down and keep your attention on the present moment so we can feel more peaceful and think more clearly." The exact wording is up to you, but the essential part is to tell your body or mind what you want it to do, and then give it a good reason for doing it.

THE SECRET OF SELF-HYPNOSIS

A prominent hypnotherapist, T. X. Barber, has suggested that there is no such thing as hypnosis. One reason is that an analysis of brain waves shows absolutely no distinction between a normal waking state and a state of hypnosis. What, then, explains why people do all those strange things that we see a stage hypnotist put them through? Doesn't the hypnotist have some sort of mysterious power?

Let me tell you what happens during a stage hypnotist's show, because this will help you understand the power of self-hypnosis. First, except for those dragged along by their spouses, all the people in the audience want to see this kind of show. Thus, a select group of people is in attendance. Typically, the hypnotist asks for a group of volunteers to come on stage, perhaps ten or twelve, depending on the size of the audience. People willing to do that make up an even more select group. Then he waves his hands and makes some suggestions about relaxation to put them into a "light trance." He doesn't have to wave his hands, but it looks good and it may help to get the attention of his subjects. A "light trance" means your eyes are closed and your body is calm. Next, he will take them through an exercise to see how deeply "hypnotized" they are. In a typical situation, he has them hold both arms out in front of them and think of one being connected to a balloon and the other to a heavy weight. It's usually surprising and amusing to watch some of the arms drift upward and some of them drift downward, and some of them not move at all. This exercise and others like it can actually be done without any preparation, but because it's unusual it gives people the impression that something special is happening. After a bit, the hypnotist will give some suggestions for the volunteers to "wake up" when he claps his hands or snaps his fingers. They weren't really asleep and he could have just told them to open their eyes, but he has to main- tain the illusion that he is controlling the process.

After this exercise, and perhaps a few more, the hypnotist will keep the three to five best responders on stage and ask the rest to go back to their seats. In terms of hypnosis, those remaining are called the most "suggestible." That means they have good imaginations and are more responsive to authority. The hypnotist will give this group more relaxation suggestions to put them into a "medium trance," meaning their eyes are closed and their bodies are relaxed. He will proceed to take them through some more exercises, usually including the very impressive one in which a person is made to lie "stiff as a board" with his or her shoulders on one chair and feet on another. This also can be done in a full waking state by anyone with good imagination and determination, but it certainly is impressive if you haven't seen it done before.

In taking the subjects through more exercises, the hypnotist is trying to determine which individuals seem to have the strongest imagination and response to authority. Usually there will be one or two exceptionally responsive people out of such a group, and these will become the stars of the show. By this time they may be in a "deep trance," meaning that their focus of attention is very narrow, their imagery is intense, and their bodies are very, very relaxed. Everything else that happens is the result of excellent imagination and the body's atavistic desire to please the leader of the pack or the tribe.

During, or at the end of the show, the hypnotist may give a "post-hypnotic suggestion." This is a suggestion that at a certain signal from the hypnotist or when the subject sees or hears a certain thing or goes to a certain place he or she will do something, usually absurd, such as barking like a dog when entering a bank. If the authority of the hypnotist has been well enough established the person may consciously forget the suggestion, especially if told to, and be genuinely surprised when the body remembers. In the movies, an innocent person may be hypnotized and given a post-hypnotic suggestion to, for example, set off a bomb that will kill a lot of people when the person hears a special word said over a telephone. Then you see the person's face go blank as he goes into a trance and sets off the bomb like a zombie. In reality, it doesn't happen that way. Post-hypnotic suggestions are the verbal equivalent of tying a string around your finger. They are no different than your boss telling you to punch the time clock when you get to work. You may forget about it until you actually see the time clock. If a suggestible person under the influence of a hypnotist were given a suggestion to set off a bomb at a certain signal, he might make a face as he suddenly thought of doing such a thing. However, unless the person was already a terrorist, the urge would be ignored just as any suggestion would that goes against his personal ethics. A lot of disappointed teenage boys have found out that hypnosis won't make girls do what the boys want them to if the girls don't want to do it.

The power of hypnosis is not some mysterious form of thought control that the hypnotist has. It is the power of authority, imagination, and words to direct one's focus. Now that you have some understanding of what hypnotism is and is not, I can introduce you to therapeutic hypnosis, the use of hypnosis for healing.

THERAPEUTIC HYPNOSIS

Therapeutic hypnosis got its start by accident. Although the basic technique is very ancient and can be found around the world, it wasn't until the 1800s in Europe that it developed as a specifically Western process. In the previous century a man named Mesmer was experimenting with healing energies using magnets and other items. In his healing practice he found that, although the energies did have therapeutic effects, he could amplify the effects a great deal with low lights, colorful robes, weird music, strange gestures, and a commanding voice. Soon others found that they could get the same healing effects by omitting the energy devices. More experimentation whittled the necessaries down to the gestures and the commanding voice, and even more showed that the gestures could be replaced by anything that could fix the patient's attention. Because the early practitioners were gentlemanly medical doctors, the most popular object for fixing attention for a long time was a pocket watch on a chain, which later became a pendulum. At first the process was called "mesmerism" after Mesmer, which aggravated him greatly since he wanted to be known for his energy work. Later the word "hypnosis" was coined from "Hypnos," the Greek god of sleep, as deeply relaxed people with their eyes closed do look as though they are asleep.

In the early days of hypnosis, doctors reported astounding successes involving such things as painless surgery, extremely rapid recovery from illness and injury, and amazingly accurate self-diagnosis. This is not too surprising, considering that their early subjects were peasants and nervous women who were awed to the extreme by the god-like presence of a doctor who gave commands with a voice like thunder. As it is practiced now, therapeutic or clinical hypnosis is a quieter art and the benefits of the process are available to everyone. And those benefits include anything that it is possible for the mind and the body to do.

It is said sometimes that certain people cannot be hypnotized. This is simply not true, because hypnosis is no more than a state of relaxed focus in which a person is open to suggestions related to something they want to do, be, or have. All you have to do to hypnotize someone is to get their attention on something they are interested in. A person watching a soap opera they like on television is just as much in a hypnotic trance as someone in a hypnotherapist's office.

> You can perform some good therapeutic hynosis in as little as a minute, though you can take as long as you want.

Hypnosis can be either guided or self-directed. The only difference between self-hypnosis and hypnosis guided by someone else is that in the former you have to be both the guide and the subject. Some people find it easier to let someone else do the work while they just relax and respond. Others feel they need the authority of someone else to help them focus and take in the suggestions. Otherwise, self-hypnosis is just as effective. Self-hypnosis can be used for a myriad of ailments. You can try it on anything.

The Process of Self-Hypnosis

Without all the fancy trimmings, the basic elements of self-hypnosis include:

1. relaxing your body

2. closing your eyes

3. focusing your attention on something

4. relaxing your body some more

5. giving or receiving suggestions

6. giving yourself post-hypnotic suggestions

7. opening your eyes and being aware of your surroundings

Using the above process, you can perform some good therapeutic hypnosis in as little as a minute, though you can take as long as you want. Read on for an elaboration of the various steps.

1. For the first step, just take a deep breath and relax your muscles as well as you can. I recommend doing this sitting up, because if you lie down, you are likely to really go to sleep.

2. For the second step, just close your eyes. Some hypnotherapists take as long as twenty minutes trying to get you to close your eyes involuntarily, which is a big waste of time. Just go ahead and close them and be done with it.

3. The third step has a lot of possible variations. One of the most common is to count backward from ten or some larger number. This is

because it takes more attention to count backward than it does to count forward. Some people like to imagine a blackboard and write numbers on it and erase them. Others like to walk up or down stairs. Actually, the third step is where hypnosis and meditation meet, so anything you use in meditation to start focusing will work well here. Examples are the repeating of a word or phrase, imagining a candle flame or flower, and feeling the movement of your breathing. Or you can use a favorite memory that gives you a good feeling. The most important thing happening in this step is that your attention is drawn away from external distractions and into a narrow focus where anything that comes into your awareness will have greater importance.

> Give your suggestions in the form of words that evoke images, either memories, detailed plans, or fantasy symbols.

4. In this step you make a quick check of your body to notice any tension areas, then either hold the intent to relax or tell you body to do so. You can also remember or imagine in detail a peaceful, relaxing experience, such as lying on the sand at a beach or walking along a forest trail in springtime.

5. Now you are ready for the main event. It is best to decide before the session what kinds of suggestions you want to give yourself. Give your suggestions in the form of words that evoke images, either memories, detailed plans, or fantasy symbols.

For example, if you are helping your body to cope with cancer, you could tell it to remember all the things you could do and how good you felt before you had it. You could visualize and verbalize your plans for treatment and tell your body to cooperate so you can do things and feel good later on. As an alternative, you could fantasize your white blood cells as excavators and bulldozers taking the cancer apart and hauling it away, and yourself being applauded for your success at a victory celebration by friends and family. The words help you to keep your focus and the imagery helps your body to incorporate the suggestions. The most powerful suggestions will be the ones that evoke the strongest positive emotional responses in you, so they should be personally tailored to your experience and desires. Be sure to have the suggestions include sensory benefits to motivate the body in the form of physical or emotional pleasure as a result of or as a reward for the healing. This could include a food treat (unless you are trying to lose weight), a special movie or fun event, purchase of something that would give you pleasure, or anything you would consider a reward. Once I promised my body a trip to an amusement park. Although I was unable to arrange the actual trip, I discovered that my body was just as happy with a detailed imaginary experience of the rides and the cotton candy.

If you are unsure about the form the suggestions should take, use the ideas given earlier under the headings of Interpretation, Affirmation, Direction, and Blessing. They will have even more power as part of a self-hypnosis process. Some people, including myself, have had good results by incorporating suggestions into a relaxing scene from Step 4. For example, while lying on the beach, some dolphins could pop out of the water and give the suggestions, and they might also be written in the sand; or in the forest, animals could give the suggestions and they might be written on trees and rocks.

6. Post-hypnotic suggestions are very useful as reminders to your mind to focus on what you want, and to your body to remember what you want. Relate the suggestion to something you'll encounter infrequently enough that it will grab your attention, and not so frequently that you'll quickly ignore it. For example, your birthday would be too infrequent, but your breathing would be too frequent. You might try something like, "Every time you smell a flower you'll

remember these suggestions," or "Whenever you sit down to eat you'll remember these suggestions." You can also end the session with a suggestion to come back to full awareness quickly and easily. This will be helpful for getting ready to open your eyes.

7. When you open your eyes you may feel a little spacey because of the transition from deep focus and relaxation to normal distractions and activity. I have found that the quickest way to get reoriented is to look at things around you as you move your hands and your feet.

Responding to hypnosis is a skill, just as meditation is a skill. Some people learn to do it and gain the benefits very quickly, while others have to practice a lot. You'll know how skillful you are when you start to get results. It took me a good while to learn it well, and it has become one of the most valuable skills I have. Sometimes the results are instant, sometimes rapid or fast, and sometimes—when there is a lot of emotional clutter to deal with—it takes a lot of time and persistence. Nevertheless, it is definitely a skill worth developing.

CHAPTER FIVE

Instant Healing with the Power of Imagination

I magination is one of the greatest abilities we have, because we can imagine what was, what is, and what isn't. As I pointed out in chapter 3, what the mind does well is imagine, and imagination affects the body. So, if you use your imagination skillfully, you can help the body to heal itself. In this chapter I'll give you a number of different techniques that use imagination for instant, rapid, and fast results.

INTENTIONAL REVERIE

The deliberate use of memory to elicit a healing response in the body is a sadly neglected area of healing practice. Healers rely on the body's memory whether they realize it or not, but very few use it on purpose. Ignoring memory as a resource when you need healing is akin to trying to build a house without any reference to basic principles of construction. Of course, you can do it, but you're making it a lot harder than it has to be.

Everyone has experienced times of wellness and times of illness, at least relatively speaking. I believe that the body remembers every single detail of those experiences, right down to the cellular level. No one knows if this is actually true, but I do know this: if you imagine that the body can remember everything, then it acts like it can.

When I was doing hypnotherapy, I found that one of the best ways to aid the healing of a wide variety of complaints was to help a person recall a time when the complaint didn't exist and/or a time when the person was in a high state of health. The key to the healing effect was a vivid re-creation of the memory. That does not just mean visual images. The body remembers visual data as well as every other sort of sensory data imaginable. I suspect that the body even has pheromonal memory.

A man I worked with suffered from what is now called "fatigue syndrome." He was in a perpetual state of low energy and could barely even make it to my office. He said that medicine and counseling hadn't helped, so he figured what the heck, why not try me? Well, we got his energy back in one session. In talking about his past, he mentioned that he had been pretty good at basketball, so I helped him to recall his best game.

> Take some time and deliberately recall every detail that you can bring up of when you didn't have the problem you have now.

For a first session, I had him remember the sights and sounds, smells, touches, feelings, and movements involved in preparing for the game, playing the game, winning the game, and celebrating the win in the greatest detail possible. By the end of the session he was full of energy and feeling better than he had in a long time. There was more to his problem than that, however. The issues in his life that caused the stress that led to the fatigue took longer to resolve, but when he needed energy he could recall the game and be charged up again in practically no time.

In using this technique yourself, first assume (imagine) that your body can remember everything. Then take some time and deliberately recall every detail that you can bring up of when you didn't have the problem you have now, or when you felt really good, or when you had been healed of something similar. Be sure to include all of your senses in your recall, especially any physical movement that may have been involved (walking, running, dancing, change of posture or position, and the like) and positive emotional feelings. Because memory works by association, you may remember apparently unrelated bits and pieces at first. These will normally be the elements with the strongest sensory content, including emotions. Keeping your attention on them will help lead you to more detail. You can use your mind to organize the memory into a chronological sequence if you want, but it isn't necessary. The aim of this exercise is to recall memories that will help you change a current physical, emotional, or mental state and/or which will help your body to evoke immune responses, relaxation, strength, energy, sexual responsiveness, or whatever else you need that you have a memory about. This will help to evoke the health and healing responses that the body holds in memory and activate them in the present moment. Do this until you start to feel or experience changes in your condition, no matter how small. Then you can continue if you have the time, or plan another time for doing it again. You are not looking for miracles (although be prepared to accept them if they happen). You are looking for any changes for the better, because that indicates progress. There may be other areas of your life that you will have to work on as well to reduce your overall stress, but this technique will be a great help in mobilizing your body's healing resources.

INTERIOR REDECORATING

About ten years ago I read a book that impressed me very much. It was *Using Your Brain—For a Change,* by Richard Bandler, well-known for his system of Neuro-Linguistic Programming. In it, Bandler described a method for what I would call instant emotional healing that involved recalling a memory and changing various aspects of it such as brightness, color, size, sound volume, and others without actually changing the content of the memory itself. The idea, as I interpret it, is that memories are stored as patterns of experience and emotional charge. Experience provides the content and emotional charge determines the "packaging." For example, important memories, whether good or bad, are remembered by many people as being brighter or bigger than other memories. Bandler discovered that consciously making such memories dimmer or smaller usually resulted in a permanent change in emotional and/or behavioral response to them. Reactions and behavior based on unhappy memories were changed in virtually the flick of a thought.

I taught the process to students in my workshops and it worked very well. It was, however, tedious to work through a whole group of visual, auditory, and kinesthetic cues, so I experimented with variations that eventually led me to the idea that whatever you do to alter the mood of the memory will alter your reaction to it. And that led me to "Interior Redecorating." Some of the most universally successful applications of this idea follow. There are three critical issues to be aware of, however:

- some memories are so traumatic that a person won't want to or won't be able to make the changes

- some people have so much of their identity invested in a memory that they will either pretend to alter it or refuse to try

- you can make up any variations that work for you

Circus Décor

Recall a memory in which someone has really upset you or hurt you emotionally. Without changing the event, put antlers on the person involved and dress him or her in a clown costume. Have some other clowns come into the picture behind the person and make faces while circus music plays in the background. When you are ready, drop the memory for a few moments and then recall it again with the changes you made. Usually, your feelings about the event will have changed and this memory will no longer bother you like it did as long as you always recall it with the changes. Soon, you will probably even stop bothering to recall it.

Scene Change

Recall an unhappy or unpleasant memory. Without changing the event itself, change the context by placing it in a location that contrasts as much as possible with the mood of the event. If it's a noisy event, put it in the middle of the desert or in a quiet mountain meadow. If it's a quiet event, put it in the middle of Times Square on New Year's Eve. Any peaceful or happy surroundings will usually work well, as long as you can maintain the mood of the surroundings in your recall.

> Recall an unhappy or unpleasant memory. Without changing the event itself, change the context by placing it in a location that contrasts as much as possible with the mood of the event.

Flash Freeze

Recall an unhappy or unpleasant memory. Freeze it into a thin sheet of ice. As your current self, step up with a hammer and break up the sheet into little pieces. Sweep the ice into a bucket and set it out into the sun to evaporate or on a fire to boil away.

RADICAL RECALL

There is a way of consciously working with memories that can have dramatic effects on physical healing. It's very easy to do, and it's also very hard, depending on how you relate to memories. I call it "radical" because it consists of changing the content of the memory, in essence, imagining that it happened differently. This might seem like denial or escapism at first, but the intent and the process are quite different.

It is well known that nearly all of the cells of the body regularly die and are replaced by new cells. As I understand it, the brain cells don't actually die, but their contents are replaced. In any case, the body you have today is, physically and literally, not the same body you had last year. It is common to say that your body replaces itself every seven months or so, but that is misleading. Actually, different parts and organs of your body replace themselves at different rates. It is said that your skin, for example, replaces itself completely every six weeks. But this statement is also misleading because individual cells and groups of cells are dying and being replaced by new cells every day. Fortunately, skin cells are replaced by skin cells, liver cells are replaced by liver cells, bone cells are replaced by bone cells, etc. The new cells know what kind of cells they are supposed to be. How? By memory, of course. Thus, if the cells of your body are damaged by injury or disease and the damage lasts beyond the normal time for the cells of that area to die and be replaced, the only way that can happen is because new cells carry on the memory of the damage. Therefore, if you can find a way to provide the new cells with a memory of not being damaged, they will form without the damage. That's the theory, anyway.

However, there's a hole in that theory. In practice, the cells can change faster than the time it's supposed to take for new cells to be born. Okay, so it's not a perfect theory. I'm still working on it.

First, I would like to give you some examples of radical recall that I am personally familiar with. In one case a friend of mine was suffering from a weeping wound that was three months old. When getting off a motorcycle, she had burned her bare leg by hitting the hot manifold, causing the wound. She had tried a variety of medicines, but nothing seemed to help. Because radical recall was cheaper than a visit to a doctor she decided to try it first. So one day she sat down and recalled the incident when she was getting off the motorcycle, only this time she changed the memory so that when she got off the motorcycle her leg didn't touch the manifold. It wasn't easy, of course, because the memory of what had actually happened was very strong. But she persisted, and I mean she really persisted. She reworked the memory forty times, until she could easily remember getting off the cycle without brushing her leg against the manifold. Nothing happened right away so she just forgot about it. Within three days, however, the wound had healed up completely, which qualifies it as a fast healing.

The next case concerns a student of mine. I debated with myself as to whether I should even mention this one because it sounds so far out, but it did happen, so here goes. This person was a fireman in a major city. His crew was called to put out a fire in a warehouse and he was in the process of spraying water into a storeroom when the stream of water hit a pool of burning oil that he hadn't seen. The force of the water caused the oil to ricochet against a wall and splash back on the fireman, burning his face, his hair, and his arms. The burns were bad, especially on his arms, but he refused treatment and decided to go straight home. As he left, his friends joked about his frizzy hair. Once he was home— he washed, drank some water, and did a radical recall four times in a row in which he was in the same place doing the same thing, except that in the new version of the memory, the oil missed him completely. Then he went to bed. In the morning he got up, noticed that his arms looked fine, combed his hair and noticed some burnt hair coming out in his comb, and went back to the station. He was greeted by gasps of surprise and wonder. His friends made him look into a mirror and he saw that his hair and face looked normal. This was a good case of rapid healing. This story is somewhat remarkable, but I'll be the first to acknowledge that this person did have an extremely vivid imagination.

Now I'll share one of my own experiences. As I've studied my body's reactions to events in my life, I've found a direct correlation between "cold sores" and the suppression of anger. In particular, if I get angry with someone and keep quiet about it, both internally as well as externally, I tend to get a cold sore in my lip. I know they are supposed to be caused by viruses, but perhaps the tension of the suppressed anger prevents my body from taking care of the virus on its own. Whatever. What I know with certainty is that if I do something to relieve the tension, the cold sore goes away. If I'm aware of being angry with a particular person, the process is easier. In one dramatic incident I got a bad cold sore and I knew with whom I was angry. In front of a mirror I imagined that I had not suppressed my anger, but that instead I had told the person how angry I was and what I wanted him to do about what had upset me. I think I did this three or four times in a row. The reason I'm not sure is that I was distracted by watching the cold sore fade away from my lip in less than a minute. Now that is instant healing.

Radical recall requires:

- a willingness to change a memory

- the use of as much sensory detail as possible in the re-creation of the event

- sufficient repetition to "stabilize" it as a new memory that the body will respond to

The amount of repetition varies with individuals and even for individuals, because it seems to be dependent on how vivid, sense-laden, and emotionally stimulating you can make the re-creation. I don't know what its limitations are, so experiment freely. There needs to be a lot more experimentation and more experience with it to understand it better.

HEALTHY FANTASY

An exercise I used to do in my workshops was to have everyone turn their head to the right as far as they could and pick a spot to look at that marked how far they had turned. Then I had them face front and close their eyes and imagine that they were an owl, able to easily turn their head around a hundred and eighty degrees with no effort. I had them imagine doing that without actually turning their head, and then I had them open their eyes and turn their head to the right again. Almost always, 100 percent of the class found that they could turn their head much farther the second time. So what happened?

The body is constantly reacting to the mind. Every thought, idea, image, daydream, night dream, plan, or fantasy produces a physical effect according to what the mind is doing. Just the thought of getting up to get something to drink activates the muscles that would be involved and the appropriate chemical reactions, perhaps including salivation, that would relate to the actual experience. If you think a lot of stressful or conflicting thoughts, your body can go haywire trying to act on every one of them. However, if you can make your body go haywire by what you think, then you can also make it healthy. In this section I'm going to show you how to take advantage of a most curious aspect of the body: it doesn't make a clear distinction between reality and fantasy.

Another workshop exercise I did was to guide my students through a fantasy experience. Most often I had them imagine that they were on a sailing ship anchored in the lagoon of a South Pacific island in the nineteenth century. During the less than five-minute exercise I had them see, hear, feel, smell, and taste in great detail. Then I had them open their eyes and reorient themselves to the classroom again. Next I asked them to recall a vacation, a trip, or a party they had experienced some time the previous year. Then I had them recall the lagoon experience; then the real experience;

> Every thought, idea, image, daydream, night dream, plan, or fantasy produces a physical effect according to what the mind is doing.

then the lagoon; then the reality. Finally, I asked if anyone could tell me the difference between the two experiences as memories, regardless of content. Except in cases where the real experience or the lagoon experience was exceptionally emotional, no one could. Then I had them compare the lagoon memory to a memory of lunch two weeks ago Tuesday. In this case, unless that particular lunch was especially traumatic or joyful, the lagoon memory seemed more "real."

It turns out that the body doesn't determine reality by the same rules that the mind uses. As far as the body is concerned, reality is determined by sensory stimulation, and it isn't particular about where that stimulation comes from. A highly emotional reaction to an ordinary event will have a greater influence on the body's ongoing behavior than a lukewarm reaction to an extraordinary event. And a really good fantasy can change the body in ways that mundane experience may not be able to. Personally, I can keep my body in much better shape with exciting fantasy exercises than I can with boring physical ones, as long as my fantasies have a high degree of sensory stimulation in them.

> For me, one of the quickest ways to take care of a stiff neck is to imagine, with great attention to detail, that I'm getting a neck and shoulder massage from a favorite actress or model.

Really effective healthy fantasy involves making up experiences that are either highly unlikely or, in terms of ordinary reality, utterly impossible, but which contain a large degree of intense sensory stimulation related to healing. Some of my favorites follow.

Magnificent Massage

When I'm home, I spend a lot of time at my computer, and if I get too involved for too long a time my neck and shoulder muscles get stiff and sore. One of the quickest ways to take care of this is to imagine, with great attention to detail, that I'm getting a neck and shoulder massage from a favorite actress or model. This can ease all the tension in less than a minute. Of course, I always have the option of having them do a more extended massage if I choose. Although I have great respect for the art of real therapeutic massage, my fantasy masseuses do a better job then most of the ones I've been to, because I can imagine exactly what I want and how I want it.

Techno-fantasy

One time I was in bed with a bad chest cold, so I conjured up a team of scientists from the future who set up a healing apparatus over my bed and zapped my chest with an energy ray, complete with spacey sound effects. I also imagined that I could feel the ray penetrating my chest and dispersing the congestion. Not only was it great fun, but I was able to breathe easily and go back to work within a half-hour.

On another occasion my oldest son challenged me to arm wrestling at a time when he was working out and I was desk-ridden. There was no question that he would be able to beat me under ordinary circumstances, so I created extraordinary circumstances. As he told me later, he was using a martial arts technique to send a powerful flow of water through his arm to increase his strength. I suspected as much, so I imagined a band around my wrist that was attached to a rod in the direction I wanted to go, both band and rod being made of titanium steel and connected to a miniature nuclear engine at the end of the table. Well, flowing water didn't stand a chance against that. When I turned on the engine and put his arm on the table without any apparent effort he reacted with great shock and surprise. In fact, that event didn't have anything to do with healing, but the same concept can be used to increase strength and endurance, speed up healing processes,

> All you need to do is be able to imagine a technology that, if it existed, could do what you want.

or make repairs to the body. All you need to do is to be able to imagine a technology that, if it existed, could do what you want. I've found that this works best when you use it to do something positive instead of trying to use it against something or to try and get rid of something. For instance, my healing ray filling my chest with light wasn't directed at destroying the illness. The nuclear engine wasn't working against my son's arm—it was simply pulling my arm, and took my son's arm with it. If you use a techno-fantasy device to repair your body, keep it focused on the result you want, and not on the illness or disease or condition that you don't want. As with every technique in this book, sometimes you get quick results and sometimes you have to keep doing it for a while.

Fantastical Magic

Some people are not into technical stuff and would rather play with magical imagination, which works just as well, as long as you put enough sensory data into it. A long time ago I led a series of role-playing games for a group of teen-age boys in my neighborhood. One of the boys usually played the role of a druid with magical powers. He came down with chicken pox and had to leave the game for a while, but he returned sooner than anyone had expected. As he told us later, he was lying on his bed at night feeling miserable when he suddenly thought, "Hey, I'm a druid. I can make this stuff go away by magic!" He knew he was just playing, but he made up a spell and ordered his spots to fly off his body and stick to the ceiling, seeing that happen in his mind's eye at the same time. Then he smiled to himself and went to sleep. The next morning his chicken pox was gone (however, there were no spots on the ceiling). The key factor was that, even though he was doing it for fun, he didn't actively deny or doubt what he was doing.

Just a few moments ago my body was feeling out of sorts because of stress and lack of sleep, so to go along with this section I got a glass of water and pretended that I was casting a magical spell on it to turn it into a healing potion. I said the magical words, "Abracadabra, sis boom bee, turn into a healing potion for me!" and I imagined the water becoming all bubbly and golden. Then I drank some of it and imagined I could feel the potion going through my body and making it feel better. And right now I feel great.

Symbolic Logic

One of the most amazing instant healing techniques of all has to do with the use of inner symbols. It's possible to turn this into a very complex procedure, but I'm going to give you the simple version that usually works just as well. First I'll explain the concept and the process; then I'll give some examples.

I said earlier that the body judges reality by the intensity of sensory experience, and not by whether the experience happens outside your body or inside your mind. In addition, the body can respond to symbols of a condition as strongly as it can to the condition itself. That's why dreams can have such a powerful influence on health, and also why an encounter with something associated with an event can reproduce the effects of the event. Some people get allergic reactions when looking at a picture of a cat. Some people get depressed when they hear a bit of music that was playing when something bad happened. Some people get drunk from non-alcoholic drinks that they think contain alcohol. Some people smile when they smell a particular fragrance. In all of these cases, something unrelated became a symbol for an experience and the body reacted to the symbol when the experience itself wasn't happening. The responses I'm describing are suggestive of simple behavioral conditioning, like when Pavlov's dog heard a bell every time he was fed and then learned to salivate when there was only a bell and no food.

Ah, but there's a very clever way to turn the use of symbols into a healing technique. If the body reacts to a particular experience and you change the experience, then the body changes its reaction. And, if the body reacts to a symbol as if it were the real experience and you

> If the body reacts to a symbol as if it were the real experience and you change the symbol, then the body also changes its reaction to the experience as if it, too, had changed.

change the symbol, then the body also changes its reaction to the experience as if it, too, had changed. Because the body doesn't care if the symbol is external or internal, providing it's vivid enough, you can imagine a symbol of the experience or condition and change the symbol to get a healing effect.

When my mother was alive, there was a time when she was having chest pains. I asked her to tell me what it felt like, that is, what did she think could cause a pain like that? She immediately said that it felt like a big box of books was sitting on her chest. So I told her to imagine a couple of big, husky Hawaiians coming over to lift it off her chest, and I had her repeat that as a detailed experience three times. By the end of the third run-through, a few minutes later, the pain was all gone. Days later she told me that her doctor had found tumors in her chest before I had seen her, but when she was checked after the "box of books" technique, the tumors were no longer there.

Many times, people I've been with have had headaches and they have told me that it felt like their head was in a vise. So I told them to imagine that there really was a vise there and to imagine they could reach up and loosen it. In almost every case, after repeating it three times to "set" the experience in memory, the headache was relieved. Similarly, people have told me that they had a stabbing back pain, as though there was a knife in them, and I had them repeatedly imagine they could reach back and take the knife out and the pain went away.

During a class, a woman complained of a pain in her knee that had been there for months, making it hard for her to walk. I asked her to imagine that an object was in her knee causing the pain and to tell me what shape it was. She said it was like a wedge. I asked her to tell me how much it weighed and she said five pounds. I asked her what color it was and she said it was red. So I told her to imagine that she was reaching into her knee with her hand, taking out the five-pound, red wedge, and throwing it away. I had her do that three times in detail and then asked her to get up and walk and tell me how she felt. She got up without pain and walked without pain for the first time in three months.

In all of these cases the pain or discomfort has not been suppressed. To suppress pain, you have to divert attention away from the pain through distracting activity or a mental process, use a drug that blocks awareness of the pain, or tense muscles so much that you can't feel the pain. None of these changes the condition. On the other hand, symbolic imagination actually induces relaxation that allows the body to get on with healing.

CLOUDS OF COLOR

People who get involved with metaphysics learn of an imagination technique that is generally called something like the "white light of protection." It consists of imagining that you are surrounded by a white light or, in some variations, a white cloud, a sort of energy shield, or a kind of mirror. Metaphysically, it is supposed to set up a "high" vibration around you that repels negativity. Practically, it lowers anxiety and stress to the degree that it makes you feel safer. However, its range of use is limited, because all you can use it for is protection.

When I was much younger I learned a Hawaiian technique that I call "clouds of color." Instead of protecting, however, these imaginary clouds that you put around yourself or around parts of your body are used for physical, emotional, and mental healing. There are two aspects to the technique: color and intent, and each draws upon memory associations to produce its effects.

There are a lot of color systems in the world and I am not going to invent another one. If you have already learned a particular system of associating colors with specific qualities and you like the system, you can apply it to this technique. But if not, or if you want to try something different, you can work with fundamentals that are not based on philosophy or culture. Fundamentally, colors can be divided into warm or cool, bright or dim, and hard or soft. Red, orange, and yellow tend to be more stimulating—physically, emotionally, and mentally—and green, blue, and violet tend to be more soothing in the same areas. Brighter colors are more stimulating and dimmer colors are more soothing. "Hard" colors, that is, colors that are more pure, are also more stimulating, while "soft" colors, those that are mixed with a small amount of white, gray or black and which may be called muted, are more soothing. Mixing the preceding characteristics allows for a huge number of variations, but the main effects to remember and use are stimulating or soothing. Physical colors can produce these effects, and so can imagined ones.

Intent, in this case, simply concerns imagining the specific healing effects that you want the imagined colors to have. Imagining yourself surrounded by a cloud of bright orange or yellow, with the intent that it should increase your strength and endurance, will help to produce that effect by stimulating physical processes in your body and evoking appropriate memories that will alter your behavior. Imagining a soft green or blue cloud in or around a part of your body which is swollen or infected with the intent that it heal the condition will help to reduce tension and mobilize the body's healing resources. Doing the same thing with the intent to heal any related emotional conflicts will help to resolve them without your having to understand them or even know what they are. You'll find that some cloud colors will help you reduce

> Imagining yourself surrounded by a cloud of bright orange or yellow, with the intent that it should increase your strength and endurance, will help to produce that effect.

anger and some will help to reduce fear; some will help you to increase tolerance and some can help to resolve confusion and doubt, all depending on your associations with the colors and the intentions you have. In short, you can use the colors in any way that you want for any purpose that you want.

TAKE ADVANTAGE OF YOUR IMAGINATION

Whether you choose to alter a memory or surround yourself with clouds of color, you can use your imagination to get excellent healing results. As with all healing techniques, sometimes the effect will be immediate and sometimes you will have to keep it up, steadily or intermittently, until you get results.

CHAPTER SIX

Instant Healing with the Power of Touch

I t is good for your health to be touched. Being touched by another person produces more physiological, emotional, and mental changes in your body than input from any other sense, and unless you have mental or emotional resistance to that touch, those changes are always beneficial. Even when the touching seems superficial the body-mind response can be significant.

In the book *Healers on Healing*, Dr. Bernard Siegal tells the story of a colleague who had been using talk therapy for several years to treat a woman for the psychological effects of severe burns. After hearing Dr. Siegal speak about love, the colleague started the next treatment session by giving the woman a hug. He reported later that that single hug did more good for her than all the other sessions.

At a university in Florida, volunteers were brought in to gently stroke the skin of premature babies for ten minutes a day, while a control group of babies was left untouched. The results showed that the stroked babies gained weight faster and were ready to be discharged days earlier than the babies that were not touched.

An experiment carried out by UCLA researchers at the Santa Monica Library in Southern California consisted of having the person checking out the books contrive to make hand contact, however slight, with one hundred people who were borrowing books, and then being careful to avoid contact with the next hundred. Outside the library, students interviewed each person exiting to find out what they thought of the library's services. The overall satisfaction of the hundred who had been touched was dramatically higher than those who had not been touched, even though the touch was unobtrusive and had nothing to do with the services. That small human contact was enough to alter perception on a much larger scale.

Strong responsiveness to touch is normal in human beings, but for a variety of reasons some people grow up with a fear or dislike of it. Part of a person's response to touch draws from his cultural background. Northern Europeans and northern Asians tend to severely limit touching in family groups and avoid it whenever possible among non–family members. When it can't be avoided, as on crowded trains, it is studiously ignored. Some people, such as the British and French, engage in ritual touching (the handshake, the shoulder-grab with a quick peck or near-peck on the cheeks). Other groups, such as the Japanese, avoid even that by substituting it with ritual bowing (except when they have to deal with Westerners). However, even though the Japanese don't go in for public touching, they do have a strong cultural tradition of massage, which puts them way ahead of the British in the touching department. Compared to the British, Americans are touchy-feely fiends, with their back-slapping, arm-grabbing, rough hugging manners, but compared to the Italians, Americans are very stiff and reserved.

Excluding those with severe mental disorders, all people will respond well to touching, even public touching, in the right circumstances. Quite intimate touching seems to be okay among athletes, for example, touching a stranger while dancing is normal, and group sing-a-longs often result in more physical contact than usual in a crowd. I remember a workshop I led in Japan where the response really surprised me. Ordinarily I end my workshops with people holding hands in a circle, and to finish I have everyone hug the person on either side of them. I had ended this workshop with a circle, but I was going to end without the hugs out of deference to Japanese custom. However, my wife signaled me to go ahead with it (you'll remember that she is not to be ignored), so I explained to the group that this was a Hawaiian custom and they had to do it as part of the workshop. They did it, with a fervor and excitement that I couldn't believe. It was as if my giving permission to touch let loose a powerful force of suppressed inclination. They hugged on either side, they hugged across the room, and they hugged me over and over again.

Apart from cultural resistance to touching and being touched, there is the resistance that comes from bad experiences. Unfortunately, it seems as though nearly every culture has people so selfish and cruel that they take advantage of positions of authority and responsibility to exploit the natural impulses of others to love and be loved. They do it for their own personal pleasure and without regard to the consequences for the other person's life. They can be found in the ranks of parents and siblings, relatives and friends, educators and administrators, and wherever people have incorporated separatism to such a degree that there is no longer any empathy, compassion, or respect for others. The saddest results are when the ones exploited try to clamp down on their feelings to the point where their bodies carry the tension of a time bomb. Some victims turn to exploiting others themselves, perhaps out of revenge, or perhaps because they think that is the only way they can get touched; some, apparently calm and nice people, explode without warning in a furious attack on whoever is nearby; some live lives of unhappy isolation, fearful of the slightest human contact; some are healed by compassionate healers; and some even heal themselves. If our society had more safe and acceptable ways of touching and being touched we might have a lot less despair, violence, and illness to deal with.

Oh well, part of my small contribution toward that will be the techniques I share with you in this chapter.

SELF-TOUCH

In the absence of someone else to touch you, the thing to do is to touch yourself. Touching benefits your mind and your body because of endorphins and other substances released when your skin is touched, even by yourself, and, while your body and mind probably have preferred touchers, you can still gain a lot of benefit from touching yourself. So here is a non-sexual, self-touch exercise you can perform alone (I have nothing against sexual self-touch exercises; I'm just not going to teach you any). Every step will help to relieve a lot of tension. You can do this with or without light clothing. It also has a much better effect if you can do it with a real sense of caring about yourself.

> Massage your hands by "dry-washing" them, and be sure to squeeze each finger.

1. Start by massaging your scalp or pulling your hair (gently or strongly, your preference). An amazing amount of tension accumulates in your scalp and because of this, some people find this exercise very pleasurable.

2. Place the fingers of each hand along the center of your forehead and drag them outward and across your temples. Drag your fingers down along the sides of your nose, out and across your cheekbones, and down your jaw line. Drag from the center outward along your upper and lower lips.

3. Massage your ears.

4. Massage your hands by "dry-washing" them, and be sure to squeeze each finger. Rub the center of each palm and the area on the back of your hand between the thumb and forefinger.

5. Run your hands slowly or quickly over the entire front of your body, right on top of your clothing if you have any on.

6. Use a towel to rub the entire backside of your body, again over any clothing you have on. If you have a so-called Chinese back-scratcher, use that, too. It's a wonderful device for relieving back tension even when you don't itch.

7. Massage your feet, if you have time, and wash your hands before you eat anything or touch anyone else.

If you don't have time for all this you can do a quickie by massaging your arms and hands, and giving yourself a fast hug.

HUDDLING

Huddling is great for two or more people. It takes us way back to our primitive origins. Some monkeys like to do it for hours. As extremely simple as it sounds, you may expect some mind-blowing and body-boggling experiences, especially if you do it for extended periods. Clothing is optional. So is music and aroma.

- Version 1—For two people. Sit on the floor, supporting each other back-to-back. Stay there as long as you like, but give it at least five minutes to get some effects. You may feel warmth after a short time, of course, and perhaps tingling. Some people will eventually feel waves of energy, relaxation, or pleasure.

- Version 2—For two people. Get into a comfortable mutual holding position, on the floor, against a wall, or in a chair. Don't do anything except be with each other. If you need to move after awhile to get more comfortable, do so gently and minimally. In addition to the effects mentioned above, there may also be a sensation of merging with the other and it is easy to enter a state of dozing or daydreaming.

- Version 3—For three or more people. Use any combination of back-to-back, holding, draping, leg/arm entwining, comfortably close positions and just be there for a while. Breathe, but don't speak. Move slowly and minimally when you have to. This usually works best on a floor, with or without pillows. Go to the bathroom before you start. Share your experiences afterward. Besides warmth, tingling, relaxation, pleasure, dozing, daydreaming, and merging, the group experience in particular lends itself to the potential for visionary and blissful experiences.

The main benefits from huddling, from the point of view of this book, are physical and emotional healing.

Oh, I almost forgot. Huddling also tends to stimulate sexual feelings in some people. Depending on who's involved and what the circumstances are, you'll have to judge for yourself what kind of behavior is appropriate. Just remember that it's possible to experience sexual feelings without doing anything about them. Stay relaxed and just let them be there and enjoy them without obligation. The sexual energy itself can be very healing for your body.

Sit on the floor, supporting each other back-to-back. Some people will feel waves of energy, relaxation, or pleasure.

HEALING HANDS

People often tell me that they think they have healing power, or that a psychic has told them they have healing power, and they ask me what they can do about it. I usually tell them to start healing.

Your Hidden Talent

It's easy to say that everyone has the ability to heal. How do I prove it? Well, I don't have to prove it to you. You can prove it to yourself with a few experiments. If you are widely read, or a workshop junkie, you've probably come across the following ideas before, so this section is for those who aren't sure what I'm talking about.

1. Rub the palms of your hands together and hold your hands with your palms facing each other about six to eight inches apart. You should be aware of a tingling sensation from the rubbing, but now move your hands toward each other in a slightly bouncy kind of way, as if you were thinking about clapping but couldn't make up your mind whether to do it or not. Pay attention to anything you may feel with your palms. If you are like most people, you will feel a slight sensation of resistance, like you were squeezing a soft balloon or pushing similar poles of two magnets together. This is an energy field you are feeling, and it's what healers use for healing (at least, some healers).

2. Line up three glasses of orange, grapefruit, or apple juice; three cups of coffee or tea; or three glasses of chablis wine. You could use plain water for this, but the experimental results are more definite when something has a bit of bite to it. Rub your hands together and then hold one of the cups or glasses in your hands for one or two minutes and taste the liquid. Then taste the liquid in the other two containers. Taste the first one again. Notice any difference? You have just "healed" the liquid (one person may

not notice a difference, but another person usually can).
The reason I suggest two controls is so you can be more
certain the difference is real. Typically, the "healed" liquid
has less bite or bitterness; it becomes more mellow. Some
people think it tastes sweeter. Some don't think that the
change is an improvement.

Everyone has healing power. Not only is everyone's body constantly
engaged in healing itself, often in spite of all the things a person may be
doing to interfere with it, but everyone has the power to help others
heal themselves, too. Right now. This minute. Without any fancy rituals.

Rituals are good. They have authority and they can convince unknow-
ing or uncertain people that they have the power and the right to start
helping people. There's nothing wrong with that. People also have the
right to charge whatever they think they or their services are worth, and
people have the right to pay whatever they think a person or a service is
worth. No problem so far.

My only beef is when people think they can't or are not allowed to
heal without a ritual or someone else's permission (I'm not talking about
legal issues here; they're another mat-
ter). The fact is, if you're human, you can
heal (this is a book for humans, by the
way. If you are an animal or a plant or a
rock or a star you need to be reading a
different book). Of course, as with anything, some people are naturally better at
it than others, but everyone has the talent to some degree.

Rub your hands until
they tingle and just lay
them on a person's
sore area (this works
even through clothing)
for a minute or two.

The next time you are around someone who has an ache or a pain, and who

is willing to let you experiment on them, rub your hands till they tingle and just lay them on the person's sore area (this even works through clothing) for a minute or two. You will get much better results if you keep your attention on what you are doing. I know some systems teach that the energy just flows through you so you can let your mind wander, but energy flows where attention goes, and your hands will have more energy if you stay focused. If the person experiences any relief at all, the experiment is a success. And by employing the techniques in the next section, you can amp up the power of this kind of healing touch.

HANDY VIBES

Many people have tried to find a way to use sound for healing, and there's no doubt that it can have a beneficial effect on the body. "Music soothes the savage breast" and it can also calm you down or lift you up in a very short time, but it's not really touch therapy. Another kind of sound therapy called "toning" consists of someone using his voice to make sounds in your direction and this is supposed to have a healing effect, but I have never observed nor experienced any pronounced short-term healing benefits from it.

Humming

Something that does work very well is the combination of sound and touch. All you have to do is hum while your hands are touching yourself or someone else. That's right, just hum while you touch. To get a direct sense of what the effect is, hold your palms apart and facing like I described above, without rubbing them first. Now hum. In addition to the vibration in your body, you

Wherever you have aches or pains or places that need healing, you can put your hands on them and hum your way to health.

will feel a tingling in your hands and perhaps even the soft pressure sensation between them.

Wherever you have aches or pains or places that need healing, you can put your hands or fingers on them and hum your way to health. Actually, it will help to relieve tension and speed up your body's natural healing process faster than touch alone. You can experiment with humming high notes or low notes, or even your favorite tunes. I've found that the effect is stronger if you keep your attention on where your hands are touching while you hum. The effect is also stronger when you hum with your mouth closed because this produces a stronger vibration within your body, which transfers more energy to your hands.

Mumbling Mode

A variation on humming is mumbling. Mumbling is speaking with your mouth closed and your lips moving. It produces an effect like humming with the added benefit of subliminal (subaudial for the perfectionists) suggestion. When you apply your fingers or hands to an area of the body for healing, instead of humming you mumble affirmations, blessings, or directions. I did this in a taxi for a friend who had sudden stomach cramps and in about three minutes she was fine again. It's a very handy technique for all kinds of situations.

I use it on my own neck and shoulders when I'm at the computer for too long and often, right afterward, I just turn my neck and my spine adjusts itself. It's also great for easing sore muscles after a workout and relieving your own headaches. However, be aware that some people may be distracted or irritated by the mumbling and will not respond well to it.

BLANKET FORGIVENESS

Blanket forgiveness is an awesome instant healing technique that uses both touch and words. It is awesome because it works so quickly and it is awesome because you don't even have to know whom you are forgiving for it to work. It is based on an assumption that any physical condition involving swelling or infection also contains an emotional component of repressed anger or guilt. Notice that I didn't say it was caused by emotions, just that it can be useful to assume that emotions are involved in causing at least some of the stress that is maintaining or aggravating the condition. If you can relieve the emotional tension, it will help the body heal more quickly.

The actual technique is very simple. With your hand or fingers, you lightly touch the area that needs healing while at the same time you repeat the words, "Whatever this is related to, I forgive it completely," for as long as you can or until you get some relief. It's likely that you'll feel various sensations as you do this, such as tingling or movement or relaxation, and maybe even pain relief. The more that anger or guilt is connected with the condition, the more quickly and dramatically you will experience healing effects. Even if angry emotions are only a small part of the malady, there will be some degree of benefit. As I said, you don't have to know consciously who or what the emotions are directed at. Just holding the idea of forgiveness while touching the infected or swollen area is enough to cause subconscious changes that will ease a lot of stress. The touch itself provides a certain amount of energy as well as helping to keep your mind focused on forgiving.

Of course, if you do know who or what you are resenting or feeling guilty about, then forgiving him or her or it can make the technique even more effective. The most astounding personal experience I had with this technique was when I woke up one day with an abscessed tooth and extreme tension in my jaw. My teeth were so sensitive that I could barely close my

> With your hand or fingers, you lightly touch the area that needs healing while at the same time you repeat the words "Whatever this is related to, I forgive it completely."

mouth because the slightest touch of my upper and lower teeth set off waves of pain. Obviously this called for a trip to the dentist, and even though I had a good one in mind I decided to try something else first. To begin with, I assumed that there was anger involved. Then I asked myself with whom I might be angry. Immediately a woman came to mind who had reneged on an important commitment the day before. I thought I had handled it with peaceful forbearance, but my body was now telling me that all I had done was to suppress my anger. So, very gently, I placed one finger against the place on my jaw where the swelling of the abscess was most tender, and began to repeat my forgiveness affirmation, directing it toward the woman in question. As I recall, the phrasing was something like "Whatever so-and-so did or didn't do, I forgive her completely." The reaction was so sudden that even I was stunned. The pain immediately began to ease off and I could feel the swelling start to lessen. Within thirty minutes there was no trace of an abscess, nor any pain or tenderness. It was as if the condition had never existed. So my dentist didn't get my business that day, but I eventually used his services for other things.

Although knowing whom or what it is that needs forgiving is not really necessary, there is a way to narrow down the choices. Because of deep, cross-cultural associations, many people around the world make a conscious or subconscious relationship between women and the left side of the body, and men and the right side of the body. It's very useful from a healing point of view to assume that problems on the left side of the body have an emotional component that relates to women in one's life, and problems on the right side have to do with men. I have also found that an emotional conflict with a strong woman may be part of problems on the right side, and similar conflicts with a meek man may be part of problems on the left side. If you are working on a physical problem on one side of your body or the other, let your mind play with the idea that your relationship with a man or woman might be involved on the appropriate side and see what comes up. In the case of my abscessed tooth, the problem was on my left side. In the case of a Mongolian shamanness I helped who had an infection in her right eye, another shamanness with a very strong personality was involved. In any case, consider the possibility that emotional conflict, usually anger or resentment, is at least partly involved in a problem you might have and try to relieve that before you go on to other healing methods. At the very least it will help to make any other methods you use more effective.

ENJOYING THE WONDERS OF TOUCH

Touch is one of the most powerful of all healing modalities in any form it takes, from a handshake to a hug to a full-body massage. There is the effect of exchanging energy, of course, but even more important is the way in which touch serves as the bridge between beings. In a world where ideas of separation have such great influence, touch becomes the surest way of making connections. A healing touch, empowered by love and compassion, becomes a means to greater awareness and a source of joy for the reacher and the reached.

CHAPTER SEVEN

Instant Healing with the Power of Energy

The powers of words, imagination, and touch have this in common: they each produce physical, emotional, or mental changes, and therefore they each produce a movement of energy.

Healing is a process of making changes in the body, the feelings, and the mind. Instant healing is simply a way of making those changes more quickly. Whenever there is change, energy is involved, and there are ways of working more directly with energy in order to produce those changes. In this chapter, the movement of energy becomes the primary focus.

Before I look at specific applications of energy to the instant healing process, it would be useful to take a closer look at energy itself.

WHAT IS ENERGY?

Humans are conditioned to think of matter as something solid, and so it is sometimes very hard to get away from the idea that the smallest bits of matter must be solid somethings. It is even harder to get away from the idea that energy is a something. Energy is defined in physics as the capacity to do work, that is, the property of one system that enables it to influence another system. Examples of energy are rain falling because of gravity and eroding a hillside, and adrenaline releasing sugar into your bloodstream to be used as fuel by your cells to give your brain and body a boost. Nonetheless, many people persist in thinking of energy as something, like a brick. If you have a brick and you hand it to someone else, now he has a brick and you don't. But energy isn't like a brick at all.

Energy is much more like an ocean wave that gets its energy from the wind, that gets its energy from something else, and so on. Where there is energy there is movement, or change, and where there is movement or change there is energy. Because everything is apparently moving or changing, it's easy to see everything as a potential source of energy. Also, all this movement seems to be in the form of waves.

As humans we experience life primarily through sight, sound, and touch. To see, hear, and feel there has to be a particular kind of phenomenon existing at a particular range of frequencies that can be perceived by specially organized receptors. In other words, seeing, hearing, and feeling require a nervous system that can process information received by the eyes, ears, and skin. That information reaches those receptors in the form of light waves, sound waves, and vibration. Of course, it's more involved than that, but those are the basics.

If energy is movement and matter is moving, then matter is energy. If movement occurs in waves (also known as frequencies or vibrations or radiations), then what we perceive as matter consists of different kinds of waves. And if one kind of wave can influence the behavior of another kind of wave, as wind influences water or fire influences wind, and if humans can find a way in which they themselves can generate waves that will influence the behavior of other waves, why, then, maybe they can use that ability for instant healing. In any case, I am going to use those assumptions as a starting point for the subject of this chapter.

Where Do Waves Come From?

Waves are started by other waves. If you have ever watched a field of grain or grass being buffeted by the wind, you may have noticed how the pressure of the wind rolls across the field in waves, not as one solid flattening effect. That's because wind moves in waves. Earthquakes move in waves. Sunlight moves in waves. According to our assumptions, everything moves in waves, and waves make waves.

In earlier chapters, I discussed how stress produces tension that interferes with healing. Stress was defined as resulting from mutual forces working against each other. In terms of the present chapter, I would say that the tension of stress comes from two waves colliding. If you can use another wave to redirect or modify one of the colliding waves, then the natural process of healing can take place. And the more quickly you can do that, the more instant the healing will be.

For the practical part of this chapter, I'll consider three sources of energy that can be used for instant healing: physical, emotional, and mental.

PHYSICAL ENERGY

There are a myriad number of ways in which physical energy can be employed for healing purposes. As with the following discussions of emotional and mental energy, I'll concentrate on a few very useful specific methods, rather than provide an exhaustive survey of all the possibilities.

Water

Yes, I know that practically everyone is aware of the importance of drinking more water to avoid dehydration, and bottled water is available almost everywhere. On a recent trip to China I had no trouble finding bottled water at a market stall in every town I visited, and even some airlines

A glass or two of water will often produce instant benefits for backache, headache, joint pain, nausea, cold or flu-like symptoms, and anxiety.

make sure their passengers are supplied with plenty of water. It's easy to forget that this is a very new phenomenon. However, in my classes and courses I've found that many people, including those who bring their bottles of water to class, still aren't aware of some of the instant healing benefits of water.

When the body gets dehydrated, it goes into a state of stress and the resulting tension can produce symptoms that may not seem to be associated with a lack of water. One of the things I discovered on my own was that if I wake up in the morning with aches and pains, a glass or two of water will almost always make them disappear as if by magic. The effect seems to take place much faster than the time it would take for the water to get from my stomach to the cells that might need it. If I were to assume that the water acts like a wave of energy, then I could say that the water energy moves one or both of the colliding stress waves and the release of tension allows the body to heal itself. A physiologist might throw fits at such a theory, but it doesn't hurt to play with ideas. The fact of the matter is that it works.

In addition to morning aches and pains, I have found that a glass or two of water will often produce instant benefits for backache, headache, joint pain, nausea, cold or flu-like symptoms, and anxiety.

Another healing characteristic of water is its ability to neutralize a positive electric field. Under certain conditions, a static electric field can build up on and around the body and cause considerable stress. This can happen during dry winds such as the Santa Anas of California, the Konas of Hawaii, the Harmattan of West Africa, and the Scirocco of North Africa. It can also happen when winds blow through natural canyons or the concrete canyons of a city, and when air blows through air-conditioning ducts in buildings, planes, and cars. Such fields may build up as well during a high-pressure weather system when the air doesn't seem to be moving at all. Although a positive electric field may build up around the body as a whole, it tends to concentrate wherever there is metal in contact with the skin (rings, necklaces, bracelets, watches, and the like). The emergence in the electric field may cause you to feel some of the symptoms I mentioned above, such as headache or nausea. Taking a shower or bath, wiping the skin with a damp cloth, and touching the metal that is in contact with your body with a wet finger are all good ways of discharging the field and producing an instant feeling of relief.

Breath

Yeah, sure, it's important to breathe. And?

Of course it's important to breathe, so important that a lot of different cultures have developed special breathing exercises that are supposed to make you healthy, wealthy, wise, and full of super powers. Over the years I have experimented with quite a few styles—yogic breathing, tantric breathing, taoist breathing, gnostic breathing, rebirthing, and others too obscure to mention. By my analysis all of their benefits can be derived from one master technique: deeper breathing.

Breathing occurs in waves. In addition to the cycle of inhaling and exhaling there is a wave pulse that goes up and down the torso when you breathe, sometimes in sync with the breathing and sometimes not. The primary benefit of breathing is the provision of oxygen to your cells, and a major secondary benefit is the fact that breathing acts as a pump for your lymph system, helping to eliminate toxins from your body. If the breath waves are small, i.e., if your breathing is shallow, you take in less oxygen and get rid of fewer toxins. This makes you more susceptible to illness, lowers your pain threshold, reduces your physical strength, and fogs your brain. Deeper breathing (just deeper—not more rapid) helps to change all that. The problem, naturally, is that under

It might be a good idea to train yourself to remember to breathe more deeply whenever you feel under stress, as a kind of self-help first aid technique.

stress we all tend toward shallow breathing, and for many people shallow breathing becomes a habit. Deeper breathing often requires conscious effort. It might be a good idea to train yourself to remember to breathe more deeply whenever you feel under stress, as a kind of self-help first aid technique. Instead of a sign saying "Think" above your desk, put one that says "Breathe."

In addition to just plain deeper breathing, there is one breathing exercise that I have found to be extremely useful. Some yogic techniques emphasize holding the breath at one or both ends of the cycle for a certain number of counts. So you would inhale and hold for four counts, and exhale and hold for four counts, or more. According to my research, there is a valuable physiological benefit to this, at least at the inhalation end. In simple terms, when you hold your breath for a few moments at the top of the inhale, there is a mixing of oxygen and carbon dioxide which enables more oxygen to be absorbed by the red blood cells. The instant healing benefit of this is more energy, faster pain relief, and clearer thinking. In my experience, holding the breath for three or four counts is sufficient for the effect to be felt. However, it does usually take more than one breathing cycle.

Strange Waves

I had a really hard time figuring out how to present this next idea. Although some of the concepts in this book are rather unorthodox, I wanted to keep the techniques as practical and understandable as possible without sounding esoteric or too far out. What I'm about to describe is so practical, however, that I'm going to risk sounding weird to those unfamiliar with subtle energy research.

To keep it simple, not all forms of energy are understood or even acknowledged by mainstream science (or by anyone, for that matter). Even things that are not understood, however, can be put to practical use as long as their effects can be shown to be beneficial. What follows are some simple ways of using a source of energy for healing that doesn't seem to make any sense according to conventional knowledge. These ways have been experimented with and experienced by thousands of people all over the world with good results. Those who would like more background can read my book *Earth Energies*. Otherwise, you can just try them out for yourself. Theoretically, the "devices" I'll describe generate waves that tend to relieve tension and thus assist the natural healing process of the body.

The Wavepad

Take one square foot of aluminum foil and cover it with one square foot of plastic cling wrap (the clingy kind works best). Now fold it over several times to make a square or rectangular pad suitable for placing on a part of your body where you are suffering discomfort. It doesn't matter whether the foil is on the inside or outside. You can attach it with tape or any other way you choose and leave it in place until you get relief. This is particularly good for helping aches, pains, bruises, and nausea, and for helping to speed up healing of any kind.

> Attach a wavepad with tape or any other way you choose and leave it in place until you get relief.

The Waveplate

Cut two six-inch squares of acrylic or styrene plastic (the kind used for window panes or in picture frames is good) and one six-inch square of aluminum foil. Sandwich the foil between the plastic and tape the plastic pieces together. Use this plate as a coaster for water and other liquids. Allow about 30 seconds for the liquid to be "charged" with energy. Drinking the "energized" liquid will provide a subtly beneficial effect for your whole body, helping to keep tension levels down, and the "energized" water can be used topically on the skin. Many people will notice that coffee, tea, or young wine will have a more mellow taste after sitting on the waveplate for a while. You can also expand the size of the waveplate to twelve inches square and use it as a foot pad at your desk, in front of the TV, or by your bed. Many people will immediately feel an invigorating effect within a minute or two of resting their feet on the plate, whether they are sitting or standing.

EMOTIONAL ENERGY

The same people who think of energy as bricks tend to think of emotions as chicken feathers. Good emotions mean you are full of soft, dry feathers that give you a warm, fuzzy feeling and bad emotions mean you are filled with damp, lumpy feathers that give you an unpleasant feeling. By this reasoning, if you feel bad and you want to feel good you have to take out the wet feathers (release or get rid of the bad emotions) and replace them with dry feathers (put in good emotions). As a theory about emotions, it doesn't work very well, because an emotion isn't a thing any more than energy is. If you gain any healing benefits from expressing anger, grief, sadness, or whatever, it isn't because you've gotten rid of anything. It's because you've changed behavior and started energy moving and have released tension that came from trying not to feel the emotion. The potential for the same emotion to reoccur is still there unless you change your relationship to the memory that triggered it. However, immediate healing benefits can come from moving directly into a positive emotion without even bothering to "release" the negative one.

At a conference in Colorado, I attended an evening discussion on how to be happy that was given by a young Frenchman. His message was deceptively simple: if you want to be happy, just be happy. Most of the evening's discussion went like this in a question and answer format: Q—"How can I be happy if I've lost my job?" A—"Be happy." Q—"How can I be happy if I'm all alone?" A—"Be happy." Q—"How can I be happy if I'm sick?" A—"Be happy." A lot of people left the discussion just shaking their heads. They couldn't grasp the idea that happiness is a choice. It comes from dwelling on what you like, rather than on what you don't like. Outside events or the behavior of other people are not what make you unhappy. Unhappiness derives from actively or passively resisting events and behaviors. Resistance creates tension. And enough tension creates or amplifies illness. Happiness, and other positive emotions, relieve tension and support the body's natural healing abilities.

The theory sounds good, but what about the practice? It's one thing to tell someone to be happy and quite another for a person to be able to do it. It's like advising someone to be well when he's sick. Without a way to do it, the advice is empty. The following are some ways to generate positive emotional states to help with instant, rapid, or fast healing. If you're in a bad emotional state you won't feel like using them, so it might be helpful to think of them as emotional medicine that you "take" if you want to get well.

> If you are hurting, physically or emotionally, it really does help you feel better to think of your favorite things.

Favorite Focus

If you are hurting, physically or emotionally, it really does help you feel better to think of your favorite things, whether they're brown paper packages tied up in string or anything else. It does much more than just distract you. It relaxes muscles, releases endorphins, and stimulates lots of other good healing stuff. The "catch" is you really have to take the time to do it. Take at least a minute, anytime or anywhere, to fill your mind with memories or imaginings of things you like. For healing purposes, the more time you spend on it the better, but try it in one-minute chunks to start, at least.

Love Power

Some years ago my organization received an unsolicited box full of red pin-back metal buttons with the words "I am loved" written on them. With them was a story about a man whose wife was critically ill in a hospital. On one visit he told her, "Just remember you are loved." When he left she took that idea and dwelt on it as much as she could, especially when fears came up. According to the story, her recovery was fast and was called miraculous. We were asked to distribute the pins in the hope that they might help other people, which we did. And they did. Since then I have used this idea on myself and taught it to others with extremely good results. Because it isn't easy for many people to just start thinking that way, I developed the following approach to make it easier. Take a good look at your present life, including your immediate environment and significant people in your life, then carefully note everything you can that provides you with any kind of benefit, and, finally, interpret that benefit as a sign that you are loved by the source of it. Assume that the fragrance of a flower is a gift of love; assume that the air you breathe is a gift of love; assume that all the things that people do for you, from the strangers who provide electricity for you to the help of friends and family, and all the good that the universe provides, are signs that you are loved. To the degree that you can make the signs of love more important than any other assumptions about your world, you'll experience a remarkable increase in healing.

Positive Posture

Fairly recently I was on an extended trip that was physically exhausting and mentally stressful. After two weeks I began to come down with cold symptoms, such as nasal drip, stuffed sinuses, and sneezing. Because of past experience, I knew that these were stress symptoms and not a "bug." Of all the techniques I used to relieve the stress, the most instant relief came from shifting into a feeling state of confidence. It was not a matter of feeling confident about any particular thing. It was simply a confident feeling. Within seconds of shifting into that feeling state, all of my cold symptoms were completely gone, and that's about as instant as you can get. My nose was dry, my sinuses were clear, and the tickling urge to sneeze disappeared. I had been able to bring on the state by merely thinking about it, due

Of all the techniques I used to relieve the stress, the most instant relief came from shifting into a feeling state of confidence. It was not a matter of feeling confident about any particular thing.

to a lot of practice doing so. However, as soon as I let my attention wander from the feeling of confidence, all the cold symptoms immediately came back. Fortunately, in learning how to share this technique with others, I have discovered that the easiest way for most people to enter and sustain this state is by assuming a confident posture. The assumption of the posture of confidence reminds the body of the feeling of confidence, and as long as one maintains the posture, the feeling remains—with all of its healing benefits.

MENTAL ENERGY

Perhaps to your surprise, I am not going to discuss thoughts or telepathy in this section. I am going to talk about attention.

When you put attention on something, a vitally important event occurs. That event is a wave. It's a wave of energy and I'm not going to discuss what kind of energy because I don't know and no one I know knows, although theories abound. For the sake of convenience, I call it mental energy, but so far it can't be directly measured or sensed and there's no way to scientifically prove it exists. However, and that's a big "however" so I should say *however*, a wave happens when you put your attention on something and we know that because of the effects. When you put your attention on something, that something changes, often in ways that can be measured scientifically. Using my wave theory, attention directs a wave of mental energy toward whatever the attention is on, and that influences the wave energy of the object of the attention. The nature of the effect depends on the degree of attention, the duration of the attention, and the information carried by the wave of mental energy.

The Power of Your Will

Here are some experiments you can perform yourself to test the power of will. You can use words, imagination, and/or touch to direct your will, but remember that they are not the source of power here. Your results will be determined by the intensity of your intent.

1. Opening a jar. Find an unopened jar of something, one that is very hard to open. After your first, unsuccessful try (if your first try is successful there's no point to the rest of the exercise), mentally tell the cap to open easily or tell your hand to open it easily, and/or imagine seeing and feeling it happen. At the same time, will it to happen. The strength of the seal and the strength of your hand are factors to take into account, and it might possibly take you more than one try, but the difference from the first try will be very noticeable.

2. Lifting an object. Pick up any fairly heavy object that you can lift with one hand, such as a rock, or a full bottle of wine, or a statuette. Then will it to be lighter and lift it again. The difference will be very noticeable.

3. Making your finger grow. Just so you don't freak out, I want you to know that the effect you are about to produce is only temporary. The point here is to demonstrate the power of will to influence your own body. A few rare people don't seem to be able to produce the effect for some reason. It could be that their doubts are interfering with the process. Anyway, you start by finding the more or less horizontal crease on both wrists that is just below your palm. You bring both wrists together at the crease and flatten your hands together like you were going to pray. Pay attention to your middle fingers. For most people they will be the same height. In that case, leave one hand up and put the other one down. If one of your middle fingers is longer than the other, leave the shorter one up and put the longer one down. Now, put all of your attention on the middle finger of the hand that is up and will it to grow. Tell it to grow, imagine it growing, and most of all want it to grow. Keep this up intensely for one minute. Then bring up your other hand, put your wrists together at the crease, and flatten your hands against each other. Surprise!

Attention itself is moved by one of the most mysterious forces of the universe—the will. The main characteristic of the will is that it starts energy moving; it creates waves. You can have an intention, but it takes will to carry it out. You can have a desire, but it takes will to achieve it. You can have a wish, but it takes will to fulfill it. You can make a decision, but it takes will to implement it. And even though one can find ways to rationalize it or to justify it, no one knows where it comes from. So forget about that part. Assume that the power of will exists. What then?

Then comes applying it. There are two vital aspects to effective willing. What follows is one of the most useful secrets you will ever encounter in your whole life.

The first aspect of willing is intending something to happen (or not happen). This is not just having an intention or holding an intent. Those are weak-willed variations that may or may not have an effect over a period of time, depending a lot on the strength of other forces. No, I'm talking about actively intending with as much confident expectation as you can muster. It's not an easy idea to get across in English, but I hope it's clear enough. The second aspect is just as important. You apply your will to forces that already exist or that you are going to use. Many people give up on willpower because they try to use it directly to make something change, and that's not how willpower works best. It works best by generating waves that influence waves of existing or potential energy. Instead of willing a cancerous tumor to instantly disappear, it's more effective to will your body to use all its resources (which could include its own immune system, medicine you are taking, or even surgery you are going to have) to make it disappear. Your will, added to your body's natural inclination to heal itself, makes a very powerful combination.

Will directs your attention and attention influences events. The following techniques for directing and strengthening attention have proven very effective in instant healing. I'll warn you in advance that the last one is a stunner.

The Eye Relaxer Technique

In an earlier chapter I mentioned that when my eyes get stressed I do something to relax them and my vision comes back to normal (which for me is 20-20). With this technique I can read six-point type at a distance of six inches without glasses, contacts, or surgery, although my eyes are over sixty years old.

Sometimes, for a quick relaxer, I squeeze my eyes shut tightly three to five times and that generates relaxing waves of energy that improve vision, but that's not the technique I'm talking about. For a longer lasting beneficial effect you have to look at things differently.

A whole lot of people develop the habit of trying to grab things with their eyes. They treat the verb "to look" as if it meant "to lock." The effort of trying to hold on to what they see and even pull it toward them creates a great amount of tension in the eye muscles. The tension, in turn, often distorts their vision.

Actually, everything that you see is coming to you. You don't have to do a thing other than receive it. However, if you've developed the habit of "eye-grabbing," or if your eyes get stressed

> Just put your attention on the back of your head and keep it there while you are looking at something. Breathing deeply and slowly while you do that is helpful.

or strained for any other reason, you may want to do something a little more active to relax your eyes and obtain better vision.

The process, however, isn't really very active. Just put your attention on the back of your head and keep it there while you are looking at something. Breathing deeply and slowly while you do that is helpful, and so is imagining that your eyes are sitting at the back end of long tunnels leading to the back of your head, or putting your hand on the back of your head to help you maintain the focus. The main effect, however, comes from sustaining the back-of-the-head focus. At first it may take awhile to obtain a good improvement in your vision. With practice, however, you'll find that you'll be able to see better very quickly. Instantly, so to speak.

The *Pikopiko* Technique

Only move your attention from your head to your navel. Don't try to move the energy. This technique is useful for mild anxiety and low levels of tension.

Pikopiko is a Hawaiian word meaning "center to center," and I learned the technique from my uncle. Basically, it consists of shifting your attention from one place to another in conjunction with deeper breathing. The breathing assists in maintaining the attention and seems to amplify the mental energy. There are numerous variations to this technique and many applications. Below I will list three that are most useful for instant healing. Any of them can be used while sitting, standing, walking, or lying down.

The Pikopiko *Tune-up*

Inhale with your attention on the top of your head; exhale with your attention on your navel. Intend to relax or be energized, as you wish. A lot of people try to visualize energy moving from the top of the head to the navel while doing this, but not only is that unnecessary, it can even interfere with the process. *Pikopiko* works best when you give up trying to make something happen and just let the attention do the work. Only move your attention from your head to your navel. Don't try to move the energy. This technique is useful for mild anxiety, low levels of tension, when you need a quick energy boost, and for practicing the technique.

The Pikopiko *De-stresser*

Inhale with your attention as far above your head as you can (I often use the stars as a focus, but the clouds or sky are also good). Exhale with your attention as far below your feet as you can (the center of the earth works well, and so does the ground beneath your feet). Intend wellness. In Mongolia I taught this technique to a local shaman who had a sudden onset of headache and nausea symptoms. In her belief system this might have been a psychic attack from an enemy, but I suggested that she try this technique before doing anything else. If she was just experiencing heavy stress—and we were in a stressful situation—then the technique would help. If the technique didn't change the way she was feeling, she could still do her own thing. The technique worked in a few minutes, so she didn't have to engage in any defensive rituals that time. I have used it myself in many severely stressful situations and so have others with instant to rapid healing effects.

The Pikopiko *Harmonizer*

Inhale with your attention on your navel, exhale with your attention on any part of your body that needs tension release or healing. Because this helps to increase circulation instantly it is very good for stiff or sore muscles, but it really shines as an instant healing technique for numbness of the limbs due to a cramped position while sleeping or sitting. If I wake up in the morning with a numb arm or hand, all I have to do is less than thirty seconds of this *pikopiko* and the numbness is gone—without any pain or excessive tingling at all.

The Pikopiko *Incorporator*

Inhale with your attention on something outside of yourself that has qualities or associations that you desire. Exhale with your attention on a part of your body where you want those qualities or associations to manifest and imagine the external object of attention in miniature at that location. Intend the appropriate effect. In London I was walking in a park with some students during a break in a seminar and one of them told me he had

Inhale with your attention on your navel, exhale with your attention on any part of your body then needs tension release or healing.

a badly strained back. He showed me that he was unable to bend forward more than ten degrees without a sharp pain. There was a breeze blowing and I pointed out the leaves of an oak tree that were fluttering in the wind. I taught him this technique and told him to use the moving leaves for the focus of his attention. He did the technique during the fifteen-minute walk back to the classroom and by the time we arrived he was able to bend over almost ninety degrees without pain. He had inhaled with his attention on the moving leaves, and when he exhaled he had imagined those leaves moving in his back.

On another occasion, I woke up with a painfully stiff neck after moving furniture the day before. While still in bed, I played one of my favorite CDs and did this technique, inhaling with my attention on the source of the music, and exhaling with my attention on my neck while imagining that the music was playing in my body. After half an hour the painful stiffness was gone. Objects of attention suitable for many healing needs are anything that moves, anything that melts or dissolves, anything that is peaceful or quiet, anything energetic, and anything that is strong.

The Mindblower Technique

In the past I have called this "repatterning" or "the repetition technique," but neither of those does it justice so I changed the name to reflect its awesome power. What else would you call a technique that enables you to heal burns, cuts, bruises, and even broken bones in just a few minutes? This will probably produce more skepticism than anything else in this book, but the proof is in the practice. Several times I have said that the body has a natural inclination to heal itself. Now I'm going to rephrase that a bit. Based on empirical research I am convinced that the body has a natural inclination to heal itself instantly. Unfortunately, in the healing field it is taken for granted that the body needs time to heal. I disagree. I think that what takes time is reducing stress and redirecting energy waves so that the body can do its healing without restraint. Experience indicates that the sooner you can reduce stress and redirect energy, the more quickly the body will heal, and this technique can help people to do that with amazing speed.

When the body is injured it immediately mobilizes all of its available resources to repair itself. However, the body gets its information about current reality from three sources: immediate sensory data from the environment, its own memories of sensory data, and the mind's imagination regarding past, present, and future sensory data. It then attempts to correlate the information from these three sources in order to respond appropriately to a given situation. Ideally, the memory data contains valuable information on how the body has coped with such situations before, and the mind's imagination can reinforce past success, reinforce present coping strategies, and guide future progress. That's how it could work (and even does, on rare occasions with rare individuals). Fortunately, the body usually does its part of the healing job quite well. Unfortunately, the mind seldom does. Instead of helping the body, the minds of most people hinder it. (I feel safe in saying most people. Otherwise, the state of health and healing in the world would be very different.) Most often, what happens is that while the body is busy coping, the mind is re-creating the injury in imagination, reacting with anger, and anticipating fearful results, all of which add tremendous additional stress to the situation and inhibit the healing process. As if that weren't bad enough, the body also has to deal with memories of past mental reactions to an injury.

One solution would be to quiet the mind and put it to work at helping the body, rather than interfering with it. That's what the mind-blower technique does. I know it doesn't sound very mind-blowing, and the name is only valid because the effects are astounding in terms of current expectations. As more people become familiar with it and use it, I'll have to change the name again. First I'll tell you how it works.

When you receive an
injury, relax your mus-
cles and do a "quasi-
repetition" of the
action that produced
the injury. The idea
behind it is to create a
new experiential memory
in which the injury
doesn't take place.

When you receive an injury, what you do with your body in this technique is to, insofar as possible, relax your muscles and do a "quasi-repetition" of the action that produced the injury. A quasi-repetition is an action that almost duplicates the original action. The difference is that you complete the action by stopping short of, or bypassing, the original traumatic contact. For example, if you burnt your finger by touching something hot, you would immediately repeat the action of moving your finger toward the source of heat and stop short of touching it again by a safe distance, doing this again and again until the pain subsides, which usually happens in less than a minute (if you do the rest of the technique properly). If you got your fingers caught in a door, you would leave your fingers in place and repeat the movement of the door until just before it touched your fingers. If you stubbed your toe, you would repeatedly swing your foot toward whatever you stubbed it against, stopping short of contact. If you hit your finger with a hammer you would swing the hammer toward your finger in the same way without contact. If you cut yourself with a knife, you would repeat the cutting action without contact, stopping the blood flow first, if necessary. In all these cases and others, you would continue the repetitive action until the pain subsides. If, for any reason, it is impossible or inconvenient to interact with the original object that caused the injury then you can substitute a different object to represent it, such as a free hand to represent a hammer or a knife, or a glass jar to represent a hot pot. The idea behind it is to create a new experiential memory in which the injury doesn't take place.

The mental side of the technique is really the most important because it's the mind that causes most of the ongoing stress. This consists of two parts, to be carried out as simultaneously as possible.

One part is to bring all of your attention into the present moment in which you are repeating the alternate, noncontacting action. The success of the technique depends primarily on your ability to keep your mind on what is happening, and not on what happened when the injury occurred or what might happen as a result of it. Doing this well requires an act of will. You must choose not to think of anything other than the repetitive, noninjurious action you are currently involved in. If stray thoughts come in, don't get upset. Just choose to bring your mind back to the present as often as necessary.

The other mental part has to do with using words to help maintain your present-moment focus and to help your body heal itself. My students and I have experimented with a lot of word combinations, but the all-time favorite remains "Nothing happened! See! Nothing happened!" repeated over and over until the pain is gone. This was first used spontaneously by a woman whose friend was cut badly on the forehead when he fell while they were both waterskiing. In this case the man was dazed and could not do anything for himself, so the woman held him up in the water with one hand and repeatedly moved her other hand toward his head as if it were the ski that had cut him while shouting the above phrase. When they were back on shore after being picked up by a boat, the blood on the man's forehead was wiped away and there was no sign of a cut. The fact that the man was dazed obviously contributed to the success of the technique because his mind was not able to get in the way. Naturally, you can use any other words or phrases that work for you. The purpose of the words, remember, is to help keep you focused in the present moment and to give a clear message to your body which reinforces its healing work.

You may have noticed that several times I mentioned continuing the process until the pain subsides. In most cases, this is all you need to do because when the pain is gone the mind gets occupied with other things and the body can do the rest of the healing on its own. Often, in a very short time and to the degree that you are able to keep your mind off of the original trauma, the redness of burns fades away and no blisters are formed, blood stops flowing from a cut and the edges mend, and bruises don't form discoloration from broken blood vessels. The more severe the injury the longer or more often you may need to do the technique simply because it's a lot harder to keep your mind off the event or off the possible consequences.

You may also have noticed that I haven't mentioned the healing of broken bones yet. That's because this use of the technique deserves special attention. I wouldn't expect instant or even rapid results with a compound fracture (when the broken bone has pierced through the skin), and even fast results are probably unlikely in most cases because of the degree of trauma and generalized stress involved. However, I would expect that using the technique to whatever degree possible would greatly help to reduce the stress and aid the healing. The technique has been used very successfully with simple fractures of leg bones, arm bones, and finger bones. Normal medical attention, if available, is always called for in such cases, and setting the bone (if appropriate), ought to be done whenever possible. Nevertheless, I'd like to share a story about myself in which this technique was all I had to work with.

The event took place on a very strenuous hiking trip up the Wailua River on Kauai. On the return near the end of the day, I decided, foolishly, to take a little-used branch of the river by myself. In this part of the river there were no trails on the banks, and it was necessary to walk in the river itself, clambering over the rocks in the stream. I was wearing hiking sandals that had already proven themselves very slippery on the stones. At one point, when I was climbing over a boulder, I stood up . . . and slipped off. As I came crashing down, I put out my right hand to break my fall and the first three fingers crumpled under the impact. The pain was intense and my fingers were twisted in all directions. I sat down and immediately began swinging my right hand downward to the boulder—without contact—over and over. At the same time I shouted, "Nothing happened!" at the top of my lungs and struggled to keep my mind in the present. It was a hard struggle, because images of the fall and remembrance of the impact kept trying to intrude, but I kept going for about twenty minutes. At the end of that time almost all the pain was gone and the first two fingers looked and felt normal. The third finger was straight, but swollen. I made my way home, kept up the work, and in three days my hand was completely normal. Curiously, a week after the event, I was sharing this experience with some friends when my third finger instantly became swollen. I used the technique again right then and the swelling went away. Since that time I have had to retrain my body's response to the event so that my finger doesn't swell up any more when I tell people about it.

A number of people have asked me whether children can learn this technique. First I say yes, and then I share this true story told to me by a Hawaiian friend. One day in a park, her seven-year-old grandson had been told to watch his baby sister while their mother went to the restroom. The baby was squirming around in her stroller and the boy's attention was wandering. Suddenly the stroller tipped too far and the baby fell out, hitting her head on the walkway. While horrified onlookers watched, the boy immediately lifted the baby by its ankles and lowered its head up and down toward the concrete. When some people came running up to stop him he said, "It's okay, my grandmother told me to do this!" And the baby did stop crying.

PART THREE

Leaping Ahead with Instant Healing

CHAPTER EIGHT

Mastering the Power of Words

I n old Hawaii, there was a form of verbal therapy called *ho'opono-pono* which, in Hawaiian, means "to set things straight." It was used in many ways, but it is best known as a sort of group or family therapy. The practice has seen a resurgence in recent years, as Hawaiians strengthen their cultural identity.

The best known description of the group form comes from a book called *Nana I Ke Kumu* (Look to the Source), published by the Queen Liliuokalani Children's Center. The book was published for the use of people in the healing and social services professions as a means of understanding important concepts in Hawaiian culture that affect their Hawaiian clients, consciously or subconsciously. The primary source for the information was Mary Kawena Pukui, a Hawaiian lady of noble lineage with an abundant store of knowledge about her people and their ways. *Ho'oponopono* is a very formal process. As Mrs. Pukui described it, the process consists of the following steps (I will leave out the Hawaiian words):

1. A prayer, and/or the reason for coming together.

2. An explanation of the rules.

3. A clearing of the air, in which all participants have a chance to state their grievances, offer their points of view, or make comments. This takes place one at a time, in turn, with no one else allowed to speak except the leader until the person whose turn it is has finished. In addition, each participant speaks only to the leader unless the leader directs otherwise. This helps keep emotional outbursts and conflicts to a minimum.

4. Confession or acknowledgment, in which a person admits that he or she has done something to hurt or offend another person in the group.

5. Restitution, in which the offender does something or promises something to make up for the offense.

6. Forgiveness, in which offenders are forgiven. This is often accompanied by hugs, kisses, and tears. As a part of the forgiveness, the leader tells the participants never again to bring up the offense that has been forgiven.

7. Closing, usually done with a prayer of thanksgiving or an acknowledgment of what has been accomplished, and some kind of snack, meal, or feast.

In actual practice, such a session could last thirty minutes or so or days, depending on the number and seriousness of the grievances, because steps 3 to 6 could be repeated many times. What to do if someone refuses to forgive? In old Hawaii, that was the gravest of social offenses, and the ultimate solution was banishment. Today there has to be a sincere desire by all parties to find a solution before the process can begin, except where the offenses are not so severe, as in an argument among children that has led to lost tempers and fighting.

Another form of the process was used by the Hawaiian spiritual teacher Morrnah Simeona. Her version centered around forgiveness, and she taught that this could be done by anyone at any time to heal relationships not only with people, but with objects and land as well.

A MODERN VERSION OF AN ANCIENT PRACTICE

My Hawaiian family taught a personal form in addition to the group form. Because it is somewhat different from both the Pukui and Simeona versions, I have named it *kupono*, after a Hawaiian word meaning "to move straight toward a goal." The personal form is used to help individuals heal any relationships that may be causing mental and physical distress (remember that in my thinking emotional distress is an effect of one of the other two). The elements of *kupono* are similar, but not identical, to those for group *ho'oponopono* given above. The process assumes the presence of someone who can guide the individual through the process. It is not impossible to do alone, it's just much easier with a guide. I'll describe the process in terms of someone working with a client. This person serves more like a guide or a mediator than a therapist, although *kupono* works very well as an adjunct to therapy. I'll assume that the guide and the client are male only for the sake of convenience in describing the process.

The Assumptions of Change

The *kupono* process is based on seven assumptions:

1. Everything can be viewed in terms of relationships, such as relationships between mind, body, spirit, environment (including other people), and circumstances. Disharmonious relationships are produced by disharmonious behavior based on disharmonious ideas, and harmonious relationships are produced by harmonious behavior

based on harmonious ideas. Therefore, the role of the guide is to help the individual to change his ideas in order to establish harmonious mental and physical behavior.

2. The guide helps the client take into account the influence of past circumstances, present relationships, and future expectations on the current problem, and helps the client to remove any perceived limitations due to these influences. The idea that effectively changing one side of a relationship changes the whole relationship is implied. This means that the physical presence of any other party to the relationship is not necessary because the assumption is that as the client heals he will be able to deal more effectively with any other relationships that are involved.

3. Attention energizes ideas, and sustained attention strengthens those ideas and, therefore, the resulting behavior and experience. The guide helps the client to shift focus from negative ideas to positive ideas, to focus on what is desired and away from what is not desired, to use positive actions to reinforce positive ideas.

4. We can only live and act in the present moment. The guide helps the client realize that the present is more important than the past, and that it is in the present that we plant the seeds for the future. All experiences, including memory and anticipation, exist only in the present, and change can only occur in the present. Therefore, the guide emphasizes living more fully in the present moment in order to diminish any negative influences from the past, and to rehearse in the present for a better future.

5. Love is expressed by being happy with someone or something, not just by doing something for someone, and a happy relationship produces harmony. The best way to become happy with someone or something is to reduce judgment and/or increase appreciation. The guide helps the client reduce criticism and increase appreciation of

self and others in order to resolve conflicts. In addition, the guide will be more effective to the degree that he or she can suspend any critical judgment of the client.

6. In order for the client's experience to change, the client must change, because existing personal ideas and behavior have given rise to the present situation. Outside people and events are factors, not causes. Therefore, the guide orients the process toward self-confidence, self-empowerment, and self-determination.

7. There are numerous ways to achieve any goal, and so the goal is more important than the plan or techniques used to reach it. Because the goal of *kupono* is harmony, the guide uses any harmonious technique that helps to achieve the goal.

The Rules of *Kupono*

The seven assumptions of *kupono* are followed by the seven rules (have you noticed that I like the number seven?):

1. The purpose of the session is to resolve specific issues in order to create harmony in the mind, body, and behavior of the client.

2. All comments and questions shall be directed only to the guide unless he or she states otherwise (important only when two or more people are participating in the session).

3. When a person holds the talking symbol only he or she has the right to speak, except as noted below (this is mostly for when two or more people are involved, but it can be used with just a guide and an individual. The talking symbol is a stick, shell, or other object that represents the authority to speak. It gives some people the confidence to speak more freely).

4. The guide has the right at any time to interrupt the speaker by touching or taking the talking symbol (always courteously, of course).

5. When the guide declares "Peacetime!" all talking must cease until the guide starts the process again (this is to provide time for emotions to calm down, if necessary).

6. When the guide declares "Finished!" the resolved issue is not to be brought up again, in or out of the session.

7. If an issue cannot be resolved for any reason, the guide may move on to another issue or end the session.

The *Kupono* Process

Here it is at last, in seven steps. Depending on the circumstances, the process can be performed very formally or very informally. Much of the effectiveness depends on the structure, however, so it's a very good idea to stick to the sequence as given:

1. Opening. There is both a conscious and subconscious benefit to having a clear beginning to the process. Consciously, it helps to focus attention on the process, and subconsciously it helps to give the process a sense of importance. The guide can use a prayer, a blessing, or a statement of welcome, or anything appropriate to the background and beliefs of the client. It could be set up like a ritual or it could be as simple as "Okay, let's begin." It's a good idea to include a statement of the purpose of the session, described in terms of the relationship to be healed and/or the effect to be achieved.

2. Preparing. Next, the guide explains how the process works and helps the client to relax. As a guide, you may want to provide the client with a handout of the assumptions and the rules. The client must accept the rules before continuing. If not, the session ends or you can use some other process to help him. You can use any good technique for relaxing the client. I will describe my favorite one below.

3. Organizing. It is extremely useful to establish an agenda, a list of issues to work on during the session. This was an integral part of the process even in old Hawaii, because it helped to maintain the focus on the healing. Keeping the process aligned to the agenda is an important part of the guide's role. If you are doing it on your own, make an agenda yourself and keep it where you can see it during your session. If the list seems too long for the time available, more sessions can be scheduled. When the client has accepted the agenda, the session can continue.

4. Clarifying. The next step is to clarify the issues. The client can start talking about the first issue on the agenda, aided by the guide's questions and comments to increase clarity and, if necessary, redirect the discussion back to the issue at hand. It isn't necessary to let the client talk himself out before doing anything. Be alert for opportunities to resolve conflicts, even for part of an issue, while the client is talking (see methods below). If the discussion gets too emotional or if there are other forms of distraction, declare "Peacetime" and impose a one- to five-minute break or period of silence before continuing. When the client is ready to make changes in his thinking or behavior, no matter how small, you can move immediately to the next step, even if the issue is not ready to be completely resolved or if all the issues have not been discussed yet. Treat each potential change or resolution, no matter how small, as a separate event or a separate healing. By immediately taking advantage of every little opportunity for change, big issues become less intimidating and healing becomes easier.

5. Reconciliation. This is the act of changing mental behavior with respect to a relationship. The guide can help the client to resolve mental conflict and emotional reactions by changing words and images in regard to a relationship. This could include statements

and visualizations involving forgiveness, apologies, confidence, courage, or whatever is appropriate. You know when reconciliation has occurred because the emotional response to thinking or speaking about the relationship will have changed for the better (see techniques below).

6. Empowerment. Empowerment is the act of changing physical behavior in regard to the relationship issue being worked on. In this part of the sequence, you can guide the client through a ritual symbolizing a change in the relationship, or through a detailed mental or physical rehearsal of a change in the relationship. Be sure to include postural changes in both the ritual and the rehearsal. After each empowerment change, declare "Finished" for that issue or portion of an issue. Then return to Step 4 for another issue or move on to the next step as appropriate (see specific techniques below).

7. Closing. When the session is about to end, either because everything has been done or you have run out of time, you can do a prayer, blessing, statement, summation, action, song, dance, ritual, or food-sharing to signify the end of the session. Include this step even if the session ends early because of an unwillingness of the client to continue. This step is important because there is a great subconscious value in emphasizing and reinforcing any positive changes that have been made, even those that seem insignificant. Whenever possible, schedule one or more sessions to address unresolved issues on the agenda.

TECHNIQUES FOR THE *KUPONO* GUIDE

Any technique can be used by the guide to help the client with relaxation, reconciliation, and empowerment, including those provided earlier in this book or any others with which the guide may be familiar. However, to assist the guide in this process, I am going to provide some of my favorites that I use for *kupono*.

Stillpoint for Relaxation

Stillpoint is a very simple, very fast, relaxation technique that uses a form of *pikopiko*. It can be used any time you want to relax, and it serves as a good prelude to self-hypnosis or meditation. I'll describe it as if you are doing it for yourself, but it's easily adaptable as a guided process. You start out by sitting comfortably and closing your eyes. It doesn't matter what you do with your legs, your feet, or your hands.

1. Be aware of your navel. Touch it physically if that helps you to become better aware of it. Now inhale slowly with all of your attention on your navel. At the end of your inhale, shift your attention to the top of your head and hold it there as you slowly exhale. As you exhale, say to yourself "rest and relax" or any other short phrase that helps you to calm down and feel more relaxed. You can physically touch the top of your head if that helps you to center your attention there. At the end of your exhale, shift your attention from your head to your navel again. The same thing applies to the steps that follow.

2. With your attention on your navel, inhale. Pause for a moment at the top of the inhale (count to three, four, or five if you wish), then shift your attention to your left shoulder just before you start to exhale and keep it there the whole time you are letting out your breath. Tell yourself to rest and relax. At the end of your exhale you can pause again if you want to, but it really isn't necessary. Shift your attention to your navel here and after each exhale.

3. Inhale with your attention on your navel, exhale with your attention on your right shoulder.

4. Inhale with your attention on your navel, exhale with your attention on your chest.

5. Inhale with your attention on your navel, exhale with your attention on your left hip.

6. Inhale with your attention on your navel, exhale with your attention on your right hip.

7. Inhale with your attention on your navel, exhale with your attention on the base of your spine.

8. Inhale with your attention on your navel, exhale with your attention on your navel. At this point, relax your attention and just be aware of your body. If you can still feel tension in any part of your body, tell that part of your body, gently and persistently, to relax until it does. It's okay to use imagination as an aide in this technique. When you feel as relaxed as you can, start any other process that you want to.

Biodynamic Feedback for Reconciliation

This extremely effective technique for inner reconciliation is based on the natural learning process of the body. The body learns behavior by associating a stimulus with a response. The stimulus is any form of energy that the body reacts to, and the response is the pattern of behavior that the body develops in regard to the stimulus. The response is based on the body's current state of tension, memories related to the stimulus, and the mind's reaction to the stimulus. Generally, the body reacts to any stimulus in terms of pleasure or pain. And generally, it tends to move toward pleasure and away from pain. However, in actual experience it's a lot more complicated, because the body can learn to respond to a particular stimulus, for example, a spouse, with a very involved combination of both pleasure and pain simultaneously. In addition, a stimulus is usually thought of as something external, such as sight, sound, touch, movement, smell, taste, and the like, but people probably react more strongly to their own thoughts than they do to outside sensory input.

The biodynamic feedback technique is designed to help a person change his or her behavior in relation to something by helping a person change the body's behavioral responses to thoughts or emotions about it. When you can think about someone or something in detail without a stress response, your ability to handle the live event with little or no stress is greatly enhanced. The following description is based on you serving as a guide for a client.

Instructions that the guide gives to the client:

1. "Take a deep breath and relax. Close your eyes if you wish."

2. "Think of an issue (a relationship), or some aspect of an issue (this could even be a person's name) that is a problem."

3. "Be aware of any tension or discomfort in your body and locate it clearly."

4. "Relax the tension any way you can and tell me when it's better." (I usually leave this up to the clients. They often use creative ways I wouldn't dream of.)

5. "Think of the same thing again, and tell me if there's any tension." (Often the tension or discomfort seems to move to another location. I treat this as a different layer of tension and keep going through steps 4 and 5 until all tension and discomfort are gone when the person thinks of the same thing.)

6. At this point the guide takes the client back to Step 2 and repeats the process with a different aspect of the same issue, or with an aspect of a different issue. For example, if the issue is a relationship with a person, I begin by having the client reconcile a vague thought about the person (one aspect). I follow this by having the client reconcile a clearer memory of the person (another aspect), then being with the person, then speaking to the person and hearing the person speak back, then, if appropriate, touching the

person (not hitting, just touching) until the entire relationship with that person is reconciled. In some cases this may take more than one session.

7. "When you've had enough, take a deep breath and open your eyes."

The results of this process can be truly amazing. By changing the body responses to all the thoughts surrounding an issue, very profound changes can occur in a person's mental and physical behavior with little actual effort. Even more amazing, you, as the guide, can use this technique without even knowing what the person is thinking about. It is the ultimate form of client confidentiality.

Individual Teamwork for Reconciliation

Individual teamwork is another reconciliation technique that can be guided or performed on one's own. This time, I will describe it as if you were doing it on your own.

It can be very useful at times to look at yourself in terms of body, mind, and spirit. One of the ways to use this arbitrary division is to think of these three aspects or functions as a team and to identify with each in turn in order to improve communication and cooperation, especially with respect to health. The following method is one way to do it.

Start off by taking the role of your spirit. As spirit, you are the source or channel for creativity and inspiration and your motivation is harmony. You are very much in the present moment. Only when body and mind are in harmony can you really do what you do best. With this viewpoint, take a position or posture that helps you to assume this role (some people like to stand on something and speak down to body and mind). Tell body and mind to air their grievances and express their needs so that the whole self can get well.

Next, take the role of mind. As mind you are very concerned about effectiveness, obligations, and responsibilities. You want your body to function properly and you want to do things right. You also are concerned about the future, in terms of goals or how events will evolve. You are basically a problem-solver and you want to know what you can do. With this viewpoint, take a position or a posture that helps you think of yourself as your mind and talk to your other two parts (some people like to talk up to spirit and down to the body, for example). Air your grievances, if you have any as the mind, tell the other parts what you need from them to do your part in the healing and tell them that you are willing to help them in the overall purpose of getting well.

Finally, take the role of body. As body you want to feel good, but you also want to follow the rules you've learned from family, society, and mind about right and wrong, good and bad, love and hate, and so on, and sometimes these interfere with feeling good. You are grounded in the past and you basically want to protect the whole self from harm. With this viewpoint, take a position or posture that helps you assume the role of body and speak to the other two. Air any grievances, express your willingness to change so that the healing can take place, and tell the others what they can do to help you change.

Finish by taking the role of spirit again. Now you act as a sort of mediator, participating with the other parts in working out an agreement in which every part has a role in the healing process. End this technique with one full minute or more of complimenting body and mind for all their good qualities and skills (as spirit you totally ignore any faults).

Often this technique helps to reveal a lot of valuable information and insights of which you were not consciously aware and that can be of great benefit for the healing. If one is willing to make significant new choices in attitudes, behavior, and plans, instant results are definitely possible.

Power-Right-Desire-Will for Empowerment

This technique for the empowerment stage is designed to strengthen your inner authority, which can produce both immediate and long-range benefits for mind-body interaction.

The body is extremely responsive to authority, a quality that may relate to the animal troop ancestry of humans. The trouble is that the body gives authority to anything or anyone that speaks or acts with authority. The body typically gives authority to DNA, sensory-rich memories, parental declarations and those of other important people, repetitive experience (internal or external), and the emotionally-laden or energized thoughts of its companion, the mind. On the positive side, it is this acquiescence to authority that enables it to learn new behavior; on the negative side, the new behavior that it learns isn't always positive.

In chapter 4 you learned some ways of using words to influence your body. The things you learned there are going to be applied here, as well, but in a much more structured context with a twist. The power-right-desire-will technique is a way of evoking (or provoking) a response from your body in connection with a healing issue, and then changing or modifying that response so that your body improves its healing function. It was designed particularly to elicit verbal responses and that's how I will describe it, but if you should get a visual or kinesthetic response while using it you can incorporate one of the techniques discussed in the following chapter.

The process involves making a statement to yourself and listening for an internal—I'll call it subconscious—response. It's as if you said to yourself, "I think I'll go on a picnic this weekend," and a voice inside says, "You can't do that . . . you have too much work to do!" At this point, you could say, "Right, I'd better not" or "The work can wait; I need to get out." If you have enough inner authority, the inside voice will back down after the last statement and probably won't bother you again, except to cause you a few twinges of guilt now and then. If your inner authority is weak, you'll back down and stay home to work even if it increases your stress severely.

The body needs direction and it will take it from any authoritative source, even directions that are bad for your health, because it fears criticism and rejection even more than it does feeling bad. It's up to you to take charge and guide your body out of fear and into better health. Power-right-desire-will helps you pinpoint and resolve areas of conflicting beliefs and attitudes that are causing unnecessary stress. And here's how it works.

1. Get comfortable and relax. I'd like to take this opportunity to mention a few things about getting comfortable and relaxing. First of all, it doesn't matter how you do it, as long as you are comfortable and relaxed. Some therapists insist that you uncross your arms and legs and put your feet flat on the floor under the strange notion that this will let your energy flow more freely. What's strange about it is that yogis don't seem to find crossing their legs a problem at all and, in fact, they say you are supposed to cross your legs while doing inner work. My research with a lot of different postures seems to indicate that crossing or uncrossing really doesn't matter, and neither does a particular way of holding your body. If uncrossing your legs helps you to relax more, then do it. If crossing them yogi-style helps you to do inner work without falling over, then you can do that, too. Just don't be uncomfortable because someone tells you his way is the right way. Oh yes, it's alright to move around and change your posture or position if that helps you relax more, also.

2. When you are ready, make the following statement silently, three times, as if you were speaking to your subconscious (whom we will assume is inside you somewhere): "I have the power to heal myself—I can do it!" Say it slowly enough to be aware of any response or reaction. You can, of course, substitute any other words for those above, as long as they are related to the condition you want to heal.

   Although this statement sounds like an affirmation, its purpose is to evoke or provoke an internal response. If this statement is in accord with your inner beliefs, you will feel a rush or glow of good feeling and/or hear an affirmative response from your subconscious, such as "Of course you do," or something else along those lines.

If the statement is not in accord with your subconscious beliefs or behavior patterns, it will cause stress. This may occur in the form of actual, physical discomfort and/or words that indicate non-agreement, such as "No you don't."

3. Respond to whatever your subconscious says. Don't bother trying to analyze the source of the subconscious reaction to your statement. Maybe it came from a parent or teacher; maybe it came from an actor in a movie who said something that made an impression on you in a weak moment . . . who knows? Who cares? Take action now to change the pattern. How you respond to your subconscious depends a lot on what it says and your own degree of self-confidence, but if you don't respond strongly and firmly your subconscious will keep the pattern of belief or behavior and that will continue to interfere with your healing. The following are some ideas for responding that have worked for a lot of people:

- The Overriding Reply. If your subconscious says "No you don't" or makes any other negative response to your statement, then you can reply "Yes I do!" or any other appropriate, positive affirmation. It sounds like something kids do, but kids can be pretty smart. They know that whoever repeats a statement the longest wins. Most people give up when their subconscious disagrees with them once or a few times. My advice is, don't give up. You can outlast your subconscious by simply responding positively for as long as it takes. In practice, you may be surprised at how quickly your subconscious backs down and begins to accept your response.

- The Shout. Another technique that kids use, and that your subconscious may be impressed by, is shouting down your opposition. When you get a negative response, shout your affirmative reply—silently, please—as loud as you can, until your subconscious changes its response to a better one.

- Rules Rule. All of your beliefs, attitudes, expectations, and behavior patterns can be defined as rules. Whatever reply your subconscious makes to your statement, you can purposely interpret it as a rule that your subconscious is following, and then you can take charge as "the supreme rulemaker" and initiate a change in the rules. For instance, if you say "I can do it" and your subconscious says "No you can't," you simply stop and say to your subconscious, "Ah, you have a rule that says I can't do that. As the supreme rulemaker, I now declare that old rule null and void, and I further declare that the new rule about that is I can do it." Or words to that effect. The success of this particular approach depends a lot on your confident attitude when you change the rule. Make the original statement again, and check the response. If your subconscious agrees, you're home free. If it doesn't, interpret its response as a rule again (it may be a different response/rule this time) and declare a new rule again. Keep this up until you get cooperation.

4. After you've cleared the first statement with your subconscious, go on and clear the next three that follow in the same way:

- "I have the right to heal myself—I deserve it!"

- "I have the desire to heal myself—I do want it!"

- "I have the will to heal myself—I will do it!"

Be advised that the power-right-desire-will technique may evoke emotional issues that you could have a hard time dealing with. If at any time you feel too uncomfortable with it, just stop and take a break. Go back to it if and when you want, or try something else. Not every technique will work for everyone under all circumstances. That's why I give you so many different ones to choose from. When power-right-desire-will does work, however, its effects can range from instant healing to a release of tension that will pave the way for more healing by another means.

CHAPTER NINE

Mastering the Power
of Imagination

T he mind has some very peculiar characteristics that are often used, but seldom discussed. For example, we all have ideas, but we usually don't question where they come from unless they are startlingly different from our ordinary way of thinking. Those who do wonder about it tend to come up with answers ranging from memory, stimulus-response, indigestion, telepathy, spirits, or God, depending on the idea in question and the person's personal background. However, these answers assume that ideas are like prewrapped packages carted out of a warehouse or sent from a gift shop. If you really pay attention, you'll find that the process of thinking produces ideas, just as the motion of the earth produces a sunset, or as the growth of plants produces fruit. Moreover, ideas don't come from outside of us, but they are certainly influenced by our environment in the same way that the color and duration of a sunset is influenced by location and atmospheric conditions, and the size, shape, color, and taste of a fruit is influenced by weather and soil conditions. Your ideas can be influenced by your memories, your beliefs, the state or condition of your body, the place in which you live or work, the weather, the people around you, your goals and plans, and a host of other factors. Your ideas themselves, however, are generated by your intentional and habitual thinking. Intentional thinking and the ideas that arise out of it are the main focus of this chapter.

Another peculiar mental characteristic of the mind is that when you intentionally think about a particular subject for any length of time, a stream of related and apparently unrelated ideas flows into your awareness. Sometimes this happens immediately, and sometimes it takes awhile. In my own case, I occasionally write poetry as a result of inspiration or conscious purpose (it isn't great poetry, but it usually rhymes). Inspiration for a poem seems to come up suddenly sometimes, but I've had enough experience with it to know that it's always related to something of importance to me. It's as if a kind of subconscious thinking has been going on that has finally gathered enough force to break through into my awareness, perhaps triggered by an environmental event. Once the inspiration is in my awareness, the process of turning it into a poem (or a novel, or a project, or a song, or a painting, or whatever) involves more thinking, which generates more ideas and a further process of refinement (meaning changes and modifications) until it's suitable for publication or presentation. When I consciously decide to write a poem (or a book or whatever) I keep my purpose in mind and, immediately or eventually, ideas begin to flow and the thing begins to take shape and then I refine it until I like it. I will sometimes purposely let environmental factors in the form of other people's opinions, reading about other people's ideas, or just time itself influence the process. Similarly, once you begin to intentionally think about healing, ideas about that healing start to flow.

A third peculiar characteristic of the mind is that the process of thinking, and the resulting ideas, are an environmental factor that influences the functioning of the body. I have claimed that throughout this book, of course, but now I'm going to put it to use in a rather different way.

In chapter 5 I introduced you to the concept of "symbolic logic." Symbols, by which I mean images or experiences that represent something else, are a kind of language that the body understands very well. Music, poetry, storytelling, photographs, and paintings can all evoke very powerful physiological responses, even though they are only symbolic representations of actual experiences. Oh yes, so can fantasizing. When you fantasize, or make up an event in your mind, your body responds to it like a real event in the outside world, depending on the degree of sensory or emotional intensity contained in the fantasy. (This is the same process that makes mental rehearsal for a speech or a sporting event so effective.) Note that the body doesn't care whether the fantasy is "realistic" or not. That's why your body can respond so strongly to a horror movie or a nightmare or a good story about love and adventure on a distant planet.

What is so wonderful is that when you intentionally create a fantasy designed for a healing purpose, the body responds by increasing its healing activity. The following techniques are designed to bring together the three peculiar characteristics of the mind described above. They are all forms of symbolic fantasy that have consistently produced helpful (and frequently astounding), health benefits for myself, my family, my friends, and my clients. They involve intentional thinking, idea flow and refinement, and physiological response. In carrying them out, remember that their purpose is to create a powerful experience for your body. You might have a strong urge to analyze the experience as it is happening, trying to understand what it means. Don't bother. It doesn't matter. Analysis will only get in the way. If you absolutely must analyze it, wait until after the experience is over.

If you start to lose your focus at any time during any of the following experiences, you can regain it by narrating to yourself what is happening and what you are doing. Of course you want the experience to be as vivid as you can make it, but don't worry if it isn't particularly sharp. If you can't make something clearer visually, for example, then emphasize another sense like touch, hearing, or feeling. Overall, intention matters even more than intensity. The actual content of the fantasy will emerge from a combination of conscious direction and subconscious responses using material already in your memory. Don't be surprised if the results of this combination are sometimes surprising.

THE PATH OF POWER

Imagine that you are standing on a path that leads to a building some distance away. Tell yourself that the path represents the direction you are heading in your life, and what's inside the building represents the achievement of whatever particular healing goal you have in mind. Let the building itself represent the ideas you will need to achieve the healing. Be aware of the condition of the path. Is it concrete, asphalt, stone, gravel, or dirt? Is it in good repair or run-down? What kind of terrain lies to either side? Grass? Trees? Hills? Houses? Something else?

Start walking and feel the path beneath your feet. Are you barefoot? Wearing shoes or sandals? Keep walking for a while. How far away is the building? Can you make out what kind of building it is? Are there any other people about?

Suddenly—you decide the moment—imagine that a barrier of some kind springs up across the road, blocking your way. This barrier represents all the conditions that are in the way of the healing, including your fears and doubts, so pay close attention to it. Is it a boulder or a mountain? Is it a wall of some kind? Is it a bottomless chasm? Is it a fire or a storm? Is it a person, an animal, or a monster? Is it big or small? Is it scary or just sitting there? Is there a barrier at all? If there is one, get as detailed a sensory experience of it as you can. As well as you can, look at it, touch it, even smell it and hear if it makes a sound. Now comes the most important part: take some action to get beyond the barrier. Do whatever you can do to get over it, under it, around it, or through it. Even remove it if you can. Whatever you do, don't just imagine yourself on the other side. This part of the fantasy is designed to create a strong experience that will convince your body that changes have been made in the condition or conditions that may be hindering your healing. If you just bypass this part of the experience the technique won't do you any good, so in getting beyond the barrier be sure to imagine it with all the "realism" you can muster.

If there is no barrier, or if you find that getting beyond the barrier is very easy, then this technique probably won't affect your healing very much. If you find that you are having a great deal of difficulty getting past it, don't give up, because getting through will have a strong effect on your condition. Feel free to use tools, heavy equipment, future technology, and even magic if you like. You can also call on help from friends, real or fictional heroes, angels or elves, according to your fantasy preferences. In confronting biological barriers, warrior types will tend to use weapons and force, while peacemaker types will tend to use negotiation and persuasion. In one group I was teaching this technique to, one person used a laser cannon to blast through a wall and another simply asked the wall to form a doorway through itself. Regardless of how, do whatever it takes to get beyond the barrier.

Once you are beyond the barrier, keep walking toward the building. Some people will find that other barriers will spring up on the way. If this happens to you, get past them, too, and keep going. When you get to the building, pay attention to detail and go inside. Somewhere inside there will be an object or an experience that will represent the healing you seek. When you find it, do your very, very best to generate a feeling of happy accomplishment. Add a crowd of applauding fans if that helps you get the feeling. Here is where you are convincing your body that a healing is taking place, or will happen shortly. In some cases, people will experience an immediate change in the condition of their body. In other cases, people use this technique as one step in the healing process and as an aid to other things they are doing. The more difficult it is to get past the barrier, the more useful it would be to repeat the technique as often as feasible. In most cases of repetition, the path, the barrier, and the building appear differently each time, which indicates that you are confronting other issues related to the healing.

In a recent use of this technique, I closed my eyes and told myself to create a path leading to a resolution of something that needed healing. After a few moments of nothing, I was suddenly surprised to find myself whizzing down a sort of "techno-tunnel" of the type that is popular in certain science fiction movies. I couldn't tell if I was in a ship or not, but the sense of movement was strong, the tunnel was lined with metallic projections, and I had to dodge occasional laser fire. Finally I could see that I was heading for the cavernous interior of a gigantic spaceship (resembling scenes of several sci-fi movies in my memory). The moment I wondered about a barrier, I found myself slowing down, almost as though I was caught in a magnetic web, and then I was rushing backward away from my destination. There wasn't anything definite to fend off, so I simply willed myself forward and it worked. Soon I was in the interior space and I flew up to a catwalk leading to a sort of windowed pod in the center. Some people were on the catwalk and at first I thought they would try to stop me. Instead they opened the door to the pod for me, greeted me as the captain, and showed me to the captain's console where I sat down, turned on the microphone, and gave orders for the healing to happen. In that case there was no immediate change in circumstances, but there was a significant increase in my confidence that changes would occur, and about a week later they did.

REDREAMING THE DREAM

Anything that you imagine is constructed out of memories, fears, and desires, all built on a foundation of beliefs. Many people have the strange notion that beliefs can only be expressed in words, and certain kinds of therapy will continue the therapeutic process for ages until the beliefs of the client can be expressed in verbal terms that satisfy the therapist. Actually, beliefs can be expressed in any medium because in and of themselves they are only ideas about something. Essentially, beliefs are symbols of attitudes toward experiences. One of my favorite demonstrations in a seminar is to ask if there are any musicians among the students. I then ask if any of the musicians are familiar with Beethoven's Fifth Symphony, and finally I ask a student who is familiar with it to describe it in words to the class. Confused or frustrated silence is usually the result. Some experiences, and beliefs about those experiences, simply cannot be translated verbally. It is common for people to have a dream or visionary experience quite clearly in mind and for them to be unable to describe it in words. In the realm of imagination, beliefs appear as symbols, and as symbols they can be changed to produce healing results.

The factors of memory, fear, and desire may or may not be apparent in a particular imaginary experience. Nonetheless, they are always present, whether the imagination takes the form of a dream, a fantasy, a plan, or a carefully constructed mental training program. Purposely changing any one of these factors causes changes in the others, which produce repercussive changes in your body and perhaps your life. Conversely, the act of making changes in your body or your life by whatever means causes changes in the nature of your imaginary experiences. However, it is the former phenomenon that is of more interest here as an instant healing technique. In this section I will apply it to dreams, but keep in mind that it also applies to any imaginary experience.

While you are dreaming, anything that you do to modify your experience has the effect of altering the foundation—the belief system behind the dream. Unfortunately, the ability to willfully change your dream in the midst of dreaming is a rare, but learnable, talent. Fortunately, there is an excellent alternative to spending the time and money to attain this ability. All you have to do is recall the dream and change the recollection. Your body doesn't care how long ago you had the dream or when you change it. All it cares about is the experience.

When you change your memory of the dream, you are changing the beliefs that were the basis for it, as long as you are working with the same symbols that were in the original dream. And if the dream is related to a physical, emotional, or mental condition in need of healing, changing the symbols will help the body to heal. Often instantly.

A long time ago, I was in a very confused mental state (some people think that it wasn't so long ago) and when it was at its worst, I had a dream in which I was all alone inside a prison yard that was filled with waist-high weeds. The prison yard image came from a movie I had watched the evening before, but it still represented my belief about being trapped. The weeds represented the fear that I was wasting my life, and the open yard represented my desire to be free. You could say that being alone meant that there was no one else to blame for my situation and that I was on my own for a solution. The feeling I had from the dream was one of great helplessness. After I woke up, I recalled the dream and intentionally called in a helicopter to lift me out. In keeping with the theory of intensifying the experience, I watched the helicopter move, heard the engine noise, felt the wind from the blades, and experienced climbing aboard and flying away in great detail. It was one of the most liberating experiences of my life. After I freed myself from my own prison, I was able to make and carry out plans that helped to increase my income, improve my relationships, and keep me focused. That day I was able to see my situation clearly and make changes that affected the rest of my life for the good.

One of the best areas for using this technique is in helping children to cope with nightmares. Most of the time parents or guardians try to convince the child that it was only a dream and that there is nothing really to be afraid of. The only benefit of this approach is for the parent or guardian: the child will usually stop bothering them with it. Simply telling the child that the experience wasn't real will not heal the child's fears and sense of helplessness. For the body, at least, it was real, and the beliefs are still there and may remain for many years. If you can guide the child through a recall of the nightmare in which he or she can change the dream from a frightful experience into a successful adventure, with help from angels or super-heroes or cartoon characters if necessary, the effects of the nightmare will dissipate "instantly" and you will be helping the child to grow into a more self-confident, self-determined individual.

ORGANIC DREAMING

One normally associates dreaming with night dreaming or daydreaming, but some cultures believe that everything is alive and that everything dreams. Whether you take to that idea or not, it can be turned into a very useful healing technique because of those three peculiar mental characteristics mentioned above.

For this one technique, go ahead and assume that every part of your body is capable of dreaming. It doesn't hurt and it doesn't cost anything, and you can always go back to another way of thinking whenever you want. So now I'll assume that you've made the assumption. The next step is to turn your attention to a part of your body in need of healing and to wonder what it is dreaming. You could simply imagine that you are able to speak to it and say something like "Hey, elbow, what are you dreaming right now?" Then close your eyes or gaze into space with the intent of being aware of its dream until some kind of image, symbol, or story comes into your mind. You could also say to yourself something like "If my elbow were dreaming, what might it be dreaming about?" Then close your eyes or gaze off in the same way.

For this to be effective, it is important to accept whatever comes to mind as being the dream of the part of the body you are focused on, however strange, weird, ordinary, or unrelated it may seem to be. After allowing the dream to be whatever it is for a few moments, you work with it in the same way you did with the recall of the night dreams described above. That is, you change the symbol, the story, or the outcome until the condition changes or you at least feel a release of tension. Also as above, leave off analyzing until it's all over.

A woman to whom I taught this technique had a swollen thyroid gland that caused a lump on the side of her neck. She asked the gland what it was dreaming and got an image of her boyfriend trapped in the gland itself. After considering what to do for a while, she used her imagination to open a door in the gland and let her boyfriend out. In the dream of the gland he was reluctant to leave, so she had to use persuasion. When he finally left, she closed the door and immediately felt a tingling in her neck. A short time later—several days as I recall—the swelling was gone entirely.

A man I know had a severe pain in his lower back and he was considering surgery because it had been going on for a long time and pills weren't working. Now, surgery can be an important and valuable process when it is needed, but it does no harm to try a safe alternative first. The man in question learned about organic dreaming and decided to give it a chance. He asked what his lower back was dreaming and got a scene in which a train was speeding along a track so fast that it derailed and crashed. The man tried to keep the train on track, but he couldn't do it, even with willful imagination. He tried to slow it down, but it still derailed. Finally, he introduced another track into the dream that led to a peaceful valley and a village with friendly people and placed a switch on the first track. The train kept going so fast that it took him three tries before he could pull the switch in time for the train to get onto the other track. When it did, it slowed down all by itself and pulled gently into the village station. The man felt good about being able to make that happen, but he was really surprised when he came back into full awareness. He had been so involved in remaking the dream that he never even noticed his back pain had disappeared.

CREATIVE CLEARING

The technique I call creative clearing requires very little time and no special preparation, yet the results can be dramatic. You start out by imagining a clearing of some sort, anything that appeals to you. It doesn't even have to be the same one every time you do it. Frequent favorites are a stretch of beach, a meadow, a garden, a space in a forest, a desert oasis, or even an empty room (tastefully decorated if you like). You can get the intensity started by putting your attention on something that you can see, hear, and touch in the clearing (three different things are fine). In seminars I suggest looking at a tree, a rock, or a flower; hearing the wind in the tree, water flowing over the rock, or a bee buzzing around the flower; and touching the bark of the tree, the surface of the rock, or a petal of the flower. Don't worry if these sensations of sight, sound, and touch are not absolutely clear. Just do your best. Sometimes you only need to relax a bit more to help clarify the experience.

When your attention is centered in the clearing, ask for a symbol that represents the current state of the condition that needs healing (don't even bother to ask me who to ask; just ask!). Be prepared for anything. Ninety-nine percent of the time a person asking for a symbol in this way receives something unexpected. Observe how the symbol is acting and ask the symbol how it feels. If it isn't doing what it wants to do or if it isn't feeling good, ask it what it needs in order to do something better or to feel better. Then use your creative imagination to help the change come about. After the change, pay close attention to any changes in the state of your own body, mind, or feelings. Changes for the better, even tiny ones, indicate that you are making progress. Changes for the worse indicate that you have made contact with some very sensitive areas in your belief system and those are also signs of progress. When changes occur, you can keep working with the same symbol or ask for a new symbol directly related to the changes.

While working with one client, he asked for a symbol that represented his current health condition and a turtle appeared that was withdrawing back into its shell because it didn't feel safe. He asked what it would need to feel safe and the turtle said it needed to be in the ocean. When asked what it needed to get to the ocean, it said that it needed to turn around. The man helped it to turn around and the ocean appeared, so the man helped it return to the ocean. Not only did the turtle feel better, but the man also immediately felt a great release of tension, accompanied by awareness of a related problem. The man asked for a symbol of that problem and an owl appeared that looked disgusted. The man asked the owl what it would need to feel better and the man's attention was suddenly drawn to a metal collar around the owl's neck that was attached to a heavy weight. The man strengthened the owl's beak and had it snap through the collar, releasing the weight. The owl felt better and the man felt very light and free. On returning to a normal state, the man had more energy and a much improved attitude, as well as the tools to continue his healing on his own.

THE ASCENT TO AWARENESS

Sometimes when a healing is called for, what you really need is instant advice on what you can do in a practical, external way. The usual method is to seek external advice from a recognized expert, or at least from someone that you trust or respect. With today's enhanced communication options, external advisors abound for every sort of health problem. However, there is also another source for advice: internal advisors, who have the advantage of being cheap, fast, and more directly involved in the problem. An internal advisor is a symbol that helps you access information about the condition that you may not have known you had. Generally the information comes from memory, a direct body knowing, or, according to some theories, an innate human ability to tap into a larger, more nonpersonal database. The more serious the health problem, of course, the more advice you want to get, both external and internal, to help you make the best decisions for your situation. Which raises a rather important point: advisors are meant to advise, not to make your decisions for you.

The ascent to awareness technique makes use of the very common human notion that associates wisdom with height. This idea probably relates to the association of knowledge and intelligence with the brain, which is at the top of the body. In any case, wisdom is usually sought on top of a mountain, in the clouds, or, in modern times, in outer space. Almost no one seeks wisdom underground or at the bottom of the ocean. Many cultures and traditions use variations of this technique that employ a "wise old man" or a "wise old woman," but you are going to be more creative than that.

It's very useful to begin with the "creative clearing" described earlier to help you get focused in your inner world, and then to use that as a starting place for your ascent. Depending on your preference, you can climb a mountain to a ledge, ride a rainbow up into the clouds, take a spaceship to another planet, or go up in any other way to any other place. Once you get there, ask for a symbol of a source of information for your particular problem. You are likely to get a human being, but allow for the possibility that the symbol may take another form, such as an animal or a plant or a crystal or a computer. When the symbol appears, ask for advice on what you can do to speed up the healing (you can ask any question you like, naturally, but I'm assuming that you are more interested in healing than in conversation). The answer will most likely come in the form of words, but some people get pictures or feelings. Thank the source symbol and bring yourself back into normal awareness (it isn't necessary to go back to the clearing, but go ahead if you want to). An instant way to get reoriented is to move your hands and feet and look at objects around you when you open your eyes, if they were closed. Treat the advice as you would advice from any other source and judge for yourself if you want to follow it.

A woman with a patch of discolored skin—the result of a prolonged irritation that had been removed—climbed a mountain in her mind to a spot that she knew from memory, sat down at a picnic table, and asked for a symbol of the discolored skin that she could talk to. Immediately a big, ugly insect was sitting across from her, the same color as the skin. After getting over her shock, she asked the insect why it took that form and it said, "Because the problem is bugging you." It's curious how many "inner selves" have a quirky sense of humor. Anyway, she asked the bug if it was happy the way it was and it said no, because everyone thought it was ugly (this is the patch of skin speaking, remember). So the woman asked how she could help it become more beautiful and it told her to keep using the salves and ointments she had recently bought, and to talk to the skin every time she applied them and tell the skin how beautiful it was going to become. The insect reminded her that skin cells renew every six weeks and all she had to do was be patient and persistent. In this case the advice was instant, but the healing was not. Within a week, however, the patch was much smaller and lighter in color, whereas there had been no progress before talking to the symbol.

In another case an emotional and physical healing occurred as soon as the advice was given. A man was suffering from acute anxiety and a painful constriction in his chest. He also climbed a mountain, but he decided to go to Mt. Everest and speak to "the wisest man in the world." After an arduous trek to the top of the mental mountain he came up behind a man sitting on a bare rock under a clear sky. When the man on the rock turned around, the man who was seeking advice was startled to see that he was facing himself. His other self smiled wisely and said that he was a symbol of the man's own deepest wisdom. The wise self told the scared self that he was afraid because he thought he was all alone in a chaotic universe. The wise self told the man that he was never alone, that he was always connected to his source, that everything was going along as it ought to, and that there wasn't anything the man could do to mess it up. The wise self admitted that the man might delay certain things and change certain things, but he assured the man that things would turn out right no matter what. And with that, the man's anxiety disappeared, he heaved a great sigh, and in his physical body all the pain and tension eased away.

CHAPTER TEN

Mastering the Power of Touch

How would you like to learn a form of massage that really isn't massage as most people understand it? This would be a type of massage that would produce deep relaxation in an hour or less, sometimes very much less. It would not require a special room, a special time, special equipment, special oils, or anything special at all, other than your hands and someone to work on. You could even use it on yourself and get dramatic effects. It would never be painful and both you and the person receiving it would end up feeling much better afterward. It could be done by virtually anyone of virtually any age. And you could learn how to start doing it by reading a chapter in a book.

I have to admit that it took me longer than that to learn it. For me it began with my Hawaiian auntie when I was in my early twenties. I was in the Marine Corps in California at the time and she was living in the Los Angeles area. I would visit her on weekends whenever I could and I would usually either get worked on myself or watch her work on someone else. What she did was so soft and gentle and simple that I never even thought of it as massage for quite some time. Sometimes she would work on a person lying on a bed or on the floor, sometimes the person would be sitting down or standing up. Sometimes she did what she did for a fairly long time (although I never saw her do it for more than an hour) and sometimes it took only a minute or two. After about a year of scattered visits, she even let me try it.

Hawaiian-style learning is very different from our modern system of schooling. In the Hawaiian style, you learn by doing, and very little if anything is explained until you become competent enough to ask intelligent questions. Some people get very competent without ever asking questions, but they aren't very good at teaching people who were raised in what I'll call Western-style learning. Fortunately, I asked a lot of questions and, also fortunately, my auntie was willing to answer most of them. So I took everything I had learned piecemeal from her, added more things I had learned piecemeal from my Hawaiian uncle, and organized it into the system I call *kahi loa* so that it could be taught quickly and easily to Western-style students. Should the question arise, I didn't need permission to do this, but my auntie and uncle gave it their blessing anyway because both of them believe that the more people there are helping others to feel better, the better off the world will be.

THE MAGIC TOUCH

In my book *Urban Shaman*, I introduced a form of healing I called *kahi*. That was one small part of the much larger massage system I learned from my Auntie Laka to which I have given the name *kahi loa*, or great *kahi*, because she just called it "helping people." Those who experience it often call it "the magic touch."

Kahi is a Hawaiian word that refers to a light touch or a light pressure of the hand during massage. It also means "fire," which is appropriate because it stimulates the body's healing system; it means "the flow," which is appropriate because it induces a flow of energy through the body; and it means "oneness" which is appropriate because it helps a person feel whole and complete. *Kahi loa* is quite different from the Hawaiian form of massage known as *lomi-lomi* and the form known as "temple-style." It is also distinctive from other types in several ways:

- it works on the skin, instead of the muscles, lymphatic system, or bones

- it uses no oil (although talcum helps on bare skin)

- it can be done in any position

- it can be done with the recipient fully clothed

- it can be done as a completely separate system, in pieces, or integrated into other systems

- communication is maintained with the recipient throughout the session

- its effects are rapid and deep; it can, as we say, "reach the bones through the skin"

Although *kahi loa* can be performed in different ways, the description below will assume that a practitioner is working with a recipient on a massage table. Further on I will discuss other alternatives.

As a general rule in doing massage I strongly recommend not touching the breasts of women, the nipples of men, and the genitals of either sex unless the recipient is your willing lover or spouse. Also, be very, very careful with, or avoid altogether, any areas of pain or injury.

Preparation for Performing *Kahi Loa*

Have the recipient lie face down on the table, fully clothed, partially clothed, or unclothed, as he prefers. In addition to a covering for the table you might want to have a sheet or light blanket available for covering the recipient in case he feels too cool. Tell the person before you begin that you are going to be asking for his participation and feedback during the massage. Soft lights, slow instrumental music, and an aroma pleasing to the recipient are always helpful. My wife tells me that what ruins an otherwise good massage for her is vocal music, which distracts her, and incense, which she can't stand.

Energizing

Use a preferred technique to relax and increase your energy before and during the practice. This can be something as simple as deep breathing or something more elaborate. I recommend the technique called *pikopiko* described in chapter 7, particularly the *pikopiko* de-stresser. As a reminder,

- think of the sky above as you inhale

- think of the earth below as you exhale

- repeat as desired

During the practice you can do this between segments (see below) as a way to reenergize yourself.

It will be beneficial to get your recipient to energize also, if you can. A *pikopiko* variation called "head to feet" is good for this:

- inhale with attention on the top of the head

- exhale with attention on the soles of the feet

- repeat as desired

Verbalizing

Ask the recipient to name a goal for the session or segment. The goal might simply be relaxation, or it could be healing or pain relief in a specific area. Tell the recipient to repeat a mental affirmation or blessing related to the goal during the session or appropriate segment. In its simplest form this would be a single word or short phrase to help keep the focus. Here are some examples:

- "Relaxing" or "I am relaxing"

- "Feeling good" or "I'm feeling good"

- "Healing" or "Healing is happening"

Symbolizing

Ask the recipient to imagine a positive symbol, picture, or memory representing or related to the element of the segment you are in as you work (this will be made clear later on). You will also imagine a related symbol. Try to feel the symbol at the point where your hands touch or approach the recipient's body. Make it as vivid or "energized" as you can.

Vitalizing

To the best of your ability, involve your whole body in the practice, as if you were dancing with the energy of the recipient.

THE *KAHI LOA* SEQUENCE

Kahi loa is divided into seven segments related to the seven elements as I learned them from my Hawaiian family: fire, water, wind, stone, plant, animal, and human. Formally, as described here, they are performed in sequence, first all seven on the back of the body, and then all seven on the front.

A vital part of the practice is to ask for feedback from the recipient before, during, and after each segment. This allows the practitioner to modify the work according to the needs of the recipient, and to introduce subsets as necessary (see below). To get feedback, the practitioner merely asks appropriate questions, such as, "Do you want me to pay attention to any particular area?" "Is that better?" "What did you experience?" Feedback also has the effect of helping both the practitioner and the recipient to keep their focus and energy on the process (refer to the Healing Hands section in chapter 6).

As described above, the recipient is also asked to silently repeat a healing affirmation and/or hold the image of a symbol related to the segment in progress throughout the session. This makes the recipient an active participant in the healing, reinforces the effect of the affirmation and the bodywork, and helps keep the energy and attention of the recipient on the process.

Here are the segments in their proper sequence. First the symbol or symbols to be used by the practitioner and the recipient for that segment will be given, followed by directions to the practitioner for moving the hands, plus any pertinent comments. For the sake of convenience, the recipient will be assumed to be male.

The Touch of Fire

1. The Goal—ask the recipient if he wants to name a goal for the segment or if there is a particular area he would like you to pay more attention to. You might also ask if there are any areas of tension he would like you to work on. Then suggest an affirmation for him to mentally repeat.

2. The Symbols—for the practitioner, imagine glowing heat or embers at the fingertips, hot enough to warm, but not to burn; for the recipient, any positive symbol or memory related to fire, such as a candle flame, a campfire, or a hearth fire, or just the sensation of warmth.

3. The Movement—hold your hands like rakes or claws. With the recipient lying on his stomach, start at the front of the scalp and rake your hands along the skin, always moving downward. Use the pads of your fingers and not your fingernails, though in some areas the backs of your nails may work well. You can use a long, slow raking

movement, or a slightly faster hand-over-hand movement. Adjust the pressure to the desire of the recipient. Generally, men like a stronger touch than women, but ask for feedback if in doubt. Remember that you are stimulating the skin and not working on the muscles. When you have raked all areas of the body accessible from the back at least three times, moving around the table as needed, ask for feedback, tell the recipient which element you are going to do next, and proceed to the next segment. When it is time to do this element on the front of the body, rake the face, chest and abdomen gently outward from the center, and all other areas downward as on the back. If the recipient is ticklish in any area, move your fingers in very short increments over those areas and tickling will usually not be a problem, especially if you pause between increments.

The Touch of Water

1. The Goal—ask the recipient if he wants to name a goal for the segment.

2. The Symbol—for the practitioner, imagine water flowing out of your hands, and the recipient's body as pool of water; for the recipient, any positive symbol or memory related to water, such as a waterfall, a stream, ocean waves, or a fondly remembered event in, on, or near the water.

3. The Movement—starting at the head, gently and slowly caress his entire body as if your hands were made of water, flowing over all the contours of his body, giving good attention to the hands and feet. Keep your knees bent and, as best you can, let your body feel like liquid, too.

   - Eddies variation: Eddies are soft little whirlpools that may form in a flowing stream. With your fingertips you may make eddies— little circular movements on the skin—at joints and places where you feel, or the recipient mentions, that there is tension. Opinions differ as to which direction is best for making the circles, but I find that clockwise works very well.

The Touch of Wind

1. The Goal—ask the recipient if he wants to name a goal for the segment.

2. The Symbol—for the practitioner, imagine that your hands are the wind itself; for the recipient, any positive symbol or memory related to wind, such as a gentle or refreshing breeze, or even flying or gliding through the air.

3. The Movement—tarting above the head, make "wind-like" movements over the whole body about four to six inches above the skin. Believe it or not, many people will feel definite sensations when you do this, perhaps more at some places than at others, because you are influencing the electromagnetic field of the body. Areas of the body with a lot of tension seem to produce a sort of "standing wave" pattern above that area. Moving your hands through the "standing wave" causes a disturbance that sends tension-relaxing signals to the body. Waving your hands over other areas of the body will provide a healing benefit of increased circulation. Some practitioners can learn to feel these "standing waves" as a subtle sensation of resistance or "roughness," or an even more subtle "knowing." Don't feel bad if you don't feel anything. You will be having a good effect anyway, which you can check by asking for feedback during or after the segment.

   - Breezes variation: If you do feel a "standing wave," or if the recipient directs you to a tension area during this segment, you can rapidly shake one or both hands over the area, as if you were creating a breeze. Do this until you feel a change or your hands get tired.

- Whirlwinds variation: Over these same "standing waves" or tension areas, or areas that may need strengthening, you can use whirlwinds. In this case you simply whirl your hand in a circle with your fingers pointed toward the body. The generally accepted way is to make a clockwise whirlwind (from your point of view) to strengthen, and a counterclockwise whirlwind to relax.

The Touch of Stone

1. The Goal—ask the recipient if he would like to name a goal for the segment.

2. The Symbol—for the practitioner, imagine that your hands are glowing or radiating crystals or gemstones; for the recipient, any positive symbol or memory related to stones or crystals or gems.

3. The Movement—his is the segment that I described in *Urban Shaman*. Place one hand (or one or more fingers) lightly at the site of a healthy joint, organ, pressure point, or navel and the other hand or fingers at a site of tension, pain, or malfunction. Inhale with all your attention on the healthy point, and exhale with all your attention on the healing point. Imagine that your hands/fingers are, or are holding, powerfully energized crystals, stones, or gems. If you like, you can actually hold some at the two sites. Do this for four complete breaths and ask for feedback. Repeat as needed. Usually there will be some relief, and often there is complete relief, after only four cycles. In the absence of major stress areas, do this between joints along the length of the body (for example, from shoulder to hip or knee to ankle) or across the body (for example, from shoulder to shoulder or hip to hip). If you are familiar with acupressure, you can do it between points and you won't need to do any painful pressing. This is excellent for foot reflexology because it eliminates any need for causing pain. Probing gently with your fingers, determine by the recipient's feedback when a point is stressed or sore. Do a few cycles

as described above between points on the body or the feet with a very light touch and you will find that the stressed points are painlessly relieved in short order. In this case it doesn't matter whether both points are sore or not because both will be relieved.

The Touch of Plants

1. The Goal—ask the recipient if he would like to name a goal for the segment.

2. The Symbol—for the practitioner, imagine that your hands are a cluster of soft and aromatic flowers or leaves (this segment provides a good opportunity to add aromatherapy to your session if you haven't already); for the recipient, any positive symbol or memory related to plants, flowers, or their aromas.

3. The Movement—brush the skin from head to foot with your fingertips and/or the sides of your hands. The brushing should be fairly rapid, yet light, depending on the preferences of the recipient.

   - Sunlight variation: On areas of weakness, or to stimulate a particular area, raise one hand up like a leaf receiving sunlight, and place the other on an appropriate area of the body. Then inhale with your attention on the upper hand, as if you were drawing in the power of the sun, and exhale with your attention on your other hand, as if you were directing the sun's energy to where it was needed.

   - Roots variation: This movement is especially useful where there is a lot of tension or heat or pain. In this case, place one hand or your fingers on the body area you want to relieve, and point the other hand toward the ground, imagining that it has roots extending into the ground. Inhale with your attention on your hand touching the body, imagining that you are drawing out the excess energy which is causing the tension or pain, and exhale with your attention on your other hand and its extended roots, imagining that the excess energy is being transferred to the ground. Don't think of it as "bad" energy or this probably won't be a good technique for you to use.

A Scientific Twist on the Touch of Plants

You may be aware that in addition to taking in solar energy, leaves also give off oxygen as a waste product. Accordingly, the first subset could be used to relieve pain and tension just as well as the second by reversing the breath cycle with appropriate imagining. Similarly, roots not only give off stuff like nitrogen, they also take in nutrients. So the second subset could also be used in reverse. Therefore, feel free to apply this segment according to your scientific preference, or to ignore this note if you don't really care.

The Touch of Animals

1. The Goal—ask the recipient if he would like to name a goal for this segment.

2. The Symbol—for the practitioner, imagine that you are an animal of your choice helping another animal of your choice (allow for some fantasy in this); for the recipient, any positive symbol or memory related to animals, especially those who are relaxed or playful.

3. The Movement—gently squeeze and stretch the skin all over the body, from the scalp to the toes. Pulling the hair to stretch the skin of the scalp will be appreciated very much by some people (I love it), but ask first and make sure you are not pulling too hard. Be sure to squeeze and stretch the fingers and toes individually.

Remember that you are working on the skin, so don't get into massaging muscles or stretching joints.

- Rollover variation: On the back, and possibly on the thighs and calves, you may be able to produce a roll by squeezing the skin between your thumbs and fingers. If you can, try moving that roll forward as far as you can, as if a wave were traveling across the skin. It is easier to do this from the hips toward the head when working on the back, and sideways on the legs. Make as many rolls or waves as you can across the back and legs. This is a very good stretching exercise for the skin. However, some people have so much skin tension that this might be quite painful at first, so be considerate. And some people are so slim that you won't be able to do it.

- Shaking variation: All over the body, or in certain areas that the recipient directs you to, hold your hands or fingers on the skin and rapidly shake it or vibrate it in short bursts of motion. Do this as many times as you feel like or until the recipient's feedback tells you there has been a change.

The Human Touch

1. The Goal—ask the recipient if he would like to name a goal for the segment.

2. The Symbol—for the practitioner, imagine that you are a wise and powerful healer touching the person with heartfelt caring; for the recipient, any symbol or memory of a loving touch from an angel, a healer, or a loved one.

3. The Movement—this is the finishing touch for both sides of the body. Imagine yourself filled with as much love as possible while you are doing it. Each touch should last about one full second (you can silently count, "one one thousand, two one thousand," etc.) but

not much longer. All you need to use are the fingertips. You can use one hand along the center of the body, alternating hands if you wish. On the sides of the body you will use both hands at the same time.

On the back, touch the top of the head, the base of the neck, the middle of the back, and the base of the spine. Then touch the shoulders, hips, backs of the knees, and the soles of the feet. Finish with a sweep of both hands in the air above the body downward from the head toward the feet. Wait a few moments and ask the recipient to turn over.

On the front, touch the top of the head, the forehead, the base of the throat, the center of the chest, the solar plexus (just below the rib cage) and the navel. Then touch the jaws, the shoulders, the wrists, the hips, the knees, the ankles, and the toes. Finish with a sweep as above. Wait a few moments and ask for feedback for the session. Help the recipient off the table whenever it's appropriate.

KAHI LOA VARIATIONS

Clearly *kahi loa* is a highly structured process. However, there is no reason that you can't employ derivations of *kahi* when you like.

Informal *Kahi Loa*

Any segment of *kahi loa* can be done on its own when a situation calls for immediate help. Fire *kahi* on the back of someone standing up is a terrific tension releaser at any time. If you know a person well enough, water *kahi* caresses around the shoulders while he or she is seated, accompanied by a few animal *kahi* squeezes, will be greatly appreciated. Downward sweeps of wind *kahi* all around a standing person can be very refreshing and upward sweeps can be quite invigorating. Stone *kahi* is very useful for relieving pain for a person who is standing, sitting, or lying down, and you can substitute your own navel for the healthy point if that's more convenient. The root variation of plant *kahi* can be done very unobtrusively when help is needed in a public place, and human *kahi* works well as the finish to any kind of healing session and as a calming technique on its own.

Concentrated *Kahi Loa*

The concentrated version of *kahi loa* is a technique that can be used for quick relief of pain or discomfort. In this variation, rapidly use each segment in the formal sequence on a specific area of the body. In this case you can use only one or two passes of each one, ignoring the subsets, and ending with a single loving touch. So, for a sore shoulder you might do a couple of fire rakes, a few water caresses, a bit of wind movement, a little plant brushing, an animal squeeze or two, and a loving human touch. The results are usually surprisingly good in a very short time.

When I am teaching *kahi loa* to a class, I always include a set of guidelines based on a philosophy that my Hawaiian family taught me. They can be useful to anyone who does massage or any kind of healing:

1. Your thoughts affect your performance, so be aware of what you are thinking.

2. You and the recipient are exchanging energy and ideas, so be free of fear and tension.

3. Your energy follows your attention, so be focused on the effect you want.

4. The more you are in the moment, the more power you have, so be present with all of your senses.

5. The more you enjoy what you are doing, the more benefit you provide, so be happy with yourself and with your work.

6. People always heal themselves, so be confident of your skill to help them do so.

7. If the method you are using isn't working, be flexible and try something else.

CONCLUSION

So there you have it. A collection of my best ideas and techniques for healing yourself instantly, rapidly, fast, and any other way you can. There's a lot to remember, so I am going to condense the whole thing for you in the form of a simple Hawaiian proverb:

Ua ola loko i ke aloha.
Healing comes from within by means of love.

Instant Access to
Instant Healing

The following appendix is designed to help you find quick and simple techniques for instant (under an hour) relief in many cases for common ailments. Of course, you will need to read the material within the main text of the book to best understand how to perform most of these healing techniques and to understand how your body and mind are interacting. Some of the techniques are variations of healing methods that I talk about. To help you along, a reference to the pertinent section of the text is included as appropriate.

Finally, don't be discouraged if a particular technique seems difficult to do. These techniques usually produce instant, rapid (less than three days), or fast (less than a week) results and are simple enough to remember easily. I do not promise that doing them will necessarily be easy because you may have a lot of resistance to changing your habits. Use your common sense when applying these techniques. If the technique you try doesn't seem to help at all, use another technique. Please remember that the following is intended as a reference guide and is not intended to replace any other form of treatment. When in doubt, always seek professional help. Getting well is more important than proving a point.

AILMENTS AND HEALING TECHNIQUES

Look for your particular malady and a quick way to overcome it in this alphabetical listing of common ailments.

Allergy

- The Admiration Effect—with your full conscious attention, admire or compliment, aloud or silently, someone or something in your life or in your immediate environment. Do this as frequently and abundantly as possible until you get relief. At the same time, greatly reduce or eliminate criticism of anyone or anything. For more information, see Healing by Blessing, chapter 4.

Anger

- Water Power—drink a glass of water. Repeat if that helps. For more information, see Physical Energy, chapter 7.

- Tension Drainer—inhale with your attention on your navel, exhale with your attention on tense muscle groups while mentally willing or telling them to relax. In particular, direct your exhale-attention to your jaw muscles, shoulders/arms/hands, and your lower back. Repeat until you feel relief. For more information, see Mental Energy, chapter 7.

Anxiety

- The Harmony Pattern—take a handful of small items like paper clips, pebbles, or coins, and arrange them in front of you randomly until the pattern they form just "feels" right even though it doesn't resemble anything.

- Tune in to Curves—be aware of any curved lines or surfaces in your immediate environment. "Trace" these lines and surfaces with your eyes and, where feasible, with your hands and fingers. Continue until you get relief.

- Tune in to Movement—be aware of movement in your environment (such as the movement of the clouds, leaves in the wind, the air you breathe in and out, the movement of your body as you walk) and maintain the awareness without thinking about it until you get relief. For more information, see Mental Energy, chapter 7.

Asthma

- The Admiration Effect—with your full conscious attention, admire or compliment, aloud or silently, someone or something in your life or in your immediate environment. Do this as frequently and abundantly as possible until you get relief. At the same time, greatly reduce or eliminate criticism of anyone or anything. For more information, see Healing by Blessing, chapter 4.

Backache

- Water Power—drink a glass of water. Repeat if that helps. For more information, see Physical Energy, chapter 7.

- Gentle Stroke—gently stroke or caress the area that hurts until you get relief. For more information, see Self-touch, chapter 7.

- Melting Ice—imagine that the hurting area is a block of ice and imagine the ice melting away. For more information, see Healing by Direction, chapter 4.

- Touch and Forgive—gently touch the area that hurts with one hand and repeat these words to yourself until you get some relief: "Whatever this is related to, I forgive it completely, and it doesn't matter anymore." For more information, see Blanket Forgiveness, chapter 6.

Blurred Vision

- Backward Focus—inhale with your attention on your navel, exhale with your attention on the back of your head. Repeat until vision improves. For more information, see Mental Energy, chapter 7.

- See Passively—remember that the light from your environment is coming to you and that you don't have to hold things with your eyes, then practice passive seeing—being aware of things without straining to look at them. For more information, see Mental Energy, chapter 7.

- Squeeze and Breathe—squeeze your eyes shut 5 to 10 times, take a deep breath and look again. For more information, see Mental Energy, chapter 7.

Broken Bone

- Quasi-Repetition—when feasible, immediately repeat the action or movement that caused the injury, making sure to stop the action or movement just before the point of contact. Do this over and over until pain is relieved or until the initial reaction to the injury has changed.

  Note: For this to work, it is very important that you keep your mind from re-creating the event. You can use your will with the aid of a forceful, repeated statement, said aloud if possible, such as "Nothing happened!" or "I'm okay!" Use whatever additional treatment may be appropriate or necessary. For more information, see Mental Energy, chapter 7.

Burn

- Quasi-Repetition—when feasible, immediately repeat the action or movement that caused the injury, making sure to stop the action or movement just before the point of contact. Do this over and over until pain is relieved or until the initial reaction to the injury has changed.

Note: For this to work, it is very important that you keep your mind from re-creating the event. You can use your will with the aid of a forceful, repeated statement, said aloud if possible, such as "Nothing happened!" or "I'm okay!" Use whatever additional treatment may be appropriate or necessary. For more information, see Mental Energy, chapter 7.

Cold

- Water Power—drink a glass of water. Repeat if that helps. For more information, see Physical Energy, chapter 7.

- Friendly Persuasion—assume that the condition is at least partly related to suppressed anger. Assume that you can talk to your body and that it will listen to you. Persuade your body that it doesn't have to stay angry and promise it some pleasurable reward as soon as it gets well. Persuade frequently and provide a reward of some kind, no matter how small, for each positive change in the condition. Even praise and appreciation can be used as rewards. For more information, see Healing by Blessing, chapter 4.

- Relax and Be Loved—relax as best as you can, close your eyes if you wish, and repeat these words to yourself until you get relief "I am loved and I am okay." For more information, see Healing by Blessing, chapter 4.

- Touch and Forgive—gently touch the area that hurts with one hand and repeat these words to yourself until you get some relief: "Whatever this is related to, I forgive it completely, and it doesn't matter anymore." For more information, see Blanket Forgiveness, chapter 6.

Confusion

- Imagine Beauty—remember, imagine, or look at a beautiful, quiet place in detail. Use a photo or painting if that helps. Even if this is difficult at first, stay with it until you get relief or fall asleep. As an alternative to a quiet place, remember, imagine, or look at something very small, like a stone or a flower, in great detail. For more information, see Emotional Energy, chapter 7.

- Inhale at the Top—inhale slowly with your attention on the top of your head, exhale slowly with your attention on your navel. Repeat until you get relief or fall asleep. For more information, see Emotional Energy, chapter 7.

Cut

- Quasi-Repetition—when feasible, immediately repeat the action or movement that caused the injury, making sure to stop the action or movement just before the point of contact. Do this over and over until pain is relieved or until the initial reaction to the injury has changed.

    Note: For this to work, it is very important that you keep your mind from re-creating the event. You can use your will with the aid of a forceful, repeated statement, said aloud if possible, such as "Nothing happened!" or "I'm okay!" Use whatever additional treatment may be appropriate or necessary. For more information, see Mental Energy, chapter 7.

Depression

- The Admiration Effect—with your full conscious attention, admire or compliment, aloud or silently, someone or something in your life or in your immediate environment. Do this as frequently and abundantly as possible until you get relief. At the same time, greatly reduce or eliminate criticism of anyone or anything. For more information, see Healing by Blessing, chapter 4.

- Affirm Ability—silently or aloud, repeat the statement "I can do it!" until you get relief. For more information, see Individual Teamwork, chapter 8.

- Positive Posture—assume a confident, positive posture while being still or moving around. Maintain this posture for as long as you can or until the depression begins to lift. For more information, see Emotional Energy, chapter 7.

Diminished Self-worth

- Self Appreciation—immediately begin acknowledging and appreciate as many of your good qualities, skills, abilities, and actions from the past or present as you can think of. At the same time, greatly reduce or eliminate any self-criticism. Repeat this process, going over the things you appreciate again and again as necessary, until you get relief. For more information, see Healing by Blessing, chapter 4.

Discomfort Around Others

- Exhale with Light—inhale with your attention on your navel, exhale while imagining yourself surrounded by a cloud of light or a field of energy—it is not necessary to "see" it, just imagine that it's there. Assume that this field or cloud can do what you want and tell it to harmonize the energy, feelings, or circumstances around you. Continue until you get relief.

- Play Director—pretend your immediate environment is a movie set, and you are the director. In your mind, tell people and things to be what they are and to do what they are doing as if everything that is happening is under your direction.

- Be Here Now—focus your awareness on the details of your immediate surroundings, including perceptions of sight, sound, touch and smell. Keep your attention on the present and away from the past or future.

Environmental Sensitivity

- The Admiration Effect—with your full conscious attention, admire or compliment, aloud or silently, someone or something in your life or in your immediate environment. Do this as frequently and abundantly as possible until you get relief. At the same time, greatly reduce or eliminate criticism of anyone or anything. For more information, see Healing by Blessing, chapter 4.

Eyestrain

- Backward Focus—inhale with your attention on your navel, exhale with your attention on the back of your head. Repeat until vision improves. For more information, see Mental Energy, chapter 7.

- See Passively—remember that the light from your environment is coming to you and that you don't have to hold things with your eyes, then practice passive seeing—being aware of things without straining to look at them. For more information, see Mental Energy, chapter 7.

- Squeeze and Breathe—squeeze your eyes shut five to ten times, take a deep breath, and look again. For more information, see Mental Energy, chapter 7.

Fear

- Exhale with Light—inhale with your attention on your navel, exhale while imagining yourself surrounded by a cloud of light or a field of energy—it is not necessary to "see" it, just imagine that it's there. Assume that this field or cloud can do what you want and tell it to harmonize the energy, feelings, or circumstances around you. Continue until you get relief.

- Play Director—pretend your immediate environment is a movie set and you are the director. In your mind, tell people and things to be what they are and to do what they are doing as if everything that is happening is under your direction.

- Be Here Now—focus your awareness on the details of your imme-diate surroundings, including perceptions of sight, sound, touch, and smell. Keep your attention on the present and away from the past or future.

Fever

- Water Power—drink a glass of water. Repeat if that helps. For more information, see Physical Energy, chapter 7.

- Gentle Stroke—gently stroke or caress the area that hurts until you get relief. For more information, see Self-touch, chapter 6.

- Melting Ice—imagine that the hurting area is a block of ice and imagine the ice melting away. For more information, see Healing by Direction, chapter 4.

- Touch and Forgive—gently touch the area that hurts with one hand and repeat these words to yourself until you get some relief: "Whatever this is related to, I forgive it completely, and it doesn't matter anymore." For more information, see Blanket Forgiveness, chapter 6.

Flu

- Water Power—drink a glass of water. Repeat if that helps. For more information, see Physical Energy, chapter 7.

- Friendly Persuasion—assume that the condition is at least partly related to suppressed anger. Assume that you can talk to your body and that it will listen to you. Persuade your body that it doesn't have to stay angry and promise it some pleasurable reward as soon as it gets well. Persuade frequently and provide a reward of some kind, no matter how small, for each positive change in the condition. Even praise and appreciation can be used as rewards. For more information, see Healing by Blessing, chapter 4.

- Relax and Be Loved—relax as best as you can, close your eyes if you wish, and repeat these words to yourself until you get relief: "I am loved and I am okay." For more information, see Healing by Blessing, chapter 4.

- Touch and Forgive—gently touch the area that hurts with one hand and repeat these words to yourself until you get some relief: "Whatever this is related to, I forgive it completely, and it doesn't matter anymore." For more information, see Blanket Forgiveness, chapter 6.

Frustration

- Water Power—drink a glass of water. Repeat if that helps. For more information, see Physical Energy, chapter 7.

- Tension Drainer—inhale with your attention on your navel, exhale with your attention on tense muscle groups while mentally willing or telling them to relax. In particular, direct your exhale-attention to your jaw muscles, shoulders/arms/hands, and your lower back. Repeat until you feel relief. For more information, see Mental Energy, chapter 7.

Hangover

- Water Power—drink a glass of water. Repeat if that helps. For more information, see Physical Energy, chapter 7.

- Gentle Stroke—gently stroke or caress the area that hurts until you get relief. For more information, see Self-touch, chapter 6.

- Melting Ice—imagine that the hurting area is a block of ice and imagine the ice melting away. For more information, see Healing by Direction, chapter 4.

- Touch and Forgive—gently touch the area that hurts with one hand and repeat these words to yourself until you get some relief:

"Whatever this is related to, I forgive it completely, and it doesn't matter anymore." For more information, see Blanket Forgiveness, chapter 6.

Headache

- Water Power—drink a glass of water. Repeat if that helps. For more information, see Physical Energy, chapter 7.

- Gentle Stroke—gently stroke or caress the area that hurts until you get relief. For more information, see Self-touch, chapter 6.

- Melting Ice—imagine that the hurting area is a block of ice and imagine the ice melting away. For more information, see Healing by Direction, chapter 4.

- Touch and Forgive—gently touch the area that hurts with one hand and repeat these words to yourself until you get some relief: "Whatever this is related to, I forgive it completely, and it doesn't matter anymore." For more information, see Blanket Forgiveness, chapter 6.

Infection

- Water Power—drink a glass of water. Repeat if that helps. For more information, see Physical Energy, chapter 7.

- Friendly Persuasion—assume that the condition is at least partly related to suppressed anger. Assume that you can talk to your body and that it will listen to you. Persuade your body that it doesn't have to stay angry and promise it some pleasurable reward as soon as it gets well. Persuade frequently and provide a reward of some kind, no matter how small, for each positive change in the condition. Even praise and appreciation can be used as rewards. For more information, see Healing by Blessing, chapter 4.

- Relax and Be Loved—relax as best as you can, close your eyes if you wish, and repeat these words to yourself until you get relief "I am loved and I am okay." For more information, see Healing by Blessing, chapter 4.

- Touch and Forgive—gently touch the area that hurts with one hand and repeat these words to yourself until you get some relief: "Whatever this is related to, I forgive it completely, and it doesn't matter anymore." For more information, see Blanket Forgiveness, chapter 6.

Insomnia

- Exhale with Light—inhale with your attention on your navel, exhale while imagining yourself surrounded by a cloud of light or a field of energy—it is not necessary to "see" it, just imagine that it's there. Assume that this field or cloud can do what you want and tell it to harmonize the energy, feelings, or circumstances around you. Continue until you get relief.

- Imagine Beauty—remember, imagine, or look at a beautiful, quiet place in detail. Use a photo or painting if that helps. Even if this is difficult at first, stay with it until you get relief or fall asleep. As an alternative to a quiet place, remember, imagine, or look at something very small, like a stone or a flower, in great detail. For more information, see Emotional Energy, chapter 7.

Irritability

- The Harmony Pattern—take a handful of small items like paper clips, pebbles, or coins and arrange them in front of you randomly until the pattern they form just "feels" right even though it doesn't resemble anything.

- Tune in to Curves—be aware of any curved lines or surfaces in your immediate environment. "Trace" these lines and surfaces with your eyes and, where feasible, with your hands and fingers. Continue until you get relief.

- Tune in to Movement—be aware of movement in your environment (such as the movement of the clouds, leaves in the wind, the air you breathe in and out, the movement of your body as you walk) and maintain the awareness without thinking about it until you get relief. For more information, see Mental Energy, chapter 7.

Joint Ache

- Water Power—drink a glass of water. Repeat if that helps. For more information, see Physical Energy, chapter 7.

- Gentle Stroke—gently stroke or caress the area that hurts until you get relief. For more information, see Self-touch, chapter 6.

- Melting Ice—imagine that the hurting area is a block of ice and imagine the ice melting away. For more information, see Healing by Direction, chapter 4.

- Touch and Forgive—gently touch the area that hurts with one hand and repeat these words to yourself until you get some relief: "Whatever this is related to, I forgive it completely, and it doesn't matter anymore." For more information, see Blanket Forgiveness, chapter 6.

Nausea

- Apply Wavepad—lay a foot-square sheet of cling-type plastic wrap on top of a foot-square sheet of aluminum foil, scrunch it up into a ball, flatten the ball, and hold it lightly against the affected area until you get relief. For more information, see Physical Energy, chapter 7.

- Inhale the Pain—place one hand on the area of pain or discomfort and the other on the ground, a wall, or a solid object. Inhale with your full attention on the first hand, exhale with your full attention on the second hand. For more information, see Mental Energy, chapter 7.

Nervousness

- Imagine Beauty—remember, imagine, or look at a beautiful, quiet place in detail. Use a photo or painting if that helps. Even if this is difficult at first, stay with it until you get relief or fall asleep. As an alternative to a quiet place, remember, imagine, or look at something very small, like a stone or a flower, in great detail. For more information, see Emotional Energy, chapter 7.

- Inhale at the Top—inhale slowly with your attention on the top of your head, exhale slowly with your attention on your navel. Repeat until you get relief or fall asleep. For more information, see Mental Energy, chapter 7.

Numbness

- Inhale at the Navel—inhale with your attention on your navel, hold your breath for about four seconds, and exhale with your attention on the affected part. Repeat until you get relief. For more information, see Mental Energy, chapter 7.

Rash

- Water Power—drink a glass of water. Repeat if that helps. For more information, see Physical Energy, chapter 7.

- Friendly Persuasion—assume that the condition is at least partly related to suppressed anger. Assume that you can talk to your body and that it will listen to you. Persuade your body that it doesn't have to stay angry and promise it some pleasurable reward as soon as it gets well. Persuade frequently and provide a reward of some kind, no matter how small, for each positive change in the condition.

Even praise and appreciation can be used as rewards. For more information, see Healing by Blessing, chapter 4.

- Relax and Be Loved—relax as best as you can, close your eyes if you wish, and repeat these words to yourself until you get relief: "I am loved and I am okay." For more information, see Healing by Blessing, chapter 4.

- Touch and Forgive—gently touch the area that hurts with one hand and repeat these words to yourself until you get some relief: "Whatever this is related to, I forgive it completely, and it doesn't matter anymore." For more information, see Blanket Forgiveness, chapter 6.

Restlessness

- Imagine Beauty—remember, imagine, or look at a beautiful, quiet place in detail. Use a photo or painting if that helps. Even if this is difficult at first, stay with it until you get relief or fall asleep. As an alternative to a quiet place, remember, imagine, or look at something very small, like a stone or a flower, in great detail. For more information, see Emotional Energy, chapter 7.

- Inhale at the Top—inhale slowly with your attention on the top of your head, exhale slowly with your attention on your navel. Repeat until you get relief or fall asleep. For more information, see Mental Energy, chapter 7.

Stomachache

- Apply Wavepad—lay a foot-square sheet of cling-type plastic wrap on top of a foot-square sheet of aluminum foil, scrunch it up into a ball, flatten the ball, and hold it lightly against the affected area until you get relief. For more information, see Physical Energy, chapter 7.

- Inhale the Pain—place one hand on the area of pain or discomfort and the other on the ground, a wall, or a solid object. Inhale with your full attention on the first hand, exhale with your full attention on the second hand. For more information, see Mental Energy, chapter 7.

Stress

- The Harmony Pattern—take a handful of small items like paper clips, pebbles, or coins and arrange them in front of you randomly until the pattern they form just "feels" right even though it doesn't resemble anything.

- Tune in to Curves—be aware of any curved lines or surfaces in your immediate environment. "Trace" these lines and surfaces with your eyes and, where feasible, with your hands and fingers. Continue until you get relief.

- Tune in to Movement—be aware of movement in your environment (such as the movement of the clouds, leaves in the wind, the air you breathe in and out, the movement of your body as you walk) and maintain the awareness without thinking about it until you get relief. For more information, see Mental Energy, chapter 7.

Swelling

- Water Power—drink a glass of water. Repeat if that helps. For more information, see Physical Energy, chapter 7.

- Friendly Persuasion—assume that the condition is at least partly related to suppressed anger. Assume that you can talk to your body and that it will listen to you. Persuade your body that it doesn't have to stay angry and promise it some pleasurable reward as soon as it gets well. Persuade frequently and provide a reward of some kind, no matter how small, for each positive change in the condition. Even praise and appreciation can be used as rewards. For more information, see Healing by Blessing, chapter 4.

- Relax and Be Loved—relax as best as you can, close your eyes if you wish, and repeat these words to yourself until you get relief: "I am loved and I am okay." For more information, see Healing by Blessing, chapter 4.

- Touch and Forgive—gently touch the area that hurts with one hand and repeat these words to yourself until you get some relief: "Whatever this is related to, I forgive it completely, and it doesn't matter anymore." For more information, see Blanket Forgiveness, chapter 6.

Worry

- Exhale with Light—inhale with your attention on your navel, exhale while imagining yourself surrounded by a cloud of light or a field of energy (it is not necessary to "see" it, just imagine that it's there). Assume that this field or cloud can do what you want and tell it to harmonize the energy, feelings, or circumstances around you. Continue until you get relief.

- Play Director—pretend your immediate environment is a movie set and you are the director. In your mind, tell people and things to be what they are and to do what they are doing as if everything that is happening is under your direction.

- Be Here Now—focus your awareness on the details of your immediate surroundings, including perceptions of sight, sound, touch, and smell. Keep your attention on the present and away from the past or future.

INDEX

ABOUT THE AUTHOR

Serge Kahili King has a doctorate in psychology from California Coast University, a master's degree in international management from the American Graduate School of International Management in Arizona, and a bachelor's degree in Asian Studies from the University of Colorado.

King has written extensively on the topic of *Huna*, the belief system of the Hawaiian shamans. His well-known previous books are *Urban Shaman, Kahuna Healing, Mastering Your Hidden Self,* and *Imagineering for Health*. He also wrote and designed *Search for Pele,* a computer game on CD-ROM.

King lives on the island of Kauai where he is the executive director of Aloha International, a worldwide network of healers, teachers, and students of *Huna*. In his spare time he manages a Hawaiian cultural museum, is the Web master for a family of Web sites, and continues his teaching, writing, and healing work. He can be reached through www.huna.org or www.huna.net.